The Toothpaste of
Immortality

The Toothpaste of
Immortality

Self-Construction in the
Consumer Age

Elemér Hankiss

Woodrow Wilson Center Press
| *Washington, D.C.*
The Johns Hopkins University Press
| *Baltimore*

EDITORIAL OFFICES
Woodrow Wilson Center Press
Woodrow Wilson International Center for Scholars
One Woodrow Wilson Plaza
1300 Pennsylvania Avenue, N.W.
Washington, D.C. 20004-3027
Telephone: 202-691-4010
www.wilsoncenter.org

ORDER FROM
The Johns Hopkins University Press
Hampden Station
P.O. Box 50370
Baltimore, Maryland 21211
Telephone: 1-800-537-5487
www.press.jhu.edu/books/

9 8 7 6 5 4 3 2 1

The author and publisher are grateful to the following for permission to quote copyright passages from the publications named here below:

The *Financial Times*, "How to Talk Yourself Up," July 3, 2002 (chapter 3, "Elevator Speech"), pp. 62–63

Elemér Hankiss, *Fears and Symbols*, Central European University Press, 2001

Mark L. Leary and June Price Tangney, *Handbood of Self and Identity*, Guilford Press, 2003 (table 10.1, p. 203)

Library of Congress Cataloging-in-Publication Data

Hankiss, Elemér, 1928–
    The toothpaste of immortality : self-construction in the consumer age / Elemér Hankiss.
        p. cm.
    Includes bibliographical references and index.
    ISBN 0-8018-8420-9 (cloth : alk. paper) — ISBN 0-8018-8421-7 (pbk. : alk. paper)
1. Self. 2. Civilization, Modern. I. Title.
    BF697.H347 2006
    302.5—dc22   2006002667

Woodrow Wilson International Center for Scholars

The Woodrow Wilson International Center for Scholars, established by Congress in 1968 and headquartered in Washington, D.C., is a living national memorial to President Wilson. The Center's mission is to commemorate the ideals and concerns of Woodrow Wilson by providing a link between the worlds of ideas and policy, while fostering research, study, discussion, and collaboration among a broad spectrum of individuals concerned with policy and scholarship in national and international affairs. Supported by public and private funds, the Center is a nonpartisan institution engaged in the study of national and world affairs. It establishes and maintains a neutral forum for free, open, and informed dialogue. Conclusions or opinions expressed in Center publications and programs are those of the authors and speakers and do not necessarily reflect the views of the Center staff, fellows, trustees, advisory groups, or any individuals or organizations that provide financial support to the Center.

The Center is the publisher of The Wilson Quarterly and home of Woodrow Wilson Center Press, dialogue radio and television, and the monthly news-letter "Centerpoint." For more information about the Center's activities and publications, please visit us on the web at www.wilsoncenter.org.

To my mother and father,

who had the courage

to live in freedom and dignity

Contents

Tables

Acknowledgments

I would like to express my sincere gratitude first of all to the Woodrow Wilson International Center for Scholars, which provided a uniquely inspiring environment for completing this book. Without the simultaneous peace and excitement of the Center, the stimulating discussions with other fellows, the flow of books coming from the Library of Congress, and the lively atmosphere of Washington, this book would be much poorer in ideas and more limited in its scope.

I am especially grateful to Samuel Wells and Joseph Brinley. Without Sam's help I would not have had the privilege to spend a second term at the Center. And without Joe, who encouraged me to work on the manuscript and had the courage to accept it as a Woodrow Wilson Center Press publication, this book would have had a thornier path leading from my desk to the readers. I thank also staff editor Yamile Kahn, as well as Alfred F. Imhoff, who copy edited the manuscript with exceptional expertise, indexer Enid Zafran, and Debra Naylor, who designed the interior and exterior of the printed volume.

I would also like to thank the members of the Woodrow Wilson Center staff—Rosemary Lyon, Janet L. Spikes, Arlyn Charles, Dagne Gizaw, Michelle Kutler, Lindsay Collins, and others—who had the moral strength to smile and help me even if I disturbed them with my questions and requests for the thousandth time. I am also sincerely appreciative of the help given to me by Henry Tom and Kathy Alexander of the Johns Hopkins University Press.

I am deeply indebted to those thinkers of earlier ages who have helped me understand the transformation of Western civilization and of the human condition since the mid-nineteenth century. I think first of all of Kierkegaard and Nietzsche, Weber and Simmel, Scheler and Gehlen, Adorno and Habermas, Heidegger and Cassirer, Jaspers and Sartre, Patocka and Tillich, Voegelin and Löwith, Polanyi and Popper, Daniel Bell and Foucault, Baudrillard and Lyotard.

I have received extremely valuable comments from friends and colleagues who took the time to read all or part of the manuscript: Neil J. Smelser, Philippe C. Schmitter, Joseph P. Forgas, Constantin Fasolt, Robert Picht, Árpád Szakolczai, Csaba Pléh, László Bruszt, Ferenc Miszlivetz, Robert Manchin, and László Füstös.

Special thanks are due to my students at Stanford University, Georgetown University, the European University Institute in Florence, the College of Europe in Bruges, and the Central European University in Budapest. They witnessed the birth of many of the ideas discussed in this book and were tough and, at the same time, extremely helpful critics. My thanks also to the staff of Osiris Press in Hungary, who took care of the Hungarian version of this book.

I am thankful to my wife Lili, who has ever been an inexhaustible source of inspiration for me, and last but not least, for the irreverent, kind, and insightful comments of my daughter and son, Catherine and Adam, who convinced me not to take my work, and myself, too seriously.

The Toothpaste of
Immortality

Introduction:
Trivialities Are Not Trivial

And who are you, said he?
Don't puzzle me, said I.

—*Laurence Sterne*

The Trivial and the Existential

The aim of this book is to study the human self, and the ways in which people protect, shape, and construct their selves, in a radically new situation: the emerging consumer civilization. The analysis is based on a hypothesis about the interaction of the trivial and the existential in human life; an interaction that plays a crucial role in the self-construction of human beings and that has become especially dramatic and spectacular in our contemporary civilization of consumption.

I will argue, throughout the book, that human beings simultaneously live on two levels; they act, at the same time, in two plays. On the "trivial" surface of their everyday lives, they keep working for the survival of their families, communities, and themselves. They make money, raise their children, travel, build their houses, smoke or don't smoke, go to the cinema or the pub, work in their offices or workshops, take a walk, read their newspapers, and do a lot of other things.

1

Yet at the same time, with everything and anything they do and say, they also act in another drama, the "existential drama" of their lives—even if they do not necessarily know that they are doing so. They keep constructing and reconstructing their selves; they strive for authenticity, for the intense experience of being, for self-esteem, dignity, meaning; and yes, also for (the hope, or at least the illusion of) immortality.

Paraphrasing a famous Hungarian humorist—who once remarked that "no nonsense with nonsense, please! . . . humor is no laughing matter"—we could also say: No nonsense with trivialities, please. Trivialities, too, are serious business. They may have and, as we shall see, they do have, a deep structure reaching down into the depths of human existence.

I will also argue that human life has ever had this duality of the trivial and the existential. During most of their lives, people would be absorbed in their daily tasks of survival and would be reminded of the underlying depths of their existence only, or mainly, by the myths and rituals of their tribes, the teaching and ceremonies of their churches, or by sudden changes of fortune: by a serious disease, the death of their beloved ones, a natural catastrophe, and the like. These are the moments when the ultimate concerns of their existence—usually well hidden under the trivial surface of their everyday lives—burst into the open.

Strangely enough, though in their real lives people tend to ignore the existence of this latent, existential sphere of their lives, they do love to be submerged in it, or to watch the interaction of these two spheres of their lives "through a looking glass," in a virtual way, so to speak. Think, for instance, of the duality of the Roman *"Panem et circenses!"*—where *"panem"* may be interpreted as the metaphor for everyday survival and *"circenses"* as the exciting existential drama of life and death in the form of gladiator fights, predators killing defenseless human beings, galleys being sunk, martyrs being crucified, and so on and so forth.

Or, to give another example, the same is true of Greek, Roman, or modern tragedies. All, or most, of them start on the more or less peaceful and practical level of human life—Oedipus is a happy king, Hamlet is a careless Renaissance prince, the Prince of Homburg is a victorious young officer, Albee's Martha and George are an American middle-class couple. And then, suddenly, their world collapses. They find themselves in a fearful and dark universe where they are confronted with the ultimate questions of human existence. In general, the main characteristic, and worth, of art and artworks consists in their unique ability to make our everyday life "transparent" so that the profound lights of our "human condition" may shine through it. I will argue in this book that, in a special way, even the most trivial genres of our consumer civilization are capable of this magic.

Let me stop here and—before my argument becomes too philosophical—make it clear, in a simple and matter-of-fact way, what I mean by this interaction of the "trivial" and the "existential." I am going to give an example that, at first sight, may be shockingly trivial in a scholarly book, but it may help me to develop my argument.

A Trivial (and Existential) Example

For a long time, I did not understand why my wife loved our washing machine so much. I did understand that it was great to take care of one of the worst household chores and read the latest issue of *People* or *Vanity Fair* while the machine was doing the job. But there was a deeper fascination here. And then, step-by-step, I began to understand the magic.

A new washing machine is definitely and glamorously beautiful. It dazzles us with its shining and sparkling whiteness. It stands there with dignity and modesty, though it has tremendous and demonic powers within. With its round porthole-like door and rectangular form, it is a "mandala," the symbol of the perfection and harmony of the universe. It is impeccably clean, innocent, white, not yet spoiled and defiled by life. I could almost say that it is prelapsarian. It comes from a world without guilt. Corruption has not yet attacked, indented, eroded it. It is untouchable. Its purity is almost transcendental. And like a virgin martyr in a white gown, it is ready to sacrifice itself for us and launder our defiled and guilty lives. It is certainly not a coincidence that on a famous poster there is a washing machine standing in the middle of a majestic Celtic forest, shining like the Holy Grail. (Only the timid roe-dear with great ears and eyes is a bit out of place there and spoils part of the symbolic effect of the Holy Washing Machine.)

And, believe it or not, washing machines are able also of much more heroic deeds. They are, for instance, able to stop and even reverse time. In other words, they are able to triumph over mortality and death. And they do so with ease and elegance. They need only the help of the latest brand of detergent. Who would not remember those television commercials that repeat, invariably, the following sequence:

> A horrendous catastrophe occurs: black coffee, greasy oil or some other alien matter splashes on a beautifully pink, light blue or white bath towel (we, viewers, are prompted to experience this incident like the drama of the Fall, the Original Sin, the defilement of everything that is clean and innocent in the world.) — First Housewife is smashed with despair. There is no possible repair (Paradise Lost.) — Second Housewife suddenly shows up, bringing a new brand of detergent (the Guardian Angel appears.) — They wash the towel. Transparence and crystalline beauty fill the world, sparkling bubbles rise up in the blue sky. — The towel emerges from the machine impeccably, angelically, transcendentally, innocently clean. The miracle has happened: Its metaphysical purity and fragrance trumpet the good news: Hallelujah, Evil can be defeated, decay, destruction can be halted, time can be reversed, the world may resurrect in its original beauty, purity, and innocence. Time, decay, mortality, death are defeated. — First Housewife romps, Second Housewife smiles gently, baby in pink jumper giggles in the background. We are back in our soft, happy, innocent universe.

Thanks to the washing machine, the detergent, and, last but not least, the magic of advertising, we are spiritually reinforced and may continue our everyday existence. Later in this book, I will analyze dozens of similar examples—examples of the way in which the trivialities of our everyday lives intertwine with our underlying fight with the existential problems of our existence.[1]

The famous psychologist Abraham Maslow (1954, 80–107, 146–55), with his hypothesis about the seven levels of needs, may have been wrong. Human life or human history is not a process of climbing the pyramid of successive, higher and higher needs, starting with our physiological needs and ultimately attaining the highest degree of more spiritual needs: "self-actualization." In each and every moment of our lives, and with each and every act of ours, we satisfy several categories of needs—physical, biological, and social ones, as well as the "higher" spiritual, existential, and transcendental ones.

The trivialities of our lives are not trivial at all.[2] Or are they?

The Duality of the Self in Philosophy

I am, of course, not the first to embark on the exploration of this latent sphere of everyday life. The question of the duality of human existence, understood in many different ways, has ever been present in philosophy. To tell the story of these ideas would almost amount to the history of philosophical thinking. Let me mention only a few recent examples.

According to Sartre and his fellow existentialists, human beings can live an "authentic" life only if—beyond their practical, utilitarian everyday activities— they do not relent in their efforts to create and re-create themselves, their selves, in an incessant series of courageous and autonomous acts of choice. Ernst Cassirer (1944, 222–23 and passim) claimed that, throughout their lives, human beings, as "symbolic animals," keep building—consciously and unconsciously—an "ideal world" for themselves. In the same vein, Clifford Geertz (1973a, 30) showed, on the example of a great variety of human communities, that they were preoccupied, even in their everyday activities, with spinning a latent "web of significance" around themselves. According to the founders of philosophical anthropology, Max Scheler (1961 [1928]) and Arnold Gehlen (1988 [1940], human beings are "handicapped" as compared with other creatures of the animal world and, as a consequence, to survive they have to create their selves and build up their own world, in a permanent, though not necessarily conscious, everyday effort.[3] Developing their ideas, Peter L. Berger (1967, 3, 6, 19, 27) described human society as "an enterprise of world-building," and human life as something that transcended people's practical, daily problems. Life is, at its very essence, a continuous effort to transform "a world of disorder, senselessness, and madness" into a universe that is "humanly significant" (pp. 22, 28).

In his famous book, *The Denial of Death* (1973), Ernest Becker described the world as "overwhelmingly tragic and demonic" and went so far as to state that the fear of death was the main, unconscious or semiconscious, motive force in human life.[4] This fear, and people's efforts to overcome it, to "defeat death," were present in every moment and every act of their lives.[5] Paul Tillich (1951–63, 1952), the famous theologian and philosopher, wrote about the fundamental and fearful ambiguities of human existence that hide under the surface of our everyday lives.

Much earlier, Kierkegaard warned people that they are "diverted" from the all-important and fearful drama of their mortal human condition by the trivialities of their everyday lives. In a similar sense, Heidegger spoke of a dangerous penchant in human beings to "oblivion," that is, to be forgetful of the ultimate questions of existence. They both acknowledged that it was a difficult exercise to escape from this state of amnesia and inauthenticity. According to Kierkegaard, only a deep spiritual experience and faith can help them do so. The Heideggerian path may be even thornier. If I understand him well, his message is that human beings have to escape from their daily lives of trivialities into Nonbeing, and only there can they experience, and only for brief moments, Being in its fearful silence and magnificence.

These verdicts would condemn most of us to a life of inauthenticity, because we—most of us—are philosophical basket cases. But perhaps we are not entirely hopeless. We are not because, as I have mentioned above, there is a second, underlying sphere of people's everyday lives, where they keep struggling with the major, ultimate problems of human existence even if they are not necessarily aware of the fact that they are doing so. Human beings live on two levels: on the levels of the trivial and the existential.[6]

Developing my argument, I shall walk on a narrow path, for two reasons. The first is because I may hold myself up to ridicule. I shall have to speak about trivialities without becoming trivial. Second, I shall have to speak about an "existential drama" underlying people's everyday lives without becoming too philosophical. As a consequence, I have to firmly anchor myself in the findings of the empirical social sciences, particularly personal and social psychology. I have to check how the hypothesis about the duality of the human self, and about the existential drama of self-construction in the consumer age, fit into our existing body of knowledge. And here I may come up against a series of difficulties.

The Duality of the Self in Psychology

The study of the human self within the behavioral sciences is a buoyant intellectual universe, full of lively controversies, hypotheses, and counterhypotheses, new ideas and approaches, attempts at classification and system building. Professionally, it is among the outstanding achievements in this field of scientific research. But it has also its limitations. Let me say a few words about both these achievements and limitations.[7]

In the past hundred years or so, psychoanalysts and psychologists, social psychologists and cultural anthropologists, linguists and literary critics have discovered and described a great number of phenomena that do indicate that there is a second layer, a layer of significance under the surface of our everyday lives, deeds, and words. Think of ancient spells, rituals, and all kinds of symbolic action; think of parables, allegories, emblems, and also of lies, irony, and double talk: They all mean something else than they say or display on the surface. It was Freud and his followers who had the merit of discovering a whole ocean of hidden meanings beneath people's words, dreams, and deeds. They directed the attention of the students of the human being to this interaction of the conscious and unconscious realms of the self. Freud's contribution is especially important for our present project (though we do not work with his concept of the unconscious), because he called attention to the fact that even under the seemingly trivial phenomena of everyday life great emotional dramas are being enacted in the human psyche.

Not less important, Jung and his followers, and a great number of cultural anthropologists and experts of comparative religion, have argued and proved that symbols, archetypes, and myths play a major role in shaping people's lives and selves.[8] Or think of Carl Rogers (1951, 1961, 1980), Abraham Maslow (1999 [1968]), Rollo May (1953, 1969, 1983; May, Angel, and Ellenberger 1958), and other representatives of the school of humanistic or existential psychology, who examined how people—even while running about on their daily business—kept constructing and reconstructing their selves and the world around themselves. They studied how people reconfirmed their identities, their freedom, and the meaningfulness of their lives, and how they tried to assuage their profound anxiety about the fragility of their selves and their very existence.[9]

This combination of psychological experiments and philosophical ideas could not really break through then, in the 1950s and 1960s, and in the following two decades or so. The majority of psychologists focused on the study of observable and measurable facts.[10] Behaviorism, which dominated the field in those decades, questioned even the very existence of the "self." The rise of cognitive psychology in the 1970s did not help much either because, though its representatives rehabilitated the concept of the self, they considered it—at least in their early years—as "an essentially 'cool' cognitive, unmotivated knowledge structure—an information processing machine based on computer analogs,"[11] and they discarded the existence, or at least the relevance, of any underlying noncognitive spheres of the self. In the 1980s, however, more and more psychologists began to explore this at least partly hidden layer of motives, emotions, goals, and values. The study of these noncognitive, nonconscious, semiconscious, "implicit" processes has since then become an important field of research. To see the extent of this change, it is enough to check the main professional journals, recent handbooks, and collections of papers in personality and social psychology,[12] along with some of the best books, studies, and monographs published in the past two decades dealing with the self.[13]

In their excellent overview of the field, Mischel and Morf (2003, 23, 24, 26) describe this complexity of the contemporary approach to the self. According to them, the self is seen nowadays as being "stable *and* variable, consistent *and* inconsistent, rational *and* irrational, planful *and* automatic, agentic *and* routinized." And they add that in "the present view, . . . while the meaning system of the self requires as its sine qua non self-awareness and conscious self-thinking, it is not necessarily always either conscious or self-aware, and often operates automatically and non-verbally (e.g., Uleman and Bargh 1989)." Defining the self as a complex "psycho-social dynamic processing system," they argue that the self as a system "functions at multiple levels and subsumes a number of subsystems that operate concurrently and in parallel."

As we see, the idea that the various subsystems of the self operate simultaneously on multiple levels is already present in contemporary experimental psychology.[14] But Mischel and Morf are in this respect ahead of a great number of their colleagues, who—if they speak about an underlying, nonconscious or less conscious layer of the self—think mainly or exclusively of various nonconscious "automaticies" or routines, and of hidden genetic, social, and cultural influences of which the self is not aware.

The same cautious approach to the latent realms of the self may also be observed in the study of motives and motivation. After the brilliant initiatives of Freud, Lewin (1935, 1951), Sartre (1953), Maslow (1954), and Cattell and Child (1975), motivation research temporarily lost part of its momentum. It had its comeback in the 1980s and 1990s. Nowadays it is a must to include chapters on motivation in monographs and handbooks on personality and social psychology.[15] But, understandably, experimental psychologists avoid the latent and dangerous realm of Freudian and other "demonic forces"[16] and focus their attention on less turbulent, and better defined, specific motivations of the self.

More or less the same could be said about the study of emotions. Robert B. Zajonc (1998) writes in his chapter titled "Emotions" that this "is the first time a chapter on emotions appears in *The Handbook of Social Psychology*" (Gilbert, Fiske, and Lindzey 1998), the first edition of which was published in 1954. But in the past two decades, a number of fundamental books have been published in this field.[17] I still have the impression, however, that the role of the most "fundamental" emotions (e.g., existential fear, or the intense experience of life) in shaping the human self has not been researched with the same ardor as—I presume—more situational emotions like shame, guilt, embarrassment, pride, joy, anger, love, and hate have been.

One important exception to this rule is the work of Tom Pyszczynski, Jeff Greenberg, and Sheldon Solomon. In a paper published in *Psychological Inquiry* (1997), they presented experimental data supporting their "Terror Management Theory." They claimed that below their everyday struggle for survival, the latent primary drive of human beings was to cope with "an existential dilemma," that is, with the "paralyzing terror" deriving from the knowledge of "the inevitability of death."[18]

As is usual in *Psychological Inquiry*, the article was followed by peer commentaries, giving the floor to some of the best specialists in the field. Nobody questioned the importance of this study, and the fact that it meant a real challenge for personality psychologists.[19] But the general reception was also strongly critical.[20]

What is really important here is that—after the early attempts of the humanistic school of Rogers, Maslow, and May, whose ideas clearly resonate in this recent theory[21]—a new channel between experimental psychology and philosophical thinking has been opened. I speak of a "new" channel because there is a field in which contacts between experimental psychology and philosophy have been established much earlier, though mainstream experimental psychologists did not pay too much attention to it. I think of the comparative study of various civilizations, which has shown that these various cultural traditions and contexts were powerful, though partly latent, forces in shaping people's behavioral patterns, attitudes, religious beliefs, visions of the world, and—last but not least—their identities and selves.[22]

The Method

Due to the goals to be achieved, and the nature of the discipline, the majority of experts working in the field of psychological research prefer laboratory over field experiments. There are, of course, other methods in use as well. And there is an ongoing controversy about the advantages and disadvantages of laboratory versus field research, or experimentation versus other approaches: observation, interviews, surveys, content analysis of texts and other documents, introspection, sociometry, oral history, life course analysis, and the like.[23]

The present book does not come out of a laboratory. It comes much more from the world of Georg Simmel and Walter Benjamin, Carl Jung and Erving Goffman, Margaret Mead and Clifford Geertz, Paul Ricoeur and Norbert Elias, who were unsurpassable masters of simultaneously analyzing the simple events, and unknown depths, of everyday human life.

In this book, we shall not dissect life into isolated psychological events in order to test and retest them under sterile laboratory conditions. We shall start from the other direction: from the side of the human being in her or his everyday life—from simple facts, events, situations, and, even more important, from the *continuum* of everyday life. We shall follow human beings through their daily activities and shall try to find out how they shape their selves by what they do, even without necessarily knowing that they are doing so. This "peripatetic" observation will not allow us to investigate each specific problem or strategy of the human self with the same precision as experimental and nonexperimental psychologists do; but—so I hope at least—studying the daily process of self-construction, the concatenation of self-constructing strategies, may shed new light on how human beings shape themselves, their worlds, and their lives.[24]

We shall see that—even without necessarily knowing what they do—people play on the keyboard of almost numberless self-constructing strategies like virtuosi play on their Steinways. Unfortunately, however, they blunder much more frequently, and with more serious consequences, than Liszt, Chopin, or Rachmaninov ever did.

The Self in Everyday Life

More concretely, and less poetically: In the first part of the book, we shall follow the life of a human person, woman or man, throughout one single day; from morning till night. We shall describe, step by step, what she does from the moment she gets up in the morning to the moment she goes to sleep in the evening. We shall watch how in the morning she prepares herself for the day; we shall shadow her in the street, on her way to her office, and observe her at her workplace; and we shall follow her, after work, on her way home, shopping, meeting friends, caring for her garden, and finally concluding her day.

Our goal in doing so will be to explore under the surface of these everyday events, acts, and situations the underlying—conscious, semiconscious, unconscious—strategies of self-construction; the "existential drama" in which—according to our hypothesis—human beings are permanently involved.

In the course of this narrative combined with analysis, we shall ask a great number of questions, some of which may seem trivial at first. They will not be as shockingly trivial as the two questions we have raised just above ("What has our washing machine to do with the construction of our selves?" "What has the latest brand of detergent to do with immortality?"). They will be more serious but will sometimes have a funny turn. Let me give a few examples.

What happens to our personalities, our selves, during the night? Do our selves change or disintegrate at night? Do we have different diurnal and nocturnal selves? In the morning, do we have to "pick up" the pieces of our disintegrated selves? And if we have to, how do we do it? How do we "reconstruct" our selves? How many faces do we have? And how many roles? What does our morning shower have to do with the *Magic Flute* of Mozart? And what do perfumes have to do with mythologies? Why do we watch weather forecasts at least three times in the morning? Why is it so important for us to complement our morning cereals and ham and eggs with reading our favorite paper and crunching the lives of the victims of the latest political and/or sexual scandals?

What do cell phones and laptops have to do with the construction of our selves? Why do we hide ourselves? And why do we disclose our selves? Why do we like to stroll in the streets? What is the magic of shopping? What happens to our selves in the pubs or the movie theaters? Why is gossip so important for shaping our selves? What kind of books are on our bookshelves? And why are just these books there? What happens to our selves while we are watching soap operas, action movies, catastrophe films, love stories? And last but not least: What does all this have to do with the "existential drama" that takes place under the surface of a simple, normal weekday? How does all this help, or impede, human beings in their conscious and unconscious striving for the freedom, dignity, and fulfillment of their lives? And ultimately (though such sentences should not be printed in a serious scholarly book), how does all this help or impede humans in their everyday struggle with time and death?

The Self in the Consumer Age

In the second part of the book, History with a capital "H" will enter the stage. In the past half century or so, Western civilization has undergone a dramatic transformation. We now live in a world that is radically different from the world in which our grandparents lived fifty years ago.[25] And in this new world, in this new civilization, people have to respond to new challenges. They have to develop new strategies to fulfill their lives and selves. We shall try to understand this new human situation, this new drama of self-construction underlying our contemporary world, underlying the trivialities of the consumer civilization. The duality of human life, the interaction of the trivial and the existential, will turn out to be even more dramatic and astounding in the spectacular scenery of this civilization than is shown and described in the first part of the book. It is not a coincidence, nor is it an empty metaphor, that philosophers and cultural critics with a slightly romantic penchant have spoken in this context about a civilization that is both an ongoing cheerful carnival ("the trivial") and a fearful dance of death ("the existential"). This is a fascinating but, at the same time, difficult situation for a human being who wants to shape, develop, and actualize her or his self.

My approach will significantly differ from the mainstream assessment of this emerging new civilization. The majority of cultural critics[26] paint a rather gloomy picture of contemporary consumer civilization and—among many other objections—deplore the fact that it paralyzes, distorts, and destroys the human self. In many respects they are right, of course. But I think that their criticism is biased in several ways. Sometimes it is elitist (protecting the values of "high culture"); sometimes it is republican (accusing "consumerism" of undermining civic virtues and a citizen's responsibility); it may be conservative (condemning it for the destruction of traditional communities and values); or it may build up a militant and radical criticism claiming that consumerism is an instrument of domination in the hands of the lords of "late" or "global" capitalism.

There is much well worth considering in what they say. But—at least according to my intentions—a less negative and more articulate picture will emerge in this book of how the consumer civilization helps and hinders, hinders and helps, people in their efforts to construct their selves.

Let me give an example of this ambivalence. One of the dominant schools of postmodern thinkers argues, for instance (and I agree with them), that contemporary civilization is a world of ambiguities and uncertainties, simulacra and role playing, flux and fragmentation, difference and chaos, language games and irony. Baudrillard (1994), for example, claims that *even tragedies have become trivial simulacra* in our postmodern age, and he may be right. But I shall try to show that the opposite is at least as true; that *the trivialities of our lives are not trivial at all.* They may even be tragic, sometimes. Their roots reach down into the unknown depths of human existence.

Here again a number of questions will arise. Questions like: How have the norms of self-construction changed in the past few decades? How does the emerging consumer civilization shape, build, or destroy people's selves? What are the motive forces that prompt people now, at the turn of the twentieth and twenty-first centuries, to keep constructing their selves throughout their lives? Wealth? Power? Success? Fame? Vanity? Sex? Fear? Longing for love? Or what? Are people free to construct their selves? What role do boundary situations play in the world of self-construction? Why do peoople like to flirt with danger? How is it possible that death is one of the dominant topics in the illustrated weekly magazines of this age of "happyism"? How can people actualize their selves in the civilization of consumption, in a world that is both "disenchanted" and "reenchanted"? How do their present ways of caring for their selves differ from those of their predecessors—the Greeks, people of the Middle Ages, of the Renaissance, of the nineteenth century?

And finally, do we know at all what we speak about when we speak about the "self"? Does it exist at all? Is it true that there are such things as "visible" and "hidden" selves? Are there "transparent" or "looking-glass" selves; "minimal," "marginal," and "saturated" selves; "imagined" or "elusive" selves; "prelinguistic," "semiotic," or "narrative" selves; "multiple," "hierarchical," or "parallel" selves? Are there "united" and "fragmented" or "decentered" selves; "existential," "transcendental," or "Faustian" selves"? And if there are such strange things, what are they like? And what role do they play in people's lives, and in the civilization of consumption?

We shall not be able, of course, to answer all these questions. What we can do is to ask them, try to answer them, and first of all call attention to the efforts of human beings who shape, construct, and fulfill their selves in a rapidly changing world full of new opportunities, new challenges, and new dangers.

What Is Missing

This book is not a general discussion of the problems of the human self. It is a study focusing on how people protect, construct, and actualize their selves in their *everyday lives,* and do so in the *consumer age.* The field to be studied is so large even with this restriction that I will have to concentrate on certain phenomena and—for the time being—neglect a great number of others. Let us look briefly at each.

Pathologies. First, I shall strictly limit the discussion to the so-called normal aspects of self-construction and leave aside the huge literature on the pathologies of the self, and on the psychological and psychoanalytic attempts at healing them.[27]

Education. It would be important to study how education (at home, at school, at church, in communities of a more or less traditional character) interacts nowadays with the forces of the civilization of consumption in shaping people's selves. Beyond a lack of competence, my excuse for not dealing with this field is that in the first, narrative part of this book, I focus on one single day of an adult person, who did go through this educational process long before we meet her or him in this book.

Language, speech, and communication have an overwhelming impact on the human personality and play a major role in shaping people's selves. Words can order, praise, ask, prohibit, promise, question, wound, and sometimes even kill. Hundreds of works on rhetoric, the sociology and psychology of language, speech act theory, communication, communicative action, and advertising have studied the power of language. But I still have the feeling that language's major role in shaping the selves of human beings has not yet been sufficiently explored.[28] In this book, there are only a few references to this important dimension of constructing contemporary human selves.

Social interaction. Another, less justifiable, limitation of this book is that it does not devote enough time and attention to the role of human interactions in shaping people's selves. This is especially true of the first part of the book, in which we study one single day of an individual's life and observe how she or he keeps constructing her or his self from morning till night. My only, and not really relevant, excuse is that thousands of papers and chapters, and hundreds of books, study the human self as a "social self," in its interaction with a social context. As we have seen, social psychology and the psychology of personality tend to overlap with each other more and more.[29] As far as the specific problems of self-construction in the interpersonal contexts of consumer civilization are concerned, studies of peer communities, "cohorts," "gangs," fan clubs, discos, e-networks, and consumer groups are among the most interesting ones from our point of view.[30]

Gender, too, plays an important role in molding one's self. It is a common everyday experience as well as a fact proven by scientific experiments that women and men use both specific and common strategies in this field. In this book, I focus on these latter ones and analyze only a few situations in which women and men have characteristically different strategies of self-construction. In feminist literature,[31] and in popular self-help books, this is already a central topic.

Age. Psychologists and psychoanalysts have shown that people's strategies of shaping their selves change over time. Children, teenagers, young adults, adults, and elderly people have, at least partly, different strategies for protecting and molding their selves. Sudden changes or shocks, and the so-called liminal or transition periods ("teen-age crisis," "midlife crisis," and the *Torschluss Panik*" are the best known among them) may have a particularly strong impact on the formation, or deformation, of human selves. In this book, however, average adult persons are the exclusive subjects of observation and analysis.

Social environment. Without any doubt, people's selves are strongly shaped by their social and political environments as well. Living in a rich or a poor country, in a democracy or an authoritarian state, let alone despotic regime, in peace or in continuous fear, in freedom or in servitude, having and not having opportunities, being the member of a well-to-do middle-class family or being a pariah: These facts may, and in most cases do, leave a deep imprint on people's selves. And even more, to grow up and live in an environment of starvation, epidemics, and no hope for the future, may rule out *ab ovo* any real possibility of developing one's self.[32] In spite of the importance of this field, I focus almost exclusively on the cultural context and refer only to a few social and political factors that may play a role in shaping people's selves in our consumer societies.

Civilization. As it has been mentioned above, civilizations have ever set the framework within which people could, and had to, develop their selves. They have provided them with those ways, means, skills, and rituals that shaped their selves in conformity with the traditions of their community. The works of cultural anthropologists, from Fraser to Geertz and beyond, are treasure troves for personality and social psychologists who want to understand the human self in its multifaceted complexity. More and more psychologists (and other behavioral and social scientists) have realized this in recent years; "cultural" or "cross-cultural" psychology is rapidly becoming an independent discipline.[33] There are already important comparative studies of the different ways in which various civilizations allow, impede, or prompt people to construct their selves, but the impact of the emerging "consumer" and/or global civilization on self-constructing practices around the world has not yet been sufficiently explored. Due to a lack of competence, and of space, this comparative aspect is reduced to a few paragraphs in this book.

Change over time. The forms and contents of self-construction have significantly changed throughout the centuries, especially in our Western civilization.[34] The Greeks, Socrates or Aristophanes; the Romans, Nero or Marcus Aurelius; medieval knights, monks, burghers, and serfs; Renaissance lords and artists; seventeenth-century Puritans and Catholics; the rising middle and working classes; Voltaire and Rousseau; Byron and Baudelaire; Dickens and Dostoyevsky; Churchill and Picasso; green activists and rappers—each has had a radically different strategy of self-construction (and destruction). It would be fascinating to explore all this variety of the ways and means of shaping the human personality. I shall come back several times to this issue on the pages of this book.

—

I should like to emphasize that, although this is a scholarly book, I have done my best to also make it readable for the larger public. The argument meanders along the events of a day, and the scenes of an emerging new civilization. It can be read and—so I hope—enjoyed as a narrative, with occasional free falls into the depths of theoretical problems. A relatively great number of notes and references to important works may help those readers who want to climb out of these abysses.

And finally, let me mention that one of the questions mentioned above asked whether such a thing as the "self" exists at all. I am not certain, but I do hope, that the answer will be a definite: Yes, it does. Because if there were no self, then this book would be about something that does not exist. And to write about "Nonbeing" and "Nothingness" is the privilege of existentialist philosophers.

PART I

The Self in Everyday Life

The Morning Reconstruction
of the Self

> "Who are you?" said the caterpillar.
> Alice replied rather shyly, "I—I hardly know,
> Sir, just at present—at least I know who I was
> when I got up this morning, but I think I must
> have changed several times since then."
>
> —*Lewis Carroll,* Alice in Wonderland

The Jungle of the Night

In the evening, when we go to bed, before falling asleep, why do we take leave of our husband or wife, of our children? We stay in the same house, perhaps even in the same room; we do not go anywhere. Or do we? Are we embarking on a journey on unknown waters, in the mysterious land of dreams?[1] And in the morning, why do we greet the members of our family? Do we come home from somewhere? Are we the same persons as we were before falling asleep in the evening? Or has something happened to us, to our personality, to our self? Do we have to "pull ourselves together" because our self has somehow fallen asunder during the night? And if it has, then the sooner we start picking up the pieces and reconstructing our self, the better. But it may turn out to be a rather difficult task.

If self-awareness, self-control, the capacity to think consciously about itself is a basic characteristic of the self, as many scholars assert nowadays,[2] then we have to state that at night, while they are sleeping, people's selves fall apart. They become submerged in the world of nonbeing, in a dark, unknown, and alien world. They lose themselves. They lose their control over their bodies, their minds, their selves, and their world. Their muscles slacken, their faces lose their traits, and their thoughts go berserk; their minds, in a wild cavalcade, jump to and fro between the most absurd paths of associations. They are engulfed by a world where the laws of their daily lives do not hold. In their dreams, they do things that would be incomprehensible and unacceptable in their daily lives. They are tossed on the waves of a dark sea, which, while awake, we call, faute de mieux, the "subconscious."[3]

This nightly disintegration of the human person already puzzled philosophers and scholars in the seventeenth century. Descartes wrote, for instance, in his *First Meditation* (1641):

> I am accustomed to sleep and in my dreams to imagine the same things that lunatics imagine when awake, or sometimes things which are even less plausible. . . . I realize so clearly that there are no conclusive indications by which waking life can be distinguished from sleep that I am quite astonished, and my bewilderment is such that it is almost able to convince me that I am sleeping.[4]

Roy Porter (1997, 9) quotes a slightly later example:

> Working with the Lockean tradition, Augustan satirists and philosophers like David Hume were . . . deeply troubled by the possibility that the individual was nothing more than an unstable heap of impressions. Under such circumstances, what guarantee was there that the same person would wake up as the one who went to sleep the night before?

Two centuries later, Marcel Proust gave a more brilliant description of the ordeal of waking up from sleep:

> In my own bed, my sleep was so heavy as completely to relax my consciousness, for then I lost all sense of the place in which I had gone to

sleep, and when I awoke at midnight, not knowing where I was, I could not be sure at first who I was. I had only the most rudimentary sense of existence, such as may lurk and flicker in the depths of an animal's consciousness; but then . . . memory . . . would come like a rope let down from heaven to draw me out of the abyss of nonbeing. . . . In a flash I would traverse and surmount centuries of civilization, and out of a half-visualized succession of oil lamps, followed by shirts with turned-down collars, would put together by degrees the component parts of my ego.[5]

Recently, the daily struggle for the reintegration of our personality has been described by a number of scholars in a more prosaic and scholarly way; in Patrick H. Hutton's words (1988, 134), for instance: "Each day we make ourselves anew in fresh formulations."

In the popular imagination, and in the folklore of various civilizations, the night was the time of darkness, of dangers, of the realm of evil spirits, temptations, and death. And, accordingly, people protected themselves against these dangers with various rituals.[6] The belief that one embarked on a dangerous journey every evening was strong in the Christian tradition as well. There was a rich literature of evening prayers, in which the faithful prayed to God and asked His protection "in the night of sorrow and anxiety, when we are surrounded by darkness of doubt and temptation and the bitter night of death."[7] And in the morning, they thanked God that He had protected them at night "against the acts of darkness," the "harmful" spirits, "all kinds of evil, dangers, the temptation of the Devil, and sudden death."[8]

In our contemporary civilization, we may be less anxious about these metaphysical dangers. But we, too, go through a chaotic experience during the night, and in the morning, when we emerge from the world of dreams, when we arrive at the threshold of our daily lives, we may be lost, we as well may be uncertain about who we are. Our limbs are lax, our muscles do not obey our torpid will, and we feel weak, disintegrated, and perhaps even miserable. We have to pull ourselves together. We have to reconstruct our selves.

Our mood depends on several things, however; on our age, on our lives, on the day ahead of us. And we may react in different ways to the necessity of getting out of our bed. Let me describe a scenario known to most of us over thirty or thirty-five. It may have some lessons even for those who are world champions in the not-yet-Olympic event of the Morning Hurdle of Self-Reconstruction.

Kings, Zebras, Humans

In the seventeenth and eighteenth centuries, the French called *"lever"*[9] the morning ceremony in the royal palace in the course of which the king was woken up, washed, clad, and prepared for his daily duties by a whole army of courtiers and ladies in waiting, as well as the royal physicians and servants.[10] It was a great privilege to be among the guests of honor who could watch the ceremony. The king, and among them Le Roi Soleil, rose from his bed and from the darkness of night, as the Sun rose over the country and the world. The ceremony reconfirmed every morning the might and majesty, the dignity and (almost) divinity of the king. But we do not know how all this fanfare and hocus-pocus shaped the king's character and self. The recurrence of Caligula-, Henry VIII–, or Ivan the Terrible–type royal figures may indicate that this process has not always been beneficial.

Are everyday people in a better position? Is it easier for them to develop and maintain a harmonious, open, well-balanced self that is rich in ideas and emotions, quick in responding to the challenges of a changing world, and able to help them achieve a life of dignity and fulfillment? Yes, perhaps, they are in a better position. But self-construction, or the care for one's self, is a difficult process and task at any time, in any human situation.

Like it or not, it seems to be a fact that we, humans, spend more time on the construction and daily reconstruction of our selves than, for instance, cats and wild ducks spend on caring for their fur or plumage. And they care a lot. As I write these lines, I look out my window on a lake. It is the misty early morning hours. I see flocks of wild ducks preening themselves with great care and devotion. They seem to have their own problems of morning self-reconstruction. But all this seems to be a trifle as compared with our morning ordeals.

We may be those beings on this planet who are likely to have the most fragile selves, and this fragility may be the source of our obsession with these selves. When they awake in the morning, lions, zebras, and finches may immediately recover their strong and sound lion, zebra, or finch identity, whereas when it is our turn to awake, our identities as human beings usually lie in ruins. We have to go through a ritual every morning in the course of which we must reconstruct ourselves from scratch. And we have to make haste because we usually do not have too much time at our disposal. As the heroine of a famous novel answered her husband, when he scolded her for starting the day by smoking a cigarette: "I have to immediately make my life tolerable."[11]

Prayer

There are many among us who begin their day by saying a prayer. Reestablishing their contact with the celestial powers, they may feel safer in this world still submerged in the twilight of the dawn. Confessing their sins, they may leave behind their burdens and start a new page in their lives. The morning prayer may purify them of their unconscious thoughts, wishes, temptations, of the chaos and demons of the night. And it may help them feel safe in a world of order and Providence.

In earlier centuries, people may have been in a better position. Think, for instance, of how many symbols and symbolic spheres protected people living in a medieval European city. First, there was God governing the whole universe. Then came the choir of angels, the cosmic spheres, those of the fixed stars, the *Primum Movens,* the planets, that safely surrounded the world. The city and the guilds had their patron saints. The churches and sanctuaries in the city assured the personal presence of the divinity within the community. The walls of the city, and the houses, were consecrated every year. People got a patron saint at their baptism. Guardian angels, icons, holy objects, amulets, relics, and a wide range of superstitions protected them throughout their lives. The sound of the tolling bells chased the evil spirits from the city several times a day. Various rituals did the same at certain points in the year. Religious ceremonies reconfirmed people's close links with the divine. . . . Shall I continue?

In comparison with this multilayered protection, this multiplication of protective symbolic spheres and magic forces, what protects people and their selves in our contemporary societies? Our first reaction would be to say that people now have much less protection against the dangers and evils of an alien world. But we might be mistaken.

In many ways, people live nowadays in a safer world than their ancestors did. They, their rights, their interests, their persons, their freedom, and their dignity are much better protected now, at least in the developed world, than they were before. Social safety, too, has dramatically improved in the more affluent parts of the world; most of the diseases are not so fearful as they used to be; physical survival and well-being are much better guaranteed than they were before. And so on.

But what about the equally important symbolic protection? Is it less watertight, or anxiety-tight, now than it was before? I am not sure, but it certainly is stronger than is usually presumed. Religious faith is still important for a great number of people. Superstitions have survived several centuries of modernization.[12] Traditional ceremonies are still in use, though they have lost some of their mystique or magic power. In spite of centuries of enlightenment, myths still play a major role in people's lives. Experts even speak of a new "symbolic revolution" and of the "reenchantment" of the world, which we shall analyze in detail in part two of this book, where we discuss the situation of the self in our contemporary consumer civilization.[13]

The First Cigarette

There is a large literature on the methods psychologists may use to help people quit smoking. But only a few important studies I know of also study the role smoking may play in *shaping* people's selves and lives (beyond the health consequences).[14] It may politically incorrect to say, but it seems to be a fact that beyond being a dangerous and destructive addiction, smoking is also a means—even if an elusive and deceitful means—of self-construction.

For those who smoke, lighting a cigarette may be of great help in their morning reconstruction of their selves. The flame of the match may be the first warm and friendly signal in a yet alien world. The rituals of lighting and smoking may reassure them that they can act and move around as human persons of character and dignity. The elegant gestures start rebuilding their egos and self-confidence. The transparent blue smoke curling up philosophically tells them that life may be full of strange and sweet mysteries, that it is more than physical existence; it is also a world of harmony, freedom, and spirituality. And smoking the cigarette may be a brief moment of meditation on life, on the passing of time, on their situation in the world, their selves. Such moments may be less frequent in the lives of nonsmokers, who keep running after their business and do not stop for these brief moments of silence. But this does not mean, of course, that there are not better, and less dangerous, ways of meditation and self-construction. The morning cup of coffee is not necessarily one of them.

The First Cup of Coffee

After waking up, and if the alarm clock has not jump-started us, we begin the ordeal of picking up the pieces of our selves. Many of us have special programs for this purpose. We may have an algorithm of how to proceed with the least effort and anxiety, and with the greatest efficacy. We may first decide which of our feet to stretch out first from under the blanket; and also of how to open our eyes, how to succeed in sitting up and, which is even more difficult, how to stand up and look around in a room full of the litter of the previous evening and the shadows of the night. A glimmer of sunshine through the shutter may be of great help in finding our way back into life. After reposing for a moment, we may totter out in the kitchen, make and drink a cup of coffee, which is euphemistically called the "sunshine" of people living in the North. And even if it is not sunshine, it fills us with the warmth of life; its sweetness suggests that the coming day may have its delights, and its bitterness warns us that we also have to be prepared for the darker sides of life.

Mugs and cups, too, play an important role in these moments. If we have a favorite one, perceiving it in its usual place on the shelf may be the first, friendly, heart-warming message of a world that we lost during the night. It may be the first link between our former selves and us. The mug may be sunshine-yellow, life-red, sky-blue, and meadows-green; it may shine as the symbol of life and the pristine beauty of the world. We may prefer china ware; its white brilliance, fragility, and elegance may be the first glimmer of hope that we may disentangle ourselves from the formlessness of the night and recover, or recreate, the reassuring forms of our daily lives and selves.

But these peaceful moments will not spare us a serious shock.

The Mirror

The shock comes in the moment when we enter the bathroom and look in the mirror over the basin and stare at the ruins of our face.[15] The face is undoubtedly ours, but it is entirely unacceptable. Our hair is disheveled, our face has shrunk into a maze of wrinkles; it has the taint of a cave dweller, and our eyes are looking at us out of pits of swollen flesh.

First, we close our eyes in horror. Then we cautiously open them and have a closer look at our wrinkles and try to find out if they have recently deepened or not. And then, with a sigh, we go on with the rituals of reconstructing ourselves.

There are merciful and merciless mirrors. The merciful ones smooth the wrinkles of our face and envelop them in the soft and mysterious light of a portrait by da Vinci or Rafael. The merciless ones show us ten years older than we are; they parch our skins, shrink our eyes, and discolor our skins. But they may have the advantage of forcefully prompting us to immediately go on with the reconstruction work. There are gentle and pleasant, and there are more radical and not at all pleasant, ways of doing this reconstruction.

The Magic Shower

As a pleasant solution, people may take a hot and cold shower and thereby achieve several things. First, in most cases, they will feel themselves better in their hides after, than before, the shower. Second, the shower will mobilize their vital energies and make them feel stronger and more athletic, even if they are not particularly that type of person. Third, a cold shower releases endorphins in their bodies so that they suddenly feel themselves victorious and ebullient; they may even suddenly feel that their lives have a meaning and purpose. Which probably is not the case. Fourth, taking a shower has also a mythical dimension.

It is a kind of a "rite of passage."[16] The morning shower is a water curtain between the darkness of the night and the lights of the new day. We pass through it as mythic heroes; as youngsters in the rituals of initiation; or as Mozart's Pamina and Tamino in *The Magic Flute* pass through waterfalls and fire walls. The shadows of the night are washed off us, and we are reborn to the new day.

The Toothpaste of Immortality

If people are asked in focus groups why they buy and use toothpaste, most of them give a conservative and almost anachronistic answer. They say that their purpose in doing so is to cleanse their teeth therewith. And in the course of the discussion, they are (usually pleasantly) surprised to discover a deeper layer of meaning under the surface of this trivial everyday exercise.

First, brushing our teeth and feeling the fresh taste and piquant fragrance of the white foam, a glimmer of hope may flash up in us: In spite of the long night, there may be joy, sunshine, and springtime in this gloomy world. Second, we go on washing our teeth with the—unfounded—conviction (generated by TV commercials) that our teeth will become, and remain, snow white. Third, at a certain point, when we have already the impression that, due to brushing and thanks to the paste, they already shine beautifully, we begin to regain our self-confidence; we look in the mirror and we may (try to) like what we see; the Big Bad Wolf is looking back at us, full of energy and self-confidence, smiling maliciously and flashing his (or her) teeth; we are almost ready for the daily fight in the arena of life. Fourth, a brilliantly white row of teeth helps us reenter the social space, whereas decaying, yellowish teeth would exclude us from it. In other words, by brushing our teeth with the right brand of toothpaste, we are on the best way to transform ourselves from disintegrated, alien, sleepy biological beings into human persons and citizens with rights and duties. Fifth, if we use the right brand of toothpaste, which is allegedly used by, say, Julia Roberts or the latest version of Agent 007, then we have found our place not only in our small community but also at the very center of the world; in the center of beauty, wealth, and success, in the midst of the jet set, where the real people live and the real things happen. Our egos fill in, more and more, our hides. And last but not least, a top brand of toothpaste is capable of even more spectacular feats. Believe it or not, it is able to stop the wheel of time. It will—at least if we watch enough commercials, which make us believe that this or that special brand of toothpaste preserves our teeth, and *per metonymiam* ourselves—make us young and beautiful indefinitely. And then, for a fleeting moment, there, in our bathrooms, we experience the sweet and melancholy illusion that we may stay young and beautiful forever; that we may defeat mortality; we may defeat decay and death. The toothpaste may help us enter the sacred fields of eternity.

The trivial and the existential interact in our daily lives and shape our selves, even if we do not know that they are doing so.

Exercise

Human beings have ever been concerned with the shape, health, and appearance of their bodies. But it is a relatively recent discovery of psychology and psychiatry that our body—that is, the perception of our body, our "body image"—plays a major role in shaping our personality, our self.[17] With the exception of cultural anthropologists, social scientists were relatively late to follow suit. But the importance and preeminence of the human body has become so obvious in our contemporary consumer civilization, in the world of television, advertising, cosmetics, "makeover programs," the cult of fitness, beauty, and sexuality, that sociologists have also started to explore this field and investigate the relevance of the human body. Philosophers, conversely, have ever considered the human body, and its relationship with the human soul, or self, as a fascinating and difficult problem.[18]

In the morning, the world is big and strong and we are small and weak. We have to redress the balance. Flexing our muscles, a bit of aerobic flinging and kicking about, a short visit to our fitness room, or swimming a few laps may provide us with the illusion that we are strong and young and invincible. (And we may have even acquired a certain degree of immunity against the attacks of feelings of guilt when we start eating a heavy breakfast.)

And we do not even need to bother too much. In our modern consumer civilization, we may acquire a stronger and more beautiful body without any effort. Table 1.1 quotes a typical text that advertised an exercise machine in a

TABLE 1.1

A Magical Machine

New
ULTRATONE FUTURA
The *Ultimate* Bodyshaper

Ultratone is the exercise machine with a difference.
It does the exercise for you. In days rather than
weeks you can trim your waistline. And build up
your biceps at the same time.

Want to turn a midriff bulge into a firmer, flatter
stomach? Like to strengthen your leg muscles?
Pack power into your thighs?

Ultratone's the answer for all that, too.
You'll also be reassured to know that it's the only
system of its kind approved to the
Highest Medical Standards.

So why spend weeks in the gym when
Ultratone can get you into great shape at home?

No sweat.

lifestyle magazine.[19] Beyond the usual advertising tricks—using superlatives ("*Ultratone*," "*ultimate*"); stressing the uniqueness of the commodity ("*with a difference*," "*the only system*"); promising beauty, youth, strength, power, a better self-image, self confidence ("*trim your waistline*," "*build up your biceps*," "*firmer, flatter stomach*," "*strengthen your leg muscles*," "*pack power into your thighs*," "*get you into great shape*"); legitimizing itself with mystique scientific authorities ("*approved to the Highest Medical Standards*"); promising the solution of all our problems ("*Ultratone's the answer for all that*")—it also emphasizes the fact that one can achieve all this without any effort: Ultratone *"does the exercise for you." "In days rather than weeks." "No sweat."* And the picture in the advertisement sweetens the whole business with a bit of sex appeal.

There are, however, and have ever been, more radical and brutal ways of transforming one's body to conform to social and cultural norms or to protect oneself, one's self, against the dangers and anxieties of human life. Gehlen (1988 [1940]) and Scheler (1961 [1928]) were right in describing humans as premature beings, who have to create themselves, and their world; but as far as I remember, they did not include the physical transformation of the human body as part of this self- and world-creation. They did not, despite the fact that their fellow humans may have felt the need of it since prehistoric times. Think of the various ceremonies and techniques of cheek-piercing, lip-enlargement, neck-elongation, foot-distortion, and the like. Western civilization was not completely void of these practices, but in the past few centuries it did not go beyond distorting women's bodies by corsets and high-heeled slippers. The change has come only recently, with the spectacular development of cosmetic and (the more radical) plastic surgery, and the new pressures, desires, and fears in the emerging consumer civilization. Due to these changes, the number of cosmetic interventions has grown almost exponentially. When I am writing these lines in Washington, several series on "makeover" and "extreme makeover" are running on the TV channels. Transforming one's body has become the rage, and sometimes almost a duty. People, and in this case especially women, have to obey the expectation of the new age. They have to be young, fit, and beautiful if they want to be accepted and successful in their societies, if they want to "actualize their selves" and fulfill their lives.[20]

It is understandable, then, that scholars have recently devoted more and more attention to the human body. They argue that the importance of one's body image in shaping one's self cannot be overemphasized. The way in which one perceives one's body profoundly affects one's self. It is a common experience of ours that our self-image may substantially change depending on how we feel. Aging, fatigue, illness, fever, injury, let alone a trauma, a paralysis, alcoholism or drug addiction, may radically change, or distort, one's self and self-image.[21]

One may get ill if one has a negative body image; vice versa, if one is ill, one's body image may deteriorate. A body injury may cause a deep personality trauma. The majority of people, more women than men, are dissatisfied with their bodies, and some of them develop serious neuroses in trying to conform themselves to the (changing) cultural norms of an ideal body shape. There is empirical evidence according to which in the past two decades American women have wanted to become slimmer than the male population's image of the ideal woman would have suggested, and, vice versa, men have wanted to be stronger, bigger, and more muscular than their female partner would love them to be.[22]

Social and cultural norms are very strong in this field. They do not leave much choice for people, and especially for women. There have been civilizations and historical periods, for instance, in which corpulence, fat, and bulging hips and bosoms were almost compulsory, while in the last hundred years an opposite trend has set in. The ideal body shape has become thinner and thinner. This has led to the paradoxical situation that in our consumer civilization, in which everything prompts us to consume more and more, and TV commercials overflow with foamy ice creams and chocolate rivers, women are forced to slim themselves to skeletal skinniness. They may be the victims of a deep human striving for equilibrium; in this age of overconsumption, we probably feel the necessity of counterbalancing our physical repletion with the ascetic and spiritual thinness of women.

The Coiffure

Our mirror, and our civilization, prompt us also to care about our forelock. This is a difficult job. This is the part of the body with which humankind has never been able to really get along. It is the only part of the body that has kept changing throughout human history. People have tried to find new and newer solutions, experimenting with various ways of cutting, combing, fixing, curling, crisping, dying, and braiding it. But—at least in the last centuries of Western civilization—they have not found a solution that could survive for more than a generation.

This has been a real failure, because the state of our coiffure seems to be, par excellence, an important part of our self-image and public appearance. The fact that—as opposed to other parts of our bodies—it can be formed, deformed, and transformed with ease and without too much pain has lent it a preeminent role in our efforts to construct our selves. Humankind has copiously availed itself of this opportunity. There were times and places in which it was used to indicate social rank. It has been both a source of erotic charm, and, on the contrary, a sign of discipline and moral rigor. It can freely fly and flame and stream in the wind, or be twisted into a decent plait, or be hidden under a timid veil. It can be used to enhance a beautiful, and hide a plain, face. It can be combed, curled, waved, tousled, trimmed, cut, or shaved to suggest freedom or discipline, frolic or dignity, caprice or languor, male power or womanly charm, bohemian nonchalance or philistine orderliness. It can be towered up like a queen' crown or sleeked like a frisky cap; it can wave mysteriously or stand up like a clown's hair, flame fiery red, shine like gold, or be submerged in the night. It can float softly like a cloud or pour down, heavily, like a waterfall. What a fantastic material for shaping and constructing our selves!

And what an anxiety when in the morning we have to handle it, invent its shape that would best suit the role we want to play that day. It is not by chance that the cosmetic industry—which flies to our assistance with all its shampoos, vitamins, and vitamin-pros; conditioners, jellies, sprays, tonics, mousses, dyes, and gadgets—makes billions of dollars in profit.

There are human beings among us for whom this everyday struggle is even more exhausting. They are doomed to failure *ab ovo,* but they are unable to accept and acknowledge this fact. They are unable to confess it to themselves, and to the world. They are unable to do so because their self-image would be deeply wounded if they did. I speak of the miserable souls who are dangerously getting bald.

Why does he, who is one of these victims, comb desperately the rest of his hair, getting thinner and thinner every week, from his nape to the crown of his head and to his forehead? The comb-furrowed thin hair sets off his baldness even more. It betrays his vanity and the weakness that he is ashamed of being a baldpate; that he may be a general or the prime minister but has miserably failed, has been defeated, is lying on the floor, is humiliated. The last starveling lad with a fine head of hair victoriously steps over him, in the limelight of all the beautiful young ladies of the world. Life has humiliated him; time has put the stamp of mortality on him. Under the uniform of power and wealth, a weak, frail, mortal being has been revealed. The king is naked. The cloven hoof is showing, the mortal being under the public gloss and mask.

Hypocrisy and lying are written all over his face. He wants to cheat us. And what is much worse: He is seen trying to cheat himself. He throws himself on our mercy because we already know that he is weak and mortal while he is still deluding himself, closes his eyes, and buries his (bald) head in sand. We see his foolishness, his lack of judgment. He believes that by combing the rest of his hair on his forehead he increases his market value, while just the contrary happens. His weakness betrayed, his market value decreases. He harms himself, but he cannot help doing so. Because the loss of youth, the loss of life, the terror of transience, the desire to stop time is stronger than anything else.

Yes, ultimately, we all want to defeat time and death by painstakingly combing and dressing our hair. We want to intensify our lives; we try to stay in the thick of life. We do not want to accept and acknowledge that we are losing ground, are sliding down in the hierarchy of life, that we are not any more the kings of life; that our life forces are oozing away.

Power and wealth may help a lot, however. They may partly offset the loss of hair and turn the glitter of a bald head into a glamorous aureole. There are people who were bald in their twenties and made brilliant careers. But don't envy them for their morning ordeals.

There is, of course, a method that radically solves the problem: One may shave one's head. In this way, one may transform oneself from a pitiful victim into a hero, who has freely decided to mutilate himself. And history, too, may come to one's aid, as has happened, for instance, in recent years. In a slightly perverse way, and perhaps partly due to the success of the *Kojak* cop show on TV, the bald head has become a symbol of male vitality, aggression, and even beauty. Poor Samson is turning in his grave.

Makeup

To make up: a curious and ambiguous term. According to *Webster's Dictionary,* it may simply refer to a process of constituting, composing something (and thus it fits well in the process of self-construction we are discussing here).[23] It may also refer to the final stage, the completion of a process (of self-reconstruction). It may mean that the subject adjusts, corrects, and compensates for a deficiency.[24] It may also suggest that the subject prepares a guise, a mask for herself.[25] Whatever the motive, making up is part of women's morning ritual of self-reconstruction. It helps them enter the world with a stronger self-confidence—and find the roles they think to be optimal. As so many Botticellis and Titians, they paint themselves into angels or demons, femmes fatales or reliable businesswomen, primae donnae or ingénues, nice housewives or bluestockings. After all, it is easier to build up and play a role than to build up one's genuine self.

Perfumes

Women have an additional wonder weapon for their morning self-reconstruction: a liquid, which is called perfume. On the surface, people like perfumes for their fragrance, which may be light or heavy, fresh or luscious, spiritual or sexy. But perfumes are much more than that. They have a long history of magic and mystery, which have been developed in the past decades into a rich and holistic mythology through the efforts and ingenuity of the art of advertising.[26]

Perfume posters and commercials enchant you with the magic messages of self-actualization and personal fulfillment. It is enough to touch yourself with the stopper, and your spirit or inner splendor is set free.[27] You become *"une femme imprévisible,"*[28] a "tender and wild amazon," or "tender and savage" as a panther,[29] bright, wild, flirty, and eccentric,[30] an "easy-going and nature loving woman at ease with life and in harmony with herself."[31] The perfume may be "soft, feminine and created for fulfilled, contemporary women."[32] It may "redefine" your femininity and celebrate your beauty.[33] Perfumes may help you escape from the boredom, vulgarity, and emptiness of your everyday world and experience the mysterious and sensual life of never-heard-of oriental queens.[34]

Under the spell of these perfumes, you may discover yourself, your deep sensuality,[35] or even the essence of your being.[36] You may feel yourself strong enough for "changing your life."[37] You may learn the secret of seduction,[38] or the art of how to live without boundaries.[39] You may achieve the Faustian ideal of *"das ewig Weibliche,"*[40] rise up to the heights of Nietzschean superwomen, and say with pride, arrogance, and defiance: "I am as I am."[41] Your life may become authentic.[42] Or it will become more than just life: It will be "destiny."[43]

Using the right perfume, you will be different, you will be the creator of yourself[44] and achieve success.[45] You will celebrate the joy of life[46] and "radiate with happiness."[47] You will discover perfection and the harmony of your life.[48] You will escape from the bondage of a material and mortal world into the freedom of pure spirituality.[49]

The world of perfumes and perfume posters is the very apotheosis of human life. It suggests that a human being can attain the highest, ecstatic degrees of pleasure and happiness, freedom, and fulfillment. With such a message, and such self-assurance, it is certainly easier to start the day. If the fragrance in itself is not enough, there is the beauty and the splendor of the bottle and the golden liquid within it: They suggest that you live in a perfect and brilliant universe. Life is beautiful, resplendent, pure, innocent, tempting, transparent, golden, valuable. After the darkness of night, the morning world is magnificent and transparent. After the chaos of your dreams, the world is now full of spirituality and brilliance. Perfection, plenitude, and eternity have triumphed over fragmentation, the void, and transitoriness. The adventure of life is waiting for you.[50]

Let me remind the reader that we are still in the first half an hour after our hero or heroine has got out of his or her bed, and we have already witnessed a whole series of efforts at reconstructing, shaping, and protecting their selves— efforts of which the actors themselves were not conscious, or were only partly conscious. On the surface, they were running through their trivial morning routines; but at the same time, at a deeper level, they were involved in the real drama of their lives: in their fight for the fulfillment of their selves and lives. If this latent arsenal of means of self-construction means were not at their disposal, they would flock in long lines to the consulting rooms of psychiatrists in search of their selves.

The Fashion Show

The next steps in people's morning ritual bring them to their wardrobe, which may be the place of their most important transubstantiation.[51] It is not the cowl that makes the monk, but it is the clothes that make the human person. At least we, people living in Western civilization, conceive and visualize the human person as dressed. People without their clothes on lose a substantial part of their personality. This may be the reason for the embarrassment of people meeting one another in a public bath or on the beach: They may have difficulty even in addressing one another. Human language is a means of communication between people with certain social identities, and the clothes we wear are indispensable parts of these identities.

On a spring morning in 2004, former president Jimmy Carter came to the Woodrow Wilson International Center for Scholars to celebrate the twenty-fifth anniversary of the Camp David agreement. Working as a scholar at the center, I went to the meeting dressed rather casually. I wore my badge, so I could enter, but the hostesses and the security guards were at a loss to find out who I might be in my jeans and shirt in the very elegant company of guests dressed in upscale business suits. "Are you from the press?" "Are you from the media?" they kept asking, and the question "Aren't you a terrorist?" may have been on the tips of their tongues.

In earlier times, stripping people of their clothes (and of the signs of their status in their own social hierarchy, and of their names) was an important part of the ritual in the course of which a free warrior, having been captured, was turned into a slave without social identity and human personality. Mutatis mutandis, this practice is still in use in prisons, where inmates are stripped of their civilian clothes and their names; they wear prison overalls and are called by a number.

In the morning, we have to reconstruct our social identities which we lost at night. Dressing ourselves is one of the most important elements in this self-reconstruction. This is not an easy task, because we may play various roles, and each of these roles may be linked to a different style of clothing. We have to decide which of our personalities we want to assume, which of our roles we intend to play in the course of the day. That of the respectable citizen? The swinging yuppie? The big-ego manager? The nicely awkward intellectual? The melancholy person who has got a soul? The macho? The idealist? The realist?

If one happens to be a woman, the task will be even more difficult, because women seem to have a wider range of personalities and roles at their disposal. Standing before their mirrors, and trying on various combinations of different pieces of their wardrobes, they play on the keyboard of various possible personalities and roles. They may want to look smart and reliable, disciplined or *cabotine* and capricious, serene or serious, manager-like or dreamy, harmonious or disharmonious, a Cinderella or a vamp, Desdemona or Lady Macbeth, Madame Curie or Nicole Kidman. Having made up their minds, they gradually build up the self that they can best accept for that day. According to the testimony of most women, this is a delightful and at the same time anguishing experience. One may hit upon one's innermost, genuine, authentic, winning personality; or one may lose oneself, at least for a day, in a wrong and muddled identity.

And this is only part of the story. People's freedom in the composition of their wardrobes and the choice of their daily apparel is strictly limited by cultural traditions, social status, norms of subculture, fashions, group dynamics, "collective selection pressures," advertising and mass market influences, age, lifestyle, levels of affluence, and other factors.[52] In her 650-page monograph *The Social Psychology of Clothing*, Susan Kaiser (1997, 248) reports on a study in which eighty business graduate students were asked to draw the profile of people in various occupations by mentioning the products these people would be likely to own. Here are some of the product-constellations:

> For the occupational label *professional*, the products generated included a Seiko watch, Burberry raincoat, Lacoste shirt, *Atlantic* magazine, Brooks Brothers suit, Bass loafers, silk tie, French wine, and a BMW. In contrast, the label *blue collar* elicited the following products: Schaefer beer, AMF bowling ball, Ford pick-up truck, Levi's jeans, Marlboro cigarettes, RCA TV, *Field and Stream,* Black and Decker tools, and McDonald's.

Another difficulty lies in the paradoxical character of fashion. To be fashionable means, namely, two opposite, self-exclusive things simultaneously. On the one hand, it means to conform oneself to the current norms of dressing well in the social group of which one wants to be a distinguished member. But, on the other hand, to be fashionable also means that you do not conform 100 percent. "To shock is chic."[53] You have to be different, personal, and unique. Within conformity, you have to construct your special identity. Tension and balance of conformity and nonconformity, of group membership and a unique personality, is the precondition of being elegant. If you are unable to achieve this delicate and exciting balance, then you are either dull and gray and submerged in the anonymous crowd, or you are an eccentric lacking judgment, good taste, and elegance, and the group will ostracize you.[54] This is the source of the trauma of women who have bought a designer dress, an expensive and unique model, and then run up against their alter egos wearing the same dress at the next cocktail party. They are unmasked and shamed as people who have bought their identities.

It is not easy to orient oneself in the world of fashion, because fashion is a complex system of signs. In his famous book *The Fashion System,* Roland Barthes (1983 [1967]) analyzed fashion as a system of signs, a language and speech (the French *langue* and *parole*). He listed (pp. 105–10) not less than sixty categories ("genera") of pieces and articles of clothing, with several variants within most of the categories,[55] and he defined (pp. 111–60) dozens of "syntactical" rules according to which these categories can be combined.[56]

This is an extremely rich and flexible language. By combining the various pieces of clothing, one can convey a wide range of emotions, intentions, attitudes, moods, and even world views; one can assume a wide range of roles and construct one's personality in many different ways. Which does not mean that one is totally free in using these signs and combinations, because there are cultural and temporal constraints that restrict one's freedom. On the one hand, one's social and cultural context, and one's actual situation, and on the other hand the cyclical character of fashion, restrict the set of possible choices and combinations. Barthes (1983, 295) quotes Kroeber and Richardson (1940, 295–96), who studied the history of women's dress fashions[57] and found that beyond the yearly rotation, fashion has also a rotation of longer duration making a whole cycle in about one century. Depending on which cycle you are in, you have to make different choices.

If someone does not "speak" this language of fashion, she cannot know the (hidden) message that her way of dressing communicates about her to her environment. This may be a serious handicap, it may give the wrong message about her, and it may disturb her efforts of self-construction and self-presentation.

And this is not yet the end of the ordeal. Clothes are also an important tool in people's fight for freedom and autonomy. By dressing, they oppose themselves to nature; they state the fact that they are different. Jean Baudrillard claimed that fashion was the "cult of the artificial."[58] According to others, even the simplest clothing has ever been the tool for denaturalizing the body: for opposing the artificial—that is, civilization—to nature and the natural; for emphasizing the constructed nature of the human body; and thereby for convincing ourselves that we, humans, are able to subdue nature and create ourselves as autonomous personalities.

There have been ages in which the contrast between nature and the artificial was especially stressed. Think of the cult of the artificial practiced by the nineteenth century dandy, or of the increasing importance of the "pointless," "the contingent, the decorative, the futile" in the era of postmodernism.[59] Do people know that they "speak" (fluently or stammering) this complex language of fashion when they dress themselves in the morning? And how far are they aware of the fact that they construct and shape their selves by doing so?

Stripes

To dress oneself us is a dangerous profession. One has to proceed with caution. One may make serious mistakes, for instance, if one is not familiar with the symbolic functions of the various pieces of clothing. Let me give an example. What happens if you put on a striped skirt or walk with a streaked handbag? It gives you a youthful, playful look. But if you had done the same thing in the Middle Ages, you would have been looked at with horror. Why?

In his book *The Stuff of the Devil*, Michel Pastoureau (1991) tells us the fascinating history of striped cloth. In the Middle Ages, striped cloth and clothes symbolized diversity (*varietas*[60]), and for the medieval culture what was *varius* always referred to something unclean, aggressive, immoral, or cheating. "A man qualified as *varius* was a sly dog, a liar, he was supposed to be cruel or ill (suffering mainly of a mental or skin disease."[61] In medieval illustrations, traitors (Cain, Judas), cruel people (hangmen), madmen (jesters, . . .), invalids (lepers), prostitutes, Mohammedans, Jews, and clowns wore striped clothes.[62] When the Carmelite friars returned from the Holy Land in the thirteenth century, they wore habits striped in white and brown, or white and black. But such was the outrage that—after decades of resistance—they had to change to pure white.[63]

Animals suffered the same segregation. The striped (*tigridus*) and spotted (*maculosus*) animals became the symbols of bloodthirstiness (the tiger), cruelty (the hyena), viciousness (the leopard), and slyness (the snake and the wasp). Even the poor zebras were abhorred as vicious and dangerous beasts, until people in Europe saw the first samples with their own eyes in the mid–eighteenth century.[64]

In a few cases, stripes kept their negative character up to our own day. Think, for instance, of the striped overalls of prison inmates in a number of countries. But this is now the exception. In the course of the nineteenth century, stripes slowly changed their sign, and today we associate striped clothes and objects not with depravity, illness, or immorality but, on the contrary, with youth, joy, playful eccentricity, and irregularity.[65] Whereas in the Middle Ages, to be different was to be disorderly, immoral, and ill, nowadays to be different is a virtue; it is a sign of being an autonomous personality, of having a genuine self.

Jewels

Beware jewels. The love of jewels is a vicious trap for the self. Golden jewels and diamonds are especially dangerous; mainly for those who are on the wrong side of forty. Jewels have an inner fire, they have a deep inner radiation of perfection, of the intensity and fullness of existence, of harmony, significance, and, mainly, timelessness and eternity. And those who wear them may feel and believe that they, the jewels, lend them this deep radiance of beauty, significance, life, youth, and immortality. Alas, in most cases they don't. They do just the opposite. If you already struggle with age, if your beauty has been ravaged by time, if you yourself do not have an inner fire of life, significance, and energy, then, by their contrast, jewels set off the signs of decay. I think, and I may be mistaken, that with age, golden rings, bracelets, and necklaces should become more and more thin and light, fragile and transparent. Instead of youth, buoyant energy, and the fullness of life, they should radiate the beauty, harmony, and dignity of a frail human being who has accepted the human condition of mortality.

Knickknacks

Small is not only beautiful but powerful as well. In the mythic imagination, dwarfs are symbols of energy, and amulets are sources of magic power. The predilection of women for armlets, lockets, rings, and pendants may probably be explained by the fact that these small objects—and they often have some symbolic or mythic allusions as well—function as quasi-amulets. They are sources of energy, and they surround those who wear them with a magic sphere of protection. One can touch them, hold them, and cling to them as to small Archimedean points in a vast and empty universe. This may be one of the reasons of the fact that holding and manipulating small objects, such as lighters, pipes, and keys, has a stress-reducing effect.[66] They are simple, solid, tangible objects in a vague, uncertain, far-too-complex universe—let alone the fact that most of them, pebbles for instance, cope much better with time than we do. Holding them, we hold a small piece of timelessness, or almost eternity, in our hands.

Shoes

I have almost forgotten shoes. Yet there are few things more important than shoes. Shoes are telling signs and symbols of one's self. In comparison with them, everything else is of only secondary importance. Which does not mean that it is enough to put on shoes and you are ready to go for a walk on the Champs Élysées.

No. Shoes are not the whole and sufficient truth. But if we perceive new, clean, elegant, and well-designed shoes on somebody, then his trousers may be ragged, his jacket rumpled, he may wear threadbare jeans, a creased shirt, and a weather-worn coat—we know that the slovenly aura is only a camouflage, a sign of nonchalance; it hides somebody who may be able to afford not to dress too formally. And, vice versa, your clothing may be of the highest quality, expensive, of an elegant brand, but if cheap, dirty, trodden shoes peep out of your trousers, the whole effect is spoiled. Your elegance turns out to be a fake. Your shoes suggest poverty; you have an ill-groomed look. And we believe the shoes, and not the clothes.

Why? Why are shoes so important?

Perhaps—and this is only a hypothesis to be proved—because shoes touch the ground, the dusty, dirty, muddy tarmac of the street. Clean, well-polished, elegant shoes separate us from this material world of dirt, filth, and decay; they protect our personality, our selves, and our human autonomy; they emphasize that we belong to a cleaner, more noble, and spiritual world. We are different; we are independent and free.

And what about the recurrent fashion of high-heeled women's shoes? Why do women and men find those high heels so attractive?

There may be several reasons for this. The routine answer would be that high heels make legs look long, and long legs have an erotic radiance. But this is only part of the answer. High heels and elegant, light, well-designed slippers lift their wearer off the ground and lift her over a heavy and dirty material world into a world of elegance, freedom, and spirituality.[67] There is a strange dual effect here: High heels simultaneously emphasize women's sex appeal and spirituality; their bearable lightness of being.

In certain ages, the fashion of high heels may have had social causes as well. Women may have tried, for instance, to "raise" themselves to the level of men by adding a few inches to their stature. But, in doing so, they walked into a trap because, in this way, they became even more valuable sexual prey. And they became even more dependent on their male partners—because, toddling on high heels, they became even weaker, more clumsy, and more helpless (though they were lucky that in this part of the world men at least did not force them, with similar intentions, to physically cripple their feet). Men, conversely, wore heavy boots in which they could trample over hill and dale and could lend a helping hand to beauties in distress, which is a cherished macho role. The recent feminist response to this is the fashion to wear heavy military boots even at elegant parties (not, perhaps, without the hope that the clumsy boots will enhance the frail and elegant beauty of their legs and selves).

Hands

There is another point of contact between human beings and the world: the hands. Your hands should be clean; you should wash them several times a day, because the "alien world" keeps attacking you, it wants to defile you, it wants to engulf you. Clean hands separate you from this vulgar, chaotic, and dirty world and indicate that you have nothing to do with it. You are an autonomous, independent personality. Women even grow long nails, and polish them in bright and shiny colors, to keep the gray, shapeless, profane world at a distance. To avoid even the slightest contact with the vulgar, material world, people with an aristocratic penchant would wear gloves as well. And if they have a butler, he should wear white gloves when he handles plates, glasses, and bottles, lest the material world contaminate their ladyships or lordships.

In addition, our selves shape the movements and gestures of our hands, and perhaps this also works the other way around. The way in which a blacksmith shapes the iron with a pair of tongues and a hammer in his hands, or a pianist's fingers run across the keyboard, may also leave its imprint on their nervous systems, and perhaps also on their selves. Isadora Duncan would have certainly asserted, with deep conviction, that the movements of the dance play a fundamental role in shaping the dancer's soul and self.

Women's Handbags

Why do women compulsorily carry (usually big) handbags with them? The obvious answer is that they do not have pockets in their dresses in which to put their wallets, some change, tissues, and keys. Another answer may be that they need more gadgets than men do. They have to care for themselves much more than their male counterparts. They need lipstick, powder, eye shadow, combs, scents, and the like. Being socially handicapped, they have to work more on their self-presentation than men.

Or are they weaker? Are they more lost in an alien world than men are? Do they need something to hang on to? And is this handle or anchor their handbag, full of magic objects, which reassure them in an alien world? In any case, objects in a handbag may perform important functions. They may protect their owners, reassuring and reinforcing their selves.

The owner of the bag may feel and say to herself: These are my ignition keys; I can get in my car any time and drive safely home. This is the key to the front door of my house: I have a home, my castle, the framework and cradle of my life, full of meaningful and precious objects, and people whom I love and who love me. This is the key to my wardrobe, which is full of my identities, roles, and memories in the form of dresses. This is the key to my cabinet and escritoire, with their drawers hiding the sweet and painful secrets of my life. Here is my ID card: I am somebody; I have an identity. Here is my Social Security card: I will be taken care of in any event. These credit cards are passes to anything I may need in this world. With the help of these cosmetics, I can repair my personality and self-image any time. Here are my trinkets and rings: their brilliance is my brilliance; their timeless beauty protects me against the shadows of mortality. This mirror gives me control over my life and my relationships with people: I can check any time how far my appearance corresponds to expectations and suits the situation. In its absence, I would not know how other people see me, and this would give them a dangerous power over me. Here are photos of my family, my children, and my parents: They surround me with the protective sphere of love and memories. Here are diapers for the baby: I am a good mother. Here is the cell phone: It is a main source of safety; it links me with a number of important points of contact in the world. Here are a pad and pen: I can make a note if I see anything new in the world. Here is a vial of Tylenol: I am protected against sudden pain. Here are tissues: They help me get rid of any occasional defilement. And here are my sunglasses: I may disappear behind them any time.

Goals and Life Goals

Having gone through this morning ordeal, one may still not feel to be quite ready for the problems, tasks, and exertions of the day. Something may still be missing: the momentum, the starting energy. Or a goal, a kind of Archimedean point by which one can pull oneself first out of one's bed (My God! It is already half past six and I have to prepare the breakfast for my children), and then through one's day (I have a deadline at my office), and ultimately through one's life (I should attain something in my life).

Goals play an important role in shaping our selves and lives, and they are thoroughly researched by psychologists.[68] Humans are goal-setting animals. They can hardly act (and live and survive) without goals. A substantial part of their lives is spent setting and pursuing goals. To use an up-to-date image, they are like those positive or negative movie heroes who shoot a kind of harpoon up to the top of the wall of a house, or a fortress, and then pull themselves up by the cable: so do people set themselves life goals to be able to pull themselves through the maze of their lives. According to Peter Berger and his coauthors (Berger, Berger, and Kellner 1973, 75, 73), "The meanings of everyday life derive from future plans rather than from the explication of past events," so much so that people's life plans are primary sources of their identity.

It is a great advantage in life when there are strong motive forces in oneself and when one is able to mobilize these forces with the purpose of attaining goals. To set an optimal goal for oneself—the best goal that one can attain—one has to know several things. First, one has to take into account the alternatives, those goals that might be worth achieving. Second, one has to study the environment, the context in which one will have to work to attain the goal in question. Third, one has to check how far the means necessary for the attainment of the goal are at one's disposal. Fourth, one has to control whether the goal one has set corresponds best to one's basic gifts, faculties, powers, and "strengths."[69] If it does, then—using the terminology of Mihaly Csikszentmihalyi (1975, 1990, 1993, 1997, 2003)—it triggers off a joyful "flow" of creative energies in us, maximizing the chances of a high achievement and of our attaining the goal. One may make great detours and lose valuable time, years and decades, or a whole lifetime, if one forgets about the main goals(s) one has set for oneself. It is a good idea to keep one's life goal(s) in the back of one's head, check it, modify it if necessary, from time to time.

The same is true for one's everyday goals. It may help a lot if we set a goal for ourselves before we leave for our office in the morning; something we think is the most important to achieve that day. It may help focus our energies, structure our day, strengthen our self and self-confidence. And, in addition, it may rock us into the illusion that our lives have a meaning.

—

By now, armed with our handbags or attaché cases, our goals and good advice, we may be tempted to take our keys and briefcase, open the door, step out of our house, close the door, walk down the driveway, and set out to conquer the world.

But we have to watch our step. There may be no world outside. During the night, not only our selves but also our world may have been submerged in the dark and chaotic world of dreams. We may have to reconstruct our world as well. The question is: How to do it?

The Reconstruction
of the World

Architecture starts when you carefully
put two bricks together. There it begins.

—*Ludwig Mies van der Rohe*

The Family

If we happen to live with our family, breakfast may help in the process of world
reconstruction and morning resocialization. Emerging from our nightly loneliness, this is our first encounter with other people, and we suddenly realize that
we have to behave as civilized social beings. We step out of the irresponsible
and amoral jungle of our nightly dreams and are quickly entangled in the web
of the rights and duties of daily life. We may not like it—tension and aggression may rise in us—but the smile of our children or parents, the color and fragrance of the orange juice, the coffee and the ham and eggs will help us over
this small psychic turbulence: We may start feeling quite comfortable in this
day-lit world, among other human beings. Anyway, to have breakfast with our
family may be a good preliminary exercise for resuming our social skills and
roles, which we lost at night. We should not waste our time, nerves, and energy
by discussing problems around the breakfast table. We had better use this ex-

cellent opportunity for smoothly slipping back into the established patterns of our social relationships.

Social psychologists have studied hundreds of facts, facets, and strategies of people's interaction with one another, and also the role of this interaction on the formation (and deformation) of their selves. But, as I mentioned in the introduction, we shall focus our attention in this book on other issues and shall deal with this important field only *per tangentem*.

The Papers

Baudelaire was outraged by the fact that people read newspapers in the morning, which in his interpretation meant that people started their days by feeding on the misery of humankind and the filth of the world. He may have been right. A century later, Robert Musil wrote in his novel *Man Without Qualities* (1979, 257) about the role of the papers in the very disintegration of the human self:

> "One must value it if there's a man still left nowadays who is striving to be something integral," said Walter. . . . "There's no longer any such thing," Ulrich countered. "You only have to look into a newspaper. You'll find it's filled with immeasurable opacity. So many things come under discussion that it would surpass the intellectual capacity of a Leibniz. But one doesn't even notice it. One has become different. There is no longer a whole man confronting a whole world, but a human something floating in a universal culture-medium."

He, too, may be right. But it is still true that papers—tabloids or serious ones—also help people find their way back into their real lives by constructing a (virtual) world around them, reducing thereby their morning loneliness and anxiety. How do they do this trick?

First, the fact that we find our favorite paper in the mailbox, on the lawn or the porch—our example will be here an issue of *The Mail on Sunday*—gives us the reassuring signal that the world outside still does exist and works as it did before.[1] We need this "business-as-usual" feeling badly, this reassurance that we can return to a safe and solid world from our nightly free fall into the abyss of the unknown.

Second, a quick glance at the headlines is enough to see that myriad things happened yesterday around the world. Thank God, because these events articulate time, and articulate our lives. They do not let them run emptily and without any purpose out of nowhere into nowhere.

Third, glancing at the headlines, we immediately get two or three delicious shots of poisonous excitement: news about catastrophes, earthquakes, accidents, airplane crashes, shoot-outs, murders, scandals, accidents, perversions, epidemics, frauds, riots, wars, terrorism. Predator instincts prance, human emotions well up in us. We experience and absorb the powerful forces of the world. The dramatic events, destruction, tragedies, and happy solutions thrill, outrage, or delight us. We start to live.

Briefly skimming the political column, we are reassured that the wheels of power, government, and the public services are turning in a more or less orderly way; there is no reason to panic. We are shocked by news about corruption in the corridors of power but, at the same time, we are strengthened in our moral superiority. Reading criticism of the government or the opposition, we agree or protest, and we are reborn as responsible citizens.[2]

But our *Untertan* instincts are also flattered by reading that our Prince of Wales is a nice young man.[3] It is good and safe to live in a country where the royal prince is a decent young man. The report on a coming national anniversary activates for a moment our patriotic feelings and identity.

The latest juicy scandal feeds our cannibal appetites, though, at the same time, news about sick and starving children awakens our moral selves and prompts us to do something about it as responsible human beings. A report on squandering charity funds by foundation officials gives us a quick alibi to not too hastily write a check for the next orphanage.[4]

Stories about celebrities fill the morning's virtual world with the necessary heroes and gods to adore and identify with[5] (and to feel relieved that they, too, have to suffer).[6] Gossip about their sex scandals provide us with a brief experience of peep show and a kind of alibi for cautiously relaxing our own moral norms.[7] We are upset with, and enjoy, the routine news of lovers betrayed and forsaken.[8] We watch with fascination the conflicts of stars, the battles of gods.[9] We are electrified by old secrets revealed.[10] We are thrilled, and revitalized, by horror stories,[11] and we are glad to know that all these horrors happened far from our homes and, anyway, we are safe because the police arrest criminals, though regrettably they all too frequently mishandle people and cases.[12]

The travel column enchants us with the beauty of the world. Faraway islands promise the pleasures of the Garden of Eden, or those of a "fine romance."[13] Renaissance villas (transformed into hotels) evoke grandeur and luxury that could be ours;[14] we may visit the notorious hideaways of prominent people and their lovers,[15] or we could take a cruise on "a majestic superliner," where anything may happen onboard. Yes, the world is exciting and beautiful. We are at home here on the Globe.[16]

We may lose this beautiful Globe, though, if, . . . and here come a few staple news—shocking or sentimental—about the dangers threatening our fragile environment.[17] There are still a few whales in the seas, and some decent people have saved some baby seals,[18] though pollution and poachers still threaten the life of many innocent creatures. We have to make further progress.

The world is not only beautiful but it is also full of fantastic opportunities and bargains. "Bargain," "Cash back," "Save . . . pounds," this and this service is "only . . . pounds per month," are the phrases most frequently used in this paper.[19] The chance of wining the lottery flashes up.[20] Our money is safe in banks and bonds. We can make immense fortunes, though brokers sometimes cheat us out of our last pennies. This is a world of opportunities for those who have the courage to grasp these opportunities. And we should not forget: Phone tariffs will go down: another proof, and a pleasant feeling, that there is progress in the world.

If all this self-administered therapy does not yet suffice to rebuild in us the faith in the world, and ourselves, we have a further refuge: sports; the sports column of our morning paper. Sports is a world in itself, complete with its own space and time, heroes and traitors, with victories and defeats, jubilation and protest, myths and rituals, cooperation and fight, cheating and fair play, scandals and punishments.[21] It is a world of strong emotions and passions, of fascinating speculations and intellectual games; it is a world of high intensity. It cranks up one's thoughts, it jump-starts one's emotional life; it may give us a strong momentum, launching us on our daily trajectory.[22]

Reading about all this, we are more and more strengthened; we bask in the background radiation of our age's basic ideology of universal happiness and limitless self-actualization; we gather momentum; and we are ready to start the day.

We may leave for our office. . . . But we should not forget to take our umbrella with us. Just in case.

The Weather

The nice, friendly, and interesting world we have constructed for ourselves with so much care in these morning hours may be ruined in a trice. It may be ruined by an almost tragic uncertainty in our lives—by the whims of the weather.

As far as their relationship with the weather is concerned, there are three types of people. First, there are forecast addicts. Second, there are stoics. And third, there are people who love extreme sports.

The forecast addicts are absolutely at the mercy of the weather, and even more of morning forecasts. Looking out their windows, in the morning light, they do not really believe their own eyes. They may see a sunlit garden or street, but they still fear that rain, snow, a storm, or a "system" may come up in the next hours. They cannot make up their minds whether they may happily open up to a beautiful, sunlit world of joys, or have to shut themselves up and take all the possible precautions before they enter a hostile and aggressive world. They trust only the TV forecasts, repeated every half an hour on the morning programs (only national or international emergencies get this level of obsessive attention); they have to see on continental and global maps projected unto magic blue boxes where the systems are and in which direction they are moving. They are relieved only when they have been assured a half dozen times that in the next twenty-four hours there will not be any unpleasant (or even pleasant) surprises.[23] They live in a state of a latent, vague, and permanent anxiety that things may go wrong, that the world may go wrong.

This forecast addiction may be due to the fact that weather is one of the last things in the world of people living in the highly developed countries that eludes the grasp of human technology. In our ultraorganized world, almost everything is strictly controlled. The weather is one of the last major uncertainties in our lives (beside volcanoes, floods, earthquakes, stock exchanges, viruses, and terrorists). In spite of all our efforts, satellites, and weather balloons, we are unable to control it. We may reduce the risk, though, and protect ourselves against the raw and rude impact of the forces of nature. We may get from our weatherproof garages to the weatherproof garages of our offices in our weatherproof cars. We may reduce our weather anxiety by moving to a part of the world with *"bleu fixe,"* as the French refer to regions with a permanent, beautiful Mediterranean sky. Or we may air (and weather) condition, if not the world, at least, our homes, offices, and public spaces, thus creating a constant and constantly pleasant climate around ourselves. But our anxiety about an impending catastrophe will never totally subside.

The Mirror, Once More

For a last check before we leave our home, we may look in a mirror in the hall. It is an important control, but we should not trust it too much. In a mirror, we do not see ourselves as other people will see us. We see our self "through a glass, darkly," having a cast in our eyes; our self-love gilds the picture. But our fellow beings gaze at us with a hawk's eyes, or they give us the go-by. It may be Narcissus' brook reflecting our image, or Snow White's stepmother's mirror, which keeps telling us that we are the most beautiful creatures in the world—which, perhaps, we are not.

The Self in the Public Space

There will be time, there will be time
To prepare a face to meet
the faces that you meet. . . .

—*T. S. Eliot*

Which World?

After so much preparation, we may take our keys, coats, and umbrellas, open the front door, and enter the world. But I warn again that we—people living in the age of globalization and in an emerging new civilization—have to watch our steps.

Fifty or a hundred years ago, it would have been easier to enter the world. Then people knew the community, the locality, the environment, the *"milieu"* (Scheler), the "lifeworld" (Husserl, Habermas), the *"Umwelt"* (Goffman), the "symbolic space" (Cassirer), the "biographical space" (Schutz), that they entered. But with the major changes that have been taking place in the world, and which are summed up under the name of globalization, people have been uprooted, "deterritorialized," "disembedded," "delinked" from their local communities, and they have been left alone in a more or less chaotic global space.[1]

In this global space, they have to create and continuously recreate for themselves a "nonterritorial," virtual lifeworld, a nonlocal community, within which they may again feel at home, where they have the necessary competence to control their lives and can form and pursue their life plans. Being bombarded by a heterogeneous multitude of ideas, ideologies, values, worldviews, and lifestyles, they have to create their own framework of values, their own symbolic space, their own lifestyle, which may have some roots in the history of their traditional, local communities but which must be able to respond to the new challenges of a rapidly changing world.

In this global world—wherever we live—we may, or must, know more about Singapore and San Francisco then about our neighboring village; a colleague of ours in Cape Town or Stockholm may be nearer to us by phone or e-mail than our brother-in-law who lives two blocks away; our life and future may depend more on the American president and the German chancellor than on the mayor of our city; we have to find our ways in a world of new ideas, new concepts, new techniques, and new values coming from all over the world. Hollywood stars may play a more important role in shaping our selves than the heroes of our national history. We enter in a nonterritorial world—in the field of force of powerful global institutions, trends, and influences—in a global crowd, in which our local identity counts less and less. We have to prepare ourselves for this encounter.

And we should not forget that the world is not a peaceful and harmonious Garden of Eden and life is not an idyll. When we leave our homes, we enter an arena where we have to fight and win; we enter a savannah, where there are both predators and grass eaters. Both have chances of survival, but they have to behave in different ways. We'd better decide whether we want to be leopards or antelopes. Both are noble and beautiful animals, but they live radically different lives. And there are also elephants and giraffes, monkeys and eagles, ants and crickets. And there are also parasites. We have to decide which role we want to play in our lives, or at least in the public place.

A Framework

Besides our umbrella, it is a good idea to take with us, in our minds, the "framework" within which we think we are able to act. This framework is a set of beliefs and facts about the world, about how it works, how one can move around in it, how one can handle it, cope with it, control it, what are the opportunities and the dangers in it, and so on and so forth. According to Barkow, Cosmides and Tooby (1992, 106), a

> frame provides a 'world-view': It carves the world into defined categories of entities and properties, defines how these categories are related to each other, suggests operations that might be performed, defines what goal is to be achieved, provides methods for interpreting observations . . . provides criteria to discriminate success from failure, suggests what information is lacking and how to get it, and so on.

Peter Berger and his coauthors (1973, 15) describe the same phenomenon in the following way:

> Any specific knowledge has a *background* (phenomenology calls it a *horizon*). That is, whatever is specifically known assumes a general frame of reference. . . . In other words, the individual needs overarching reality definitions to give meaning to life as a whole. These overarching definitions are essential to hold any society together and, for that matter, to keep any particular social situation going. Together they make up an individual's or a society's *symbolic universe*.

There are several levels of these frames. First, there is a simple, everyday knowledge of the world, a set of basic information about the characteristics of the world—the knowledge, for instance, that objects drop on the floor if we let them go; that after a certain period of time, the sun will rise; that certain objects may hurt, cut, or bruise us; that we may eat certain plants and should not eat other ones; that people may be hostile or friendly. Overarching this simple frame, there is a more or less complex set of beliefs about the world, about human life, about where we come from and where we may be heading, about what is not only useful or harmful but also good or bad from a "higher" perspective, and finally also about the "ultimate concerns" of the human condition in this universe, in time and eternity.

These frames guide us in our everyday proceedings, help us orient ourselves, avoid dangers, feel more or less safe in this world, and set and attain goals. They may also help us feel that we are at home in this universe and that our lives have a meaning.

We are not quite free in selecting our "framework." The civilization, the age, the society, the environment in which we live, our parent's example, other models, our education, and many other facts play an important role in shaping the way in which we see, and think of, the world. If we want to know more about this field, one of the best introductions is certainly Karl Jaspers's (1960) famous book *Die Psychologie der Weltanschaungen*, written in 1919; but unfortunately, as far as I know, it has not been translated into English. In this book, Jaspers analyzes the psychological sources and characteristics of various attitudes toward the world. His concepts and their arrangement would not be considered up-to-date nowadays, but they may give us an idea of the many ways in which people can see the world. According to him, for instance, our attitude may be "objective," "active," "mystic," "contemplative" "intuitive, "aesthetic," "rational," "scholastic," "experimental" "dialectic," "reflexive," "self-reflexive," "hedonistic," "ascetic," "self-creating," "historical," "systematic," "enthusiastic," and so on. Our vision of the world may be "sensible-spatial," "spiritual-cultural," "metaphysical," and so on.[2]

Scholars working in the field of cultural anthropology and cross-cultural studies were the first to explore the relationship between such frameworks and the development of the human self. In spite of the fact that these frameworks seem to play a crucial role in shaping people's selves, psychologists were lagging behind their colleagues. But in recent years, comparative or cultural psychology has emerged and has become an important field within experimental psychology.[3]

The Private and the Public Self

When we step out the front door of our homes, we have to switch over from our private to our "public" selves—the selves that we want to show to the world, the role we want to play in the world. Carl Jung (1971a) called this public self the "persona."

A large scholarly literature analyzes the complex relationship between these two selves.[4] They speak of the difficulty to integrate these two selves (Schlenker 1985). They try to answer the question whether only the private self is a "genuine" self and the public is a fake, a mask, a playing of roles. Or, on the contrary, our real, genuine self is being created in the public sphere, in our interaction with other people, in our responding to the various challenges of the world.

If it is difficult to construct one's private self, it is at least as difficult, or even more difficult, to build up, maintain, and protect one's public self. At home, our family members know, or think they know, us and more or less accept us as we are. In the public sphere, we have to start from scratch. We are alone in an—if not hostile—at least competitive and not too friendly environment. If we want to have a place in this community, if we want to make it, to succeed, then we have to construct for ourselves adequate public selves. And we have to keep protecting, asserting, and presenting these selves in, and to, this ever-changing community.

And the time is here whenever we enter the public space.

The Presentation of Self

One has to construct and continuously reconstruct one's public self and present it to the world in an optimal way.[5] "You'll never have a second chance to make a first impression," a TV commercial warned us. And as Erving Goffman (1959) put it, with much more authority, we have to learn "the art of impression management." If one fails to do so, not only one's carrier opportunities and survival chances but also one's self-image and self-esteem may be seriously impaired. So before leaving one's home, and entering the public sphere, one has to make important decisions.

If we think that we have a genuine private self, an essential or "core" self, then we have to decide how far we want to present or hide this self when we move around in the public sphere. We may have a wardrobe of public selves and roles that reveal or hide our real self to various degrees and in different ways: We have to pick the self or role that we think best suits our mood or purposes, and optimize our chances, on that particular day.

We may also need several selves and roles among which we want to switch in the course of the day. We should not leave at home the paraphernalia necessary to play these roles (for women, a pair of high-heeled shoes in their handbag or car, for instance, may be indispensable for transforming themselves in a trice from low-heeled Cinderellas into nimble fairy queens).

We have also to decide whether we want to be different, to "stand out" of the crowd, or disappear in it.[6] We may also wish to emphasize our membership in a particular social group, community, nation, subculture, or culture because it may lend us a feeling of belonging and security. The uniform is the hundred-percent solution in this case, but much less may also suffice. We may dress ourselves in the style of a certain region or ethnicity, or hint at our affiliation only with a scarf, a color, or even only a badge. The same piece of clothing may allow us to blend in with a community or stress our being an outsider. Put on Bavarian leather shorts in Munich, in New York, and in Tokyo and you will see the difference.

Once we have made up our minds, assumed our chosen selves, and shut the front door of our home behind us, we will find ourselves in an arena that is not very dissimilar from the arenas of Nero in which gladiators killed one another and wild beasts tore martyrs to pieces. Beware of *homines sapientes et non-sapientes*.

But the public space is an important forum for self-construction as well. We may use it for improving our self-image and self-perception, strengthening our self-esteem, and boosting our self-confidence. We do so, for instance, when we meet a friend of ours, whom we have not seen for a while and want to get the better of him or her at any price (even without knowing that we behave in this ridiculous way). We start boasting as children do when they brag about their bikes, their baseball skills, or their parents' social position. We are in a haste to prove to our friend that we have made it, that we will be soon appointed to the head of our department, that we have a fine house and family, our children went to the best college, and the like. And, in the meantime, we feel a pang in our hearts whenever we hear that he or she has got a bigger house, a better job, more successful children. During the conversation, we feverishly keep balancing the books of his and our assets. And this is not a question of envy. No. We are just frail, fragile, and mortal human beings; we have to strengthen our selves, our self-esteem, day in and day out. We do not want to be losers, we want to have as much of "life" as possible. If others achieve and fare better, this means that we have lost a part of the life that we might have had. We do not envy their success; we deplore the fact that we have less of life, which is short anyway. We boast with what we have done or acquired because we are prompted by a deep and unconscious desire to believe, to delude ourselves with the illusion, that we are the kings or queens of life.

One may lose or gain a lot, and one can seriously hurt one another, in these symbolic duels. Education, good manners, tact, and political correctness are the means through which society tries to keep them within civilized boundaries.

We are not left alone and helpless in the public space. In the course of human history, an arsenal of behavioral patterns and strategies has been developed that may help us in protecting and reinforcing our selves and optimize our chances in our interaction with other people. Most of these patterns and strategies developed spontaneously, but people could also get advice from great teachers like Socrates or Saint Francis, Castiglione or Erasmus, Lord Chesterton or Carnegie—as well as from sixteenth-, seventeenth-, and eighteenth-century devotional manuals and guidebooks for the personal and social conduct of the faithful Christian, moral treaties on virtues and vices,[7] from the popular seventeenth-century genre of "Characters,"[8] from eighteenth- and nineteenth-century novels describing the everyday lives of people, Victorian self-help books, nineteenth-century etiquette books,[9] and from the how-to-be-successful-and-happy, and the how-to-make-everybody-your-friend, type books published by the dozens and hundreds since the second half of the nineteenth century.[10]

In spite of all this good or bad advice and help, it is not easy to safeguard our dignity, protect and reinforce our selves, survive in the social space. In the past half century, hundreds of scholars—social psychologists, human ethologists, ethnomethodologists, symbolic interactionists, communication experts, sociologists of everyday life—have studied the social behavior and interactive games of people. And they have discovered a theater full of fun and intrigue, maneuvering and jockeying for position, cooperation, and struggle. To show how difficult it is for human beings to survive and succeed in the public space, to safeguard their selves, let me quote some of the main headings of one single book in this field. The book is *The Self* by Jonathan D. Brown (1998).

Among the strategies of self-presentation, Brown mentions, beside others, "self-promotion" versus "self-protection," "self-monitoring" (Snyder 1987), "self-verification," "ingratiation," "intimidation," "exemplification,"[11] "supplication,"[12] and so on. He describes the role of "sincerity and authenticity versus pretense and deceit." He points out the "risks of both being sincere and presenting a false impression." Commenting on people's "identity repair tactics" and acts of "symbolic self-completion," he gives further examples of how people state and stress their identities and selves. He argues that even obvious and strong identities "require social validation." To get this, people also use symbolic means. Physician wear white lab coats, stethoscopes round their necks, and so on. Wearing badges serves the same purpose. Among the "identity predicaments,"[13] Brown describes how people "apologize" and "claim innocence," and "reinterpret—that is, alter the meaning of an event," "justify" or "legitimize" their behavior, "excuse themselves by denying intentionality," "make preemptive excuses,"[14] or even handicap themselves."[15]

Seeing this welter of strategies and counterstrategies, it is not surprising to learn that experts speak of a ""self-presentational anxiety" as a common phenomenon in contemporary societies.[16]

People who lived in traditional, more or less closed, communities had fewer problems presenting themselves than we do nowadays. Their roles within the community were given once for all, and the community prescribed how they had to behave and present themselves in the public space. People moving around in the anonymous crowd of our contemporary metropolises, and nervously switching to and fro between various situations and human relationships, are in a much more difficult situation. They have to perpetually respond to new and newer challenges; they have to protect and assert their selves in an ever-changing environment. And with the acceleration of time, they have to act very quickly; they have to respond with lightning speed. They have to "sell themselves" in the twinkling of an eye. Let me illustrate this last point by referring to a new genre called the "elevator speech."

The Elevator Speech

To present ourselves in a surprisingly and fascinatingly favorable light is nowadays a must. We should be very good at that. In this accelerating world we have to make a very good first impression. A few years ago, I read in the *Financial Times* a brilliant feuilleton by Lucy Kellaway (2002, 9) about a new fast-lane strategy of self-presentation. It is called, the "Elevator Speech" and is meant to impress your boss in 30 seconds, while—the chance of your life!—you happen to ride with him in the elevator. What she writes about this precarious situation is so enlightening, and so witty, that I quote from it at a bit more length than is usual:

> You are riding up in the lift at your office. The doors glide apart and in steps your CEO. What do you do?
>
> If you are in Britain you stare at your shoes. Or you make some daft pleasantry, or comment on the weather. Or wait for him to say something. Above all you hope he gets out quickly . . .
>
> If you are in the US you deploy the latest weapon of the thrusting business person: the elevator speech. This is a 10–30 second commercial for yourself . . .
>
> Craig Harrison, a Californian self-help guru, introduces himself in lifts. "Hi. I market confidence! I'm a motivational speaker and trainer who helps others aspire and achieve. . . . Here's my card, let me help transform your world!"
>
> The only British person I can think of who is good at the art of the elevator speech is the Queen. This is a bit odd since I very much doubt she has ever taken an elevator in her life in which she ran any risk of an unexpected encounter. . . .
>
> She resists the temptation to say anything like: "Hello. I am the Queen. I have been on the throne for 50 years, some of which have been good and some have been *anni horribiles*. I own various palaces and don't pay inheritance tax." It might be a good speech but she does not make it. Instead she says, "And what do you do?" . . .
>
> That being the case, any attempt to establish difference in a 16-second elevator speech seems doomed to failure. And the more people who try to do it, the more tempting it becomes for everyone else to take the stairs instead.

What would be your elevator speech? Have you got one?

Anyway, people are likely to make clowns of themselves in trying to make a good impression; to present themselves in a favorable light. When they are in public, politicians—and not only the younger ones, like Clinton or Bush, but the old and potbellied ones as well—lightly and nimbly skip and hop up the stairs of the speaker's platform, gracefully alight from the helicopter, and advance with dancing steps on the emerald lawn of the White House or the residence of the Bundeskanzler, sending enthralling smiles to the TV cameras and playing a bit with their freshly laundered dog, because they, too (I mean the presidents), are humans. The message is that they are young and energetic, they easily take the hurdles, and they are in full control of themselves, the situation, and the world (which usually is not the case).

"Preedy"

Whatever self one wants to assume, whichever role one decides to play, one should not forget about the importance of self-restraint. Overdoing one's part, being overconcerned with fondling and exalting one's self, may be counterproductive. It may reduce the chances of finding one's place, improving one's position in the community, and thereby boosting one's self. Let me reproduce here a brilliant text, quoted by Goffman (1959, 4–5), describing the tragicomic case of somebody who was blindly enamored of himself. Preedy is an Englishman; he is the hero of a novel.[17] The text in question describes his first appearance on the beach of a summer hotel in Spain:

> In any case he took care to avoid catching anyone's eye. First of all, he had to make it clear to those potential companions of his holiday that they were of no concern to him whatsoever. He stared through them, round them, over them—eyes lost in space. The beach might have been empty. If by chance a ball was thrown his way, he looked surprised; then let a smile of amusement lighten his face (Kindly Preedy), looked round dazed to see that there *were* people on the beach, tossed it back with a smile to himself and not a smile *at* the people, and then resumed carelessly his nonchalant survey of space.
>
> But it was time to institute a little parade, the parade of the Ideal Preedy. By devious handlings he gave any who wanted to took a chance to see the title of his book—a Spanish translation of Homer, classic thus, but not daring, cosmopolitan too—and then gathered together his beach-wrap and bag into a neat sand-resistant pile (Methodical and Sensible

Preedy), rose slowly to stretch at ease his huge frame (Big-Cat Preedy), and tossed aside his sandals (Carefree Preedy, after all).

The marriage of Preedy and the sea! There were alternative rituals. The first involved the stroll that turns into a run and a dive straight into the water, thereafter smoothing into a strong splashless crawl towards the horizon. But of course not really to the horizon. Quite suddenly he would turn on to his back and thrash great white splashes with his legs, somehow thus showing that he could have swum further had he wanted to, and then would stand up a quarter out of water for all to see who it was.

The alternative course was simpler, it avoided the cold-water shock and it avoided the risk of appearing too high-spirited. The point was to appear to be so used to the sea, the Mediterranean, and this particular beach, that one might as well be in the sea as out of it. It involved a slow stroll down and into the edge of the water—not even noticing his toes were wet, land and water all the same to *him!*—with his eyes up at the sky gravely surveying portents, invisible to others, of the weather (Local Fisherman Preedy).

This desperate search for a good role, a good public self, is both ridiculous and tragic. But Preedy is only an extreme case; we all suffer, more or less, from this self-presentational compulsive neurosis.

An opposite case would be an agoraphobic, or autistic person, who hides himself in his hotel room, shutters closed, and does not dare to poke his nose out of the room throughout his holidays. This latter behavior may do even more harm to one's self than Preedy's narcissistic clownery.

Fortunately, there are more, and also much better, models of life and behavior than offered by the example of Preedy.

Models

Several patterns of social and individual life have been discovered by social and behavioral scientists. Bourdieu (1984, 1991), for instance, described various social "schemata," which regulate to a certain extent the ways in which people of a given society act and live. Eric Berne (1972) developed a "transactionalist" approach, according to which people live their lives, without knowing it, according to a latent "script," which has been implanted in them by their parents.

Charles Taylor (1989) proposed a more philosophical approach. He described three possible patterns of human attitudes: the "Biblical," the "Utilitarian," and the "Romantic-expressive." Bellah and his coauthors (1985) added one more: the "Republican." And one could add further ones: the Stoic, for instance, or the Nietzschean-existentialist, which is included by Taylor in the Romantic-expressive group. But Nietzsche's or Sartre's tragic confrontation with death and nonbeing is not necessarily an "expressive" or "Romantic" attitude. And in which category should those hundreds of millions of people be ranged who lived—throughout the history of humankind—in slavery or serfdom, who were exploited and oppressed and had no opportunity to develop strong and rich personalities? Most of them would probably fit in the category of Biblical selves, and some of them in the Republican, Expressive, or Utilitarian categories. But what about the rest? They may belong to another category, which could be defined as the category of Anomic or Stunted selves. Millions among us are threatened by the danger of being caught in, or lapsing into, this category.

These latent patterns of behavior may crystallize into real or imaginary persons, transforming them into life models of intense radiation. When people identify themselves with one or another of these models, they knowingly or unknowingly accept the fact that their selves will be shaped by the patterns underlying their ideals or models: the hero or the martyr, the missionary or the world-saving prophet, the priest or the knight, the soldier or the seafaring adventurer, Robin Hood or the revolutionary, the Grand Inquisitor or the successful businessman, the macho or the philosopher, the scholar or the pop star, the honest merchant or the con man, the virtuous housewife or the bluestocking, Sleeping Beauty or the vamp, Caesar or Croesus, Leonardo da Vinci or Byron, Napoleon or Catherine the Great, Churchill or de Gaulle, Rockefeller or Einstein, Picasso or Bill Gates, Sherlock Holmes or Al Capone, Hemingway or Antonioni, Margaret Thatcher or Julia Roberts, Bill or Hillary Clinton, Schumacher or Beckham, and the like.[18]

Literature is an especially rich source of life strategies and behavioral patterns. It is because writers usually work in the following way: They take a usual or unusual life situation, put their hero in it, and then observe how the hero responds to the challenges of this situation. People in everyday life go through a similar experience: They get into various life situations and have to successfully respond to them. In this effort of theirs, situations and human responses described by novelists and playwrights may be of great help, even if people are rarely conscious of this help.

Let me briefly describe a few literary models for self-construction; I shall mainly refer to works of a high literary value, but later in this book we shall see that similar models also recur in the popular genres.[19]

The ambitious self. Balzac's Rastignac wanted to make it, to make a career at all costs, to get into the higher circles of society. He became the model for thousands or millions of young men in the nineteenth and twentieth centuries. But his market value could even be higher nowadays, in our consumer civilization, where wealth, success, power, and fame have become the principal values. Many people follow his example even without knowing that they are doing so.

The rebellious self. Stendhal's Julien Sorel revolts against a social order that he considers unjust. Rebelliousness is at the center of his self. This has been an attractive model for young people. To rebel in the name of justice may give one an exceptionally strong feeling of identity. The identification with a sacred cause may even replace a weak self or substitute for a missing one. Rebels may be not only "without a cause"; they may also be "without a self."

The anchored self. Electra adored her father; she was dependent on him, her self was anchored in his person. After his death, she lost her balance, her fixed point in the universe. She wanted to reestablish the harmony of the world by any means, and this led to destruction and tragedy. Her story may serve as a warning for people, for whom a father or mother figure has been a rich and indispensable source of identity. They have to know that after the severing process, it will be difficult to develop their autonomous adult selves. In tribal societies, the rites of passage and the rituals of initiation helped young people in making this transition. In our contemporary societies, they are more or less left alone.

The genuine self discovered. Throughout his life, King Lear had been a childish, spoiled, conceited person, living in complete "oblivion." Then he suddenly discovered the tragic depths of the human condition and, in the horrendous ordeal that followed, he achieved, without knowing it, an "authentic" self in the Kirkegaardian or Heideggerian sense of the word. This warning may be especially important nowadays, in our civilization of consumption, which—with its powerful means—prompts people to self-dispersion and oblivion.

The split self. As a victorious general, Othello had a strong and autonomous self. He exchanged it for the weak and dependent self of a lover; he became entirely dependent on Desdemona's love. She became his world, and the source of everything that was valuable in the universe. Her supposed betrayal destroyed his self, and destroyed his whole universe. When he learned that she had been innocent, his self split in two: He began to address himself in the third person singular:

> Othello: That's he that was Othello: here I am.
> . . . . I pray you in your letters,
> When you shall these unlucky deeds relate,
> Speak of me, as I am. Nothing extenuate,
> Nor set down ought in malice.
> Then must you speak,
> Of one that lov'd not wisely, but too well. . . .
> . . . . Of one, whose hand
> (Like the base Indian) threw a pearl away
> richer than all his tribe. . . .

An then, his stronger, martial self kills his weaker self for having "thrown away" the pearl of life.[20] The punishment of oneself by oneself is a well-known and strongly researched psychological phenomenon, and it has its normal and pathological versions.

The vicarious self. Martha and George in Albee's *Who's Afraid of Virginia Woolf?* are unable to accept their own selves. George is a flop, Martha is an alcoholic. Their lives are in ruins. To be able to survive, they construct an imaginary self, a son, whose existence is a proof that there are still beauty, innocence, brilliance, and love in this world. This is an extreme case of parental love, and a mirror for those people who want to fulfill their lives and realize their selves in the future lives and selves of their children. This is a dangerous but common trap. Many people give up too soon the struggle for their own lives, for the actualization of their own potentials and selves, and invest everything in the future of their children. And do not think of the possibility that their children, too, may fail to realize themselves and will leave the task of achieving authentic lives and selves to the next and next generations.[21]

The constrained self. Ibsen's Nora discovers that she has been forced into a role that thwarted her self and starts out on the quest of her real self. This was exceptional in the late nineteenth century, and it became an everyday routine in the late twentieth century. It is all the rage now, in our contemporary consumer civilization, to keep searching for one's real, authentic self. The problem is that changing spouses and jobs, and running to the astrologer, are not necessarily the best ways of finding what people are looking for.

The nostalgic self. The three sisters in Chekhov's play are convinced that they could find their real selves only if they lived in a different world, that is, in Moscow. (It would be frivolous and anachronistic to say that to go to Paris, London, or Rome would probably have been a better idea.) Nostalgias may play both a positive and a negative role in people's lives. They may mobilize them, they may compensate them for things that they miss in their lives, they may enrich their selves. But they may be destructive as well, paralyzing people, absorbing their energies, distorting their selves.

The loss of self. The loss of one's place and position in the world is a fearful experience. Literary works have kept reenacting this experience since the tragic fall of mythic heroes, through the shocking tragedies of Oedipus or King Lear losing their royal roles and selves, to the "Fall of Princes" in the Middle Ages, to the tragic fall of a Napoleon, or the tragic or scandalous fall of the rich, the powerful, and the glamorously beautiful of our own consumer civilization about which we read—shivering and with delight—in our weekly magazines.

One of the classic examples is, of course, Hamlet. He had been a happy young man, a Renaissance prince, heir to the throne. He bathed in the lights and wealth of the court, in the love of his parents and Ophelia. But suddenly the lights went out, love turned into betrayal, trust into fear, friends into foes, life into death. And Hamlet's happy, carefree, strong self suddenly turned into a gloomy, harassed, desperate self at variance with itself. He was unable to handle the new situation, he was crippled by this change of self. He lost himself, he did not know anymore who he was, he did not understand why he was unable to act. On a lower and less spectacular scale, almost all human beings undergo this fearful experience of losing their places in the world and getting into a situation with which their existing selves cannot, or have great difficulty, coping. Where can they find help in the contemporary civilization of consumption? In part two of this book, we shall study some of their attempts to do so.

The demonic self. Demons have ever fascinated, terrified, and attracted people. Shakespeare's Richard III adopted, of his own free will, the role of a destructive demon. But there were more attractive demons as well, like Goethe's Mephistopheles or Pushkin's Onegin, or a whole series of demonic characters in our contemporary cinema and television. The temptation to be a powerful (and destructive) demon may be even stronger today, in this age of "actualize-yourself-at-every-means."

The unacceptable self. Oedipus discovered too late that he was not the person he had thought to be. He was unable to accept this newly discovered self, he was unable to see himself in this new identity. He blinded himself. There are many pathological and nonpathological cases of people who are unable to accept their selves. The pathological response to this situation may be to try to repress, or to destroy, this unacceptable self. The normal response is to try to transform one's self, to develop a valuable and acceptable self. This is a strong motivation in many people's lives.[22]

The mistaken self. Flaubert's Madame Bovary thinks that she will find her real, genuine self in the love of Rodolphe Boulanger. She suffers a deep disappointment. Being deprived of this longed-for self, she collapses and takes her own life. One may fail to achieve a self that one thinks would be ideal for oneself. How could psychologists or psychoanalysts have helped Madame Bovary with all the knowledge they have accumulated ever since?

The self relinquished. People in Ionesco's *Rhinoceros* give up their individual human selves for the collective self of the rhino herd. This was a well-known epidemic in the twentieth century, plagued by totalitarian ideologies and mass movements.

The regression of the self. In Golding's *The Lord of the Flies,* children are left alone on an island. After a few weeks, their relatively weak, undeveloped selves regress into a precivilizational, atavistic state. They enslave, torture, and kill one another like brutes without any cultural or moral restraint. The question of how strong or weak the cultural frame of the human personality is, how easily the moral varnish may wear off, has ever puzzled students of human nature.

The "I" and the "Me" self. There is, sometimes, a strong discrepancy between these two selves: the "I," that is, my self as I inwardly experience it; and the "Me," that is, my self as I see it in the mirror of other people's gazes and relationships with me. Kafka described a tragic version of this duality, or discrepancy of selves, in his novella *The Metamorphosis.* The hero of the story was changed, overnight, into a huge bug. He kept his normal human consciousness and self, but the members of his family took him for a disgusting bug and treated him as such. This is an extreme case; but a great number of ordinary, everyday people suffer from this discrepancy. Some of them try to reduce this tension by conforming to the outside picture people have of them. Others opt for the opposite course: They boost their inner selves and try to make people accept it as their genuine self.

The illusory self. Blanche in Tennessee Williams's *A Streetcar Named Desire* imagines herself to be the Queen of Life. When she is cruelly forced to discover and accept her miserable everyday life, she loses her mind (and self). Self-knowledge is not our strongest virtue. We have a penchant for building not only castles but also "selves in the air." We usually have a more favorable opinion of ourselves than of others. And if everybody does so, then there is something wrong with the equation. In national surveys, usually about seven or eight people out of ten consider themselves just, honest, civilized, and more or less smart. And the same people feel and say that only about four to five people out of ten in their society are just, honest, civilized, and more or less smart. Which means that the same community is a just and civilized "we-society," and at the same time an unjust, dishonest, uncivilized "they-society." A more realistic self-assessment and perhaps a less bitter assessment of others might reduce this discrepancy, which is at the root of much resentment and conflict.

The missing self. Could we describe in this way the protagonist of Musil's *The Man without Qualities*? I do not think so. A complete absence of self can occur only in seriously pathological cases.

In quest of a self. The best literary examples are here Goethe's *Wilhelm Meister's Apprenticeship and Travel*, Gottfried Keller's *Green Henry*, Flaubert's *Sentimental Education*, Thomas Mann's *The Magic Mountain*, and other stories of the (self-)education of a young man or woman.

Experimental selves. Virginia Woolf's *Orlando*—overarching several centuries—changes his/her self several times. She/he tries to achieve the fulfillment of her/his life by experimenting with various potential selves. On a much more modest scale, teenagers and young adults do something similar. Psychologists studying life cycles have shown that even adult people "shed," or at least modify, their selves when they pass from one cycle to the other.

The faked self. This is a favorite type of playwrights and novelists. Think of Iago, Tartuffe, and all the other intriguers and hypocrites of world literature. In our everyday lives, we often struggle with the problem of how far our "public selves," the selves we present to the world, are genuine or, on the contrary, artificial, hypocritical, faked.

The composite self. There have been heated controversies throughout the centuries about the question of Jesus Christ: Was he purely divine, purely human, a combination of the two, or fully both. Tens of thousands of heretics were sent to the scaffold for holding the wrong view. The problem is still alive in debates about the divine, animal, or mixed character of the human being. To opt for one of the views may be important, even from the point of view of the everyday construction of our selves. The belief that the human being has a dual character, divine and animal, may lead to a different strategy of self-construction than the conviction that humankind is simply the most developed species of the animal world.

Playing with selves. Why are we so fascinated by plays in which an actor plays various roles, assumes various identities? Are we ravished by the virtuosity of the actor? Probably. But it may be more important that this is a delightful experience of freedom: We see and feel that we, human beings, are able to freely choose and freely construct our selves. We are not imprisoned in one single, unchangeable self.

Typologies. The freedom of playing with various selves may be not attractive for each of us. There are people who are anxious to find their only possible and genuine selves as quickly as possible. They may turn to popular "typologies" for help. There are hundreds of these typologies—serious ones, based on scientific research; and nonserious ones, offered weekly by women's magazines to their readers and television programs to their viewers.[23]

Yes, it may be an anguish-filled experience not to know who we are, what we are like. And it is a pleasant surprise when we suddenly find our place in humankind—not in a chaotic crowd, but in a population neatly divided into four or eight or sixteen or thirty-two types (the number of categories is, in most cases, well rounded off). It is a relief to feel that we live in an ordered universe and have our place in this order. And the easiest way to generate this illusion is to find our pigeonhole in a ready-made typology. We do not need to analyze ourselves; we get our portrait off the peg, and the portrait is, as a rule, flattering.[24]

Do not believe, however, that having found your slot in a nice typology will enable you to solve all your problems of getting ahead in the public space. You will still need a wide range of further strategies.

Norms of Conduct

If one wants to find one's way and succeed in the public space, it is advisable to give a brief thought to the question of how one would behave among one's fellow beings. This may be a routine question in civilizations with well-established norms of behavior. But in our contemporary civilization, with its chaotic norms of conduct, it might be important to briefly go through a checklist of some of the main, and often contradictory, norms and decide which of them one would prefer to observe in the coming hours.

According to Jorge Arditi (1999), centuries ago, rules of conduct were firmly established; they changed slowly, and people's lives had a "centeredness," turning around a central concept or virtue—around God, for instance. People in the Middle Ages wanted to behave as God-fearing, pious people of goodwill. Many centuries later, in the Renaissance, "grace" was the central concept for Castiglione's courtiers; they tried to behave gracefully in every moment and situation of their lives. In Castiglione's words (1959, 39):

> Let him [the courtier] laugh, jest, banter, frolic, and dance, yet in such a manner as to show always that he is genial and discreet; and let him be full of grace in all that he does or says.[25]

Although models open up a wide range of possible selves and ways of life, norms of conduct limit the range of socially acceptable types of behavior and restrict the field within which a human being may develop, shape, and construct her or his self. Let me illustrate this problem with a simple example. In earlier times and civilizations, the norms of behavior used to be rigid and strict. For instance, Catholics for centuries were taught to avoid by all means the seven cardinal sins:

1. pride (*superbia*),
2. greed (*avaritia*),
3. lust (*luxuria*),

4. envy (*invidia*),
5. gluttony (*gula*),
6. wrath (*ira*), and
7. sloth (*acedia*).

Nowadays, there is confusion about these concepts. They still have a residual existence in our consciousness, but the contemporary civilization of consumption keeps convincing us that they are more virtues than sins. *Pride:* The media (and our peers and model personalities) encourage us to be proud of ourselves, build up strong egos, realize ourselves; modesty is a dangerous weakness; we should have the strong self-consciousness of an autonomous human being; we are the lords of life. *Greed:* They prompt us to enrich ourselves, they tell us that the more wealth we have piled up, the more opportunity we have to enjoy the joys of life, they convince us that gold and wealth govern the world and that the poor are responsible for their poverty. *Lust:* They convince us that the world turns around sex. They urge us to seize all opportunities while we are young. They warn us not to distort our personalities by repressing our drives and instincts. *Envy:* They prove to us that there is nothing wrong in wanting to be as rich, as successful, as powerful, as beautiful, as happy as those on the peak. *Gluttony.* Their commercials bathe us in a sea of creams, sauces, yogurts, sparkling beverages. *Wrath* and *sloth* (or despair) are the only items that are still on the list of forbidden things. Wrath is a weakness; it may harm our career, so we have to behave ourselves in a disciplined and politically correct way in all situations. And sloth or despair does not fit into the contemporary ideal of a dynamic life strategy, success orientation, and compulsory positive thinking.

For people living today, it is much more difficult to find the norms and principles of a decent and rewarding life than it was for their ancestors. They live on the battlefield of two civilizations—the traditional/modern Western civilization, on the one hand, and the emerging consumer civilization, on the other—struggling and interacting with one another. They are the two variants of the same civilization, but they suggest and enforce totally different, and even contradictory, norms of behavior. And because both of them have a strong influence on us—the one derives its energy from a three-thousand-year-long tradition; the message of the other is broadcast twenty-four hours a day by the media and the advertising industry—we act in confusion, observing a certain norm in this moment and its opposite in the next. The impact of these contradictory influences on the formation of people's selves may, and should, become one of the main fields of research in the next decades.[26]

Etiquette

Above the system of moral norms and rules of conduct, there is a layer of more ephemeral but not necessarily less important rules of social behavior, which is usually called "etiquette." Its rules are less deeply rooted in the depths of holy traditions, myths, religious beliefs, social hierarchies, and idiosyncrasies; it gives more leeway to personal styles and whims; and there is a playful element in it. But woe is he or she who makes the mistake of ignoring it (only misanthropes, eccentrics, and revolutionaries can allow themselves this freedom).

Each human society we know of has had a sort of etiquette, though in early civilization it was hardly distinguishable from the basic system of religious, moral, and ritual norms. In later civilizations—in Athens, Rome, and Byzantium; in the Age of Chivalry and the Renaissance; in the royal courts of the seventeenth or eighteenth centuries—etiquette developed into a high and sophisticated art.

Later, in the nineteenth century, in the emerging new industrial societies, with millions of people looking for their place and trying to rise, or stay, in the middle classes, familiarity with the rules of genteel behavior became a must also in the lower layers of European societies. This was the heyday of etiquette books. Between 1870 and 1917, about 300 etiquette books were in circulation just in America. And *The Ladies' Home Journal,* which was one of the earliest women's magazines, with a special column on comely behavior, had a circulation of 700,000 in 1885.[27]

One of the typical etiquette books of the age, *The Mirror of True Womanhood* by Bernard O'Reilly (1877), for instance, discussed the following virtues a woman had to emulate.

> Unselfishness—Fidelity—"Vanity [is] the path of dishonor"—Justice—
> Kindness—Gentleness—"The mother should be gentle, low-voiced, and
> patient"—Sense of duty—Culture of the heart—Generosity in conquer-

ing self—Hospitality—"Simplicity in dress . . . not extravagance"—
Piety—etc.[28]

In the early twentieth century, life had become more and more "decentered,"
and etiquette books were no longer like moral treatises but, according to Arditi
(1999), read like "cookbooks," "travel-guides," or "dictionaries."[29] Emily Post,
the author of one of the most successful etiquette books of the early twentieth
century, *Etiquette: The Blue Book of Social Usage* (1928 [1922]),[30] argues, for
instance, that people have to observe the rules of various etiquettes in various
life situations. Arditi (1999, 36) sums up her views:

> There is a formal etiquette demanding a formal personality, a business eti-
> quette demanding a business personality, a travel etiquette demanding a
> travel personality, etc. . . . At home a woman should be assertive and
> strong; in leisure she should be charming and playful; in society, modest
> and measured; in business, where women occupied almost exclusively
> positions of subordination [remember that we are in 1922], she should
> have no personality whatsoever. "The perfect secretary, figuratively speak-
> ing," declares Post [1928, 549–50], "should not even admit knowingly that
> she is a human being. . . . She should respond to [her employer's] require-
> ments exactly as a machine responds to the touch of lever or accelerator.

These kinds of advice sound revolting nowadays, just as our contemporary
rules of behavior will probably sound revolting in fifty years. For the time being, fashions and norms of conduct change with a lightning speed. We live in a
"postmodern," eclectic, and multicultural age, where one can mix almost everything with almost everything. We have an exhilarating and terrifying freedom of
behaving, speaking, dressing, dancing, and living in the most diverse ways. We
have the gadgets, dresses, clothes, traditions, norms, forms, styles, and colors
of several thousand years and of several dozens of civilizations. The question is
how we can use this chaotic variety to shape our selves and build ourselves into
authentic personalities. This is a real *embarras de richesse*.

Etiquette is also a good example of the duality of our everyday lives we considered in the introduction to this book. It is a good example of the fact that we
live on two levels. On the surface, we observe the rules of etiquette because we

want to be accepted by our community, fit into this community. But while we are doing so, we also keep building our selves—even without knowing that we are doing so—on a deeper, perhaps more essential level. Strange as it may be, it is a fact that with the help of etiquette we are reinforcing our personal autonomy and transforming ourselves from "animal" into spiritual beings. How do we do this?

Etiquette is an artificial system, the essence of which is to make us behave ourselves artificially. It is a system that prompts us to curb our natural instincts, as the trainer in the Spanish riding school forces the horses to step and dance as they would never do in the pasture. It teaches us to behave as if we were completely autonomous beings, in total control of our animal instincts, as if we hovered over this vulgar material world as pure spiritual creatures. Most of the table rules are, for instance, meant to show that we are not greedy animals, we do not feed or gobble, we even do not eat, we only pick and taste the food, not because we are hungry but because we are connoisseurs, we are in search of spiritual experience in the world of tastes, and anyway, eating is just an insignificant side effect; the main thing is that we exchange elegant ideas with our host or fellow guests. Why shouldn't we take the china cup in the hollow of our hands? Why hold it, daintily, at its fragile ear? The answer may be that in this way we (unconsciously) stress our nonmaterial, almost spiritual relationship with the golden and mysterious liquid in the cup. Stretching one's little finger may still add to this airy effect. Or why do people in the highest society eat the soup from a cup and not from a bellied soup-plate? And if they eat their soup from a plate, why do they immerse their spoons in the wrong direction, that is, moving it not toward themselves, as it would be natural, but away from themselves, toward the outer edge of the plate? In all likelihood, they do so, without actually knowing why they are doing so, because they do not want to make the impression that they greedily rake everything on the table into their mouths. And they want also to emphasize, while holding the—obligatorily not brimful—spoon in the air for a fraction of an instant, that as autonomous and spiritual beings, they will freely decide what to do with this earthly something called soup, when and whether they will allow it to enter the world of their holy personality.

I may have stretched these examples a bit too far, but the fact remains that even the trivial rules of the etiquette have a double function: On the surface, they limit the range of possible behaviors and help us integrate into our community. But in the underlying "existential" sphere, they help us shape and build the autonomy and the spirituality of our personality.

The Art of Lying

I have already mentioned that in the public space we not only have to present but also hide ourselves—so much so that I would not be surprised if somebody proposed that the right to pretense should be included in the constitutions of all countries around the world. One could argue, namely, that the ability to pretend and to play a wide range of roles is an indispensable source of freedom. It protects people, their inner selves, the core of their personalities, the deep layers of their personal existence. They would be absolutely defenseless and would lose their selves if they were forced to be continuously open and sincere, if they were forced to betray their feelings and thoughts in every moment of their lives, if they did not have the right to silence, pretense, dissimulation, and—in certain situations—even to lying. Their privacy and autonomy would be impaired, if not annihilated.[31]

But there is also another reading of people's role playing.[32] As we shall see below, there are experts who claim that there is no such thing as a "genuine" or core self. In the various and changing situations of their lives, people behave in different ways, play different roles, and their self is nothing else than the sum of these roles.[33] Which means that they do not pretend and do not lie when they play different roles; they only adapt their behavior to the various situations in a way that they think may optimize for them the outcome of the situation.[34] We shall come back later in this book to the especially great importance of role playing in our contemporary consumer civilization.

Let me add here that pretense, silence, and white lies are indispensable also for social reasons. Any human community, marriage, friendship, association, club, or government would blow up in a few days if people knew in every moment of their lives what their partners feel and think about them, and vice versa. They would kill one another. It is safer to see one another darkly, through the mirror of our roles. Which does not mean, of course, that we should open the floodgates of lies. This is a paradoxical situation: We know that our partners play roles, but we also want to trust them and believe that they say what they mean. This is a perpetual comedy of hide-and-seek. We do, and do not, want to learn the truth.

We are in search of ourselves. "Be yourself!" and "Actualize yourself!" are the primary watchwords of our age. But how to do so is an anguish-filled question for millions of young and not-so-young people around the world. One of the main sources of friendship and love is the hope that she or he will help us answer this question. Over all genuine human relationships there hovers the timid or anguished supplication: Tell me, please, who I am. Or more exactly, we would say, tell me that I am valuable, interesting, smart, strong, mysterious, bright, good, irresistible, or at least acceptable; somebody of worth. We almost permanently need reassurance and confirmation. We keep fishing for compliments. Without admitting it, or without even knowing it, in searching for our selves we are also fishing for lies. Our selves are complex constructs, in which illusions and self-delusions may also be important, and not necessarily harmful, component parts.

We have to accept it as a fact that lying is almost omnipresent in the human world.[35] It may be harmful and destructive (this was called by experts *mendacium perniciosum*), or it may be a "white" or innocent lie (called *mendacium officiosum*). On the one hand, it may be destructive, it may poison people's lives and relationships, it may undermine their communities and polities, it may destroy friendships, loyalties, life. But, on the other hand, lying also has more positive forms. It is the sister of fantasy and illusion; it builds those castles in the air, those worlds of symbols, myths, and beliefs, without which our lives would be poorer and less tolerable. According to Plato, poets were liars. Renaissance poets and critics questioned this and argued in the defense of poetry, as for instance Sir Philip Sidney did, that the poet "nothing affirms, and therefore never lieth." And Sir Francis Bacon added to this: "One of the Fathers, in great severity, called poesy *vinum daemonum,* because it filleth the imagination; and yet it is but the shadow of a lie."[36]

But even if poets do not lie, a great proportion of world literature has ever turned around the comedy and tragedy of lying. We are stunned, fascinated, and mesmerized by the demonic lies of a Mephistopheles, an Iago, Richard III, Tartuffe, Don Giovanni, or by the killing fields of lies in the plays of Ibsen or Chekhov; think of the lies in *The Iceman Cometh* by O'Neill or in *Who's Afraid of Virginia Woolf?* by Albee. But think also of the great masters of the art of lying, *miles gloriosus*, Tyl Eulenspiegel, the Baron of Münchhausen, or the heroes of the film *The Sting*. We love them; we keep our fingers crossed for them.

According to Alan Ryan (1996, 619 and passim) there are, and probably we need them, "professional liars," including "doctors, lawyers, and politicians, and doubtless university teachers, too." Most of us still accept the fact, or even expect, that in ultimate situations doctors lie to us. Lawyers are trained in the art of not telling. Ryan (1996, 640) is perhaps right when he remarks that the "public presently shouts very loudly about the untruthfulness of politicians, but will not listen if it is told the truth."

It may be a shame, but it is a fact that without the art of lying, or at least without the art of not telling the truth, concealing the truth, and hiding ourselves behind various forms of semblance, we would be more defenseless in the world as it is nowadays and probably has ever been. Lying, dissimulating, hiding ourselves: This is a complex art, which we start to learn in our cradle (we cry, pretending that we suffer, but we only want to have more milk), and which we still practice on our deathbed (when we smile to conceal our pain and make the ordeal easier for our relatives). We need this art badly when we enter the public space.

Masquerades

Hiding appeals to us in many ways. Children adore playing peek-a-boo. While hiding, they enjoy the power they have over their parents, whom they see but who cannot see them. When found, they laugh happily; they enjoy being found and admitted back into the world of light and safety. Homecoming is a more delicious and intense experience than being at home. In the adult world, lovers play at hide-and-seek in the first phase of their courtship. But beyond this, masques and masquerades have played an important role in a great many civilizations. And for centuries, masked balls were also among the most exciting social events in European aristocratic courts and burgher cities.

Why were people so fascinated by putting on masks and going to these balls? Perhaps they were because they loved to escape from themselves, from their selves. They loved "to lose themselves" in the crowd. They loved to escape from their lives. They loved to escape from the cage of morality and plunge into the sea of amorality, into a prelapsarian world, where there was no identity and therefore no guilt and no responsibilities. The masked ball was a world of adventure where one could experiment with strange new roles and selves. Philistines may have paraded as princes, and princes may have relished the imagined bucolic simplicity of the lives of everyday folks. People could play with the idea that they were, and were not, themselves at the same time. It was a world of thrilling ambiguities. It was a world of flirting and delicious intrigue. It was a world where one was freed from the everlasting pressure of obligatory self-actualization—where one could play and just *be*.

Sunglasses

Masquerades are no longer in vogue——the growing popularity of Halloween costumes in the Anglo-Saxon world may be an exception—but due to a favorite gadget of the age of consumption, sunglasses, the play of hide-and-seek is still an important strategy of self-construction. Sunglasses may be the last vestige of carnival masks, or those of the traditional veil, which for a thousand years hid the faces of women—with the significant difference that traditionally women hid their faces and did not hide their eyes and gazes, whereas modern Western women hide their eyes and expose their faces. (Do they protect and hide their inner selves, their thoughts, their souls more than their predecessors? And if they do, what explains this change?)

Wearing sunglasses allows women to show and hide themselves at the same time. A pair of sunglasses is an instrument of flirtation, provocation, and seduction. It hides women's selves without hiding their beauty. It intrigues and tempts people to discover their secret, their mystery. It makes women unapproachable, though at the same time it is also an invitation to dance.

Sunglasses worn by a man have a different function. They are instruments and symbols of power. First, this is because it enables the person who wears them to see people while they do not see him. This is a situation of authority. They cannot read his thoughts and emotions in his eyes. He has the appearance of being in full control of himself and the situation. There is something puzzling and mysterious about him, he has a secret, a depth. Sunglasses function as masks; they protect his identity (or—even more often—hide his lack of self and identity). He can move around in the world incognito. They lend him the image of autonomy and dignity, the austerity of a bodyguard, a Mafioso, a godfather. With his big, dark, inscrutable glass eyes, he may even be a powerful and dangerous extraterrestrial alien.

After all, it is not a bad idea to take our sunglasses with us when we leave our home in the morning. But we should not think that we have solved all our problems by doing so. Our project of self- and world reconstruction goes on throughout the day, even if we are not aware of this latent dimension of our lives.

Cars and Bicycles

Cars, and the time during which we drive from our home to the office, may play a crucial role in the process of reconstructing our selves.[37] Cars are our alter egos. We identify ourselves with them; we live in a kind of coexistence with them. Their strength is our strength, their speed is our speed, their flashy beauty is our beauty, their streamlining is the streamlining of our lives, their elegance is our elegance, their mystery is our mystery. When they are OK, we feel OK; when they break down, we have a fit of existential panic. When we get in our new car for the first time, we feel as if we have been reborn and are young. When they have sex appeal, we have sex appeal. Their personality is our personality. It is true that there are many fewer brands and types of cars than there are human beings, and so it is certainly a self-delusion to think that they express our selves. Luckily, we can live with self-delusions quite comfortably. Nay, we cannot live without them.

Cars are not only our alter egos. They are also our private worlds. If we did not succeed in constructing a homely world for ourselves before we left for our office, our cars may help us feel, at least temporarily, that we are at home in this universe. The car is a world in itself—a closed and complete universe, well protected against the dangers of the outside world.[38] It is a microcosm moving around in a chaotic world. It cruises in the streets smoothly, silent and undisturbed, like a spaceship out in space. It protects us against rain, snow, and wind. It protects us against the gazes of the multitude, the others, the crowd. We can see them, and they cannot see us; we feel strong and safe: This is a position of power, earlier enjoyed only by royalty in the cushioned privacy of their *equipage*. In our cars, we are in charge; we despotically control everything in this microuniverse. Cars protect us also against time, decay, aging; if we have the better car, we may be old as the hills, but we will drive faster than the youngest athletes. Horsepower is our power.[39]

Cars have other attractions as well. Living creatures have the common feature that they do their best to save their energies. They try to attain their goals with the least possible effort. One could say that they are lazy. They like to repose and relax. They do not exert themselves for nothing. They move around only if it is necessary; if they have to graze, hunt, and work to survive or to feel comfortable; when they happen to have surplus energy, they blow off steam by playing and romping about. One of the sources of the pleasure, or even the bliss, of driving a car is certainly the fact that it perfectly satisfies both our need to save energy (I mean our personal energy, not the global sources of energy) and our penchant for idling. We simply have to touch the accelerator and this minimal effort triggers a huge amount of energy, which carries us smoothly and swiftly forward. (In earlier ages, human beings could go through this fascinating and almost metaphysical experience only when rafting on rapids, sliding downhill on a sledge, or on board a ship gloriously sailing in the wind.[40] It is an almost metaphysical experience because it makes us believe that we have defeated the laws of physics, the law of the conservation of energy. We proceed without effort; we do not need to defeat gravity at each of our steps. This is the magic of the wheel as well. It rolls easily and smoothly, as if it needed no energy.

Carmakers know us well and exploit this weakness of ours. They seduce us into buying their cars by adding new and new gadgets; gadgets that we have only to touch in order to produce spectacular effects. We lightly touch a knob and windows open, seats slide to and fro, mirrors readjust themselves, our car switches gears. We softly turn the steering wheel one inch and our heavy car, weighing two tons, obediently, elegantly, silently changes direction. Yuppies would touch the steering wheel with just one finger, or with the palm of one hand, and they would do so to demonstrate that they are above the laws of physics and to avoid the appearance that they have to struggle with the wheel as if it were the stilt of a plough.

Yet, conversely, one needs physical exercise to keep oneself in good shape. And so, getting out of our wonder car, we start jogging, we lift weights until we sweat and lose our wind, and then, after a quick and pleasant shower (we need not hoist water any more in wooden buckets from deep wells), we get in our cars and start pressing the magic buttons again.

Personal Music Players and Cell Phones

If we choose to walk to our office, or to use public transport. we may need some help. Recently, for many of us, a Walkman, or other personal music player, would do the job. With the earphones on our head—and the sound, melody, rhythm, and harmony of the music surrounding us with a transparent bubble—we may enjoy the trip. We are protected against the noises, the dissonance, the gloom, the sharp edges of the world. The music reverses the relationship between the world and ourselves. We no longer feel ourselves lonely, lost, insignificant, and weak in a great and powerful world; the music exalts our spirits and elates our selves. We feel as if we were at the center of the universe. And we only have to turn up the decibels if our sense of power and self-consciousness falters.

Cell phones, too, may also help a lot. They are practical and useful gadgets, but their enormous global success cannot be explained solely by the fact that they have made the organization of our lives easier. They have other, latent, functions as well.

First, they are outstanding anxiety reducers. Having one of them in our bag or pocket, or carrying it in our hands, as many people of the more anxious type do, we may reduce the uneasy feeling that we are alone and lost in the world, or in an aggressive crowd of strangers. Instead of saying a short prayer to our patron saint, we may give a couple of quick calls to one or two key figures in our personal universe—our mother, our husband, our wife, a friend, a colleague, the grocer, our hairdresser—and the anxiety will immediately subside. The friendly voices will create a warm and familiar environment, a microworld around us, in which we will feel at home.

Second, with the help of the cell phone, one can also reconfirm one's identity. In a metropolitan crowd, one loses oneself. When everybody is a stranger, then nobody is anybody. In an anonymous crowd, everybody loses her or his social role and identity. One ceases to be a human person of some distinction. One loses one's self if it is not confirmed by the gaze and words of those who know us. Giving a call to them, greeting them and being greeted by them, seeing them and being seen by them on the screens of the most up-to-date versions, fills us with the pleasant feeling of our reconfirmed existence and identity.

Third, a few years ago, talking on our handy phone in the street or in public places may have slightly enhanced our momentary social status in the crowd. It created an aura of mystery around us: We had an "online" connection with somebody in another world, unknown to those who stared at us. Our talking to somebody may have also made the impression on passersby that we had something important to say or listen to, that we were important.[41] But this is no longer the case. Talking on a cell phone in a public place now has a vulgar and proletarian aura, except if you are dressed like a banker or a broker and talk on your phone while hurrying through the crowd and making the impression that you are just selling or buying the Coliseum or the Empire State Building. If you are not a banker or broker, then you have to flash a very expensive, modish phone to make a positive impression and suggest that you belong to the swinging new generation of the Information Age, that you are in. In this case, your phone is still a membership card in the club of an imaginary elite.

Networks

What happens to us if, walking in the streets of a foreign country, we suddenly realize that all our belongings have been stolen—our handbag, our wallet, our documents and return ticket, the few dollar bills we had in our pocket? We are standing there, with nothing but shorts and a shirt on. Well, in all likelihood, we would panic, our heart would sink, our self would shiver, and we would shrink to a dwarf's proportions. The question is: Why? We, ourselves, have not changed. We are the same human being as we were an hour ago. Or aren't we?

Checking the contents of women's handbags,[42] we have already seen with how many threads, or ropes, we are linked to our world. Or, to use another metaphor, we are linked to the world by a number of capillary vessels, which all feed and reinforce our selves. If these threads and channels are broken, our self may collapse. What are these threads and channels?

Money is an important safety belt; it is one of the most important channels or sources of safety in the modern world. It may help us survive in a great variety of situations, find food, move around the world, pay for medical assistance, buy clothes and protect ourselves against the cold and the heat, find a shelter, and get out of a prison by paying the bail. And it may also help us enjoy the joys of life.

A credit card is even better if we happen to be in the so-called civilized part of the world. It links us to our bank, our bank accounts, our normal lives. It fills us with the pleasant feeling that we have, somewhere in the world, a home, a safe background. And if we have a major credit card, we may even feel that we are at home in the global world of international financial services.

The driver's license or the social security card is a major link to our own world and our old self. It anchors us in our society. It is the symbol and guarantor of our social identity, of our being a member of a human community. It is a strong link, expressed by a number. This number connects us to the world, it defines our place, our rights and duties in a community. It proves that we are a citizen of a country and are protected by its institutions. We are protected by its constitution and legal system, its health care system, its police; it offers us a wide range of opportunities and services, roads and trains, schools and hospitals. It indicates that we have a job, a profession, a role in the world. It testifies that we exist at all.

To lose our wallet, or handbag, may be a serious blow to our self. We suddenly perceive the complex structures that we have built up in and around our self, the scaffolding that, collapsing, has all at once emerged from its status of invisibility. From the surface of our daily life, we have fallen into the twilight zone of our existence, in the midst of the "existential drama" of our life, where—without really knowing it—we have ever kept constructing our self, our freedom and dignity, the meaning of our life. And then, after we have gotten safely home, renewed our documents, revalidated our credit cards, and clicked back into our daily routine, this scaffolding of our self, and the drama of our existence, will be again submerged in the twilight zone of our life.

—

Let's stop here briefly and try to answer a question while our protagonist is on her way to her place of work. In this book, we are exploring how—in an unconscious, semiconscious, or conscious way—people keep constructing their selves. But the question arises: How far are they able and free to do so? Do they, themselves, really construct their selves, or are they shaped by outside forces they cannot control?

4

The Limits and Freedom
of Self-Construction

To dare is to lose one's footing momentarily.
Not to dare is to lose oneself.

—*Søren Kierkegaard*

The Social Construction of the Self

A rich literature on cultural anthropology and sociology has shown that civilizations—Western civilization included—limit the range of roles people may assume, the range of selves they may develop. Traditional as well as contemporary societies, nations, regions, communities, professions, clubs, pubs, gangs, environments, streets, shopping malls, means of public transport, consultation rooms, and holidays like Thanksgiving or Christmas—all have their own codes of behavior, which people have to observe if they want to be accepted by the community in question.[1] As George Herbert Mead (1962, 162, 221) remarked: "A person is a person because he belongs to a community. . . . One has to be a member of a community to be a self. . . . In primitive human society, the individual self is much more completely determined, with regards to his thinking and his behavior, . . . than he is in civilized human society."[2]

Norbert Elias (1991, 60) described the power of the social environment in shaping people's selves in the following way:

> The more differentiated the functional structure of a society or a class within it, the more sharply the psychical configurations of the individual people who grow up within it diverge. But however different the degree of this individuation may be, there is certainly no such thing as a zero-point of individuation among people who grow up and live within society. To a greater or lesser degree, the people of all the societies known to us are individual and different from each other down to the last detail of their configuration and behavior, and society-specific, i.e., shaped and bound in the nature of their psychical self-regulation by a particular network of functions, a particular form of communal life which also shapes and binds all its other members.

Anyone who is a bit familiar with the works of cultural anthropologists knows that the differences between these networks of functions and rules of behavior in various civilizations are amazingly great. The very fact, for instance, that the self is such a central problem for people in the West, that they are permanently urged to care for their selves, actualize their selves, is determined by the cultural tradition of the Western world, in which they live. In Clifford Geertz's words:

> The western conception of the person as a bounded, unique, more or less integrated motivational and cognitive universe, a dynamic center of awareness, emotion, judgment and action, organized into a distinctive whole, and set contrastively against other such wholes and against a social and natural background is, however incorrigible it may seem to us, a rather peculiar idea within the context of the world cultures.[3]

Other civilizations have ever had different messages for their believers.[4] Buddhism, for instance, told people that the self does not exist, it is an illusion, a dangerous illusion, that is the main source of human suffering. For a Buddhist, the way to the "happiness" of nirvana leads through the destruction of this illusion.[5]

There were periods even in the history of Western civilization when the destruction of the human self was the dominant imperative. Think, for instance, of Saint Benedict's *Rule* (2001 [c. 530]), which urged, if not forced, the monks to work in every moment of their lives on the annihilation of their selves. Each and every monk was prompted

"to deny himself," "to climb all the steps of humility" — "to attribute to God, and not to himself, whatever good one sees in oneself" — to humble himself because human beings "descend by self-exaltation and ascend by humility" — "to keep death daily before one's eyes."

He was told "to hate his own will" — "to turn away from his own will."

He was told to "humbly confess" all his thoughts and hidden desires to the Abbot, "to hide from his Abbot none of the evil thoughts."

He was prompted "not to fulfill the desires of the flesh" — "to chastise his body" — "to fast" — "to be on his guard against evil desires, for death lies close by the gate of pleasure." — "For our sake we are put to death all the day long; we are considered as sheep marked for slaughter."

He had "to be content with the poorest and the worst of everything" and had "to consider himself a bad and worthless workman," "a beast of burden," "lower and of less account than anyone else" — he had to know that he was "a worm and no man" — "He should always have his head bowed and his eyes toward the ground" — "Feeling the guilt of his sins at every moment, he should consider himself already present at the dread Judgment."[6]

At first sight, this is the opposite of the twentieth-century and twenty-first-century cult of the self, of our contemporary apotheosis of the self. Its fundamental message is humility instead of pride; the destruction of one's will instead of the boosting of one's ego; poverty instead of wealth and comfort; self-chastisement and asceticism instead of hedonism and the cult of the desires of the flesh; obedience and self-denial instead of autonomy and self-actualization.

Yet on another level, Saint Benedict's *Rule* are also a program for the care of the self. It only defines the "self" in a different way than we do it nowadays. Self is used here in the sense of one's immortal soul, and the Benedictine rules care for the salvation and eternal life of this soul. One has to destroy, punish, limit, humiliate one's spurious, mortal, material, sinful self in order to liberate one's true self, one's soul, and achieve fulfillment beyond in the sphere of eternal life.

If the medieval repression of the (secular) self may seem pathological to us, modern self-apotheosis may also have a pathological version. Paul Tillich (1952) referred to such a case:

> There is a moment in which the self-affirmation of the average man becomes neurotic: when changes of the reality to which he is adjusted threaten the fragmentary courage with which he has mastered the accustomed objects of fear. If this happens—as it often does in critical periods of history—the self-affirmation becomes pathological. The dangers connected with the change, the unknown character of things to come, the darkness of the future make the average man a fanatical defender of the established order. He defends it as compulsively as the neurotic defends the castle of his imaginary world. He loses his comparative openness to reality, he experiences an unknown depth of anxiety. But if he is not able to take this anxiety into his self-affirmation his anxiety turns into neurosis.[7]

The Self as a Trap

Cultural critics from Adorno to Baudrillard, Lyotard or Foucault have convincingly argued that, while it is celebrating the liberation of the human personality, our contemporary civilization of consumption exercises an almost total control over people. The cult of the self has been a trap that has helped the holders of political and economic power control people and their communities. Identity and self have ever been instruments of social control.

Foucault (1974, 387) claimed that the human being, as the subject and object of knowledge, was "an invention of recent date" soon to be "erased, like a face drawn in the sand at the edge of the sea." And he argued that the emergence of personal identity and the self in the seventeenth and eighteenth centuries was not a victory of individualism and freedom—as it is usually believed—but just the contrary: Personal identity and the self were invented by the emerging national bureaucracies because they wanted to identify people as subjects of the central authority. "It is through the policing process," Foucault contended, "that the modern frame of mind has been formed."[8] "The self is an abstract construction, one continually being redesigned in an ongoing discourse generated by the imperatives of the policing process."[9] Faith "in the autonomy and centrality of the human subject," which was "the central myth of the Enlightenment," became a trap, an instrument of domination, and it has served "the interests of modern inquisitors."[10]

In a same vein, George Levine (1992, 4) paints the picture of a fierce struggle between modernists and postmodernists. Modernists argued that the "self" "was an aspect of a great enterprise of moral and political renewal, which they associated with "liberalism" and "romanticism," while postmodernists or poststructuralists contend that the modern conceptions of "essential selfhood are complicit with conservative and repressive social forces." For modernists, he maintains, "the self has a strong history of political liberation, enfranchisement, transformation. For poststructuralists, the history is different, infinitely more repressive and delusive"[11] Modernists themselves acknowledge that even if

> in its Enlightenment formation the self was a means to resist a brutal traditional autocracy, it has in our own time become the justification for moralized greed on a grand scale, an expression of the right of the individual to reject social demands except on the smallest scale by the nearest at hand. Current history confirms Howe's [1992] perception of the link between the idea of the self and the new commercial society. It has produced yuppiedom and magazines like *Self*, television programs like *Lifestyles of the Rich and Famous*, junk bonds, and corporate takeovers.[12]

Modernists reply that, in spite of this justified criticism, the "idea of the self has been a liberating and revolutionary step, perhaps the most liberating and revolutionary, toward the goal of a communal self-humanization." And the autonomous self still is the main source of human values and social innovation.[13]

Arguing in a Foucaultian manner, Nikolas Rose (1997, 246) claims that human beings are governed, and determined, by a number of "psychological machines": by "desiring machines, laboring machines, pedagogic machines, punitive machines, curative machines, consuming machines, war machines, sporting machines, governing machines, spiritual machines, bureaucratic machines, market machines, financial machines." Durkheim's contemporary followers, too, consider the human self as a "social fact" and leave relatively little room for the self-construction of the individual. In his book *Beyond Freedom and Dignity*, B. F. Skinner (1971) goes even further in describing the narrow limits between which human beings can shape their selves. Mitroff and Bennis (1989, 70–89) maintain that our contemporary consumer civilization "manufactures people."

According to social genetics, people's behavior is determined to a large extent by their genetic heritage, though—in principle—their interaction with their changing natural and human environments may leave them a certain room of more or less free maneuvering.[14] In a similar way, human ethologists argue that behavioral patterns transmitted by heredity and imprinted in the individual by group pressure, are major determinants of human behavior. In the case of humans, group pressure is further enhanced by the world of objects, symbols, beliefs, institutions, and especially by language (though most of the scholars admit that this cultural/civilizational context may also become a major source of individual freedom).

In a certain respect, members of the structuralist school of thought also deny the existence of an autonomous human self and consider it much more as something located at the intersection of, and defined by, various structures. However, they speak not so much of social as of linguistic structures, and they define the self as a "language" or "act of language."

Roy Porter (1997, 12), describes the human self as being "just a construct, a trick of language, a rhetorical ruse." Nikolas Rose (1997, 225), whom I have just quoted, sees the role of language in a different light. According to him language, or more precisely the language of a given historical period and context, is a kind of cage: People can construct their selves only in the terminology of their own age. In our contemporary world, for instance, it is modern psychology and psychiatry that provide the concepts whereby one can perceive, describe, and construct oneself:

At certain historical moments, particular issues or problems are *constructed* in certain ways—as melancholia or depression, as hysteria or post-traumatic syndrome, as cowardice or shell-shock[15]—only through the possibilities available within language: words, vocabularies, the grammars of explanation and causation, the narratives of life events that it provides. Language makes only certain ways of being human describable, and in so doing makes only certain ways of being human possible.[16]

Advertising is a good example of the social control exercised nowadays over the human self.[17] It had already become a powerful means of control in the first decades of the twentieth century. In a fascinating essay titled "The Ad Man and the Grand Inquisitor," Jackson Lears (1992) describes the double language spoken by leading advertising experts in those years. On the one hand, they spoke of "consumer sovereignty":

> The old Kings and aristocrats have departed. In the new order the masses are master. Not a few, but millions and hundreds of millions of people must be persuaded. In peace and in war, for all kinds of purposes, advertising carries the message to this new King—the people.
>
> Advertising is the King's messenger in this day of economic democracy. All unknowing a new force has been let loose in the world. Those who understand it will have one of the keys to the future.[18]

In the first half of the twentieth century, agency executives more or less believed in their missionary role of promoting economic growth and moral progress. They were confident that they had the power to shape people's lives and minds. James Wallen, a senior copywriter, wrote in 1925. "We advertising writers are privileged to compose a new chapter of civilization. It is a great responsibility to mold the daily lives of millions of our fellow men, and I am persuaded that we are second only to statesmen and editors in power for good."[19]

Lears claims that despite "all the talk of 'economic democracy,' from the 1890s to the 1930s advertisers increasingly assumed that their audience constituted an extraordinarily pliable mass of putty, and that their own power to mold it was almost unlimited." He quotes John Lee Mahin, an agency head from Chicago, who wrote in 1910 that the "consumer nearly always purchases in unconscious obedience to what he or she believes to be the dictates of an authority which is anxiously consulted and respected."[20] In 1925 Arthur Holmes, a marketing professor at Northwestern University, stated the same thing even more bluntly:

People unacquainted with psychology assume that men have the power to say "Yes" or "No" to an advertisement. The assumption is only partly correct. A man has the power to decide in the first stage of the game, not the last. . . . If the printed word can seize his attention, hold him chained, drive from his mind all other thoughts except the one "Buy this!" standing at the head of an organized sentiment from which every opposing idea, perception, feeling, instinct, and disposition have been driven out or smothered to death, then HE CANNOT SAY "NO!" His will is dead.[21]

After almost a century, experts still discuss the question of how far advertising can influence people's decisions, how far it limits people's freedom, how far it is able to shape and control people's selves. To know about this influence and danger is one of the preconditions of successfully protecting one's autonomy.

We may safely conclude that we are not completely free to choose our selves and roles. Social and cultural norms restrict our freedom. To a certain extent, we are prisoners of the society, culture, and historical period in which we live. And this is true not only of traditional cultures. We may celebrate our modern or postmodern freedom, but our contemporary cultures and subcultures also restrict our freedom and permit only certain modes of behavior. If, for instance, you are a Portuguese farmer or a banker in New York, you may not behave yourself as a Japanese samurai of yore, or as the member of a hippie community in Amsterdam would do.

Does this mean that we deceive ourselves when we believe that we can freely construct and shape our selves? Does it mean that, as a matter of fact, we are jerked like puppets throughout our lives by irresistible routines? And, speaking of our morning rituals of self-construction, is it possible that, instead of freely building our selves, all we do is to insert ourselves into the impersonal routines and disciplines of our social environment?

We may even be tempted to do so. As human beings, we are anxious to find our place and peace in a human community, and this anxiety may prompt us to conform to the expectations of this community, to act as a member of the community, to pour our selves into the ready-made molds of our community.[22] It is not easy at all to find a good balance between our personal autonomy and our being members of a community; between the bad extremes of being an eccentric or a conformist.

Self-Construction and Freedom

Rejecting the hypotheses about the strong determination of the self, a great number of scholars argue that the human being has considerable freedom in constructing her or his self. They argue, for instance, that there is a "pre-linguistic," "presymbolic" self that is not the product of social and linguistic interaction.[23] Others assert that the self of the human being is not "prefabri-cated" or "assigned" but it is being "made," "shaped," "created" "constructed," "constituted," "built," "achieved," "assembled" (Ewen 1988; Rose 1997; Weber 2000); "administered," "produced," "realized" (Horney 1950); "conceived," "as-sessed," "regulated," "appraised," "fashioned" (Greenblatt 1980); "developed" (Brown 1998); formed, unified (Schrag 1997); "organized," "achieved" (Kaiser 1997); "invented" (Lyons 1978; Rose 1996); or "improved," "actualized" (Maslow 1999 [1968]) by the human person herself or himself.[24] We all are involved in a lifelong experiment of creating, shaping, and constructing our selves. And this is not an easy exercise.

As a first step, the human being will have to learn as much as possible about herself. She will not be left alone. She will be prompted by a great number of excellent scholars, and by even more modern quack-doctors, to "know her self," "be conscious of her self," "rewrite" her self (Porter 1997) or her soul (Hacking 1995); to "map," "analyze," "explore," "verify" her self; to "image" (Spacks 1976) or "monitor" herself (Snyder 1987); to "narrate" her self and achieve a "narra-tive self-identity" (Ricoeur 1992). And her attention will be drawn to the im-portance of "self-disclosure" (Smith et al. 1981); "self-recognition" (Tiemersma 1989); "self-identification," "self-discovery," "self-awareness" (Leary and Kowal-ski 1995); "self-scrutiny," "self-problematization," "self deciphering" (Rose 1997); "self-seduction" (Taylor 2003); "self-feeling," "self-seeking," "self-description," "self-cognizing," "self-insight" (Wicklund and Eckert 1992); "self-image-maintaining" (Whitehead and Smith 1986); and "self-symbolizing" (Gollwitzer 1986)—shall I continue?

Beyond exploring herself, she will have also to "master," "possess," "disci-pline," "centralize," and "experience her self" (Kierkegaard). She has to be good at "self-inspection," "self-persuasion," "self-regulation" (Elias 1991); and "self-preservation," "self-promotion" (Baumgartner and Tice 1986). She will also have to achieve and maintain her "self-constancy" (Kierkegaard); and her "self-esteem," "self-regard," "self-strength," and "self-respect" (Wylie 1974–79; Csikszentmihalyi 1975, 1990, 1997, 2003; Mecca, Smelser, and Vasconellos 1989; Hill 1991; Dillon 1995; Kernis 1995; Keshen 1996; Seligman 1998, 2002; Peterson and Seligman 2004).

And all these efforts will be futile if she is not ready to incessantly "renew" her self; to "adapt" her self to the changing challenges of a changing world—to "exercise," "evaluate," "cure" (Rose 1997); "educate," "determine" her self; to "struggle" for her self; if she does not excel in "self-help" (Smiles 1958); if she is not capable of continuous "self-betterment" and "self-enhancement"; if her purpose is not a genuine "self-fulfillment" and "symbolic self-completion" (Wicklund and Gollwitzer 1982; Brown 1998); if she is not capable of "self-transformation" (White and Hellerich 1998), "self-transfiguration" (Lears 1992), "self-transcendence" (Sartre 1953, 1956; Csikszentmihalyi 1993); if she is not involved in genuine "care for her self" (Foucault 1988b)—all in all, if she is not ready to embark on the "odyssey of the self" (Schrag 1997).

In his later years, even Foucault stressed that human life is not determined by historical necessity, because history is not a predetermined continuity but discontinuous, random, and fortuitous:[25] "All my analyses are against the ideal of universal necessities in human existence."[26] Human communities and individuals have a certain freedom to choose between various options in spite of the strong outside pressure and indoctrination.[27] They have the option not to accept the visions of the world and of the "self" that are imposed on them:

> I don't feel that it is necessary to know exactly what I am. The main interest in life and work is to become someone else that you were not in the beginning. If you knew when you began a book what you would say at the end, do you think that you would have the courage to write it? What is true for writing and for a love relationship is true also for life. The game is worthwhile insofar as we don't know what will be the end.[28] . . . All my analyses are against the idea of universal necessities in human existence. They show the arbitrariness of institutions and show which space of freedom we can still enjoy and how many changes can still be made.[29] . . . My role—and that is too emphatic a word—is to show people that they are much freer than they feel, that people accept as truth, as evidence, some

themes which have been built up at a certain moment during history, and that this so-called evidence can be criticized and destroyed. To change something in the minds of people—that's the role of an intellectual.[30]

In a brilliant article comparing Freud's and Foucault's ideas on the "self," Patrick H. Hutton (1988, 139–40) sums up Foucault's ideas in the following way:

> The quest for self-understanding is a journey without end. Even in the deepest recesses of our psyches there are no experiences which, if evoked, will reveal our true identities. But the quest for such knowledge is itself a form of self-care. . . . We are condemned to a quest for meaning whose meaning is that our human nature is continually being reconstituted by the forms that we create along the way. The responsibility to create meanings and values anew is a perpetual task but nonetheless the foundation of all human endeavor.

Our freedom to shape our selves keeps changing throughout our lifetime. In principle, at our birth, "we have the world at our feet": A wide range of potential roles and selves are open for us. Growing up, we may develop abilities and skills, which on the one hand may open new possibilities, but on the other hand rule out other ones. Bergson, Heidegger, Sartre, and others have argued that with each and every decision of ours, we opt for one possibility and destroy all other ones. At a certain point in our life course, the number of possibilities that are still open for us start to decrease. This does not mean, however, that toward the end of our lives, we necessarily reach a zero point of freedom of choice. Until we are in control of our minds and will power, we may choose between various "selves," or at least between various attitudes toward life and death. And this is still a real and genuine freedom.

The Self as a Narrative

We have seen that language patterns may limit our freedom. But—as a great number of scholars assert—language is, at the same time, a most powerful help in freely constructing our selves.

According to Lyotard (1984), the self emerges from the "heterogeneity of language games." Heidegger thought that human beings "dwell in language." Gadamer spoke of the "linguisticality of being."[31] Calvin O. Schrag (1997, 29) characterized the human being as a "rhetorical animal" or a *"homo narrans."*[32] Anthony P. Kerby spoke of a "narrative self" (1991). Daniel Dennett (1991, 426–27) described the self as the "center of narrative gravity." Paul Ricoeur (1984—86, 1992), Kenneth J. Gergen (1991), Gary S. Greg (1991), Adriana Cavarero (2000), and others claimed that the self came into being only as, and through, a narrative.[33]

Paul Ricoeur, the most important representative of this school of thought, defines the human personality as the "who in discourse,"[34] and he agrees with those who assert that our selves are not ready-made. We do not inherit them and do not possess them *ab ovo.* The human self is being constructed through experience, education, interaction, thinking, remembering; in trying to find a center in a vast and empty universe; in fighting time and transitoriness. We construct our selves through narration. Ricoeur quotes Socrates ("an unexamined life is not worth living") but goes further and says that an "untold life" is not a real life, and an "untold self" is not a real self, just a "narcissistic ego." "What we call the *subject* is never given at the start. Or, if it is, it is in danger of being reduced to the narcissistic egoistic and stingy ego, from which literature, precisely, can free us."[35] Only through narration, and by drawing on the immense variety of narrated lives and selves in our culture, can we construct a richly articulated and autonomous self. This "narrative identity" is the precondition, and source, of an authentic human existence:[36]

> We can become our own narrator . . . without being able to become the author. This is the great difference between life and fiction. In this sense, it is true that life is lived and that stories are told. An unbridgeable difference does remain, but this difference is partially abolished by our power of applying to ourselves the plots that we have received from our culture and of trying on the different roles assumed by the favorite characters of the stories most dear to us. . . .
>
> In place of an *ego* enamored of itself arises a *self* instructed by cultural symbols, the first among which are the narratives handed down in our lit-

erary tradition. And these narratives give us a unity which is not substantial but narrative. . . .[37]

The narrative approach not only allows greater analytical rigor, it allows us to turn away from the monadic concerns of Being-towards-death
to a more fully public and social sense of our temporality. Moreover, fic-
tional narrative draws in the creative imagination, by offering us textually
elaborated possibilities of existences.[38]

In his monograph on the history of the concept of the "self," Charles Taylor
(1989, 288–89) argues in the same way: "But the new time sense has also
changed our notion of the subject: the disengaged, particular self, whose identity is constituted in memory. Like any other human being at any time, he can
only find an identity in self-narration. Life has to be lived as a story." Narration
is a source of freedom, and it turns toward life and not toward death, as for instance in the existentialism of Heidegger.

In the same vein, Calvin O. Schrag (1997, 33) stresses the fact that the self
is not predetermined by outside factors but is being created in the course of
discourse and narration:

> The presence of the who is not that of a self-identical monad, mute and
> self-enclosed, changeless and secured prior to the events of speaking.
> The presence at issue is localized neither metaphysically in a fixed, un-
> derlying substratum nor epistemologically in a prelinguistic, zero-point
> center of consciousness. The who of discourse is not a "thing," a pre-
> given entity, a ghost in a machine, or whatever. . . . The who of discourse
> is an achievement, an accomplishment, a performance, whose presence
> to itself is admittedly fragile, subject to forgetfulness and semantic am-
> biguities. But in all this there is still a unity and a species of self-iden-
> tity, secured not by an abiding substratum but rather by an achieved self-
> identity.

Let me add that narration even fills us with the benevolent illusion and hope
of a certain, modest immortality. With the dying Hamlet, we would all like to
say to Horatio, if we had a Horatio: "Tell my story."[39] Our story told, something
would remain of us; we would not disappear in the darkness and void without

leaving a trace. And perhaps even the meaning of our lives—for which we, while alive, searched in vain—would shine in this narrative.

The unscientific lesson of all this may be that, if one wants to live an authentic life and develop a genuine self, one should tell one's story—at least to oneself, once a week, a month, a year; anyway, some time before it is too late.[40]

—

Here, let us close this short survey of the problems and possibilities of self-construction, and come back to our protagonist, whom we left on her way to her office. There, a new phase of her daily efforts to care for her self will begin and later continue, in the afternoon, on her way home, and in the evening, at home. We shall follow her along this process, but I have to warn the reader that our coverage and analysis of the events and situations will be brief and superficial. Most of them have been thoroughly analyzed by dozens of books and hundreds of papers. I deal with them only to show that the conscious, semiconscious, or unconscious construction of our selves goes on throughout the day, from morning till night, and that whatever we do at work, walking home, being at home, is also part of the latent "existential drama" of our lives.

The Self at Work

You have to do your own growing
no matter how tall your grandfather was.

—*Abraham Lincoln*

The Workplace

Arriving at our workplace, we enter a peaceful haven, an exciting arena, or a
killing field. Our workplace may be a sanctuary, an *"île des délices,"* a second
home, a laboratory of creative ideas, a hothouse where our personalities may
unfold and assert themselves. It may be an arena of fascinating challenges,
where we can test our strengths, flex our muscles, corroborate our egos. And it
may also be a dungeon where our selves are put on the rake, tortured, and ultimately destroyed.

A good workplace is a fortress, within whose walls we feel safe and protected. Ideally, it is an ordered microcosm within a chaotic world, with clear
and simple rules, transparent structures and relationships, rights and duties,
where everybody has her or his place, identity, and importance. It is a closed
universe that has an obvious purpose and meaning (which the macrouniverse
may not have). The experience of order and significance is enhanced by the rit-
ualistic rotation of special events, anniversaries, company meetings, and celebrations throughout the year.[1]

Beside our own neighborhoods—where we are engaged in the all-American, all-French, all-German, all-Polish, or global lifestyle competition—the workplace (and our profession) is the most important track or court where we are engaged in a permanent competition with our peers. It holds a mirror up to us, in which we can check our performance, see our achievements, and mourn our failures. In the evening, at the end of working hours, it may give us the good feeling that we have achieved something: We have sent 65 e-mails, processed 43 applications, sold 10,000 shares, controlled 201 chips, repaired 2 cars, and the like.

If we have a service job, if we are nurses, doctors, teachers, policemen, if we are at the counter, we may enjoy also the experience of power. And, as we know well, the sense of power may very well substitute for a real self. And vice versa: We need not have a personality to have power. It is a well-known phenomenon that people with weak, distorted, or disturbed selves strive for power to fill the vacuum left empty by a missing self.

Having a job may give us the good feeling that we are useful, that we have a place and a standing in our society. If our company has a nice badge, our feeling of importance and identity may be still further enhanced. The workplace may also provide us with a "brand" and a social self. Meeting with people we have not met before, we would have serious difficulties in identifying ourselves if we could not refer to this brand, to our job, profession, workplace.

The workplace is nowadays, for many people, the village, the lost community, in which one is known and accepted, where things keep happening, where people have a role, where the continuous flow of gossip provides excitement and the semblance of life, where scandals feed one's cannibal instincts, where one can act out one's Machiavellian instincts of intrigue without running too high a risk, where there is an ongoing fashion show, which may caress one's ego or prompt us to higher efforts of self-presentation and self-construction.

Beside one's family and neighborhood, one's workplace is the third most important "social bubble" that surrounds us, and in which we may feel at home. In this private universe, we are among people whom we know, and with whom we have, more or less, the same experiences, myths, and lifestyles.

The workplace is our second home, to which we can escape from our first home. However much we love our home, we need these escapes; from time to time, we need to disentangle ourselves from the emotional web of our family relations and emerge in the workplace as independent personalities. This may be especially important for women, who have ever been the happy or unhappy prisoners of their homes. It is not only slippers and shoes, aprons and business suits that distinguish people's home selves and professional selves. Think of how embarrassed people usually are when their spouse calls on them at their workplace. They do not know how to relate to one another's workplace selves.

The workplace is also the theater of a perpetual performance of human drama, comedies as well as tragedies, or gladiator fights between overenergized human ambitions. On the Olympic upper floors of the office building, it has its gods reigning, surrounded by legends kept alive by gossip or by the efforts of the public relations department generating, and taking care of, the mythic image of the company. Our workplace is like a ship, sailing beautifully or sinking miserably. We, our social selves, fare well or perish with it.

Not all the workplaces are laboratories of creative thinking and fascinating activity. And not all the jobs offer the opportunity for a grand self-realization. But even they may be more important for people than just places issuing their weekly or monthly paychecks. A great number of workplaces offer their workers and employees only routine jobs; jobs that, after a longer or shorter period of training, do not provide too much need and opportunity to creatively respond to new challenges. They build on two factors. The first is the necessity of having a job and earning one's living; the second is the fact that routines, too, have an important role in human life. As a matter of fact, we could not survive without them. Likewise, we could not walk if we had to think over each step we want to make, how to make the next step, which muscles to activate, and so on. Routines may be useful by minimizing the energy needed to do a certain type of work. They may help us lay down the burden and duty of self-construction by keeping us on a lower level of existence. They may help us switch over to a self-saver state, hibernating ourselves as automata, working without thoughts, emotions, moral dilemmas. A bit of tam-tam music may paralyze even the last synapses in our cortex. And even routine jobs may provide us with the feeling, the illusion, that our lives have a kind of content, and we may mistake this content for the meaning of our lives.

Our workplace is also a launching pad, or a pothole, for our careers. Or it is at least a ladder. It may launch or lead us to the top floor, or let us drop to the basement.

Keep Smiling

Our workplace is not necessarily an ideal environment for character building. We have seen that it is also an arena of competition and that—besides having its positive side—an excessive competition may also create a succeed-or-perish atmosphere, which, in turn, may distort people's selves and characters. This is true, however, not only of the workplace but also of a wide range of social interactions. Let me draw a gloomy, not at all objective, caricature of this situation.

One might say, with some exaggeration, that in the social space people walk around among predators; or more exactly among crossbreeds of predators and grass-eating animals. They are called, we are called: humans. For a while, people are peacefully grazing beside one another, exchanging words, news, and smiles, but in the next moment they jump on one another's weaknesses, they luxuriate in scandals, they munch wounded lives. Other people's weakness is their strength. One has to watch out in this jungle. One has to scent the prey, look for each possible opportunity of self-boosting, and avoid the danger of becoming prey oneself.

There is a wide range of strategies of self-defense at their disposal; both at and outside the workplace. Let me mention only two of them. People may apply the strategy of power, which means that they play the strong man, show strength, and trample all resistance. If the trick works, if other people are impressed, let alone intimidated, than the actor has successfully strengthened her self. If she fails, if she makes a fool of herself, then her self may be seriously injured.

There are also various kinds of strategies of weakness. *Invisibility:* I efface myself, I move around in a way not to be perceived by anybody. I am modestly swimming in the swarm of small fish. *The innocent lamb:* I play the role of the nice, gentle, little lamb, who loves everybody, who is loved by everybody, who cannot hurt anybody. *Keep smiling:* I don't flash my teeth, I'm not morose, but I keep smiling and waving the flag of my goodwill and harmlessness. I am a nice person, you are a nice person, we don't threaten each other. *Self-handicapping:* As we have seen,[2] according to psychologists, this is a common strategy of protecting oneself against risks and failures. It consists in finding a pretext, something for which one is not responsible (a real or imagined illness, poor childhood, lack of time, etc.), which explains in advance our possible future failures, which in this way will not hurt our selves, our self-esteem. *A flattering dog:* I fawn on all the predators stronger than myself. I wag my tail. I lick their hands, I flatter them. This latter is an especially successful strategy, because even the strongest predators have their weak point: their vanity. Flattering is a wonder weapon. It can carry practically everybody off his or her feet, because almost everybody struggles with his or her self-image. Our selves, even those of our bosses, are insatiable: They devour everything, even the cheapest compliment, to inflate themselves as much as possible.

My Desk

One's office is much more than a place where one has to work. It plays a complex role in our lives. Let me present this complexity using the example of my own study. It is a sanctuary and a complete and safe universe. It is closed, well protected, but—through the phone and the computer on the desk, and mainly the books on the shelves—it has myriad openings on the world outside; on the universe, I would say in my more emphatic moments.

The bay window, where my desk stands, is a cockpit from which one can govern the world, without stirring or going anywhere. There are a personal computer, a lamp, a modem, a jar full of pencils and pens, an eraser, and paper clips. On the two sides, there are shelves within my reach, with sheets of printing paper, stationery, a cartoon, plastic folders (blue, yellow, green, red), and pads. A color printer is also there, with a scanner, a few documents, and photocopies. Behind the chair there is, still within my reach, a revolving book case, with dictionaries, encyclopedias, a few basic books; they are the last resorts if I am getting lost in a world full of too many known and unknown things and events.

All these objects have their special significance and importance in the protection and daily reconstruction of my self.[3]

The desk: It is old, with a seedy chestnut shade of color, full of scrawls and scribbles, undecipherable signs of thousands of days, evenings, and nights spent there. I cling to it as a shipwrecked sailor would hold on to a board floating in the sea.

The lamp: It is an American-type reading lamp, from the late nineteenth century, with a black wrought iron stand and a green shade. My grandfather had used it in his office, and my father wrote his books in its light. I am stunned and moved by the motionless peace as it has been standing and shedding its light for more than a century. The silent patience of an object that has kept its beautiful form throughout a century of upheavals, two world wars, and chaotic change is a warning that beyond the hectic events of our lives, there may be a world of peace and permanence, if not eternity.

The computer: It is half of my self. It remembers my thoughts and ideas better then myself. It disciplines my erratic thoughts, it prompts and forces me to translate my thoughts into strings of letters, syllables, words, sentences, and paragraphs—into a text. If it breaks down, I panic and feel lost. It is mine, and I am its slave. Ours is a love/hate relationship. If it performs its dirty tricks, I curse it.

The Internet: It is a life-saving (and destroying) new gadget. When we get in our office, we jump on our PCs or Macs and check, with pleasant expectation, our e-mail. We may thereby reduce our morning anxiety at being alone in an alien world. Opening our new-mail box, magic happens: We suddenly recover our place in a virtual world of people we know. By this Net, we are safely suspended in the universe. And in addition, opening the mailbox, we are titillated by a vague hope of hitting the jackpot of the best news of our lives in our mail.

The eraser: It is the promise that things cannot go definitely wrong, that there is always a chance to start again. (It is more and more often replaced, though, by the absolute terminator, the DEL-key.)

Pencils, pens, and pads of various sizes and colors promise exciting new ideas to be put down, new books to be written.

Photos of my mother and father and my favorite uncle: I am working in the light and warmth of their gazes.

—

We could, and should, further analyze the dimensions of our working life. But let us skip them and enter the next phase of our daily lives. Let us suppose that our working hours are over, we are ready to leave our office, or workshop. We may take the elevator, or the stairs, or just step out the front door. And voilà: The world with all its possible joys and pains, good and bad surprises, fears and hopes, lies at our feet. There is still time, there is still time to build and shape our selves and fulfill our lives.

The Self and the Articulation of Time

Time is the longest distance between two places.

—*Tennessee Williams*

In the Street

After work, stepping out of our office building, we may not yet be in a mood to go home. We may still feel that something is missing from our life that day. We may want to "really" exist, "to be," "to actualize our self" before we go to bed and lose our self in the darkness of the night. We have only a few hours at out disposal; we somehow have to slow down time and not let it flow emptily away never to be retrieved. We have to structure it and fill it with experience and (at least the semblance) of meaning and significance.[1]

Fortunately, our itinerary itself structures time and our self. We may rush along Fifth Avenue in New York; we may be strolling along the meandering streets of Prague or the Latin Quarter in Paris; we may be taking a crowded trolley bus on the former Stalin Prospect in Vladivostok; we may idle away time in La Rue de la République in Brazzaville; we may drink a cup of coffee in the Alter Markt in Salzburg. These radically different ways of structuring time and different experiences leave their imprint on our self.[2] Entering a church, we may even step out of the flow of "profane" time and into the world of "sacred" time, which has a different rhythm, that of the timeless world of eternity.[3]

The city environment may make us feel at home, or feel like a stranger, in this world. It may protect and threaten us; it may attract and repel us. It may surround us with forms, colors, and lights, which prompt or obstruct our self to develop its own forms, colors, lights, harmonies or disharmonies. It may be full of symbols of freedom, harmony, and meaning or it may oppress us with its gloom, lack of freedom, spiritual misery, and painful emptiness.

Baudelaire's dandy *flaneur* does not simply *walk* in the streets of Paris. "*Flaner*" is also a peripatetic exercise in the construction of one's self. As one proceeds in the streets, one exposes oneself to a series of impressions, impulses, effects, experiences. Strolling in the streets is a kind of inverted cinema. In the theater, the pictures are moving while we stay put. When we stroll in the streets, we move and the pictures keep still. In both cases, we are exposed to a stream of images, symbols, experiences, which—in an imperceptible but incremental way—keep articulating our time and shaping our selves. Let alone the shop windows, which, dark and mysterious mirrors, help us to experience brief but important moments of "self-reflection."

All this is especially true of our contemporary consumer age, in which the stream of pictures and symbols has swollen to a tidal wave. It overwhelms us both in the streets and in the sacred places of this new civilization.

The Shopping Center

Nowadays, shopping articulates time with a dazzling variety of forms, colors, lights, commodities, and encounters; and it is also an excellent exercise for strengthening, and caring for, our selves. A rich literature deals with the various ways in which consumer civilization helps "consume products in an attempt to acquire important life meanings." Consumers "may engage in almost pathological levels of consumption as they desperately purchase products seeking to acquire cultural meanings with which to construct a satisfactory self-concept."[4] Shopping may help people have an ultimate experience of the fullness and significance of their lives. Shopping and consumption may also be a means of "denying death" and fighting for immortality.[5] People need only to enter a shopping center.[6]

Elsewhere, I have studied the rich magic of these centers in detail.[7] Strolling in a shopping center has become such an important part of contemporary life, and of self-construction, that I cannot help taking over a few paragraphs of that text, in a shortened form.

A Human World

The shopping center is the perfect human world, a private universe, a space completely closed and protected not only by walls and a dome but also by galleries of shops running around the atrium, full of everything that is delicious, tempting, comfortable, and homely in a human-made world. It surrounds us with the protective sphere of an "unending stream of spectacles."[8]

In this world, there is no snow or sleet, there is no winter or summer, no thunderstorm or parching heat, no day or night, no disturbing change or painful transitoriness. There is eternal spring here, with torrents of flowers, bubbling springs, and the refreshing breeze of Zephyrus, a benevolent and hidden deity (represented here by a lesser deity called air conditioning). Time has stopped. Mutability and death have disappeared. They have been replaced by the illusion of eternity; or even more by a combination of eternity and the Kierkegaardian or Heideggerian moments of authentic existence. People may wander around the galleries, round and round, as if they were ambling along the archetypal paths of the "eternal return."

The mall is much more than a simple building. It is the symbol of the universe, an *imago mundi,* as medieval cathedrals were in their time. It has a strong transcendental dimension. The golden and glass elevators ascending ceremonially to the heights of the atrium, almost up to the blue sky, suggest the glorious experience of the Ascension into the sphere of the divine. Leaving this greenhouse world of the mall's comfort and happiness for the wind and sleet of a cold winter evening is like being cast out of Paradise.

The shopping center is a soft and beatific version of Utopia, "a pseudo-democratic twilight zone between reality and a commercially produced fantasy world,"[9] where everybody is anonymous and equal, where there are no feuds or conflicting interests, no social classes or inequalities, no rich or poor, no duties or responsibilities, but just the rotation of a crowd of benevolent people, who in a serene and contemplative mood roam over the galleries of the world, more as philosopher-*flaneurs* than consumers. The mall is a reincarnation of the *jardin des délices,* or of the island of the blessed souls of medieval and Renaissance imagination. There is no thirst or hunger, illness or destitution here; this closed world offers to our selves all the comforts and delights, goods and goodies of a world created by human beings for themselves. The stream of time flows far from the shores of this sacred island.

It is also a world of meaning. Strolling in the galleries, people can revel in myriad meanings, or the simulacra of meaning, because commodities are designed to suggest purpose, meaning, and the promise of fulfillment. Posters, labels, and publicity slogans emphasize and shamelessly overemphasize this dimension; they promise more than the goods can ever deliver. But this does not prevent people from being fascinated, and deluded. It helps them forget, for a fleeting moment, their own world outside the mall, and their selves, which may be chronically short of meaning.

Due to the magic of the mall and publicity, a new pullover may seem as precious as the Golden Fleece was for the Argonauts, promising fulfillment and perfection; a new lipstick may give one a new identity; a new book may enlighten the ultimate meaning of life; a new jewel may lend the brilliance of transcendence to one's self and life; a gift may be the magic wand that, back home, will fill with joy and meaning a relationship that probably has run out of joy and meaning.

The shopping center euphemizes and, as a result, tames and trivializes the problems of our everyday lives. It is full of secrets, like a jungle, yet this is not a fearful but a friendly jungle full of pleasant surprises. Here the secrets are tempting and not threatening. This is the jungle of an alien world totally domesticated and transformed into a garden of joys. Here the monsters lurking behind the palm trees are huge teddy bears, toy lions, and the dinosaurs from Jurassic Park.

Or am I mistaken? Is this innocence, beauty, and harmony only the camouflage of a hidden danger? Some experts so argue.

The Devil's World

The shopping center may be a dangerous trap as well. Instead of helping people feel themselves at home in this world, stop or articulate time, and develop their selves, it may enslave them and destroy their personalities.

With a bit of mythic imagination, the shopping mall may be seen as the place of an ongoing black mass glorifying the basest instincts, the lascivious beast in human beings, the Evil Spirit. If the Earthly Paradise is a dangerous illusion invented by Satan, then the shopping mall is his creation par excellence, because it is a world where people are lured into believing that they are innocent. And is not a world where people live in the illusion of being innocent the world of Satan? Theologians could certainly argue that in an innocent world there is no place for the transcendental drama described in the sacred books of several civilizations; there is no place for God, Christ, or any other divinity; there is no place and time for remorse, feelings of guilt, repentance, or salvation. It is not God's world. It is a trap set by Satan to make people believe that they are already saved; that they are (almost) immortal.

No doubt, the mall is an amoral world, a world trivially beyond Good and Evil. In traditional and modern societies, men and women were advised and disciplined by a system of moral laws. They were prompted to control and at least partly repress instinctual drives and libidos, to delay their gratifications and to sublimate them into socially useful activities. Drives thus became major sources of social, intellectual, and artistic activity. By immediately gratifying people's appetites and wishes, by tempting them with the delight of an eternal, happy present, Satan may prevent them from transcending the borders of their physical and instinctual selves.

Strolling in the mall, one may experience one's own apotheosis as a free and authentic personality, the protagonist of a friendly universe, while in reality one is losing, "dispersing" one's personality—in the Kierkegaardian sense of the word—in the whirl of shallow gratifications and trivial choices. Heidegger would describe the same process as losing the "centeredness" and authenticity of one's being and self.

The Negative Myth

I do not want to take this comparison of the shopping mall and the world of evil too far. But some scholars literally satanize the mall and leisure society as a whole. Mitroff and Bennis (1989), for instance, speak of "the unreality industry," which "deliberately manufactures falsehood," entrapping people by promising them power and self-control. Instead of helping them achieve perfection and fulfillment, it increases the void in their souls and leads them to self-destruction. It creates in people the illusion that they may defeat death and thereby makes them even more vulnerable.

Other scholars argue that instead of helping people create a really human universe around themselves, the shopping mall is the instrument of the dehumanization of the world; it enslaves people instead of liberating them, it distorts their selves instead of developing them. In their judgment, leisure society—and the mall within it—has become an instrument of Foucaultian domination and disempowerment. People are manipulated by political and economic powers, which infantilize them into unconscious puppets caught in the vicious circle of desires generated and gratified in a never-ending rotation. Langman (1992, 42) writes in this context:

> Hegemony now depends on the effective gratification provided by a mass-mediated popular culture whose themes express myriad deprivations, longings, satisfactions, aspirations and the desired experiences of particular taste cultures. There is love for the lonely, sex for the horny, excitement for the bored, identities for the empty and, typically, all are intertwined. There is a pop sociology that explains such megatrends and a pop psychology to soothe any remaining despair.

Due to the incessant impact of television and marketing, people may lose their social role and identity—they are more and more becoming anonymous consumers with pseudoidentities generated by the market. They are being "depoliticized" and "desocialized" and, as a consequence, more and more enslaved by the forces of power and money:

> Privatized consumption has thus become the contemporary locus of a selfhood for a hedonistic subjectivity that has withdrawn from the public realms. But this withdrawal lets the social order become more powerful with an ever more enfeebled privatized self less likely to contest major issues—as the recent Persian Gulf war showed. When the going gets tough, the tough go shopping—and at malls. It is of course no accident that after the Nintendo War, malls all over the country had celebrations of consumption for the "heroes" of Desert Storm.[10]

If these scholars are right, then the building of megamalls may prove an unsuccessful attempt to create a human world for ourselves, where we might, and should, feel free and safe at the center of the universe. On the contrary, we may realize, far too late, that we have unwittingly put our selves at the mercy of an alien world; that we are suffering "the terrors of emptiness," inauthenticity, and mortality from which we wanted to escape. This would be a tragic failure of our efforts to enrich our selves and build for ourselves a meaningful world. We had better get out of the mall and look for another place for world construction and self-construction.

Travel

Let us make a short detour. A trip abroad would not fit into the one-day framework of our present argument. But let us suppose that on our way home we plan our summer holidays and, stopping at a street corner, we suddenly ask our self: Why do we like to travel so much? Why is travel one of the key events in our contemporary civilization of consumption? Let me offer a few tentative answers.

In our consumer civilization, travel has become one of the favorite ways for people to articulate time. If one stays forever at home, in the same city and environment and job, one may slowly get bored with one's world and with one's self. One's everyday life may wear out; it may run dry, may lose its freshness and innocence. One's time may drift away imperceptibly. But by stepping out of one's routines, one may feel that one enters a new life. When one is traveling, the changing environment "brushes up" one's self. Thanks to the flow of small, pleasant shocks of new experiences, one begins to feel that one can still respond to the world, that there are new things, new experiences, new emotions—that one is still alive.[11] And—as we shall see later in this book[12]—being as much alive as possible, experiencing the flow of time and life in their utmost intensity, is the first commandment of our contemporary civilization.

In foreign lands, there still are surprises. And, more important, there are still secrets. In our own land, in our own lives, there are no surprises left. There are no mysteries that would attract us, tempt us, intrigue us, flirt with us, promise new experiences, new worlds, new lives, faraway islands, the lost Garden of Eden, transcendence, grace, the Holy Grail.[13] If there are undiscovered parts of the world, then there is still hope; then everything and anything can happen; then we still may find our genuine, authentic worlds and selves somewhere.

Travel is also important as an escape from the web of our everyday duties and routines. Travelers are free like birds; they have no duties, only rights. If they behave, they are protected by the laws of the host country. They enjoy the right of hospitality. This is a pleasant type of regression into their childhood selves. And as a matter of fact, tourists do behave like children. They are louder, they gesticulate more, they laugh more than at home. They have more fun; they dance, play, sing in the streets; they behave irresponsibly; they enjoy the "eternal carnival" of the civilization of consumption. They also expect to be treated kindly by the natives, they expect to be forgiven minor breaches of laws or custom, they do not work but only enjoy their lives, they wear more colorful dresses, and, last but not least, they relax their norms of decency and moral behavior. They may be even tempted to cast off their sexual inhibitions, to let their instincts run free. The balance within them between the EGO and the ID tips in favor of the latter. Tourists, especially if they travel in groups, are more like *homines infantiles* than *homines sapientes*.[14]

Traveling is also a glorious campaign, a conquest of the world. We march into a country like conquerors; the land lays open and unprotected at our feet, and we may take possession of it. We walk in the streets that the citizens of the country built for themselves, we enter their public buildings, we shamelessly look into their homes through their windows, we profane their holy shrines. Travel is also time travel. We go back in time, we explore *"le temps perdu,"* we relive the history of our hosts, we add their history to our own history. And, taking pictures of everything we see, we may take home their country, their houses, cities, hills, and rivers; their lives and their past; and we may enrich our selves with all this booty.[15]

It is time, however, to reenter the original framework of our argument, that is, the story of one single day of self-construction. Before making this short detour into the world of travel, we left our *flaneur* strolling homeward in the street.

The Pub

Going to a pub may seem to be a trivial way of passing our time, but spending the evening with our cronies may have a latent significance as well: It is an excellent way of articulating time and caring for our self. Our friends accept and love us, and we accept and love them. We live in the same world, root for the same football club, have the same ideas and prejudices. We fit easily and smoothly into this world. It is the best mold for our personalities. We mesh. Or we do not even need a personality here. This friendly world has its special niche for us, where we are accepted as we are. It provides us with well-known clues, to which we automatically respond as if we had a personality. We may feel ourselves bright guys because our jokes are sure to trigger an outburst of laughter. We may forget our daily lives, our families, our worries. We may forget about the passing of time and—if we feel so—the meaninglessness of our lives. We are reconfirmed in our convictions and prejudices a dozen times in the course of the evening. We have our role, our identity, our rank in the hierarchy.

And all this may be seasoned, and made more delicious and exciting, by a couple of bottles or cans of beer. These beers may help us in various other ways as well. They may very quickly kill—if not time itself, at least—our sense of time. They may transform our anxiety and neurosis about time into the comfortable and pleasant feeling that we swim in the meaningful and glorious flow of time. They may help us start deconstructing our self, relax our cognitive discipline, reduce our level of social responsibility, loosen our self-control. All in all, they may help us loosen up the rigid framework of our daily, "enlightened," rational personality. And as a result, we may slowly become submerged in the dark seas of timeless night, losing again the self that we were so busy constructing all the day.

However, we may drink with just the opposite goal as well. We may want to relax the control of our daily, "one-dimensional" self to open up the rich sources of our subconscious and emotional self, to actualize our full potentials, fulfill our life, in this way completing the process of the daily construction of our self.

By drinking, one may also enter a world full of meaning. In a half hour, a painfully empty and purposeless life can be transubstantiated into a magic world of meanings, where each word, object, and person is saturated with significance and mystery. With one or two pints of beer, one may transform an alien world into a homely and velvet world of our own.

Sports

Instead of going to the pub, we may decide to go to a gym, a football match, or a tennis court. Sports are among the most popular and efficient ways of articulating time. Psychologists working in this field have mainly dealt with the psyches of professional sportsmen and sportswomen and with how to boost their performance. They have paid less attention to the role sports play in shaping hundreds of millions of people's lives and selves, despite the fact that this would be at least as important, or even more important, as a field of research. For our present argument, it certainly is more important for at least two reasons. First, it clearly displays the duality of the trivial and the existential levels of our lives. Second, sports events and spectacles have become omnipresent and more important in our contemporary civilization than they were in earlier ages and in other civilizations.

Elsewhere, I have written about the attraction of soccer matches, about how they stagger people's selves to their very foundations, how they open the floodgates of emotions, how they combine Dionysian ecstasy with Apollonian lights and harmony.[16] Let me now turn to another popular sport, tennis. Why do people love it so much? Does it have anything to do with the construction of their selves?

Tennis may be a trivial way of passing our time but—beyond the beauty of the court, the sky, and the physical good feeling—the world of tennis enchants us in many ways. Instead of the routines and boredom of everyday life, here there are challenge and excitement. Something unexpected (but not threatening) happens every instant. We experience time, our lives, and our selves, with high intensity. We also love to fight; this is an atavistic drive in us, and we enjoy fighting even more where risks are not too high. And tennis is a test of strength, a real fight without the danger of the players being seriously hurt, without our selves being really threatened.

In the real world, life plays with us. Here we play with life; we are in total control of everything that may happen in this world. Several times a minute, we set the target, we act (strike the ball), and we attain our goal; or if we fail, we can repeat the process again and again. Here there are no unforgivable and irreparable mistakes. And our selves are reinforced by each successful strike. Tennis, being a game, is also a brilliant self-booster.

In real life, there is permanent confusion. Nothing is concluded. Everything is left open, pent up, unfinished, unconcluded. Here, everything is clear, defined, and distinct; each tennis event has a beginning and an end, a conclusion. There is no muddling through; there are unambiguous victories and defeats. If life is confused, opaque, and jumbled, here everything is transparent and geometric. This is an ordered world. Tennis articulates time in a strict, but pleasurable way. There are strikes, games, sets, matches, competitions, and tournaments; and one can start this cycle of events again and again. The fearful passing of time is tamed here, too, into the serenity of Nietzsche's "eternal return."

In real life, things are good and bad at once; they are more or less good or bad, right or wrong. Nothing is obvious. One can never know for certain. Here, in the trivial or not at all trivial world of tennis, good is good and bad is bad. The goodness or badness of a strike can be measured with precision. If the ball misses the line by half an inch, it is out. Full stop.[17]

Instead of yes-and-no answers, instead of all the "maybe," "perhaps," "if-I-may-say," "I-don't-know-but" answers, here we can give simple, strong, straightforward answers in every moment, in every situation. Is there a more resounding and convincing response to the chaotic indefiniteness of the world and our lives than a beautiful, clear, strong, successful smash?

In real life, we frequently feel ourselves weak, helpless, lost. In the world of tennis, we feel safe. We feel ourselves strong and adequate, because tennis adjusts itself to the level of our skills and strengths. One can enjoy the play the first day one starts learning the simplest strikes, and one can equally enjoy the play later on a much higher level of expertise. One's self is strengthened by these challenges that are not too weak and not destructively strong. One has only to find one's genuine partners. And a tennis partnership, just like a chess partnership or membership in a string quartet, may be more lasting than some marriages.

It is a world where one may feel oneself privileged, belonging to an almost aristocratic community. It is a universe that has no contact whatever with the real, vulgar world. It is separated from the everyday world only by wire fencing, but it is sacred ground on which profane mortals must not set foot. Here one speaks softly, as if in a sacred place.

This is also a world of justice. The rules of the game are obvious and absolutely clear. Before we enter the court, we accept these rules of our own free will, while in real life we have no choice. We have to accept the rules of a world into which we were born. And our situation is even worse because the rules of the game in real life are vague and contradictory, let alone the fact that the fundamental rule of life and death is utterly unfair: We have no chance whatever in our fight against our own mortality. But in the world of tennis, the rules are fair. Everybody has the same chance to win or to lose. And, perhaps even more important, in the world of tennis there is no death. Time is reversible. One can always begin a new game.

When we enter the court for the first time in our lives, we immediately become citizens with full rights in a fascinating universe. If we have signed up for a court, nobody can ask us to leave, not even the ruling world champion. This is a world of equality, justice, and fair play. Everybody, even the last ham-fisted amateur, has the same rights. Nobody can disturb her or him in the play. This world has its everydays and has also its mythologies; it has its stars, gods, and goddesses with all the necessary myths and gossip around them. It has also its great and sacred ceremonies at Wimbledon, Flushing Meadows, and Roland Garoche. It has its small revolutions, showdowns, coups d'état, and exciting scandals. It is a world for all seasons.

And, last but not least, there is the magic of the ball.[18] The ball is freedom, or chance, embodied. It is a demon; not Maxwell's boring and industrious demon, but a jolly goblin. It may bounce in any direction. It seems to have its "own will." It seems to be autonomous. One cannot predict its movements entirely. It is an object and, nevertheless, it seems to be free. A tennis ball is among those few objects that look as if they could challenge the forces of nature. By bouncing off the ground again and again, it seems to triumph over the iron law of gravity. It moves as if it were weightless; it can choose the most beautiful and glorious trajectories; it has the Platonic perfection of spheres.

It also has an almost metaphysical function. It spiritualizes the fight between human beings. In a real fight, the adversaries try to physically hurt and defeat, if not destroy, one another. In tennis (just as in football or basketball), the fight is no less fierce; but it is not destructive. Thanks to the ball, it is defused and spiritualized. According to the rules, players have to avoid any physical contact. There is a kind of vacuum between them, a spiritual sphere, the sphere of the ball and its movements, which keeps them apart and mediates between them. (The net is a further dividing line; if a player reaches over it, she or he is punished.) The player can touch even the ball only indirectly, with his or her racket, and the ball and its movements express, in a symbolic and indirect way, the interplay of human intentions and outside forces deployed in the struggle.

By introducing the factor of chance and unpredictability into the struggle, the ball transforms a bitter and down-to-earth human fight into an epiphany of spirituality and freedom. In the brisk movements of the ball, chance and human will interact with each other. The ball integrates in itself human freedom and limitation, success and failure, hope and also the loss of hope for a brief moment to be regained in the next.

Can something be more trivial than a ball bouncing to and fro on a tennis court? Hardly. But, at the same time, it also plays an important role in the latent existential drama of our self and life. It generates in us the conviction that we live in a world of transparent and harmonious order; that we are free; that we are in control of our time and life; that there may always be a new beginning. This is an important illusion that our self needs badly.

Gossip

Gossip is the main genre of popular narratives. It has played an important role throughout the history of humankind, and it is still an important part of our everyday lives.[19] There were ages when gossiping was persecuted as the devil's chant. Here is a characteristic title from the seventeenth century: *The Evil Tongue Tryed and Found Guilty, or, The Hainousness and Exceeding Sinfulness of Defaming and Back-Biting Opened and Declared: Wherein Is Shewed That a Defaming and Back-Biting Tongue Is a Most Pernicious and Grievous Plague to Man-Kind / Published for the Common Good . . . by Stephen Ford* (1672). In intellectual circles, gossip has ever been disparaged, mistakenly, as a primitive and vulgar form of communication and as old wives' tales. But instead of being eradicated, it has become one of the dominant genres even in our contemporary written and electronic media. Actually, its importance in articulating time and in the construction of people' selves can hardly be overestimated.

Exploration. Gossip expands the range of our organs of sense. It supplies us with indirect information about the world, the changes in our human environment, about dangers that may threaten us, and opportunities we may profit from.

Experiencing life. Our lives may narrow down. We thirst for news and new things coming from the outside world because in every event, in every piece of news, a small flame of life flares up. Even news of destruction and catastrophes thrill us, give us shots of life experience.[20]

Cannibalism. Why do we listen to, watch, or read about family tragedies, blazing towers, earthquakes, shipwrecks, volcano eruptions, floods, catastrophes, the destruction of the human world with such morbid delight? It is a fact that these catastrophes attract and fascinate us with almost irresistible force. Are we bloodthirsty sadists? Do we enjoy the sight of people suffering and dying, or the sight of life being destroyed? No, we don't and, yes, to a certain extent we do. We are predators, and injured life is an easy prey. We jump on it and tear it to pieces. We love to crunch other people's lives.[21]

Intensity and freedom. Catastrophes, floods breaking through dams, firestorms, the collapse of buildings, the explosion of bombs, earthquakes, tornadoes, and avalanches also fascinate us because we experience and enjoy their enormous energy, their intensity.[22] And we also undergo an intense experience of freedom. We enjoy the destruction of the existing order of things. It is true that we could not survive in a world where there was no order and continuity, but order and continuity are also depressing. Because they keep us in a cage, we enjoy their temporary destruction—or at least the sight of it. A real earthquake, threatening our lives, would not be enjoyable at all. But its sight or symbol enhances and intensifies our life experience. Freudians would say that the death wish is working in us. But our longing for the intense experience of life is, I think, a more important factor here.

Social justice. With the help of gossiping—and this is one of its most important functions—we may symbolically triumph over the rich and the powerful. In real life, we may be their victims; in the world of gossip, they are our victims, totally defenseless against our revenge, irony, malignity.

To be in. It is a prestigious position to be the cheerleader or the main source of information in a gossiping band. It suggests that one is somehow at home in the mysterious corridors of power. And to be well informed is to possess important social capital.

Ego boosting. Speaking ill of people behind their backs is perhaps the main motive force, and source of pleasure, of gossiping. We enjoy listening to news about other people's weaknesses, secrets, sins, fiascoes, and conflicts not because we are depraved and enjoy other people's sufferings. We are not devils either, who would triumph over human weakness and fallibility. It is not out of wickedness that we run down people behind their backs. We do so because by disparaging and degrading other people, we lift ourselves in the hierarchy of values, in several ways. First, if they sink in this hierarchy, our relative position is automatically improved. And second, finding fault with him or her, and condemning them for their faults, we maneuver ourselves into the position of a judge, who represents the spirit of law in the world and enjoys a high social prestige. This is an exceptionally efficient way of boosting ourselves.[23]

Put your hands on your heart and tell us: Leaving a party with your partner, don't you start—after a few words of empty praise, first cautiously and then more and more overtly—singling out the weaknesses of your host and hostess?

"Did you see Marianne? Didn't she look tired and a bit old for her age? I hope there is nothing wrong with her health, . . . or perhaps with their marriage? And did you see that awful new lamp? How could they put it in their living room? And the green carpet with the blue sofa on it? Where have they left their taste? And that big new digital television! Why do they throw their money out of the window? Though if I earned my living in the way they did it, I, too, would burn my money. Or I would send my daughter to a health spa if she were as fat as their little Sophie."

And in all this, there is less slander and malice than a wish to reinforce one's self. In several ways: *Physically* ("She looks seedy. She may be ill." —I am healthy). *Emotionally* ("Her husband probably is unfaithful to her." —I have an ideal husband. We are happy.) *Morally* (I don't squander. And we have made our money in a decent and legal way). All in all, we are above them in the hierarchy of health, morality, taste, and happiness. And what is more important, we have a better life. We have more of life. We have a fuller life. *"Le Néant,"*

"Nothingness," "nonexistence," and the "void of being" threaten us much less than they threaten our friends.

Community. At least two people are necessary for gossiping. Three are even better, because three people constitute a community, and if three people agree on something, their judgment is nonappealable. Let alone the fact that consensus is a great asset and a strong integrating force. It is not easy to agree with our fellow beings, but if we find somebody, a third party, whom we can disparage together, then we—the gossip partners—have found common ground; the tensions between us slacken, we accept one another, and we develop a feeling of community. These gossip communities and comradeships, held together by a common target of aversion, envy, and passion, may last for years and decades. They may be harmless tea parties or dangerously destructive conspiracies.

The passing of time. Gossiping may be a trivial activity, but it also plays an important role in our struggle with time. It articulates the invisible flow of time, it fills it with human content, it slows it down. If time flows invisibly and emptily, if nothing articulates it, we suffer. One of the best instruments of articulating, slowing down, and "killing" time is speech, discourse, conversation, tittle-tattle. Each word, sentence, full stop, and interrogation mark; each rhyme and rhythm; each story begun and concluded is a triumph over time.

The most moving example of this victory over time is the case of the heroine of Beckett's *Happy Days*. While slowly sinking into a mound, she keeps talking and talking about everything and nothing, she takes all the knickknacks from her handbag, has a story about everything, tells anecdotes, never stops for a moment, keeps desperately talking because talking becomes here the symbol and pledge of life, the only possible and ultimate means for slowing down, braking, stopping, defeating time, mortality, death. It is the same heroic fight with death that was fought by Oedipus and Antigone, by Hamlet, and by Hickey in O'Neill's *The Iceman Cometh*. The trivial (gossip) and the tragic (death) meet here under our very eyes.

The Self at Home

What we play is life.

—*Louis Armstrong*

The Home and Its Objects

As far as I know, and I may be mistaken, cultural anthropologists and students of architecture have studied the symbolic content and message of the house, and its role in shaping human selves, more than psychologists have done. Their works are full of fascinating data and hypotheses in this field.[1]

The House is not only "the image of the world," *imago mundi,* but according to Gaston Bachelard (1969, 6–7), it is "the first world of man." The

> house is one of the greatest powers of integration for the thoughts, memories and dreams of mankind. . . . In the life of man, the house thrusts aside contingencies, its councils of continuity are unceasing. Without it, man would be a dispersed being. It maintains him through the storms of the heavens and through those of life. It is body and soul. It is the human being's first world. Before he is 'cast into the world,' as claimed by certain hasty metaphysics, man is laid in the cradle of the house.

And our homes shape our selves in various ways. It is a different experience to grow up, and/or live, in a cottage, a farmhouse, a small one-bedroom apartment, or a spacious, comfortable house in a nice neighborhood. Among others, Csikszentmihalyi and Rochberg-Halton (1981) have shown that even from the psychologists' point of view, the home is a rich "symbolic environment," which—beyond protecting us against the whims of nature—provides us with privacy, where our selves can mature, and which is full of forms, colors, and objects that fill our lives and selves with a constant "background radiation" of meaning. Speaking of the "tyranny of things," Ernest Dichter (1964, 1) warns us that things can also enslave us, our selves. However, we can protect ourselves and even go on a counterattack. These things, our home, and the world not only shape us; we, too, shape them. According to Marcuse (1964, 86), we are doing so with the most aggressive vehemence:

> To be sure, the diversion of destructiveness from the ego to the external world secured the growth of civilization. However, extroverted destruction remains destruction: its objects are in most cases actually and violently assailed [think of the work of the blacksmith, for instance, or that of the bulldozer], deprived of their form, and reconstructed only after partial destruction. . . . Nature is literally "violated." . . . Destructiveness, in extent and intent, seems to be more directly satisfied in civilization than the libido.

We have, of course, less destructive methods as well. When we get home in time, we may occupy ourselves around the house. We may withdraw into the sanctuary of our garage and fix up something—our car, a bike, a bookshelf; we may restore an old cupboard, or work on the first genuine *perpetuum mobile* in the world. We may immerse ourselves in our secret world, where we are the *Primum Movens,* the Judge, the Creator, the Lord.

Weeding our garden is also a useful exercise; in several ways. On the practical level, if we keep our garden clean and free of weeds, our lawn will be greener, our flowers more beautiful, our tomatoes bigger. But this in itself does not explain the deep pleasure we feel in pulling out weeds. We feel a kind of relief, joy, freedom: We have repelled the attack of alien beings that tried to creep into our ordered, shaped, and trimmed world; we have defeated the forces of chaos, our selves have triumphed over them, we have regained control over the world. We are at home in this world. This is our world.[2]

And here again we may witness the duality of our everyday lives. Even such a trivial activity as weeding may have a deep structure and may play a role on the existential level of our being.

The Home and Its People

By the early hours of the evening, when we sit down to the dinner table with our family, we may have almost finished the reconstruction or construction of our selves. And the members of our family probably have done so, too. (Except that our teenage daughters or sons have slipped out into the night to search for the ultimate prey: the great adventure of finding *the* real life and their real selves.) But our spouse or partner remains with us.

People living together play, willy-nilly, a crucial role in constructing, and deconstructing, one another's selves. They can help each other find their genuine selves, explore the unknown regions of their selves, develop authentic selves. But this is an extremely difficult task and process. One can easily fail. One can mislead one's partner in trying to protect her or him against the pains of a real quest for her or his self, one can fan her vanity, reinforce his weaknesses. One can also cripple one's partner's self by being indifferent, by ignoring her or him. One can be cruelly sincere and thereby injure the fledgling self of one's partner. Flattering, spoiling, ignoring, and being domineering are dangerous, if not lethal poisons, for human beings. Relatively few persons have the patience, the tolerance, the wisdom, the love to be of real help to their partners in the construction of their selves.

Martin Buber (1970) argued that human beings exist as human beings only in and through their relationships with other people, in the I–Thou or I–You relationship, as he called it. This is an important message and warning in our age of radical individualism. And it is almost incomprehensible that while at school and elsewhere people learn a lot about the dangers that threaten them, which they have to avoid, in the world but learn relatively little about the dangers inherent in human relationships; about the hundreds and thousands of ways people living together may harm and obstruct one another in constructing their selves. There are few places where the duality of our lives is so obvious, where it is so evident that even the seemingly insignificant and trivial gestures and words of our daily routines can have a deep and determining impact on one another's selves.

And, in the same way, people do not learn enough about how they could easily help one another in caring for their selves. Let me give a simple example. Human beings have a relatively weak ego. They need encouragement and confirmation badly. A simple word of praise may give them momentum, may energize them, for hours and days. They thirst for praise, for recognition, and never get enough of them. Praise and recognition are commodities in short supply in our societies; this is unfortunate, because they cost practically nothing. Why should people not compliment somebody for her good looks, her new dress, her or his achievements, her or his self? A little effort on their part would generate a great amount of joy and energy in their partners. On a social scale, a better practice of mutual confirmation of one another could open new sources of joy and energy. It would boost the human resources of a society. One should believe Mark Twain, who once said: "I can live for two months on a good compliment."[3]

Self and Love

Love—both romantic and sexual—plays a major role in shaping, building, maturing, and strengthening, and also in distorting and destroying, people's selves. A systematic discussion of its role in this field would fill several volumes. A significant proportion, if not the majority, of studies in psychoanalysis would need to be covered, together with thousands of papers and books in the fields of developmental and social psychology, moral philosophy, theology, cultural anthropology, and so on. I hardly dare to touch upon this subject, and I limit myself to giving one single example of the complexity of the interaction of these two factors: sex and self.

In some ages of history, some people have believed that the moments of passionate love are the peak experiences of the human being—moments of ultimate self-knowledge and self-actualization. And to a certain extent, they may be right, because these moments, hours, days, and months may mobilize elementary emotional and intellectual forces in us. But there are scholars who claim that just the opposite is true; and several thousand years of myths, poetry, drama, and fiction support their hypothesis with innumerable examples of the destructive power of love. "When one is in love, one always begins by deceiving oneself, and one always ends by deceiving others," remarks Lord Henry in Oscar Wilde's *The Picture of Dorian Gray.* Yes, sex is a masquerade; people play roles. They deceive themselves, and/or they deceive their partners, because they see themselves in the eyes of their partners, and this mirror shows them an idealized picture. Their lovers' eyes are the best, and most benevolent, distorting mirrors. They should not believe these eyes too much if they want to know and understand themselves. People also deceive their partners by playing roles, and they play these roles because they want to fascinate their partners, to turn their heads, to make a favorable impression; or they may fake missing emotions, conceal their weaknesses, dissimulate, or even want to simply cheat on their partners. A great number of authors argue that love and sex are the greatest comedies of dissimulation and lying. According to Wendy Doniger (1996, 663, 669), world literature is, for instance, full of an extreme form of *"jeux de l'amour."* What she terms the "bed trick"[4]

> should make it onto anyone's list of the Ten Greatest Hits of World Mythology. . . . In the Western tradition alone, there are Rachel and Leah, Tamar and Judah, and (I think) Ruth and Naomi in the Hebrew Bible; Amphytrion in the Greek and Roman traditions; the begetting of King Arthur by a masquerading father, and Elaine masquerading as Guinevere with Lancelot. There are the sexual masquerades in Boccaccio and in so many Shakespeare plays, especially *All's Well That Ends Well* and *Measure for Measure,* and in opera: Mozart's *The Marriage of Figaro* and *Così Fan Tutte,* Richard Strauss's *Rosenkavalier* and *Arabella,* Johann Strauss's *Fledermaus,* . . . to say nothing of sexual masquerades in the *Arabian Nights.* . . . Lying is not simply something that occasionally happens in the course of our sexual lives, but rather its very essence.

Whoever is right, love and sex are dangerous territories. They may build and destroy, shape and distort our selves. This is a dangerous jungle, and there are many experts and books to help people find the right path through it. This book is not one of them.

Children

Here again I limit myself to just one remark. Books that could fill a library have been written on how parents form the personalities, and lives, of their children, whereas—except for studies on the periods of pregnancy and the early months or years of maternity—there are relatively few studies on the opposite or reverse process, that is, on how our children, and our preoccupation with them, shape our personalities, our selves. Bringing up our children is as much a learning process for us as having been brought up by our parents and teachers. We would be very different persons if we were not, or had not been, going through this process. Or should I call it an ordeal? It is both a source of happiness and an ordeal. Years or decades of caring for our children may reinforce our strengths and good qualities; but they may also distort our selves by overburdening us, by exploiting us, by absorbing our emotions, thoughts, and energies and thus depriving us of the time we need for our own lives and for the care of our own selves.

Psychologists have systematically studied this field. They have, for instance, compared the personalities of people with and without children, studying how the characters and selves of these two types of people develop throughout the years. But ordinary people have heard little about their results. They may read books, good and bad ones, about how to bring up their children, but they can hardly find books about protecting and developing their own selves in the course of this process. They do not know which qualities and characteristics are respectively strengthened and weakened in people with and without children. They do not know what the differences between these two groups may be as far as the richness, strength, autonomy, flexibility, spontaneity, and authenticity of their selves are concerned. And what about their self-esteem, and the fulfillment of their lives? In which group do people feel more that their lives have purpose and meaning?

From the point of view of our daily self-construction, it is important to know the answers to these questions. I do not know them. With or without children, caring for one's self is a difficult process. Let me, however, voice a warning:[5] Children may be fantastic partners; bringing them up is a unique experience. But they should not serve as alibis for giving up our own lives, for accepting the fact that we cannot achieve our own plans, cannot attain the fulfillment of our own lives. They should not be alibis for exempting ourselves from the duty and responsibility of caring for our selves, of being on a permanent quest for the meaning of our own lives. Too many people throw up the game all too early and sacrifice their lives for their children. They do so in the conviction that this is a noble role—which it is—and in the hope that they will find fulfillment in the future success and happiness of their children. But where is the guarantee that their children will attain the fulfillment and find the meaning that they, themselves, have failed to find? One should not trade in one's own self for the future, still virtual, future selves of one's children—especially because children need parents with selves that radiate strength, freedom, and harmony. Paul Tillich (1951–63, vol. 3, 43–44) speaks in this connection of the ambiguity of sacrifice: "Self-sacrifice may be worthless if there is no self worthy of being sacrificed. . . . If, however, the self which is sacrificed is worthy, the question arises whether that for which it is sacrificed is worthy to receive it."

Television

After a long day and all these serious problems, you may feel you have a right to relax; to have a second helping of spaghetti; to tell your husband or wife about what happened to you during the day, and to pretend that you, too, are interested in his or her stories; to have a beer or a glass of wine. And then you may sit down in your comfortable armchair, put your feet up on the hassock, and switch on the TV. But you should not forget that you act as if the chicken, being tired of the world, would enter the microwave oven of its own free will and let itself be roasted to a beautiful golden brown. Television is a magnificent technical invention, an outstanding instrument of public education and entertainment. But TV may also have a dangerous, if not lethal, radiation, which may both help people construct their selves and distort and destroy their selves.

Television programs may help people construct their selves because they offer a great variety of roles; those of the hero and the victim, of Dr. Jekyll and Mr. or Mrs. Hyde, the loving and the loved one, the artist, the rich or the poor, the soldier, the athlete, the president of the United States, the millionaire, the captain of a B-737, Marilyn Monroe or Robert Redford. This may be a pleasant and satisfying experience, but it may not achieve the real goal: to build, or acquire, an authentic self. One may patch up a mosaic personality out of the virtual selves on the TV screen, but this ersatz personality will quickly disintegrate and evaporate when it comes in contact with harsh and prosaic everyday reality. It may take some of the time and energy one would need to really care for one's self. Television programs may even contribute to the deconstruction and disintegration of one's personality; they may lull us into the dangerous state of "oblivion." Being a couch potato is not a Socratic, Stoic, Christian, Renaissance, Baudelarian or Foucaultian posture of self-reflective and self-constructing meditation.

All this does not negate the fact that television also plays an indispensable and positive role in our contemporary societies (even if it could multiply its usefulness with better programming). But let me stop here, because the role of television has been studied by so many excellent experts that it would be ridiculous to try to add something important to the existing body of knowledge in a few pages. Let me rather turn to another activity of ours, which may be as important in molding our selves as television itself: reading. We have already seen how important it may be for us to read our favorite paper when we start reconstructing our selves and worlds in the morning. Here I focus on an "evening genre": on the role of reading books in constructing (or deconstructing) our selves.[6]

Books

Having withdrawn to our room, we may still have a vague feeling that something is missing in our lives. The day is not yet complete. We have not yet found our selves and our place in the world. We have not yet succeeded in transforming an alien world into a friendly, comfortable, meaningful one. What could we do? Why not take a book off the shelf? Browsing or reading a book for an hour or two may successfully conclude our daily exercise of constructing our selves.

Let me give here one single example of the enormous potential of books to help us construct our world and care for our selves. It is an unusual example, but I have been authorized to discuss it by the person who would have had the right to protest against it.

My Wife's Bookshelves

My wife has an MBA, but I have found only one or two books on her bookshelves that have any relationship with economics and business, if books on managers and personality training have anything to do with economics.[7] As a matter of fact, she has been working as a journalist for twenty years, as a reporter for and editor of television and radio programs, covering mainly the cinema and the theater. For ten years, she was the editor in chief of the largest Hungarian women's weekly magazine (circulation 500,000). But I have found only one single book on the profession of journalism on her shelves.[8]

But even without titles on economics and journalism, she has constructed a universe around herself out of books. It is a complete universe—with its stars and gods; vertical and horizontal dimensions; past and present; various species of living beings, facts, dreams, and myths; and a wide range of ways and means that may nurture, strengthen, protect, and develop a human self.

Her Gods

On her bookshelves, there is a whole Olympus with, perhaps, James Dean as the king of gods, and with dozens of lesser gods and goddesses—like Humphrey Bogart, Elvis Presley, Marlon Brando, Charlie Chaplin, Michelangelo Antonioni, Federico Fellinini, Ingmar Bergman, Milos Forman, and Wim Wenders; and Marlene Dietrich, Marilyn Monroe, Greta Garbo, Shirley MacLaine, Sophia Loren, Grace Kelly, Barbara Streisand, Brigitte Bardot, and Jane Fonda.[9] This is a whole pantheon. Each god and goddess may offer my wife the vision and experience of another world, another understanding, another role to play, another opportunity to test and enrich her personality. Books on Greek, Roman, and Indian mythology complete the picture.

Her World

Landscape. Judging from her books, my wife's world consists of gardens, terraces, a collection of amazingly beautiful houses and homes, a few faraway countries, half a dozen tropical islands, and nothing in between. In this world, there are no offices or factories; no roads, cars, or newspapers; no politics, European Union, or NATO; no power plants, street traffic, or city halls. There are only "roses," "geraniums," "one-summer flowers," two-summer flowers," and "perennial flowers," "house plants," bushes," "nuts and berries," and the like.[10] And there are houses and homes; fairy tale cottages and villas in Florence, Merano, and Bellaggio; apartments that mix modestly with outrageous luxury; magic worlds of homeliness and elegance, dazzling and decadent colors, sober and exuberant, harmonious and perversely disharmonious forms; hypersoft sofas and three-inch-thick mauve and sky-blue carpets; the dazzling play of mirrors, and French doors opening on emerald lawns and purple bougainvillea, with a gentle breeze blowing translucent curtains—a beautiful, personal version of the Garden of Eden (only a bit more expensive than the original may have been).

Yes, this is an imaginary world, a world constructed of flowers and trees, colors and forms, green lawns and golden beeches. It is a world of illusions but, at the same time, it may be experienced as more true and more important than the real world. It is an ideal world where one's self can feel safe, comfortable, and at home. In this world, constructing one's self is harmonious and joyful play.

History. This world is not without a time dimension. It has a rich and interesting past. This past does not have much to do, however, with the political and social history of school books. It is a concatenation of brilliant thoughts about history from Plutarch, through Machiavelli and Macaulay, to Spengler, Toynbee, and Braudel. At the same time, it is woven out of the lives, and mainly love lives, of famous men and women; of people like Napoleon and Empress Elizabeth. It is the history of great families and dynasties. It is a series of personal testimonies, of Tolstoy, de Gaulle, and Churchill. It is a series of brilliant examples of how the great figures of history have shaped their own destinies and their selves.[11]

Transcendence one and two. My wife has surrounded herself also with a sphere of ideas. Books by the great thinkers of humankind—Plato, Marcus Aurelius, Saint Augustine, Erasmus, Descartes, Rousseau, Schopenhauer, James, Nietzsche, Heidegger, Sartre, Tillich, Popper—may help her better understand herself and her place in the world. Reading them may be an excellent exercise in self-knowledge and self-construction.

Strangely enough, these books get along very well with another group of books that open up another dimension of the transcendental. These latter are New Age–type books on the occult and the parapsychological—books that teach you "how to achieve balance and harmony" in the old Chinese way; how to learn "what the Year of the Dragon [2000] keeps in store for you." There are also books on "secret wisdoms, esotericism, oriental and western traditions" and on "dreams and nightmares.[12]

It is amazing to see how Descartes' *cogito* and Jungian dreams, William James's strict pragmatism and parapsychology, Popper's enlightened rationalism and Chinese horoscopes get on well together. It is baffling to find on these shelves—in the company of works by Voltaire and Bertrand Russell—other books with chapters titled "Love-Philters and Spells," "Sorcery," "Satanic Orgies," "Indecent Witches," "Bones in the Mortar," "Pulverized Brains," "Initiation Rites," "Infernal Love," "Black Masses," and the like.[13] But, apparently, both these works of reason and unreason may play a role in the self-reflection and self-construction of a modern, or postmodern, lady.

Fantasy. Literary works are par excellence "world builders." Each novel is a world apart, a sanctuary where one can find refuge, discovering a new universe and enriching one's personality with new experiences, emotions, and human relationships. Reading adventure books, we flirt with the dangers of the world, we test our ingenuity and strength, and we celebrate the victory of a human being over the forces of evil. Family novels enchant us with the feeling of continuity; fascinate us with the strange, mysterious meandering ways of human life; and move and elevate us with the sight of human joy and suffering, success and failure. Love stories lull us into the joyful illusion that, after all, love triumphs in this world. Or we shed tears over the moving tragedy of two loving hearts. Books on celebrities introduce us to the world of power and wealth, beauty and adventure. These lives of high intensity, glory and tragedy, fortune and misfortune, may fill us with the feeling that our life, too, has this intensity, this excitement, this significance.

And literary works know and do even more. Each poem or novel is also a victory over time and mortality—it articulates, slows down, stops, or reverses time, imprisoning it in its gestalt. And in even the gloomiest or most absurd novel or play, life has a certain significance, a hidden message, a meaning, that our everyday lives may not have.

It is then more than understandable that the owner of this small library has surrounded herself with the fascinating universes she has found in the novels of Henry James, F. Scott Fitzgerald, and Evelyn Waugh (her three favorites), and in those of Henry Fielding, Jane Austen, Emily Brontë, William Thackeray, Stendhal, Fyodor Dostoevsky, Joseph Conrad, William Faulkner, François Mauriac, John Updike, and many others.

Sounds and colors. My wife's world is not mute. Cassettes and compact discs with music by various composers and performers, from Mozart to Madonna, from Beethoven to the Beatles, from Debussy to Céline Dion, along with books on them, fill her world with traditional and modern harmonies and disharmonies.

Nor is hers a bleak, black-and-white world. The works of Botticelli and the whole Renaissance company—Van Eyck, Cranach, and Vermeer, Turner and Goya, Miro, Klimt, and Hundertwasser—fill it with forms, colors, and harmonies. Did her predecessors, women in earlier centuries, who were born long before the color-printing revolution, live in an environment much poorer in colors and forms than she does? At least they still had nature closer to them with its own abundance of colors and forms.

Her Society

Dogs. The main population of my wife's world seems to be canine. Books on dogs pop up in great numbers on various shelves. They range from matter-of-fact books titled *The Dogs of the World* (in two volumes) and *The World of Dogs,* to the less modest and more philosophical *The Spiritual Life of Dogs.*[14] Dogs must be important catalysts in the process of self-construction of human beings. Their affection for, or dependence on, their masters make these latter happy, strengthen their selves, and make them feel that they are not alone in this world and their lives have a purpose and meaning. You may feel yourself in a friendly and homely world in a vast, cold, and dark universe with even the smallest, clumsiest half-bred near you.

Birds. In an earlier cycle of our lives, when we—my wife and I—lived in the city and had only a terrace opening onto the world, birds—a great variety of goldfinches, greenfinches, linnets, chaffinches, tomtits, and siskins—were the only messengers of nature and freedom in our world. They helped us construct a wider universe around our world enclosed by four walls. A great number of books preserve their fond memory on my wife's bookshelves.[15]

Celebrities. Celebrities are located between the divine and the human species. They are demigods, or heroes, who have a human shape but whose personality and fate are superhuman. Their lives have a fascinating brilliance, intensity, and authenticity. They live mainly on the pages of women's magazines. My wife has a big collection of these magazines on her shelves—issues of *Vanity Fair*, first of all—which seem to abundantly provide their readers with valuable worldly and spiritual nourishment for their selves.

Celebrities are powerful ("The Leaders Who Shape and Rule the World Today");[16] they are famous and successful ("Rising Star Renée Zellweger's Life and Love"); they are beautiful and rich and not necessarily happy ("Julia Roberts, *Notting Hill*'s $20 Million Actress, Opens Up about Her Loves, Her Life, and Her Tabloid Lunacy"); they are involved in exciting dramas ("Mutual Treachery in the Bill Clinton–Dick Morris Saga"), or in mysterious crimes ("The Versace Murder," "The Man Who Kept the Simpson Secrets," "Murder in Big Sky Country"); they live and fight in a dangerous world (George Clooney ". . . in the Jungle" of Hollywood); they are irresistible men and women ("Leonardo DiCaprio, the World's Biggest Heartthrob"); and so on and so forth.

As I noted above, these lives of high intensity, glory and tragedy, fortune and misfortune, may fill us with the feeling or illusion that our lives, too, have this intensity, this excitement, this significance.

Women. After dogs, birds, and celebrities, the next most important group in her society is that of the feminine species. These women here are not of the everyday, homely, housewife kind; they are of the interesting, tempting grandes dames class. Her bookshelves cave in under the weight of countless books about "powerful," "dangerous," "mysterious," and "damned" women; women "who love too much"; women with interesting lives and questionable morals; the compulsory books on the innumerable wives of Henry VIII; the history, adventures, and mainly martyrdom of women from Eve to Madame Curie.[17] And here also, of course, are the evergreen stories about the melancholically beautiful Queen of the Habsburgs, Sissy, in all quantities.[18] Women writers and novels about women as well have a preeminent place on the shelves preserved for literary works.

Men. There are also male figures in this world, though they exist mainly in their relationships with women. They are likely to be, and should be, "in love."[19] Shakespeare's *Plays* are on the shelves beside the book *Shakespeare's Love Life*. A serious Napoleon biography is leaning against *Napoleon's Private Life*.[20] Casanova is here in his own right.[21]

The Care for the Self

There are also books on my wife's shelves that offer direct help in the process of the construction (and sometimes deconstruction) of the feminine self. They promise a new life, a new personality, a new, more authentic sense of being to women by opening up new sources of emotions, passions, strength, beauty, identity, happiness, dignity. The temptation to read these books may be great.

The body. There seems to be a tragic contradiction in the lives of contemporary women. Their souls are torn between two opposite messages: the message of *Enjoy your life!* and that of *Be beautiful!* These two commandments seem to tragically and mutually exclude each other in most women's lives. Eating fine meals, for instance, is likely to belong to the enjoyment of life. But enjoying fine meals almost inevitably leads to gains in weight and thus seriously threatens your beauty. And if you lose your beauty, then how could you enjoy your life?

This conflict is pushed to an almost tragicomic extreme in the world of television commercials. In one moment, women are prompted to eat, swallow, and consume all the delicious bonbons, ice creams, and sundaes available in the highly developed world. In the next moment, however, they are warned that these bonbons, ice creams, and sundaes are worse than the Original Sin; they should abstain from them and immediately go on a self-punishing diet and slimming cure.

Dozens of books, and hundreds of magazine issues, offer their help to solve this dilemma. The most ingenious solutions are those that combine cookbooks and slimming cure guides. For instance, Harvey and Marilyn Diamond's *Fit for Life* is a fitness cook book. Other books try to convince women that—like Greek goddesses—they may feed on ambrosia and nectar, that is, on ethereal substances that will make them, if not immortal, at least everlastingly beautiful; Cathy Hopkins's *Aroma Therapy* is one of the many offers in this line.[22] If none of these methods help, women may still turn to sorcery, or to the mythic examples of some celebrities. They may, for instance, follow the advice of, Chris Stadtlaender's *Sisi*—here she comes again, this tragic empress—who gives readers "the secret recipes of Empress Elizabeth and the Court" of the Habsburgs. They will read in this book about "the secret of the svelte waist," "hot slimming olive baths," "the victory of the lanolin," "the secret recipes of the gypsy woman," "Sisi's bed of beauty," and other fascinating beauty mysteries.[23] In principle, Sisi—beautiful, rich, slim, taking serious care of her body and appearance—could be a good model for the squaring of the circle, that is, the solution of the "Enjoy-your-life/Be-beautiful" dilemma. But she is not, because in spite of her beauty, she was obsessed with her appearance throughout her life, and—as far as we know—was not able to really enjoy her life.

Judging from the number of cookbooks on her shelves, my wife must be also a passionate cook. And she is absolutely not. Or she is only in principle. I mean that she is interested in the culinary arts, not so much as a practice, but as an art and narrative. Her books are not practical guidelines for cooking—they are much more poetry about the beauty, mystique, and philosophy of cooking; and of how cooking may help women develop their selves (if they do not stay too long in the kitchen).

The psyche. Two or three dozens books testify of the importance of psychology in one's life. The range goes from serious, scholarly books by and on Freud, Jung, Rank, Adler, Fromm, and others to more practical guidebooks helping people cope with their everyday problems of caring for their selves.[24] And there are also books that invite their readers to more exciting adventures in the depths of the human psyche. Let me give a bit extreme, but not uncharacteristic, example of this genre: Clarissa Pinkola Estés' *Women Who Run with the Wolves: Myths and Stories of the Wild Woman* (1995).[25]

This is a classical opus in the line of the Jungian reenchantment of the world of contemporary women. It is worthwhile to read a few sentences from the text on the dust jacket and in the preface:

There is an unbridled and timeless being in each woman, the archetypal Woman of Nature with her powerful strength, instincts, passionate creativity and timeless knowledge. . . . Our being is filled with a nostalgia for the wilderness. . . . The shadow of the Woman of Nature in the wilderness prowls about us day and night. Independently of where we are, the shadow hanging around us is definitely quadruped.

And here are the titles of a few chapters:

Song Over the Bones—The Wolf Woman—Animal Bridegroom—The Smell of Blood—The Dark Figure in Women's Dreams—Facing the Ancestral Witch—We Go Down on All Fours—The Fierce Fight—Skeleton Woman—Death in the House of Love—The Woman Returning in the Wilderness—The Riotous Dance—The Spiritual Bear—The Murderous Secret—The Girl with Golden Hair.

It may seem to be slightly humorous to imagine elegant, disciplined, goal-oriented career women as they suddenly start running with the wolves in the wilderness of "murderous secrets," perhaps on all fours, as they hunt and kill their victims with their "animal bridegrooms," "smell the blood," howl "over the bones," "dance riotously" with "Death in the House of Love." We may smile at this dabbling of a trivial genre in the secrets of the human soul and self, and we may be appalled by this almost perverse mixture of the trivial and the existential. But this submergence in the atavistic world of powerful fantasies and desires may be part of the lives of women (and, mutatis mutandis, of men), and it certainly plays a role in the process of self-construction.

Personality. Hunting parties in the world of fantasy may be exciting, but to have a strong personality and make a successful career may be even more important for most women of our age. And, of course, there are books, published by the dozens or hundreds every year, that offer potted courses in personality development promising to transform the reader into a dynamic, attractive, successful, and happy personality. If she reads the book carefully, and listens to its advice, she will be able to fully develop her potentials and "strengths" and live happily ever after. I see here, on my wife's shelves, among several similar books, Anthony Robbins' *Awake the Giant Within,* which seems to be a masterpiece of the genre. Already its title is a direct hit:

Awake the Giant Within
How to Take Immediate Control of
Your Mental, Emotional, Physical, and Financial Destiny

One may be stunned and enchanted by the happy and flattering discovery that there is a powerful GIANT within oneself. To hell with any feeling of inferiority! I am not a dwarf but a giant! I am capable of conquering the world! The title does not speak of life, which is a matter-of-fact and prosaic concept, but uses a powerful metaphor: DESTINY. If you follow me, you will be able to control—not only your life, but—your Destiny. And "Destiny" is a mythic concept;

primeval heroes and Romantic genii had destinies. Normal people have only lives. But—after buying and reading this book—you won't be any more a gray and average human being. You will have a DESTINY. And a destiny is not only much grander and more majestic than a life; it has a deep, mysterious significance, a meaning that normal human lives are not likely to have.

Your destiny will have also a fullness that lives may not have. This book will help you control not only your "physical" destiny but also your "mental," "emotional," and last but not least, your "financial" destiny. May you ask for more? Yes. You may ask that this fantastic metamorphosis take place immediately, because you do not have too much time, you are in a hurry in this hectic contemporary life. And, duly, the author promises us this "immediate control" over our lives. Read this book and you will acquire a magic power to construct your new and more authentic, or at least more successful, self.

Other self-booster books promise similar results and victories. Norman Vincent Peale's *Power of Positive Thinking* is only slightly more modest than the Robbins book: "Read It and Begin a New Life!" its subtitle tells the reader.[26] Robin Norwood's *Women Who Love Too Much* has the same message focused on women. It says of itself that it is a "life-changing book for women." Changing their lives may be an important project for women, judging from the fact that the very same message also recurs in a great number of perfume posters and elsewhere. To mention only one example, the poster for a Perry Ellis perfume reads: "Life is how you change it."

I refer here to one of Rilke's most famous sonnets, which, after describing a Greek statue, suddenly ends with the words:

Change your life.

Here we witness again the strange meeting of the trivial and the existential—the trivial world of perfumes and the existential world of a great poet who struggled throughout his life with the angels and the demons of the hidden realms of his self.

By the way, I have the impression that the wish to change their lives is stronger, and more general, in women than in men. If that is so, what may be the explanation? Historically, most of them were in a worse situation than their male counterparts; this could explain their nostalgia for change. But, at the same time, they were dependent on their spouses for their living and social position, and this must have enhanced in their eyes the value of continuity and permanence. And what about the present situation? Do women feel the necessity to keep changing because they have to play a wider range of roles than men if they want to "sell themselves" in the social and the job market? Or are they more sensitive, do they feel the need to care for their selves more than men do? Anyway—as we have already discussed in the introduction to this book—studying the similarities and differences between women's and men's strategies of self-construction is one of the most interesting, and most promising, fields of research.

Coming back to my wife's books: Browsing these shelves, reading some of these books for an hour or two, she may successfully conclude her daily exercise in self-construction.

Switching Off

After a while, watching television, or reading a book, mildly bores us, or lulls us to sleep. We do not even notice when we imperceptibly lose our selves, our personalities, and become submerged in the dark waves of the night.

—

However, this is only the end of the day, not of the story. In the preceding chapters, we have followed the life of an imaginary person throughout a day, exploring the ways in which, beyond her everyday business, she keeps constructing her self, without necessarily knowing that she is doing so. We have tried to discover and disclose this underlying, latent layer of her everyday life, the existential drama in which human beings fight, knowingly or unknowingly, not just for survival but also for the fulfillment of their selves and lives.

Our analysis has been, in an essential way, incomplete. We have put in brackets one crucially important factor. We have only sporadically referred to the fact that this process of self-construction takes place in a radically new environment, in a world where the human self has a wealth of new opportunities but also must cope with new problems and challenges.

In the second part of this book, I shall focus on how this new world—which we shall call "consumer civilization" or the "Proletarian Renaissance"—shapes people's selves; or, more precisely, how it helps or impedes them in shaping, constructing, and actualizing their selves. In other words, we restart our analysis: Now we wake up our protagonist not in her private bedroom but, so to say, in history. We shall study the process and problems of self-construction within the framework of an emerging new civilization.

We shall encounter here the same duality of human life that we discovered and described in the first part of this book. Under the colorful and trivial surface of the "Proletarian Renaissance," people are struggling—consciously and unconsciously—with the ultimate concerns, hopes, and anxieties of the human condition. They are striving for freedom and safety, dignity and meaning, for the actualization of their selves and the fulfillment of their lives. But there is a difference.

In the spectacular settings of the consumer civilization, this duality, too, will be more spectacular, astonishing, and shocking. Some scholars describe the age of consumption as an "eternal carnival." Others see it as a grotesque "dance of death." I shall try to show that it is both. People living in this emerging new civilization are pulled about by, and oscillate between, these two basic human experiences—between a trivial carnival and a fearful dance of death.

PART II

The Self in the Consumer Age

The Self in a Changing World

> Impossible is a word to be found
> only in the dictionary of fools.
>
> —*Napoleon Bonaparte*

Possible and Impossible Futures

When History enters the stage and our whole world undergoes a dramatic change, this may have a fundamental and complex impact on the formation of people's selves. Think only of the well-know fact of how different people are who grew up in times of scarcity and war from those who had the good fortune of growing up in a peaceful world and a prosperous country.

This is an issue that concerns us, people living at the turn of the twentieth and twenty-first centuries, especially strongly. We live in a rapidly changing world, struggling with increasing uncertainty.[1] We have to prepare ourselves, our selves, for various possible and (it is hoped) impossible futures. We are like weathermen who should tell what the weather will be like in a fortnight. Will there be a clear blue sky and a temperature of 90 degrees Fahrenheit? Or will it rain? Or snow? Should we wear just a T-shirt, or should we take our umbrella? Should we put on heavy boots and look for a boat because a flood may be coming? Or should we start running before the volcano erupts?

To make matters worse, let me add that not only our future is uncertain. Our objectives are uncertain as well. Are we able to clearly set our goals? Do we really know for what kind of life we want to prepare our selves? For a life of affluence? Or for a life of pleasure? For a life of power, freedom, success, glory, togetherness? Do we want to "live in truth"? To live a life of responsibility and civic virtue? A life of prestige and fame? Do we want to devote our lives to the betterment of humankind? To alleviate human suffering? Or what?[2]

These goals may overlap one another, but they are not identical. They may even contradict one another. Depending on our priorities, we must develop different strategies for ourselves. This has recently become even more difficult than it was before because events of global importance (the September 11, 2001, terrorist attacks on America; war in Iraq; the transatlantic conflict; terrorism; the emergence of would-be new nuclear powers; climate change; the growing gap between rich and poor countries and people; etc.) have raised the level of uncertainty in the world and have rendered predicting future developments even more difficult. The number of alternative futures in which we shall probably have to develop, protect, and fulfill our selves has significantly increased.

Various hypotheses and theories try to explore the main trends of change and reduce the complexity of possible future developments into simple formulas. Reviewing some of these attempts may help us better understand what may happen to us, to our selves, and to the world during the coming decades, though, as we shall see, experts are hesitating between contradictory visions of the future. Table 8.1 displays up some of these contradictory predictions and theories. This table, with all the contradictory predictions, hypotheses, and open questions, gives a good impression of how uncertain we are about our future and our future selves[3] Let me add only a few words of comment.

Modern age ↔ postmodern age. This transformation has been taking place in the last decades. At present, various features of the process of modernization (universalism, optimism, faith in the progress of humankind, a unilinear conception of history, ethnocentrism, belief in the objectivity of truth, pragmatism, etc.) are mixing with postmodern features: relativism, pluralism, skepticism, antihistoricism or a multilinear conception of history, subjectivism, multiculturalism, and so on. Some of the main values of modern Western civilization—freedom, tolerance, open minds, social justice, human rights, the apotheosis of

TABLE 8.1

Post–September 11, 2001, Scenarios

Modern Age	↔	Postmodern Age?
Age of Ideologies	↔	Age of Pragmatism?
History	↔	The End of History?
New World Order?	↔	New World Disorder?
Pax Americana	↔	Bellum Americanum?
Pax Americana	↔	War of North and South?
A World of Peace	↔	A World of Uncertainty?
A Free World	↔	"Fortress West"?
Open Society and Minds	↔	Closed Society and Minds?
Multicultural World	↔	Clash of Civilizations?
Global Democracy	↔	Decline of Democracy?
Nation States	↔	Globalization?
"I" (Information) Age	↔	"M" (Misinformation) Age?
Traditional Civilization	↔	Consumer Civilization?
Consumer Civilization	↔	?????

the human personality—are present, but have different meanings, within the two trends.[4]

Developments in recent years may reinforce the postmodern feeling of uncertainty, doubts, relativism, tolerance, cultural openness, and genuine pluralism. But the shock of September 11 may also trigger off a regression into intolerance, ethnocentrism, nationalism, and feelings of imperial superiority. It may close our minds to anything outside our own culture, it may generate in us anxieties and fears that may destroy some of the great achievements of the past two hundred years in the field of democratization, human rights, and cross-cultural understanding. We have to prepare ourselves, our selves, for both of these possible developments.

Age of ideologies ↔ age of pragmatism. In which direction will our world develop? During the past two or three decades, we have convinced ourselves that the age of murderous ideologies was slowly coming to an end and an age of enlightened pragmatism was dawning. We tried to ignore the warning signs of the rise of new ideologies. It was a mistake. September 11 shocked the world with the vision of the destructive power of these new ideologies. In its aftermath, ideological passions overwhelmed even some of the most enlightened and pragmatic nations of the world. What should we do? For which of these two worlds should we prepare our selves?

History ↔ the end of history. We were told in the 1980s and 1990s that History, with a capital H, had come to an end. We had developed the perfect model (democracy plus market economy), and all we had to do was to chisel this model; spread it all over the world; and progress step by step, with small, practical improvements. Recent developments have proved that we have not yet arrived in such a paradisiacal, ahistorical haven. We are still caught in the fearful and glorious drama of human history, with its victories and defeats, destruction and fresh starts. We should certainly not lull ourselves into the illusion that we will be spared the pains, joys, and responsibilities of history and that we can just leave behind our selves hardened in the course of history. As a warning, let me mention that the glorious end of global development had been announced already several times in the course of our history. Le Goff (1993) writes, for instance that more than a hundred years ago, at "the victory of the bourgeoisie, Guizot" believed that history "arrived at its extreme point." It is as if we were listening to Fukuyama.

New world order ↔ new world disorder. If I remember well, it was former president George H. W. Bush who promised us a New World Order. September 11 was one of the latest warnings that a New World Disorder was also in the works. Shall we supply our selves with a survival kit for a chaotic world, or should we learn how to build a New World Order? But do we know what this New World Order should, or could, be like?

A world of peace ↔ a world of uncertainty. At the end of World War II, the world entered the era called by some PAX AMERICANA, which brought prosperity and democracy to a number of nations in the world; peace, the prospect of development, and hope to others; and frustration and desperation to the rest. We may be at the end of this era, but it is to be hoped that we are not entering the era of BELLUM AMERICANUM, that of a war between the North and the South, or of a guerrilla war between terrorists and establishments. The best-case scenario would be if recent events prompted peoples around the world to lay the foundations of a PAX GLOBALIS or PAX UNIVERSALIS. What kind of selves would be best prepared for achieving this task?

A free world ↔ "fortress West." After so many centuries and millennia, the globe became a more or less free world in the last decades of the twentieth century. Not for long. We are now scared by the gloomy perspectives of the Western world closing its borders and surrounding itself by fortified walls, because this may be the only possibility of protecting its freedom, affluence, the rule of law, and its culture in the sea of global poverty and destitution. It would not be the first time in history that such a pattern developed. Highly developed civilizations used to live behind fortified city walls from the times of Uruk, Babel, or Thebes up to the modern ages. In the provinces and colonies of the Roman Empire, *castri,* and garrison cities were surrounded by walls and ramparts in a dangerous world of "barbarians." Medieval lords lived in their donjons and castles. The aristocratic and patrician families of Florence and San Gimignano lived in their residential towers, American pioneers protected their lives and belongings in their fortified settlements. The *grande bourgeosie* of some Latin American countries is experimenting with similar solutions. Should we prepare ourselves to become free-faring globetrotters and global citizens, or soldier citizens familiar with the latest techniques of global warfare?

Open society and minds ↔ closed society and minds. Will societies and human selves close down, or will open societies and open minds prevail in the coming decades? This is an open and harassing question.

Multicultural world ↔ clash of civilizations. At the end of World War II, there was a more or less general consensus that humankind would destroy itself if it could not overcome its national, ethnic, and cultural differences. In the 1980s and 1990s, the majority of Western politicians and political scientists rejected the hypothesis that the next decades would be marked by a global clash of civilizations. September 11 was a dramatic warning that such a clash cannot be ruled out. A chain reaction of wrong and paranoiac decisions by several global actors could strongly increase the probability of such a scenario. How would our "postmodern" selves cope with the problems of a world in a destructive clash of civilizations?

Global democracy ↔ the decline of democracy. We thought that after the collapse of the Soviet Union and the general demise of the communist movement democracy would continue unhampered in its triumphal march across the globe. We were inclined to ignore how fragile and underdeveloped democratic systems were in a great number of countries, and that not so far in the past, in the first half of the twentieth century, democracy still fought a desperate, and sometimes losing, fight against totalitarian ideologies and regimes.

Since September 11, the specter of a new authoritarian trend has emerged. Apart from great poverty and a high level of social inequality and corruption, few things erode democratic institutions more than fear and a feverish longing for security. This may have a strong impact on the formation of our future selves. It has become more difficult than before to build up in ourselves the right balance between freedom and the longing for security.

Nation states ↔ globalization. In the past two decades, we have witnessed the spectacular success of a new concept, globalization, which has become one of our key analytical tools for the study and interpretation of what is happening in the world. Globalization is an extremely complex process full of risks and conflicts of interests, opportunities and dangers, enormous tensions and explosive forces. It would be good to know who was right, or less wrong, in Seattle or Genoa, because we would need different selves in a well-confined, more or less ordered, traditional welfare state than in a rapidly changing, unpredictably globalizing world.

Information age ↔ age of misinformation. In the past few years, we have lived in the fascination and vertigo of the gloriously upcoming Information Age. A whole mythology has surrounded the new technologies, which seemed to promise the solution of all our problems and the coming of a world of peace and plenty for all of us. However, we have more and more realized that the new technologies may serve also purposes of control and surveillance and may jeopardize democratic freedoms.

An even more important problem lies in the fact that beyond these positive and negative mythologies we know very little about an Electronic Information Age that may become our future. Beyond technicalities, what will be the change in our lives, lifestyles, life strategies; in our selves, in our human relationships, jobs, vocations, values, belief systems; in the meaning of our lives? What will be the social and human message of this new age? We do not yet know.

Traditional civilization ↔ consumer civilization. In the past half century, Western civilization has gone through a process of radical change. As we shall see later in this book, some of the basic tenets of our civilization have switched into their opposites. "Love thy neighbor!"? No, "Love thyself!" "Discipline yourself!"? No, "Actualize yourself!" "Be modest!"? No, "Be successful!" "Repent your sins!"? No, "You are innocent. Enjoy your life." In all likelihood, the new "Consumers' Testament" will shape radically new types of selves. We are going through a great, not genetic but, "memetic" mutation.[5]

The record of this new phase or trend in the history of our civilization is mixed. Its cult of freedom and the human personality, its joy of life and Renaissance exuberance, its pluralism and tolerance, its profusion of all sorts of human experience are real assets. But it has also done harm to people by surrounding them with a world of empty illusions, by distorting the human self with its radical hedonism, by disintegrating traditional communities with its radical individualism, by generating bitter frustrations in the poorer parts of the world, and so on.

In the following chapters, we shall discuss the problems raised by the civilization of consumption. We shall try to sort out its positive and negative elements, the creative and destructive components of its impact on our selves and communities. But we shall have to admit that we can only guess—devising various hypotheses—where these developments would lead us, how they would transform the world and our lives therein. September 11 rang the alarm bells and warned us that—as a worst-case scenario—the age of peace and plenty may come to an end and be followed by a period of troubles and scarcity, turning our present hedonism into a voluntary or compulsory asceticism; and leaving our present self-actualizing selves defenseless.

This leads us back to our initial question: How should we prepare our selves for a future that is so uncertain and unpredictable?

The Self in Various Worlds

I may be wrong. I may have overemphasized the differences between our various possible and impossible futures. One might argue that irrespective of the differences in the frameworks, human life, and the situation of the human self, will be essentially the same in one or the other future world. Let me try to show that this is not the case.

To make my task easier, and the argument clearer, I shall consider only five scenarios, and I will explain in some detail what human life would be like in the five different worlds described by them. These scenarios were developed by a working group of the European Commission.[6] Here they are. They speak for themselves, I will not comment on them.

1. Triumphant Markets. It predicts the fast development of global networks; the accelerating flow of information and influence, capital and commodities; the increasing influence of multinational companies and international institutions; the decline of the nation-state; the dismantling of the welfare state; the opening of the gap between the rich and the poor; and people becoming more and more passive consumers.

2. Hundred Flowers. Globalization will lose momentum in the first decades of the twenty-first century. People will revolt against the dominance of national bureaucracies and big business and will retreat into their local and regional communities. This will be the end of the age of consumer societies and the renaissance of community life. Multinational companies, international organizations, and nation-states will have to meet the demands of local communities.

3. Shared Responsibilities. Economic and financial globalization will slow down, and a kind of social globalization will prevail. A sort of global welfare state will develop with strong social solidarity and responsibility. The accountability and transparency of governments will increase. Cooperation and contracts will be the hallmarks of the age. Various forms of direct democracy will be introduced, and the role of civil society will become more and more important. Nation-states will remain strong, but instead of dominating they will serve their citizens. There will be an intense cooperation among these new welfare states.

4. Creative Societies. People will revolt against the sclerotic routines of their states and against the dominance of global technocracy. There will be an outburst of human creative potential. New ideas will be implemented in every field. Political institutions will be renewed. Nonmarket activities will rapidly spread. The freedom of people to choose and, if they want, to change their lifestyles and careers will radically increase. Globalization as we know it will slow down. A new, "postmodern" nation-state will emerge.

5. Turbulent Neighborhoods. There will be rising tensions throughout the world; conflicts, civil wars, wars. Regional blocs, "Fortress Europe" among them, will close and protect their frontiers. Fear of immigration, isolationism, and xenophobia will increase. Globalization will come to a halt. Nation-states will form strong economic and military alliances and will develop authoritarian features.

The question is how different life—and the challenges to which the human self would have to respond—would be in these FIVE WORLDS. My method of description is simple, or even simplistic. I have a list of various features that may characterize a world, and I will check these features in the five future worlds.

This will be a subjective and unscientific procedure. But I think it may be appropriate in this case, because I want only to show that the five worlds predicted by these scenarios would substantially differ from one another and, as a consequence, they would require radically different responses from us, from our selves. This will be a thought experiment—or let me rather say that I shall play with the idea of sketching the outlines of five possible future worlds and of describing the impact they may have on the formation of the selves of future human beings.

The sets of features in tables 8.2 through 8.13 speak for themselves. I shall add a few comments only to the first one to show how these sets are supposed to work.

TABLE 8.2

Fundamental Values

Triumphant Markets	Success in business; wealth
Hundred Flowers	Community happiness
Shared Responsibilities	Social justice
Creative Societies	Self actualization; freedom
Turbulent Neighborhoods	Power; security

If the Triumphant Markets scenario prevails, then the present process of "business globalization" will continue its triumphal march. In this case the world, and our selves, will rotate, in all likelihood, around business, success, and wealth. The Hundred Flowers scenario might restore the prestige of lavender-smelling grandma values. A world of Shared Responsibilities would probably rotate around the principle of social solidarity. Spiritual freedom and the idea of self-actualization could be at the center of Creative Societies. If the Turbulent Neighborhoods scenario prevails, power and security have a good chance to become the dominant values. These various worlds would favor the development, and prompt the success, of radically different selves.

Our very concepts would have different meanings in these different worlds. "Freedom," for instance, could have the following meanings.

TABLE 8.3

Freedom

Triumphant Markets	Free market; consumer choice
Hundred Flowers	Freedom of local citizens
Shared Responsibilities	Social, political, and economic freedom
Creative Societies	Creative freedom
Turbulent Neighborhoods	Freedom of the strong

We would or could set for ourselves different life goals.

TABLE 8.4

The Goal of Life

Triumphant Markets	Bigger and bigger shopping malls
Hundred Flowers	Family bliss
Shared Responsibilities	Just and affluent global society
Creative Societies	Discovery; invention
Turbulent Neighborhoods	Defending oneself against the barbarians

---

Each of these worlds would have a different type of typical personality.

TABLE 8.5

Typical Personality

Triumphant Markets	Successful businessman; rich consumer
Hundred Flowers	Decent, kind, benevolent person
Shared Responsibilities	Responsible and active citizen
Creative Societies	*Homo creans,* full of ideas and initiatives
Turbulent Neighborhoods	Soldier of the besieged fortress

In all likelihood, the dominant mentality in these worlds would also be different.

TABLE 8.6

Mentality and *Habitus*

Triumphant Markets	Hedonism
Hundred Flowers	Epicureanism
Shared Responsibilities	Social and ecodemocracy
Creative Societies	Postmodernism
Turbulent Neighborhoods	Aristocratic stoicism

Our minds would also be shaped in different ways.

TABLE 8.7

Mind

Triumphant Markets	Pragmatic
Hundred Flowers	Emotional
Shared Responsibilities	Interactive
Creative Societies	Open
Turbulent Neighborhoods	Closed

Different skills would or could rank among the highest in public perception.

TABLE 8.8

Basic Skills

Triumphant Markets	Competitiveness
Hundred Flowers	Sensitivity—empathy
Shared Responsibilities	Responsibility
Creative Societies	Inspiration
Turbulent Neighborhoods	Discipline

We would try to score highest on various "Q-scales."

TABLE 8.9

Q-Scales

Triumphant Markets	IQ [intelligence quotient]
Hundred Flowers	EQ [emotional quotient]
Shared Responsibilities	CQ [communication quotient]
Creative Societies	CRQ [creativity quotient]
Turbulent Neighborhoods	MQ [martial quotient]

Life would have different centers in these different worlds.

TABLE 8.10

The Center of Life

Triumphant Markets	Marketplace
Hundred Flowers	Homeland; the commons
Shared Responsibilities	Civic forums
Creative Societies	Ateliers, studies, laboratories, schools
Turbulent Neighborhoods	Fortresses

The self would have to cope with different threats in these different worlds.

TABLE 8.11

Major Threats

Triumphant Markets	Global recession/stagnation
Hundred Flowers	Moral crisis
Shared Responsibilities	Social disintegration, apathy
Creative Societies	Sclerosis
Turbulent Neighborhoods	Invasions

The so-called ultimate concerns in these worlds could also be different.

TABLE 8.12

Ultimate Concerns

Triumphant Markets	None
Hundred Flowers	Life and death
Shared Responsibilities	Justice
Creative Societies	The mystery of the world
Turbulent Neighborhoods	Survival

Even the response of the self to the challenge of mortality and death would, or could be, different.

TABLE 8.13

Death

Triumphant Markets	Denial of death
Hundred Flowers	Love of melancholy country churchyards
Shared Responsibilities	Faith in the progress of humankind
Creative Societies	Immortality through creation
Turbulent Neighborhoods	*Dulce et decorum pro est patria mori*

These are very different worlds, indeed. And it is not easy to prepare our selves for so many different environments and situations.

Let me illustrate the difficulty of this task by going back into the past. Imagine that we are in the early 1920s, and we have just left behind the horrors of World War I. And we have to draw up our plans for the coming decades, let's say until the 1940s. How would we prepare our selves to have the best chances of survival and personal development? What would we teach our selves? Technical skills? Civic virtues? Survival strategies? Pragmatism and a spirit of compromise or Socratic moral courage? "*Untertan*" and subject mentality or the love of freedom and independence? The art of dissimulation or honesty? Idealism (of what kind?) or realism and critical spirit? Or Cynicism? Human solidarity, empathy, or self-defensive indifference and callousness? The importance of group identity (national, ethnic, class, religious), or the importance of personal autonomy and integrity? Would we teach ourselves hope or resignation? To hope for what? And to be resigned to what?

We are nowadays in a similar, and perhaps even more difficult, situation. How should we prepare ourselves, our selves, for all these possible and impossible futures? Could and should we construct a kit of basic skills that would help us in any situation and in any kind of worlds? Should we embark on a long journey, as ships bound for unknown, faraway lands were launched in the fifteenth or sixteenth centuries? "We have some basic skills. Here are some tools, starch, canvas and rope, a few swords and guns, a few barrels of dried pork, and gunpowder, here is some fresh water, and: Goodbye! Good luck! We are in God's hands."

What are the tools, the guns, the gunpowder, the barrels of pork today? What could and should be this universal kit of basic survival skills and of self-fulfillment in this age, in the emerging consumer civilization, with all its hopes and fears, problems and challenges, dangers and opportunities? Let us start by describing what we mean by this emerging new civilization.

9

"Proletarian Renaissance"

I can resist everything except temptation.

—Oscar Wilde

An Apology

The title of this chapter is theatrical, and it may be misleading as well. It may give the wrong impression that the "Renaissance," or the reemergence, of the proletariat will be discussed. It will not. "Proletarian Renaissance" stands here as a metaphor for our contemporary consumer civilization. I have chosen this slightly provocative title to direct attention to the dramatic changes that have taken place in the past half century or so. After having described what I mean by these radical changes, I shall discuss their impact on people's minds and behavior, and mainly on the ways in which they shape, protect, construct their selves in this new world full of contradictions and new challenges.

The Concept of Crisis

The changes I am referring to here have often been defined—probably mistakenly—as the crisis of Western civilization. The Greek word *"krinein"* meant "to differentiate," or "to decide."[1] Later, the noun, "crisis" indicated a moment or a turning point in which the fate of something important was decided; that of an illness or a battle, for instance.

Nowadays, the term "crisis" is used to denote a serious operational disturbance of a system, a malfunction that the system's own self-correcting mechanisms are unable to eliminate or find extremely hard to do. When these internal mechanisms eventually fail, and no external intervention is successful either, then the danger of a systemic breakdown is imminent. This notion of a crisis is widely used today in medicine, psychology, politics, and economics. Crisis management has become an important discipline.

It seems to be justified to talk about the crisis of a civilization or culture as well if there are grave functional disturbances in the institutions, and in those mental, emotional, spiritual, and behavioral mechanisms that help people understand and cope with this world; find their place and role in the world; care for their selves; live together with others; find answers to the existential questions of life and death; and think of their lives as having a purpose and meaning.

Can we speak in this sense of an emerging crisis of Western civilization? First we have to differentiate between *crisis* and *crisis perception*. These two do not necessarily go together. A civilization may already be in a serious crisis, though people do not perceive and experience the situation as a crisis. The opposite may also happen; that is, people may be overtaken by a sense of crisis even though the system they live in is only going through minor operational difficulties; it is not in a state of crisis. In the case of systems that are as complex as civilizations, a lack of the sense of crisis, or a false sense of crisis, may quite easily occur, and in fact they do quite often.

It is a well-known phenomenon also that the same process is experienced by one group as a *crisis*, and by another as a dynamic process of development. The Age of Romanticism, for instance, was perceived and interpreted by many as a crisis, and by others as a fascinating era of renewal. The turn of the century was a glorious period of capitalist economic expansion and, at the same time, it was experienced as decadence, a profound crisis of European culture by many among the best minds of the age. The twentieth century has been seen as the century of spectacular scientific and technological breakthroughs and, at the same time, as a period in which irrational and dark forces came back with a vengeance.

There may also be a *time lag* between various societies and social groups. Baudelaire's "dandyism" and Kafka's gloomy visions had preceded by decades the tragic life experience of the fin de siècle, and the explosion of the "absurd" after World War II, respectively.

It should be remembered also that *a crisis is not necessarily a negative phenomenon*. The crises of anachronistic and oppressive systems have been welcomed by many as a positive development. Holbach wrote to Voltaire in 1766: "The whole of Europe is in a crisis, and this is favorable for the human spirit." Roosevelt, too, was convinced that humankind had emerged from each of its crises with greater knowledge and better morals.[2] The notion of crisis also frequently has a positive connotation in psychology, especially in developmental psychology. Many see it as an indispensable condition for the periodic renewal of the self, for the growth of human personality.

This is the reason why some social scientists and historians choose not to use the notion of "crisis," that is, a term that is too emotional and overdramatizes facts. They prefer instead to speak of periods of transition in which a system proceeds from a given structure and operational mechanism—through an intermediary, more or less unstructured state, which is sometimes called the state of "liminality"—to a new structure and operational mechanism.[3] I will use the concept of crisis in this "softer" sense and shall examine contemporary Western civilization as going through a lively, and even hectic, process of transformation and restructuring.

Let me finally mention that there are philosophers, theologians, and philosophers of history—such as Heidegger, Jaspers, Tillich, Niebuhr, Löwith—who have used the notion of crisis in a radically different sense. For them, a crisis was not an occasional episode in human history, and not a simple concomitant of change, but a permanent, fundamental, ontological element of human existence and the human self. In an essay written in 1936 (one of the brilliant examples of twentieth-century "crisis literature"), the Hungarian philosopher Béla Hamvas (1983, 68–69) summarized this interpretation in the following way:

> The crisis was always there but humankind has tried to hide itself from it and ignore it. . . . Nowadays, the human being only awakens to the eschatological situation in which he or she has ever lived. . . . Our con-

temporary crisis is nothing else than the shock that forces people to perceive and acknowledge that ultimately they live in a "boundary situation" [*Grenzensituation, situation limite*]. . . . It is the human being's eternal and essential situation that is disclosed in, and by, the crisis.[4]

Existentialists would agree that by reminding us of our human condition and awakening us from our Heideggerian unconsciousness and oblivion (*"Ohnmacht"*), crisis may play a positive role in our lives. According to Karl Barth (1953, 32, 57, 65), salvation history "is nothing else than the continual crisis of history as a whole; it is not a special history in or beside history." Niebuhr (1941), Tillich (1936, 1965, 1988), or Ricoeur (1986) would add that it is the presence of Evil in the world, or that of Original Sin in our lives, that keeps us in a permanent state of crisis.

"Crises"

Several periods in the history of Western civilization have been referred to by various authors—with more or less justification—as periods of cultural and spiritual crisis: the *fourth and third centuries* B.C. in Greece, when a profound spiritual crisis accompanied the decline of the classical city state and its culture; the *fourth and fifth centuries* A.D., that is, the final decay of Roman civilization; and the *fifteenth century* in Western Europe, as the crisis of the feudal system, the medieval church, its vision of the world, and the human self itself.[5] Following the disruption of traditional social, political, and economic patterns and institutions (in the wake of the French Revolution and the Industrial Revolution), European societies went through a deep cultural and spiritual upheaval in the first part of the nineteenth century. Romantic *Weltschmerz* and hectic revolutionary utopianism characterized this age on the level of the self. Living in our own age of "crisis," it is strange to learn that people living in earlier ages complained as much about their crises as we do about our own. Jaspers (1965 [1932], 12) quotes, for instance, the view of the German historian Berthold-Georges Niebuhr as a characteristic example of the general mood that almost turned into panic after the June Revolution of 1830: "We are going to see, if God does not miraculously help us, a destruction which will be similar to what the Roman world had experienced in the 3rd century: the destruction of well-being, freedom, education and the sciences."

In the last third of the century, it was Nietzsche who painted the gloomiest picture of the state of Western civilization. His dark vision was to return over and over again during the twentieth century in the great cyclical world histories of Spengler (1926 [1918–23]), Sorokin (1962 [1937–41]), Toynbee (1934–61), and others. Fin-de-siècle decadence was also perceived by many as an emotional and mental projection of a deep crisis of the human self.

The experience, and mood, of crisis deepened in the 1920s and 1930s. Eschatological prophecies have abounded since the end of World War I. Ortega y Gasset (1957 [1930]), Paul Valéry (1924, 1951), and others saw, and feared, the destruction of the human personality and human values in the emerging mass societies. In a Tocquevillian vein, Ortega y Gasset spoke of modern politics as a "*democracia morbosa.*" Unamuno (1921 [1912], 1928 [1924]) referred to the "agony of Christianity." According to Ludwig Klages (1929–32), the pragmatic and power-oriented human mind ("*Geist*") threatened the human soul ("*Seele*") with total destruction.[6] Husserl bewailed the "destruction of the Lebenswelt." T. S. Eliot (1934, 62, 53, 60) described his own age as "an age of unsettled beliefs and enfeebled tradition," in which "most people are [spiritually] only very little alive." He deplored the loss of community, authority, and traditional values under the attacks of radical individualism and materialism. He protested against "the aggrandizement . . . of personality" and spoke of "the living death of modern material civilization."

In his famous book on the "spiritual situation" of his age, written in 1932, on the eve of the fascist takeover in Germany, Jaspers (1965 [1932], 16, 76), summed up the crisis literature of his time and painted a fearful panorama of the ordeal of the human being and self in the modern world.

It has become a more and more general feeling that everything breaks down; everything has become uncertain and doubtful; nothing substantial has remained; there is an endless whirl of illusions and self-delusions by ideologies. . . . The consciousness of the end is, at the same time, the consciousness of the nothingness of our own existence. . . . One looks for the deeper foundation [of the experience of crisis] and one finds the crisis of the state; . . . or a cultural crisis as the disintegration of everything spiritual; or, finally, the crisis of human existence itself.

The majority of these visions emerged in the circle of thinkers whom we could broadly define as "conservative" but—seeing the dramatic spread of bolshevism and fascism, the economic crisis that crippled the world, the rising specter of a second world war, and later its aftermath—liberal and leftist thinkers, too, paid more and more attention to the signs of an approaching crisis of Western societies and Western civilization. Let me refer only to the Frankfurt School, especially to the works of Horkheimer (1947, 1972, 1978) and Adorno (1991), who were concerned about the invasion of Western civilization by the irrational and oppressive forces of totalitarianism and the manipulative powers of late capitalism.

After the end of the World War II, a strange mixture of victorious jubilation and new fears prevailed in the Western world. On the one hand, the victory of Western civilization, UN and UNESCO optimism, the praise of science and new technologies, and the moral grandeur of the events of 1956 and 1968 resounded all over the world. On the other hand, the Korean and Vietnam Wars, the Cold War, tribal and civil wars around the world, the oil and currency crises, the problems of the welfare state, waves of inflation and stagflation, increasing rates of criminality, unmanageable unemployment, alarming facts of environmental destruction, rapid population growth, increasing migrational pressures, the depletion of global resources, and other phenomena have generated an atmosphere of unease and uncertainty. A great number of studies and books were born within the genre of crisis literature. Albert Camus (1971 [1951] wrote about "the loss of transcendence," and Paul Ricoeur (1986) about "the withdrawal of sanctity from the world."[7]

Even the euphoria after the collapse of the Soviet Empire was soon mixed with voices of concern. "The world is at peace, but there is no peace," Richard Cohen wrote in 1993:

> All things are important because nothing is of paramount importance. There is no absolute right because absolute wrong is gone. History has not ended, it has simply been rendered chaotic, and we are afflicted with a kind of civic depression. When the Soviet Union collapsed, we Americans lost more than an enemy. We lost a collaborator in the search of meaning.

Alarm signals were ringing on the other side of the Atlantic Ocean as well. "Our planet is in distress," Edgar Morin (1993) wrote in *Le Monde*. We face "the gigantic problems of the end of Modern Times"; we live amid "the mortal dangers of our Damoclesian age"; "the possibilities of destruction and self-destruction" have never been greater; we witness "the alliance of two barbarisms, the old, virulent again, coming from the depths of prehistoric ages, and the new barbarism, glacial, anonymous, mechanistic, quantifying"; we have to cope with "the formidable challenges of a world in crisis."[8]

How should people shape and "actualize" their selves in this fearful world? Let me also quote someone who can certainly not be accused of a propensity for decadence, fin de siècle moods, or German-type *Weltschmerz* and *Kulturpessimismus*. In a lecture at Georgetown University, given in late 1990, Zbigniew Brzezinski (1990, 3, 7), expressing "a gnawing philosophical anxiety," stated:

> Democracy has won. The free market system has won. But what in the wake of this great ideological victory is today the substance of our beliefs? To what is the human being in the democratic West now truly committed? . . . [To] hedonistic relativism? . . . I think . . . this potential emptiness, if not yet the reality, is dangerous.

And all this has not been only an intellectual fad. Already in the 1970s and 1980s, even weekly picture magazines carried articles about a global "crisis of morality," the decay of traditional values, the crisis of identity, the threat of anarchy. The experience of the potential destruction of our civilization, the loss of the meaning of our lives, and existential and existentialist anxieties are conveyed today not only by highbrow absurd dramas and philosophical treatises but also by *Blade Runner*–type apocalyptic movies and hundreds and thousands of episodes of television horror series.[9]

One thing seems to be certain: The world, and Western civilization within it, is undergoing dramatic changes in our day. "The modern world-system is coming to an end. It will however require at least another 50 years of terminal crisis, that is of 'chaos,' before we can hope to emerge into a new social order," Wallerstein (1995, 485) writes. Eric Hobsbawm (1995, 584–85) portrays this transformation in even more apocalyptic terms:

> We live in a world captured, uprooted and transformed by the titanic economic and techno-scientific process of the development of capitalism,

which has dominated the past two or three centuries. We know, or at least it is reasonable to suppose, that it cannot go on *ad infinitum*. . . . We have reached a point of historic crisis. . . . The structures of human societies themselves, including even some of the social foundations of the capitalist economy, are on the point of being destroyed. . . . We do not know where we are going. . . . If humanity is to have a recognizable future, it cannot be by prolonging the past or the present. If we try to build the third millennium on that basis, we shall fail. And the price of failure, that is to say, the alternative to a changed society, is darkness.

There are scholars—let me mention here only Habermas (1979a, 1979b, 1979c, 1987a), Dahrendorf (1997), and Garton Ash (2004)—who reject these dark visions. They, too, see the problems and dangers, but they continue to believe in the great Project of Modernization. They do believe in the human reason and goodwill that have developed the institutions of liberal democracy and the market economy, the rule of law, the welfare state, and the system of human rights and that have improved the living standards of hundreds of millions of people around the world. Others, Popper or Hayek, for instance, are not adherents of the ideology of modernization; but they trust the common sense of a humankind that, through a process of trial and error, and by learning from its own mistakes, has been able, and it is hoped will be able, to solve its problems. It certainly has good chances of coping with the present critical situation as well.

Let me, however, develop a bit further the "crisis-argument" and see what would be the impact of this crisis—if there is any—on the human being and her or his strategies of caring for her or his self.

Answers

"Providing answers" is a basic function of civilizations.[10] They have to explain how the world came about; how we humans appeared in it, where our place is in it, and how we need to act to survive in it. They have to enlighten the basic forces that move and shape the universe. They have to delineate the boundaries of good and evil and help us cope with the disturbing facts of human suffering and mortality. They have to generate meaningful roles for us in our society, and possibly also in the universe. They have to define the basic values on which we can build our selves and communities. They have to convince us that our life has a purpose.

It is a symptom of crisis when a civilization is no longer capable of answering these questions. Without these answers and guidelines, people are left alone and unprotected in a world where there is a painful shortage of trust, security, human dignity, meaningful roles, authentic selves, a purpose for life, and faith in, or the illusion of, human immortality.

However, crises may be, and often are, followed by renewals. A civilization in crisis may generate new answers, new values, new norms of conduct, new roles, and new meanings. A renewal may ensue.

In our case—and this might be the usual pattern of civilizational changes—a dual tendency may be witnessed. The "crisis" is still in the phase of deepening, the traditional forms and structures of European civilization are still in a process of disintegration, but the search for new answers is already under way. The development of a new period, or version, of Western civilization may have started. This process is still ambiguous and contradictory, however.

A great number of traditional answers have lost their relevance, and most of the traditional institutions—such as the family, the church, the educational system, and the community of intellectuals—have lost their self-confidence and struggle with the problems of their own renewal. Their ability to provide relevant answers to the existential questions of people is still impaired and limited. This shortage, or absence, of relevant answers has thrown the gates wide open for new attempts to provide these answers.

The *totalitarian ideologies* of the first half of the twentieth century, for instance, may be understood as attempts at filling this gap, at seducing, conquering, and dominating the "lonely masses" by parading as the depositories of the new answers. Though the traditional institutions were less and less able to provide answers, fascism and bolshevism—in their own distorted and satanic way—promised an all-encompassing explanation of the world, a holistic worldview, the knowledge of good and evil, new identities, new certainties, the power and the safety of the collectivity, new roles, fulfillment for the human self, new significance, freedom, the victory of justice, and the final happiness of humankind. We know that they rushed the world into a bloody and destructive frenzy. But in their expansive period, they responded to the questions and anxieties of their adherents, tens or hundreds of millions of people, and enthralled them thereby for decades.

The *fundamentalist movements* of the twentieth and twenty-first centuries have had a similar—but in most cases less dangerous—appeal. They, too, have promised a comprehensive explanation of human life, the hope of a just world or a just next world, personal fulfillment and salvation. At the same time, the traditional ideologies of the Western world—liberalism, conservatism, and social democracy—have offered only partial answers to particular economic, political, or social problems and—as a virtue or a mistake—they have kept aloof from speculating about the "ultimate questions" of human life.

Beside these movements and ideologies, two new variants of Western civilization emerged in the second half of the twentieth century. They, too, have offered all-comprising, though fragmented, visions of the world and have offered—in their specific ways—answers to the fundamental questions of human existence and the human self. The first is called "postmodernity," or postmodern civilization; the other is referred to as "consumer civilization." In the following chapters, I shall focus my attention on the latter one and shall study its role in shaping people's lives and selves. But first, I also have to say a few words about postmodern civilization. My reason for doing so is the fact that—though there are scholars who consider these two variants of Western civilization as opposed to each other—they are closely intertwined—so much so that in a great number of cases, one cannot know if one has to do with an element of postmodern or consumer civilization.

The Modern–Postmodern Dilemma

In spite of the difficulties, a great number of scholars have tried to distinguish modernity from postmodernity.[11] Some of them speak of a historical change and consider postmodernism as the civilization of the postindustrial age or late capitalism (Lyotard 1984; Rose 1991; Jameson 1991). Lash (1990) defines it as a "cultural paradigm," "cultural formation," or "regime of signification." Others describe it as a style, spirituality, approach, or "mood" characteristic of contemporary Western societies. Baudrillard (1998) speaks of a special "logic" that governs the "postmodern economy."[12] Others deal, with "postmodern politics"[13] as well as with "postmodern sociology."[14] There is confusion, or at least perplexity, even about the terms used in this field. According to Featherstone (1991), "postmodernity" may refer to a historical period; "postmodernization" to a process of change; and "postmodernism" to a new sensibility, way of thinking, or style.

More and more scholars question the independent historical status of postmodernity. They see in it the crisis or the fulfillment of modernity, a "radicalized" or "high" modernity (Giddens 1990, 150; Bertens 1995, 248); a critical transitional period within modernity (Lash 1990, 116); a modernity that "has turned its critical rationality upon itself" Bertens 1995, 247); the "clash" between "the universalizing and simultaneously self-destructive tendencies of modernity" (Bertens 1995, 245); "a way of describing . . . struggles with diverse and complex manifestations of a modernity that is still very much with us" (Smart 1993, 141); or "a fully developed modernity," a "modernity conscious of its true nature," a "modernity emancipated from false consciousness" (Bauman 1992, 187–88).

The picture is just as complex and contradictory if we try to distinguish modernity from postmodernity on the basis of their main features. According to various authors, modernity is characterized by a strong and autonomous human self, whereas the postmodern self is changing and "de-centered" (Bertens 1995, 214). Modernity tends to sharply differentiate the various domains of reality—matter and spirit, the individual and the community, life and art, the signifier and the signified—whereas postmodernity moves in the opposite direction: It blurs differences; it "de-differentiates." Modernity is discursive; it works with networks of concepts and causal chains. Postmodernity is a world of images, allusions, metaphors. Modernity strives for order, stability, and predictability, whereas postmodernity is fascinated by the unpredictable, the ephemeral, and the evanescent. Modernity is in quest for universal laws; postmodernity sees the world as fragmented, chaotic, and contingent. According to modernity, reality can be grasped, represented, and understood, whereas the postmodern mind flashes between the various aspects and experiments of an ever-changing world.

However, we should not overemphasize this contrast, because more and more scholars discover in modernity, and in other ages, features that we have just described as characteristically postmodern. They argue that modernity has ever been characterized by a fundamental duality. Two opposite trends, both with their characteristically "modern" versus "postmodern" features, have ever been intertwined in it. Giddens (1990, 49) speaks in this context of the "enigmatic core" of modernity. According to Bertens (1995, 242), modernity has ever had two contradictory "modes of thought—the one expansionist, transcendent, and omni-representational , the other self-reflexive, inward spiraling, and anti-representational."

Logically, these two tendencies exclude, but historically they have well complemented, one another. This duality has even become stronger nowadays than it was earlier. On the one hand, the search for the universal laws of the world and for the global norms of human behavior and cooperation is still going on with great momentum. On the other hand, postmodern tendencies keep "deconstructing" this self-conscious, rational universalism and propose a more pluralistic, relativistic, and ironical approach to the world and the human person.

There are scholars who see in the increasingly intense struggle of these two visions of the world the final development and fulfillment of modernity; others interpret it as its crisis. There are experts who argue that the self-reflexive tendency, which was always present in modernity, has become so strong that it is justified to speak of a new, postmodern period in the history of Western civilization. The timing of this shift is controversial. There are experts who discover a strong postmodern character already in Baudelaire's reflexivity, relativism, and irony[15]; others consider late-nineteenth-century decadence, or early-twentieth-century vanguard movements, as the first postmodern experiments. The end of World War II, the collapse of colonialism, and the weakening of Western hegemony; the spread of various human rights movements; the events of 1968; and the works of Kuhn, Foucault, Derrida, and others have also been pointed out as watersheds between modernism and postmodernism.[16]

The complexity of these processes warns us to proceed with caution when we start to analyze the other great response to the crisis of Western civilization, a response that we have proposed calling "consumer civilization." First, we must be cautious because consumer civilization is as difficult to define and to mark off from the previous stage of Western civilization as was the case with postmodernity. And second, we must be cautious because postmodernism and consumer civilization are closely intertwined. They both have been responses to the same critical situation in the Western world, they overlap in time, and in spite of sharp differences, they have a wide range of common characteristics. They are present, and mix, in the lifestyles, mentalities, and attitudes of contemporary people and societies. Later in this book, we will discuss the multiplication of the human self, the sparkling fireworks of roles, the simultaneous apotheosis and destruction of the human personality, the uncertainties of human history, the "loss of transcendence," the "cult of intensity," the importance of "boundary situations," the "reenchantment of the world"—all these are fundamental features of postmodernity as well as of the civilization of consumption. Let alone the fact that some of the outstanding students of postmodernism—Lyotard, Baudrillard, Jameson, Bauman, and others—describe the basic characteristics of postmodernity by analyzing various phenomena of the consumer society.

Consumer civilization keeps broadcasting its values and ideas twenty-four hours a day to hundreds of millions of people around the world. It trumpets the principle, the duty, the bliss of self-realization around the clock. It broadcasts a message that resembles—in a superficial or substantial way, we shall see—that of the Renaissance of yore. It has created a new mythology and a new lifestyle, which have already engulfed the world.

A Questionable Parallel

Historians generally agree that in the fourteenth century, Europe was shaken by a grave political, economic, and intellectual crisis, and that the Renaissance and the Reformation, emerging in the next two centuries, and launching the "modern age," were responses to this crisis.

I argue in this chapter that nowadays we are experiencing simultaneously the crisis of this new, "modern" variant of Western civilization, and, at the same time, in a certain sense, its ultimate golden age and fulfillment. Or, more exactly—as we have already mentioned—modernization has been a complex process in which various trends were intertwined: secularization, rationalization, individuation, industrialization, the development of the institutions of democracy and the market economy, and so on. In the second half of the twentieth century, important progress was achieved in all these fields, but serious changes also occurred. We may even speak of the mutation of certain fundamental characteristics of the civilization of modernity. I shall focus on the changes in lifestyles, attitudes, and visions of the world and shall argue that these changes can be best described as the resurgence, or consummation, of some of the basic ideas of the Renaissance—the resurgence of its vision of the world and the situation of the human being within it.

There are, of course, crucial differences between the two periods. One of the most important difference is that in the fifteenth and sixteenth centuries, the Renaissance was the culture of the very rich and educated few: kings, princes, popes, prelates, patricians, and the scholars and artists surrounding them;[17] whereas its late-twentieth-century variant became the culture of hundreds of millions of people around the world. This is why I propose to call this age, and this variant of the Renaissance, the "Renaissance of the Masses" or, more provocatively, the "Proletarian Renaissance."[18]

I am fully aware that by doing so I am entering a danger zone. A great number of objections come immediately to mind. Let me mention a few of them.

First, representatives of positivist historiography would certainly argue that the Renaissance was a historical age of its own, with its complex and specific economic, social, political, and cultural structures, and so it is unacceptable to apply this concept to an age in a radically different historical context.

Second, a cultural historian—with a penchant for *Geistesgeschichte*—might object that the Renaissance was a special and unique time-spirit (*Zeitgeist*), a vision of the world that could develop only in a given historical and cultural context.

Third, an expert in art history might claim that the Renaissance was a specific style, which could be only copied in another age. And she or he would add that there are only sporadic traces to be found of this style in late-twentieth-century Western art.

Fourth, further critics could claim that, on the level of superficial comparisons, it would be possible to find similarities with other ages as well. I will come back to this issue just below.

Without disputing the relevance of these objections, I still wish to argue that, mutatis mutandis, there is an obvious and more than accidental similarity between the fifteenth- and sixteenth-century Renaissance, on the one hand, and the attitudes, belief systems, lifestyles, *Weltanschauung,* and code of behavior of people in today's Western-style societies, on the other. The decisive difference being—as I have just pointed out—that the Renaissance was a par excellence elitist culture, available only to the outstandingly rich and educated few, whereas the "Proletarian Renaissance" is a culture of the masses, the culture of hundreds of millions of consumers around the world.

I think that, within certain limits, it is worthwhile developing this comparison because it may throw new light on the radical transformation that is taking place in our Western civilization, that is, in the social and cultural framework within which people have to care for their selves, construct their selves. We have to proceed, however, with the utmost caution.

Beyond the objections mentioned above, caution is justified also by the fact that it is difficult to clearly define the two poles of the comparison. Both the "Renaissance" and the "Proletarian Renaissance" are vague and complex notions and, as a consequence, it is questionable if they can serve at all as points of comparison for each other—and whether this comparison may help us better understand the human condition, and the problems of self-construction in our own age. Let us first look at the concept of the "Renaissance."

The Renaissance

In one of the best essays ever written on the Renaissance, and more particularly on the history of the concept of Renaissance, Huizinga (1959b) demonstrates how difficult, if not impossible, it is to precisely define what is meant, or should be meant, by "Renaissance." He states that "neither in time, extent, content, nor significance is the concept Renaissance defined. It suffers from vagueness, incompleteness, and chance, and yet is at the same time a dangerous, doctrinaire schematization. It is almost an unusable term."[19] How could, and should, we then use it as a point of reference for the study of our contemporary civilization?

The difficulty is increased by the fact that in the course of the past three centuries, the Renaissance has been defined in many and contradictory ways. According to Huizinga,

[the] Renaissance was the emergence of individualism, the awakening of the urge to beauty, the triumph of worldliness and *joie de vivre,* the conquest of mundane reality by the mind, the revival of a pagan zest for life, the developing consciousness of the personality in its natural relation to the world.[20]

It has also been described as a "stylistic term," or as "a cultural concept," "the expression of an attitude of life, . . . a notion of life, a rod and staff for all mankind, not merely a technical term for historians."[21] It has been studied as "the restoration of *bonnes lettres,*[22] the "Revival of Antiquity,"[23] one of the "four happy ages" of mankind,[24] an autonomous and "circumscribed cultural period,"[25] "a form of life" and "a cultural ideal *sui generis.*"[26] Which definition should we use in our attempt at comparing the Renaissance of the fifteenth and sixteenth centuries and the "Proletarian Renaissance" of the late-twentieth and early-twenty-first centuries?

Since Burckhardt, the Renaissance has been more and more identified with the epiphany of the human personality and the first explosion of Western-type individualism, with its program of "self-actualization" (though this term is a more recent coinage). This could be an important link between the Renaissance and the Proletarian Renaissance. However, according to Huizinga, historical facts do not justify the image of the Renaissance as *the* age of victorious and glorious individualism. "As long as individualism appears to have been just as much a dominating factor in history long before and long after the Renaissance, one would do better to declare it taboo."[27] It is not at all certain, he adds, that "the individualism of the Renaissance accepted out-of-hand is such a useful hypothesis as it seems at first glance."[28]

Huizinga speaks also of the difficulty of delimiting the Renaissance in time, as a historical period, because various scholars extended it back to the Middle Ages,[29] and others made it a forerunner of modernity, the prototype of the modern human being—in this way vaporizing its historical boundaries.

He argues also that, in many important points, the Renaissance was not at all "modern"; it was not "pagan," it was not "secularized."[30] It did not revolt against authority in general: "The turning point did not come until Descartes."[31] It is also completely false and mistaken to identify the Middle Ages with an ascetic rejection of the world, a *contemptus mundi,* and the Renaissance with an exuberant joy of life. On the one hand, "medieval Christian thought never rejected the world in its beauty and its pleasures as is usually assumed." And on the other, "was the basic tone of most representatives of the Renaissance not much graver than we imagine? The victory (was it a Pyrrhic victory?) of basic optimism came . . . only with the eighteenth century."[32] The (modern) belief in, and worship of, progress came also much later. "The two forms in which optimistic thought found embodiment, the concept of progress and that of evolution, were neither of them Renaissance forms. Also in this it is not at all possible to place the Renaissance on one level with modern culture."[33] Furthermore:

> The Renaissance was a turning of the tide. The image for the transition from the Middle Ages to modern times is (and how could it help but be?) not that of one revolution of a great wheel, but that of a long succession of waves rolling onto a beach, each of them breaking at a different point and a different moment.[34]

And his conclusion:

> But where, then, does the Renaissance stand? Certainly not on the modern side.[35] . . . The spirit of the Renaissance is indeed much less modern than one is constantly inclined to believe.[36]

If Huizinga is right, this could be one more reason to be very cautious with comparisons between the Renaissance and our contemporary "consumer civilization"; and between the Renaissance cult of the human personality and our contemporary rage about actualizing ourselves. Or, just on the contrary, could the nonmodernity, or premodernity, of the Renaissance help us better understand the eventual nonmodernity, or "postmodernity" of our own age?

Huizinga was a great admirer of Burckhardt, but he also argued against the acceptance of the ideal type of the "Renaissance Man" as it had been drawn by his famous predecessor. "It is a vain ambition to want to describe *the* man of the Renaissance," he contended.[37]

According to Burckhardt, the "Renaissance Man" was characterized by an "unbridled individualism tending toward a complete amorality; a subjective attitude toward religion—tolerant, skeptical, mocking, sometimes rejecting outright; and the paganism of the Renaissance, an admixture of ancient superstition and modern skepticism."[38] This portrait was further developed by

Burckhardt's followers and—Huizinga contends—soon took a demonic and Nietzschean turn. The Renaissance Man was portrayed then as being "demonic in his unbending pride, self-satisfied and audacious, the *uomo singolare,* the *'unique man.'*" He was imagined as a "free personality of genius, elevated above doctrines and morals, the haughty, frivolous man of pleasure who in a pagan passion for beauty seized the power to live according to his own norms."[39] He was portrayed as a man characterized by a "passion for fame . . . bravery . . . vanity . . . feeling of style . . . pride . . . enthusiasm . . . critical sense"[40] and by "the endeavor to give expression to one's life and personality by consciously developing all the abilities and potentialities one has; the awareness of personal independence and the fatal delusion of a right to earthly happiness."[41]

Huizinga proposes a much more complex approach, emphasizing the contradictions within the characters of the protagonists of the Renaissance:

> The Renaissance was one of the triumphs of the Romance spirit. Whoever wants to understand it must be susceptible to the Romance combination of stoic seriousness and a clearly focused will (occupied with quite other things than the "full expression of the personality") with light, happy gaiety; rich, broad good nature; and naïve irresponsibility. He must be able to give up seeking everywhere for the soul in order to experience a violent, direct interest in things for their own sake. He must be able to enjoy the essence of things in *their form beautiful.* Behind a countenance by Holbein or Anthony More he must be able to suspect the laughter of Rabelais.[42]

Does one or the other of these two portraits resemble our contemporary self-actualizing selves? Yes and no. There are many similarities ("pride," "self-satisfaction," "vanity," hedonism, "a passion for fame," "happy gaiety," "naïve irresponsibility"), but some essential Renaissance features seem to be missing, or to be much weaker, in us. I think, for instance, of being "demonic," "brave," and "audacious," "free personalities of genius" with "a pagan passion for beauty"; or having the spirituality of Holbein's pictures and the power and irony of Rabelais' Gargantuan laughter.

Given the vagueness of the concept of the Renaissance, we have several options. First, we may abandon our project of studying our contemporary civilization in the light of a comparison with the Renaissance as irrelevant or unfeasible. Second, in spite of justified caveats, we may try to use the Burck-hardtian ideal type, or another Renaissance model, as a point of reference and see if it helps us (or not) better understand the human condition, and the human self, in our own age. Third, we may accept Huizinga's warning that it is "a vain ambition to want to describe *the* man of the Renaissance,"[43] but we may select some individual features that certainly were characteristic of the main personalities of the Renaissance (or in some cases only of the ideal picture they had of themselves), and use these features as points of comparison when we discuss the parallels between the Renaissance and the Proletarian Renaissance. Fourth, we may use Huizinga's model, with its complexity and contradictions; this, too, may turn out to be a relevant comparison because our own age is also characterized by contradictions and a high level of complexity.

As a matter of fact, with the exception of the first alternative, I shall avail myself of all these options, cross-checking them with one another. But before doing so, I have two tasks. First, I have to say a few words about the relationship of the Renaissance and the Reformation because they were the two main responses to the crisis of Western civilization in the fifteenth (pre-Reformation movements) and sixteenth centuries and their influence in shaping human lives and selves ran parallel throughout the next four centuries of this civilization. Second, I have to reduce the vagueness of the concept of the "Proletarian Renaissance," or "consumer civilization," by drawing its boundaries as clearly as possible. This is a precondition for a relevant comparison of our own age with any other periods or variants of Western civilization.

Renaissance and Reformation

Responding to the crisis of late medieval feudalism, two great spiritual movements developed in the fifteenth and sixteenth centuries, which were to renew traditional European civilization: the Renaissance and the Reformation.[44] They had many common elements (e.g., their emphasis on the importance of human autonomy and human personality), but they embarked on different courses. They were in opposition not only to the Great Tradition but also to each other; they struggled with each other, but at the same time they were intertwined in a complex way. Both of them had a decisive role to play during the centuries that followed. The Renaissance developed a new vision of the world, a new ideal of the human self, and a new life strategy, which—as parts of a more or less latent undercurrent—played an important role throughout the subsequent centuries but—after a strange mutation—emerged as a dominant ideology only in the second half of the twentieth century. In the fifteenth and sixteenth centuries, as we have mentioned, they were adopted only by the very rich—the Medicis, Sforzas, and Pope Julians—who could afford this new lifestyle of self-actualization, and the apotheosis of the human personality.[45]

The "common people" had to wait and work hard another four or five centuries until, in the second half of the twentieth century, the material, social, and cultural conditions were attained that enabled them to switch over to a new variant of the Renaissance lifestyle. In the meantime, they had lived according to a different set of norms defined by a mixture of traditional European civilization, the Reformation, and modernization.

In its own way, Protestantism was just as much a new religion and ideology of self-fulfillment as the Renaissance. The individual, the human personality, broke out of the ideological and social constraints of the Great Tradition and took the courage to face God on his or her own. This face-to-face meeting with God boosted one's sense of value and dignity, but at the same time it also brought a torturing feeling of guilt, a tormenting awareness of human fallibility. There was no question of an immediate, joyous, victorious self-fulfillment, as in the circles of the Renaissance. First, the puritan "Soldiers of Christ" had to conquer the world; and to do so, the norms of moral discipline had to be pulled tighter than ever—the norms of self-restraint, self-control, asceticism, service, and self-sacrifice had to be strictly observed and implemented.

Protestantism played a decisive role in shaping Western minds and attitudes, and Western history in general for centuries, and it handed over its leading role to the "Renaissance of the masses" only in the second half of the twentieth century. Only then came the time for the masses to enjoy the fruits of their work without worries, or feeling of guilt—in an age when the ideals, lifestyle, and behavioral codes of the Renaissance have become the general norm as a sort of *gesunkenes Kulturgut*.[46] Only now, in the age of the "Proletarian Renaissance," can people live lives of self-fulfillment and self-actualization à la Renaissance, or at least have the illusion that they are doing so.[47]

Other Comparisons

Is it justified to posit a special relationship between the Renaissance of the fifteenth and sixteenth centuries and our contemporary civilization on the basis of these superficial and substantial similarities? Could not other parallels be drawn between the Renaissance and other periods of the history of Western civilization? There certainly are such links between the Renaissance and the Age of Enlightenment, Romanticism, or Decadence. And continuities and links could also be found between our contemporary civilization and various previous periods of European history. Franz Borkenau (1981, 332–43), for instance, argued that there is an important relationship between medieval monasticism and modernity.[48] Lewis Mumford (1963, 263 and passim) compared the medieval "carnivalesque" with certain features of late-twentieth-century consumer civilization.[49]

We could also speak of "Proletarian Romanticism," because the romantic cult of the individual is, in a certain sense, the forerunner of the contemporary apotheosis of the human self.[50] Romanticism and consumer civilization are related also by the fact that they both are elitist and populist at the same time. On the one hand, Romanticism was elitist in having discovered the sources of freedom, the meaning and mystery of life, in the genius of the great artists; and it was populist in having discovered all this also in the communities of simple uncorrupted people (*das Volk*). Consumer civilization, on the other hand, is elitist with its star cult, that is, by suggesting that only stars are able to live life in its fullness and with its highest intensity; while it is populist by offering to everybody, to the masses of the Proletarian Renaissance, the possibility of unlimited self-realization (ultimately by identification with the stars). The two ages are related also by the fact that they have both discovered beauty in the horrendous, fascinating power of the evil and demonic. And they resemble each other also in their cult of emotions, sentiments, and sentimental dramas (a contemporary variant of these latter are nowadays called "soap operas"), though Romanticism was much more cautious and shy in venturing into the depths of instincts than is our civilization of consumption.

Various parallels could be drawn also with the Age of the Baroque (with its cult of parades, the spectacular, the theatrical illusion, the irrational, and the mystical), with Bauadelairian dandyism, or fin de siècle decadence. We shall see in chapter 12 that we could also speak of a strange kind of "Proletarian Existentialism." Most of these links could and should be explored, because any of them may shed light on some important features of our contemporary civilization and the human condition in it. But I think that the relationship between the Renaissance and our contemporary civilization is stronger and more substantial than any of the parallels we have just mentioned, for at least four reasons.

First, the material conditions of a Renaissance lifestyle are now given to tens and hundreds of millions of affluent and modestly affluent people living mainly in the developed world, but sporadically also in other parts and societies of the world (mainly those who live near the centers and corridors of globalization).

Second, until the second half of the twentieth century, there was never an age in the known history of humankind in which consumption was—beyond being a necessity and a means of survival—also a means of self-fulfillment not only for a small elite but also for the majority of people.

Third, there has never been an age in which self-fulfillment was an individual and not a communal project for the majority of people; that is, an age in which so many human beings try to actualize themselves directly, by "constructing" their personalities, and not by serving others or doing their duty in the community.

Fourth, there may have never been an age in which an open, boisterous, and uninhibited individualism, exempt from any feeling of guilt, was the main attitude of the majority of people.

Proletarian Renaissance

Before starting to develop the parallel between the Renaissance and the "Proletarian Renaissance," we have to make a decision. The question is how broadly or narrowly we draw the outlines of the "Proletarian Renaissance." Do we define it as covering only the sphere of consumption, and the masses that are under the spell of the consumer industries? Or do we use it in a broader sense and say that the spirit, the values, the lifestyle, and the life strategies of the Proletarian Renaissance permeate contemporary Western life as a whole? No one can withdraw her self or his self from its influence. In one way or another, everybody lives in this civilization, struggles with the problems of this civilization, tries to find her or his place, and the answers to the problems of her or his life, within this civilization—whoever she or he is: a farmer or a banker; a skilled worker or a nuclear physicist; a film director, scientist, or philosopher; a student or the president of a multinational corporation.

I propose to work with this broader concept, mainly because it would be a mistake to make an anachronistic attempt to oppose "high" culture to "low" culture. The dividing line between the two domains has been washed away by the media and mass communications to an extent never experienced before.[51]

Having enumerated a great number of possible objections, I think we have developed the right frame of mind for exploring the analogies that may exist between the Renaissance of yore and the Proletarian Renaissance of our own days. We are already armed with sufficient skepticism for not taking this comparison too seriously. And, at the same time, we may learn something new by studying the tempting similarities between two periods, and/or variants, of Western civilization.

These similarities are striking, but they may be spurious. The danger of drawing false parallels is great. Before dismissing them as such, however, we must take a closer look at them.[52] Let us start with a few superficial and trivial similarities.

Millions of people live today in a way that only the extremely rich could afford in the old days. In the fifteenth and sixteenth centuries, for instance, only the richest of the rich had a bathroom with running hot water in it, and it needed a whole army of servants to operate it. A hundred years later, Louis XIV may have been the Sun King, but not many of us would exchange our bathrooms for his (though some of us would hesitate seeing the golden bathtub in his majesty's cabinet).

During the Renaissance, only aristocrats, high priests, and rich merchants could afford garments made of colorful and delicate fabrics, silk or velvet. Only they could afford to pay for these luxuries, and in many cases only they had the right to wear this ostentatious and incredibly expensive clothing.[53] Common people wore gray, black, or white clothes made from frieze or flax. Even today, a teenager with a modest income wears fine textiles, (artificial) silk and velvet, let alone the dazzling array of colors displayed by them. The fashion queens of the Renaissance, a Catharine de Médici or a Mary Stuart, would be amazed—and perhaps also green with envy—at the sight of the wardrobes of our teenage girls. The final shock would come when they perceived the shoes: A dozen pairs of slippers, and what fantastic shapes and designs, my God!

The majority of people in those centuries did not have to go through the morning ordeal of choosing the clothes that would best fit the role and personality they intended to play that day because they had one suit of clothes, or two at the most, one for everyday use and one for the holidays. These latter were sophisticated and ornate in certain regions of Europe, and so they could strengthen their owners' self-esteem, displaying and reconfirming their social status. But due to the fact that fashions changed much slower in those times, at least in the lower and middle layers of society, clothing may have helped people much less in experimenting with various roles and selves than they do nowadays.

In the age of the Renaissance, only the privileged, the nobility and high clergy, could move around in comfortable carriages, called *carosses* in French. Nowadays, most of us have a carriage, which we call a car, that even the richest and most powerful lords of the Renaissance would envy. The body of the car is still called in French, and in other languages, a *carosserie*. Today we have the People's Car, the Volkswagen. Back in the Renaissance, there was no Volkscarosse.

In those days, only kings, princes, and bishops had the opportunity to fight boredom by calling their clowns, storytellers, and jesters to perform for them. Today, at the push of a button, the best comedians of the world start their antics on our TV screens. We are more powerful and more ruthless than the worst Renaissance lords and ladies could have ever been; in the first instant of our dissatisfaction, we dismiss or kill the histrionics—though not by sending them to the gallows, but simply and less painfully—by zipping to another channel.

Music was also a rare delicacy, the privilege of noblemen, high-ranking churchmen, and patricians. Only they could have music in the background during lunch and dinner. Ordinary people had no means to afford this luxury; they danced only at weddings and feasts, to the sound of a lonely bagpipe or a fiddle. Today, even the poorest among us may listen to Beethoven's

Ninth Symphony, or to the latest hits from Hollywood or New Orleans; obeying our electronic demons, called Walkmen or compact disc players, we have all the musicians, bands, orchestras, and stars of the world dutifully at our disposal.

In the fifteenth and sixteenth centuries, even the richest had only a few dozen, or a few hundred, books (Shakespeare listed even his last saucepan in his will, but he did not mention one single book). Poor people could afford a copy of the Bible, at most. Later, they were able to purchase broadsides at a fair and—mutatis mutandis—these entertained and thrilled them practically with the same kinds of horror and love stories that our tabloid press and commercial TV channels entertain us with today.

The ideal of the Renaissance was a human being who—by exposing herself or himself to a great variety of impulses, various civilizations, authors, ideas, works of art, languages, and exercises—constructed for herself or himself a rich and many-sided personality. This versatility is perhaps even a stronger imperative today. The contemporary middle-class descendants of the Renaissance are continuously urged to develop their skills, to explore all the possibilities of the world, to experiment with the widest range of human experiences possible. They are being flooded with opportunities and prompts as to what they could and should learn, what they should test, where they should travel, what skills they should develop, what adventures they should embark on.

All this is, of course, only the surface. Similarities between the two eras go much deeper, and are far more essential.

The Great Transformation

There is a striking similarity in the way in which people in the fifteenth and sixteenth centuries, and in the second half of the twentieth century, respectively, turned away from the so-called Great Tradition. The new norms, the new values, and the new lifestyle emerging in our contemporary civilization have a surprising resemblance to those of the Renaissance.

Table 9.1 presents, in schematic form, the dramatic transformation that took place in the second half of the twentieth century. The column on the left lists the basic tenets, norms, and codes of behavior of traditional Western civilization; the one on the right contains those of late-twentieth-century consumer civilization. It may be observed that the concepts in the two columns clash sharply and are often the opposites of one another.[54]

It is true, of course, that in reality this transformation was not so instantaneous and abrupt. The conditions that made the emergence of the Proletarian Renaissance possible evolved gradually in the course of several centuries, together with the slow and gradual transformation of the traditional European civilization by the process of modernization. It is also true that the Renaissance ideals had a certain radiation, and a certain influence, throughout these four centuries. But the majority of people, especially those who lived in the European countryside, in small villages and small towns, continued to live essentially in their traditional culture, according their traditional values. For them, the great transformation, the crucial leap forward, the cultural explosion took place only recently, in the second half of the twentieth century. This justifies, to a certain degree, the direct, and unhistorical, comparison of traditional and contemporary values in table 9.1.

Two fundamentally different civilizations, or stages of civilization, confront each other here.[55] The first set of norms, that of the traditional ones, prompts and helps us construct ourselves as a communitarian, responsible, law abiding, unselfish, self-sacrificing person, with the drama of sin–guilt–repentance–redemption–eternal life as the main structuring force of our lives.

The other set of principles constructs us as a self-centered, dynamic, self-actualizing, hedonistic or Epicurean self, preoccupied with self-fulfillment and worldly success, being convinced of our own innocence and fundamental right to optimize our life.

These are two different, if not opposite, models of conduct and self-construction. They give us different commands, they govern our behavior, they set our priorities and shape our life strategies in different ways. Being under the influence of the one or the other, we see the world, act, speak, smile, behave, and care for our self in different ways.

The two sets of norms, opposed to one another, are not necessarily self-exclusive. We may work and at the same time enjoy our lives. We may do our duty and at the same time fight for our rights. Or we can even actualize ourselves by sacrificing ourselves for others. But in a number of situations of our everyday

TABLE 9.1

The Great Transformation

Traditional Principles	→	New Principle
Love thy neighbor!		Love thyself!
Sacrifice yourself!		Actualize yourself!
Discipline yourself!		Enjoy yourself!
You are guilty. Repent!		You are innocent!
Save! Be thrifty!		Consume!
Live in a world of scarcity!		Live in a world of abundance!
Obey! Conform!		Be free and autonomous!
Be modest!		Be successful!
Punish yourself!		Spoil yourself!
Do your duty!		Fight for your rights!
Take care!		Take a risk!

lives, these two sets of norms clash with, and extinguish, one another. And ultimately they suggest to us two fundamentally different attitudes, two different ways of behaving ourselves.

In traditional societies, life was under the constant pressure of the necessities of *survival,* leaving almost no time and energy for other things, and determining people's lifestyles, conduct, aspirations, and visions of the world. Human communities kept socializing their members for this struggle; the moral system was defined by this same purpose; the same life strategy was taught in the family, in the church, at school. People were encouraged or even forced to restrain their desires, discipline their selves, work, and do their duty.

Today, the opposite is the ideology and the rule. Instead of self-restraint and self-discipline, the curbing of one's instincts and desires, our contemporary civilization sings the praise of freedom, self-actualization, and unrestrained enjoyment of life. Hundreds of millions of people work on *fulfilling their lives* with the help of pop culture and New Age experiments, aerobics and jeans, slimming cures and perfumes, globe trotting and football games, soap operas and action movies. There is a feverish search for the wholeness of life. People want to achieve a full and authentic self and a meaningful existence here, on earth, within the short span of their lives.

In our traditional Western civilization, the principle of *love thyself*, in its meaning of today, would have sounded like an absurdity; it could have been understood even as the principle of Satan. Self-contempt, self-hate, self-mortification, self-punishment, self-tormenting, the destruction of one's worldly self, were the legitimate attitudes and acts. In our contemporary civilization, these attitudes and acts are considered pathological, and our psychologists, psychoanalysts, gurus, the media, and hundreds of self-help books keep trying to cure us of these pathologies. However, the situation is not so simple as that. The deeply religious philosopher, Søren Kierkegaard, wrote in the mid–nineteenth century: "Don't forget to love yourself." And in spite of the severe warnings of the prophets, the Rules of Saint Benedict, the admonitions of Saint Bernard, or the puritanical rigor of later centuries, the message of the Old and the New Testaments was certainly not that one had to hate oneself. They told the faithful this: "Love thy neighbor as thou lovest thyself," and the emphasis may have been both on the "thy neighbor" and on "thyself." But this was a different love of one's self than we exercise nowadays.

In traditional Western civilization, the drama of sin–guilt–penitence–salvation played a central role.[56] Today's consumer culture praises the *paradise-like innocence of humans;* there is no place in this culture for sin or the feeling of guilt as moral or psychic organizing principles. Sin is considered a kind of illness, a distortion, and a guilty conscience is simply a neurosis. "Lately I've been feeling guilty about my guilt feelings," says Ziggy, the cartoon character, echoing the dilemma of millions of contemporary people.[57]

Traditional society was organized in a *hierarchical* way, based on the principles of loyalty, patience, and the *acceptance of one's fate*. Today, almost everything pushes people in the opposite direction. One should not accept the place into which one was born; one should break out of the iron cage of constraints and aim for more, defeat everybody and every obstacle.

To a certain extent, and in a special way, most of these changes seem to relate today's "Proletarian Renaissance" to the Renaissance of the fifteenth and sixteenth centuries.

Harmony and Disharmony

The Renaissance was not only an idyllic age of harmony, the joy of life, exuberance, and the epiphany of the glorious human personality. It was also an age of wild enmities, bloody conflicts, and great contrasts. Destructive wars burned down proud cities and turned the idyllic landscapes that served as backgrounds for Leonardo's or Raphael's pictures into killing fields. Ruthless interests and foul conspiracies decimated the princes and courtiers of Renaissance courts, and plagues afflicted the inhabitants of the cities. An uncompromising struggle was going on in the world of ideas as well. The "humanists" and the "physicians,"[58] the disciples of Plato and Aristotle, idealists and naturalists, Thomas More and Machiavelli, Catholics and Protestants, the followers of the popes and those of the emperors were battling, cursing, denouncing, and excommunicating one another. This age simultaneously glorified the human personality and broke human beings on the wheel, to the delight of other human beings standing around the scaffold.

This sharp contrast between the epiphany and the destruction of the human personality, happiness and horror, harmony and disharmony, light and darkness, idealism and materialism, faith and skepticism is just as characteristic of our own age as it was of the Renaissance. On the one hand, the twentieth century was the victorious century of technological and economic development that multiplied human opportunities (and this time, it was not only Florence and Venice that achieved a fantastic affluence, but also hundreds of cities and dozens of countries from New York to Tokyo). But, on the other hand, it was also a frightening and bloody century, full of wars and genocide, economic and social crises, despair and doubt. The fundamental values, norms, and ideals of Western civilization have been shattered to their foundations.

A deep duality characterized the Renaissance, just as it characterizes our own age. On the one hand, they both proclaimed the magnificence of the human being and its (not necessarily physical) central position in a wonderful and exciting world. On the other hand, both in the Renaissance courts and in our contemporary cities, people were and are overwhelmed again and again by the anxiety that humankind is but an insignificant spot in an empty and dark universe. Both ages believed that the world was governed by the rational order of universal laws and ideas; they believed that the universe and the human mind were governed by one and the same set of laws. But, at the same time, they stood as helpless as we do in face of the absurdity, irrationality, and cruelty of the world.[59]

This duality is well reflected in the opposite worlds of the great Renaissance thinkers and artists, in those of Ficino versus Montaigne and Lipsius, Erasmus versus Machiavelli, Botticelli versus Bosch, Thomas More versus Rabelais. Elizabethan drama is perhaps the best mirror of this contrast of the world of the tragic and the comic. Some of the plays were full of the unmitigated joy of life, such as *Much Ado About Nothing* and *The Merry Wives of Windsor;* others, such as Seneca's gloomy dramas, or the tragedies of Webster, Ford, Marlow, and Shakespeare, were tragic visions of the misery and absurdity of human life.

The same, or a similar, duality radiates from the central source of light and darkness in our age, television. It broadcasts a dream world, the joy and heavenly harmony of soap operas and commercials, the hymns of human beauty and glory. But we also see hell breaking loose, on a daily basis, in the crime and action series. Perverted murderers chase down innocent people; monsters from another world swallow their victims alive; earthquakes, oceans of fire, and floods destroy the universe of humankind. In this apocalyptic world, only patrolling police cars painted innocent white and angelic blue represent some degree of hope and security.

This is the dual vision of the human being left alone in an alien world; the vision of human beings who have nothing and nobody left to hold on to, who toss back and forth between the extremes of fear and hope, arrogant pride and self-mortification. In earlier ages, this dual experience was the privilege, or burden, of the very few—the best minds of the Renaissance, the great romantic artists, the Baudelairian dandy, the great decadents of the turn of the century. It has recently become an almost general human experience.

Historically, the question of "to be or not to be" was a question of survival (and not a philosophical dilemma) for millions of people in search of their daily bread. Today, the experience of a life that has lost its meaning is shared by more and more ordinary people. Melancholy, spleen, and the pain of the purposelessness of life was the bitter privilege of the Earl of Essex, Sir Walter Raleigh, or Prince Hamlet. Today, they torment the men and women in the street. We have a new, less elegant and aristocratic word for spleen and melancholy: one of the most widespread epidemics of our time is called *depression.*

Stoicism, Epicureanism, and Neo-Platonism

The comparison between the Renaissance and the Proletarian Renaissance seems to hold less if we turn toward another allegedly fundamental feature of the Renaissance. Several authors argue that Stoicism and Epicureanism were dominant philosophies shaping the vision of the world and the moral conduct of people in the Renaissance.

"Autonomy," "freedom," "mastery over the world and over oneself," "not to depend on the outside world"—are these features characteristically present in our contemporary civilization as well? And what about "responsibility," "the readiness to accept the consequences of one's actions," "the principle of 'what I have done, I have done'"? What about self-control, self-discipline," or steadfastness, the duty to face courageously one's own mortality," "to live without fear or hope," and "without illusions"? What about "internal and external beauty," "harmony," and a "well balanced character and life"? What about accepting and living according to the "eternal laws of the universe," and "living according to nature"? What about the ideal of the "honorable man," for whom "virtue is an end in itself"? What about the withdrawal from the world?[60]

Our first reaction is that people living in the Proletarian Renaissance are much more characterized by an eager hedonism and an impatient drive for self-realization than by this Epicurean harmony and balance, or this Stoic *fortitudo*, discipline, and dignity. However, we should not conclude to quickly that the Proletarian Renaissance is essentially different from the Renaissance of yore. We should not, for several reasons. On the one hand, there may be some Epicurean and Stoic features in our contemporary culture as well; on the other hand, these features may have not been all that generally present in the Renaissance courts of the fifteenth and sixteenth centuries either.

Stoic and Epicurean codes of behavior were drawn from the classical Greek heritage by outstanding Renaissance thinkers, who then exhorted their contemporaries to follow these examples. However, as far as we know everyday life in the Renaissance, there may have been relatively few people who were willing, or able, to accept these rules of behavior and live according to them. A strong hedonism, brutal self-realization, unbridled passions, and hectic and harassed lives may have been more characteristic of some, or the majority, of people living in those courts. And if this was the case, the distance between people living then and their present-day successors may not be so great any more. The genuine care for the self, in the best sense of this term, may have been as rare in the sixteenth century as it is today.

We may add that on the level of ideas and ideals, Stoicism and Epicureanism were just two of several behavioral models current in the Renaissance. The Borgias, Machiavellis, Savonarolas, Giordano Brunos, Bacons, Jagos, and Richard IIIs lived, each of them, their "Renaissance" lives, and "actualized their selves," according to different principles. Using one single ideal type as a measure would certainly mislead us in our comparison of the two historical periods in question.[61]

Let me mention also that Stoic behavior is not unknown in, and not alien to, our contemporary culture. On the one hand, it is a well-known historical fact that in periods of dramatic and chaotic change, when traditional institutions falter, Stoicism, as an ultimate sanctuary, is likely to emerge. Thus, it has emerged in the aftermath of the collapse of the great ideologies of the twentieth century and has played an important role in shaping the visions of the world, and attitudes, of several major thinkers of the postmodern age. In Richard Rorty's philosophy, for instance, it is a major constituent.

There is also a popular version of Stoicism, which may not be bound to a historical period. The strong, short-spoken hero, with an iron will and high moral integrity, who is not a toy in the hands of fate, who is master of himself and his life (herself and her life), who cannot be tempted by the frivolities of life, who keeps a stiff upper lip in the face of danger and death: He (or she) has been an archetypal character since time immemorial and has become—in its Clint Eastwoodian or Sylvester Stallonean versions—one of the favorite characters of our contemporary popular culture in the cinema and on television. And it has become an important model of self-realization for hundreds of millions of people around the world.

I am tempted to stretch the comparison even further and argue that Neo-Platonism, which deeply pervaded Renaissance thought and art, is present in the Proletarian Renaissance as well, even if only, or mainly, in a trivial form. Elsewhere, I have dealt extensively with the mythology of the world of perfumes.[62] Among others, I have shown that the interplay of sensuality and spirituality, the "spiritualization" and "trancendentalization" of the human body and the world, are important factors in enhancing the appeal of perfumes. The parallel with the Neo-Platonism of the Renaissance is unmistakable.

Let me refer to one or two perfume advertisements out of many. This first is the poster of a Vanderbilt perfume from the late 1990s. In the absence of a reproduction, I cannot analyze here the unique interplay of sensuality and spirituality of its colors and the strong symbolism of its design. I just quote its written message: "Let it release the splendor of you." This sounds exactly as if it were a Neoplatonist principle (or a Gnostic spell). Several other examples could be cited. On the poster of "24, FAUBOURG" by Hermès, for instance, we see a woman's face and arm, in a golden radiation, and the text runs: "The inner light makes you shine." It is as if it were precisely this inner splendor that a Giotto, a Botticelli, or a Leonardo had wished to release in their pictures. Is it a blasphemy to compare the designer of this ad to the above geniuses? Maybe. But the similarity is there, nevertheless.

Visions of the World

The way in which people see the world, or as they were taught to see it, plays also an important role in shaping their selves,[63] even if they are not aware of this influence. As a matter of fact, there are moments in people's lives when they cannot avoid trying to find an answer to one or another of the "ultimate questions" of human existence; to questions like:

> Why is so much suffering in the world? Do we deserve it? Or are we just victims and non-entities in a cold and empty universe? How did the world come about? Was it created by a transcendental power? Or is it the ever changing outcome of the random or nonrandom interaction of various physical and perhaps non-physical forces and factors? Did it have a beginning and will it have an end? And what will be this end like? What is the place and role of humankind in this universe? Have we got here by chance? Do we have any role to play here? Do we live in a "just world," in which the wicked are punished and the virtuous rewarded? Are we basically good and virtuous? Or are we ferocious predators, who are tamed only by the necessities of group survival? Are we mortal beings who must perish sooner or later without leaving a trace, or do we have the hope of another life hereafter? Does human life have any meaning?

I do not want to say that people keep asking these questions, or even that they are necessarily aware of them. In their everyday lives, visions of the world are not magnificent constellations of ordered philosophical ideas. They are swirling clouds of more or less vague and more or less conscious ideas, memories, fears, and nostalgias. But in each of us, these "clouds" have a certain pattern that—in the course of a complex historical, cultural, and social process—has been formed, shaped, and articulated by myths, religions, and ideologies as well as the ideas of the great thinkers of our history. Not even the greatest philosopher knows exactly what influences have shaped his or her vision of the world and keep shaping, through them, his or her life and self. Everyday people are even less aware of these hidden influences.

In their original form, the ideas of great thinkers, for instance, were clear and accurate. Saint Augustine convinced the faithful that they were enslaved by Original Sin and their only hope was to believe in the redemptive power of Christ. In the early Renaissance, Ficino argued that a divine spirituality pervaded the universe and human life. Kant exhorted people to build their lives on reason and virtue. Hobbes warned them that the world was a struggle of all against all, and if they did not want to live in a dangerous jungle, they and their fellow beings had to agree on the main rules of the game and sign a social contract. La Rochefoucauld would have laughed at such naiveté and would have convinced his readers that only irony and self-irony could protect them against the miseries of a mortal life. Nietzsche asked people if they had the strength to break out of the cage of moral hypocrisy and if they had the courage to live the dangerous life of free and autonomous human beings. Freud told his patients that there is no such thing as happiness but, going through analysis, they can achieve at least a kind of peace of mind. Jung was one's guide in the world of archetypes, which—according to him—were the sources of inexhaustible energy and harmony. Socrates and Foucault prompted their disciples to care for their selves. Teilhard de Chardin explained that humans were parts of a divine project in the course of which the world was being more and more spiritualized. Tillich pointed out the tragic ambiguities of human life and warned people that they had to develop in themselves the "courage to be." Heidegger spoke about the enormous difficulties one would meet if one wanted to live a life of authenticity. Discussing the ways and means of how one can "care for one's soul," Jan Patocka proposed the Socratic way of withdrawing from worldly interests into one's inner self and "live in truth"—as opposed to the so-called Thrasymachean way of striving for power and wealth.[64]

These and other philosophical and scholarly ideas are alive and are floating around in our civilization of consumption, even if most people could not mention the name of one single philosopher and have not heard of any of these schools of thought. It may be surprising, but it is a fact, that the myths, ideas, patterns, and "memes"[65] of our civilization are present even in the most popular genres of our age. We have just mentioned that the mythology of perfumes is rich in philosophical ideas,[66] and we shall discuss later their presence in popular women's magazines as well.[67] Or let me mention William Irwin and his coauthors, who have studied the underlying philosophy of various popular TV programs,[68] or Chris Seay, who has interpreted *The Sopranos* as the portrayal of American society and as a contemporary version of the Judeo-Christian drama of sin, damnation, and the desperate search for meaning and salvation.[69]

These are extremely interesting studies, but they are as yet rather sporadic. Mainstream psychology and sociology are still at the very beginning of mapping the role played by the world of ideas in shaping people's selves today, in the age of consumption[70]—in spite of the fact that it would be extremely interesting, and important, to know how far we live nowadays, and construct our selves, according to the principles of an Augustinian or Kantian, Hobbesian or Foucaultian, Cartesian or Nietzschean, Marxian or Popperian, Freudian or Heideggerian vision of the world. The Proletarian Renaissance, too, has its hidden gods.

The Self in a Syncretic Age

The trouble with our times is that
the future is not what it used to be.

—*Paul Valéry*

The First Paradox

There may have been few ages in history when the human person was bombarded by so many different influences as in our own age. Traditional, closed civilizations protected their inhabitants against incoming heterogeneous influences, while—since the fourteenth or fifteenth century—Western civilization has laid itself open more and more to outside influences coming from all parts of the world. In the twentieth and early-twenty-first centuries—with the development of the media, mass communication, digital networks, globalization, and tourism—this process has immensely accelerated and has produced a by now syncretic civilization swirling chaotically with heterogeneous ideas, belief systems, ideologies, and visions of the world. In this new environment, the human self has got into a difficult and paradoxical situation.[1]

It is a strange contradiction that, on the one hand, we live in the age of the apotheosis of the human personality and, on the other, this is the very age of the deconstruction of the human personality, or even that of its annihilation. It is the Me Age and the Age of the No-Self at the same time. Seen from one angle, it is the age of triumphant self-actualization, of radical individualism, an age when the human person has become the object of cult and the ultimate source of values. Yet, from the opposite angle, we witness the self's destruction.

The Emergence and Disappearance of the Self

In our everyday lives we usually think, without really thinking about it, that we are who we are, that our existence has got a center, which we call our "self." This feeling, this experience, this belief has been one of the fundamental characteristics of Greco-Judeo-Christian civilization for three thousand years, though there are scholars who argue that the concept of self, in its more or less "modern" form, emerged only at a later date.

According to Roy F. Baumeister (1986a), for instance, the first appearance of the concept of "self" may be put in the twelfth century, in the age of the great religious renewal, with "the shift of Christian practices toward a more individualized" mode (e.g., see the spread of the practice of the individual confession of sins). And it is also the age of the Goliards and of Abelard, and the age preparing for the early Renaissance of the fourteenth century.[2]

"The word 'self' originally was a reflexive pronoun and adjective meaning 'own,' and 'same' and became a noun only late in the Middle Ages . . . Thus, in 1549 the word 'self-praise' appeared, and by the end of the century it had been joined by self-love, self-pride, and self-regard, among others."[3] In the next centuries, and especially in the early modern period (1500–1800), individuality became a major value in Western society. In the seventeenth and eighteenth centuries, the fascination with the human person increased dramatically. "There emerged a new concept of an inner or hidden self, symbolized by concern over sincerity and over discrepancies between appearances and underlying realities." This discrepancy became a primary source of human autonomy.[4]

In the Romantic era, an exaggerated, and sometimes even ecstatic, cult of the self set in. The human person was mythicized into a genius, or a hero with a tragic destiny; passionate love became one of the main sources of human fulfillment; the freedom of the individual was celebrated; and the human being found its authentic self and existence in rebelling against a society of hypocrisy and oppression.

In the second half of the nineteenth century, bourgeois individualism and self-assurance triumphed, though Victorian morals kept genuine human self-actualization and self-fulfillment within narrow limits and distorted many human selves. With the emergence of the "consumer civilization" in the second half of the twentieth century, the apotheosis of the human personality reached its zenith. The human self became the center of the world and the ultimate source of all values. But—as Peter Berger and his coauthors have argued (Berger, Berger, and Kellner 1973)—it also became "homeless."

All this does not mean that nobody has ever challenged the importance, let alone the existence, of a "self" as the center of human existence. The school of cynical thinkers in classical Greece; medieval controversies about the status of the human being after the Fall and about the relationship between the body and soul; modern philosophers like Hume;[5] the concept of the "human machine" in the Enlightenment; the ideas of Marx and Darwin, Freud and Mach[6]—all have raised serious doubts about the existence of the self. Nietzsche rejected the idea that the self was something already given; he asserted that the self was not a state of mind but a process of self-creation. The self can create itself only in a process of continuous "self-overcoming."[7]

According to Porter (1997, 10), "Freud was in one fundamental respect [still] traditionalist: he believed there was an inner truth—albeit a terrifying subterranean battleground of the id, ego and super-ego—waiting to be discovered, interpreted, and even healed." Challenging this view, Rorty (1989, 30) later claimed that Freud had "de-divinized" the self. According to him, Freud rejected the Kantian idea that the center of the self was a "common moral consciousness" and also challenged the Romantic myth that the poetic imagination was its center.[8] "Freud thus helped us take seriously the possibility that there is no central faculty, no central self, called 'reason.'"[9] If "Nietzsche de-divinized truth, . . . Freud de-divinized conscience."[10] He "leaves us with a self which is a tissue of contingencies rather than an at least potentially well-ordered system of faculties."[11] The self is an ever-changing web of contingencies, and only those who are engaged in a permanent struggle to use words that have never been used in describing themselves and the world have a chance of bringing about something that may be called a "self."[12]

In the twentieth century, more and more thinkers challenged the belief in the existence of a permanent self, of a fundamental inner personal identity. The self does not exist, they asserted, or if it does, it is not a substance but only a process of change.[13] In the process of modern individuation, the human being has lost her or his "self." Berdyaev (1927[1924]) wrote about the "loss of personality." A few years later, Carl Jung (1971c [1928]) spoke of the "the spiritual problem of modern man." Karl Jaspers (1965 [1932], 115, 145) described contemporary people as "unprotected," "helpless," "unsatisfied" beings, tormented by "the doubts of nihilism," "resisting the temptations of harmony," being at the mercy of an empty world that has lost its transcendence. "There is no God, the masses shout louder and louder; and thus Man becomes worthless and is murdered *ad libitum,* because he is nothing."[14] In 1934, T. S. Eliot (1934, 42) suggested that "with the disappearance of the idea of Original Sin, with the disappearance of the idea of intense moral struggle, . . . human beings . . . tend to become less and less real." Max Horkheimer (1947, 1972) spoke of the "mutilation of the ego," and the "dissolution" of the self. Jan Patocka (1985a) warned that Western civilization was in a deep "spiritual crisis." Much later, David Walsh (1990, 15) described the process as the "abolition of Man."[15]

Even the existentialists—for whom the authentic self, the *"für sich,"* the *"pour-soi,"* was of primary importance—thought that it was not an essence but an "existence." By an act of courage and freedom, human beings have to create their selves out of nothing. The structuralists went farther, reducing the self to a more or less significant intersection of various structures. And, finally, the poststructuralists and postmodernists set about the systematic deconstruction of the self. They spoke of the "disappearing self" (Dennett 1984)"; the "deconstruction of the self" (Derrida 1973, 1976, 1978; Sampson 1989; Sandra 2000); the "dissolution" of the self (Heller, Sosna, and Wellbery 1986); "self-destruction" (Shneidman 1967);[16] the "annihilation of the self"; the "eclipse of the self" (Zimmerman 1981); or "self-emptying" (Rudy 1996). They have also developed various "no-self" theories, claiming that the "self" did not exist at all.[17]

Summing up the discussion, Kenneth J. Gergen (1991, 7, 15–16) concludes that in our postmodern world, the self has disintegrated. The

> very concept of personal essences is thrown into doubt. Selves as possessors of real and identifiable characteristics—such as rationality, emotion, inspiration, and will—are dismantled. . . . Under postmodern conditions, persons exist in a state of continuous construction and

reconstruction; it is a world where anything goes that can be negotiated. Each reality of self gives way to reflexive questioning, irony, and ultimately the playful probing of yet another reality. The center fails to hold.

As we absorb the views, values, and visions of others, and live out the multiple plots in which we are enmeshed, we enter a postmodern consciousness. It is a world in which we no longer experience a secure sense of self, and in which doubt is increasingly placed on the very assumption of a bounded identity with palpable attributes.

According to Castells (1997, 355–56), the erosion of traditional institutions and communities has deprived people of their "shared" or "legitimizing identities" and has turned them into "identity-less individuals."[18] Ewen (1988) and others argued that metropolitan anonymity had made it very difficult for people to find, construct, and protect their selves. Baumeister (1986b, 81, 92) stated that the media entangled people in a chaotic multitude of virtual selves, "dream identities," "sham individuality," and thereby obstructed the construction of real selves. And let me add that on our television screens every night we see people, human beings, kicked, beaten, smashed, burned, and strangled to death in ferocious personal conflicts that would fit well into any Pleistocene jungle or savannah. Sex and drugs dissolve human personalities. We seem to live in an age when the human personality has disintegrated, has lost its identity and authenticity, has become a puppet, a clog in a hypertechnicized world, a torso, a basket case, or a monster in a world of hatreds and wars. The "appetite for individuality persists, but the possibility of achieving individuality has been greatly reduced. Therefore, semblances of individuality flourish. Narcissism, self-help books, personalized luggage, and the rest may have arisen from a frustrated desire for individuality."[19] Sypher (1962, 138) described even beat literature as "yet another venture in losing the self."[20]

We, everyday people, may even contribute to the deconstruction of the concept of self by destroying our own selves (if they exist at all). Scholars (and quack-doctors) keep warning people against the dangers of these "self-traps" (Swann 1996), of "escaping from freedom" (Fromm 1969 [1941]), of developing a "deceptive self" (Elster 1986; McLaughlin and Rorty 1988; Lockard and Paulhus 1988; Nesse and Lloyd 1992; Mack 1996), of "self-degradation" (Smiles 1958), of "self-undoing" and "self-dissolution" (Porter 1997), of "decentering the self" (White and Hellerich 1998; Foucault 1982, 1988a, 1988b), or of attempts at "escaping the self (Baumeister 1991a; Berofsky 1995).

The loss of self may be a shocking experience in real life but—strangely enough—it fascinates and attracts us in the virtual world of literature and television. We love to watch stories of amnesia, that is, stories in which somebody suddenly loses—in a car accident, for instance—her memory, which according to many experts is the main "glue" of our selves, and then the whole story is about how she slowly regains her memory, her previous life, how her lost self slowly reemerges. The drama, or tragedy, of this loss of memory and/or self has inspired the greatest artists as well. Think of the villagers in the *One Hundred Years of Solitude* by Gabriel García Márquez, who are losing their memory; to survive, they put labels on the various objects and animals, saying: "THIS IS THE TABLE," "THE DOOR," "THE BED," "THE GOAT," "THE PIG," "THIS IS THE COW, SHE MUST BE MILKED EVERY MORNING." Another fascinating scene of losing one's self (fascinating on the stage or screen and horrendous in reality) is portrayed in the numerous and famous "going mad scenes" of European literature. Think of Ophelia's two heart-gripping scenes in *Hamlet,* or the more sentimental but no less moving going-mad scene of Blanche in *A Streetcar Named Desire.*

Concepts and Strategies

Seeing its hectic history in the twentieth century, it is time to ask what has become of the self, and the concept of the self, in this syncretic civilization of the consumer age. Do we still know what we speak about when we speak about the "self"? What is the self? What is it like? Does it exist at all?

For answers, we have to turn to the scholarly literature (which is as heterogeneous and syncretic as consumer civilization itself). But this may prove to be a dangerous experiment. We may get lost in the teeming multitude of concepts and strategies, hypotheses and theories of, and about, the "self."[21]

"The self is a haunting problem," Allport remarked already in 1961 (p. x). A half century later, Leary and Tangney (2003b) used much harder terms. Surveying the field, they spoke of a "conceptual morass," or "a conceptual quagmire as muddy as any in the social and behavioral sciences."[22] And they added: "Just out of curiosity, we looked to see how many hyphenated 'self'-terms appeared in the abstracts in the *PsycInfo* computerized database through June of 2001. Eliminating the term 'self-report,' we found over 150,000 abstracts that contained a hyphenated 'self'-term."[23] To prove their point, in table 1.1 of their article (p. 12), they enumerate several dozens of these "hyphenated concepts"; this table is reproduced here as table 10.1.

TABLE 10.1

Self-Related Constructs, Processes, and Phenomena

Desired/undesired self	Self-blame	Self-handicapping
Ego	Self-care	Self-help
Ego defense	Self-categorization	Self-identification
Ego extension	Self-completion	Sell-identity
Ego ideal	Self-complexity	Self-image
Ego identity	Self-concept	Self-management
Ego integrity	Self-confidence	Self-monitoring
Ego strength	Self-conscious emotion	Self-organization
Ego threat	Self-consciousness	Self-perception
Feared self	Self-control	Self-preservation
Future/past self	Self-criticism	Self-presentation
Ideal self	Self-deception	Self-protection
Identity	Self-defeating behavior	Self-reference
Identity orientation	Self-definition	Self-regard
Ought/should self	Self-development	Self-regulation
Possible selves	Self-disclosure	Self-reliance
Self-acceptance	Self-discrepancy	Self-schema
Self-actualization	Self-doubt	Self-silencing
Self-affirmation	Self-efficacy	Self-talk
Self-appraisal	Self-enhancement	Self-trust
Self-assessment	Self-esteem	Self-verification
Self-awareness	Self-evaluation	Self-worth

Source: Leary and Tangney (2003b, table 1.1).
© 2003 by The Guilford Press. Reprinted with permission.

Philosophers have had at least as many problems with the concept of the self as psychologists. Agnes Heller (1992, 269), for instance, described the rich, and almost chaotic, variety of concepts surrounding the "subject" and the "self" in the following way:

> In the contemporary French (and German) debates the term "subject" takes any of the following meanings: point of view; individual; the "subject" of biography; the hermeneutical (meaning-constituting) subject; the subject who-comes-to-know (Erkenntnissubjekt); the subject of knowledge (Wissen); the political subject (both as *subjectum* and *subjectus*); the moral subject (again, both as *subjectum* and *subjectus*); person; personality; self; the mono-centered self; Ego; the man; self-consciousness; self-reflexivity; subject as Will; subject as Sovereignty; or simply the personal pronoun I. In addition, the term "subject" includes all cases of non-individual, nonpersonal subjects, such as the Kantian Transcendental Subject, the Hegelian World Spirit, or the Fichtean I; furthermore, the personal, but nonhuman subjects such as God, and the so-called universal Subjects such as History, Humanism, Rights, Art, and the like.[24]

If one still wants to know more about the problematic of the self, one may easily get lost in the jungle of definitions and concepts; such as, for instance, the "noumenal" or "phenomenal" self (Jones and Gerard 1967); the "Faustian" self or the "elusive" self (Lifton 1993); the "transparent" self (Snyder 1994); the "spectral" self or the "reflected" self (Tice and Wallace 2003); the "hidden" or "visible" self (Eicher, Evenson, and Lutz 2000); the "implicit" self (Devos and Banaji 2003); the "schizophrenic post-self" (White and Hellerich 1998); the "self-deceptive" self (Rorty 1988); the "extended" self (Belk 1989); the "created" (Weber 2000) or "creative" self (Maslow 1999); the "privatized" (Langman 1992), "embodied," or "recuperated" self (Kristeva 1991); a "full-fledged" self (Baumeister 1998); the "disenchanted" self (Leicester 1990); the "looking-glass" self (Canfield 1990); the "symbolic" self (Sedikides and Skowronski 2003); the "advertising" or "managed" self (Schelling 1978); the "normative" self (Lears 1992); the "autonomous" or "communalized" self (Schrag 1997); the "mediating" self (Aboulafia 1986); the "ego and the counter-ego" (Fingarette 1969); the "problematic" (Cole 1971), "mutable" (Zurcher 1977), "minimal"

(Lash 1984), or "marginal" self (Muller 1987, 1998); the "disembodied soul" and the "disengaged subject" (Taylor 1989); the "saturated" self (Gergen 1991); the "imagined" self (Hanson 1986); the "misrepresented" self, "evolving" self, and "transcendent" self (Csikszentmihalyi 1993)[25]; the "prelinguistic" self (Schrag 1997); the "semiotic" self (Wiley 1994); the "indexical," "metaphorical," or "ontological" interpretation of the self (Gregg 1991); the "myths of the self" (Porter 1997; Taylor 1989); the "technologies of the self," "l'écriture de soi," and "the scripting of self" (Foucault 1988b); the "historically and culturally indexed" self and the "self as memory" (Kihlstrom, Beer, and Klein 2003); the human being defined as the "center of narrative gravity" (Dennett 1991), as a "self-interpreting animal" (Taylor 1989), as a "motivated, dynamic, action system" (Tesser, Stapel, and Wood 2002), as an "organizing construct" (Leary and Tangney 2003b), or as a "psycho-social dynamic processing system"; or simply "the self-zoo" (Tesser, Martin, and Cornell 1996).

This is more than an *embarras de richesse*. This is a symptom of a syncretic civilization, which struggles—among many other challenges—with an almost chaotic plurality of approaches to the concept of the "self," the meaning of which was obvious, if not at least much less complex, in earlier ages than it is nowadays. Because the self is a, or *the* dominant, concept of the age of consumption, it may be important to have another look at this complexity.

A Multiple Self?

The possibility of multiplying oneself in several selves has excited humankind for thousands of years. In her fascinating book *The Bedtrick: Tales of Sex and Masquerade*, Wendy Doniger (2000) argues that the multiplication of the self was a frequent motif in Greek and Indian myths. The gods especially had a propensity to multiply their selves. Krishna, for instance, loved and was beloved by a number of milkmaids. To solve the problem, he multiplied himself and made love to all of them simultaneously. In a later and more decent version, he duplicated them and slept only with these doubles. Another typical tale is, for instance, the Greek myth in which Zeus took the shape of Amphytrion and made love to his beautiful wife Alcmene. Change of gender is also a common motive both in myths and, for instance, Renaissance comedies. The idea that several selves may hide in the human being also puzzled and fascinated people in the age of Romanticism. Or think of the enormous success of Robert Louis Stevenson's *Dr. Jekyll and Mr. Hyde,* Oscar Wilde's *The Picture of Dorian Gray,* or Virginia Woolf's *Orlando.* The hero of this last novel changes his/her self several times in the course of several centuries. On a philosophical level, it was Nietzsche (1968, section 490) who made the strongest statements about the multiplicity of the human self:

> The assumption of one single subject is perhaps unnecessary; perhaps it is just as permissible to assume a multiplicity of subjects, whose interaction and struggle is the basis of our thought and our consciousness in general. . . . *My hypothesis:* The subject is a multiplicity.[26]

Among psychologists, William James was one of the first to argue that the human being had "several selves" and, as far as I know, he was the first to make the distinction between the "I" pole and the "Me" pole of the self[27]; he stated that an individual "has as many social selves ["Me"-selves] as there are distinct *groups* of persons about whose opinions he cares."[28] George Herbert Mead (1962) developed these ideas and stated that we "divide ourselves up in all sorts of different selves with reference to our acquaintances. We discuss politics with one and religion with another. There are all sorts of different selves answering to all sorts of different social reactions. . . . A multiple personality is in a certain sense normal."[29]

Since Mead, a great number of scholars have asserted that, instead of having one single self, the human being has a "multiple self," or a number of "hierarchical," "parallel," or "successive" selves. One may have, for instance, a "physical self" (I am an athlete), a "psychological self" (I am an introvert), a "professional self" (I am an engineer), a "collective self" (I am Portuguese), a "spiritual self" (I am a Protestant), an "astral self" (I was born under the sign of the Bull), a "relational self" (I am a mother), and so on. One may discover in oneself an "emotional," "moral," "conscious," or "cognitive" self as well.

Within this variety of definitions, scholars have argued that the human self is well integrated, consistent, coherent, "united," "unified," "self-identical," "discrete," "self-enclosed," "immutable," "changeless," "indivisible," and "monocentered."[30] Some among them claim that this one and indivisible self is an "inner" and "authentic self," a "genuine self," an "essential self," (Baumeister

1986a); a "kernel self," a "deep self, an "existential self" (Muller 1987); and that it has a permanence and identity with itself over time.[31]

Others have affirmed—on the contrary—that the self is not, or is only "loosely," integrated. The frontal attack against the concept of a unified, "sovereign," "monarchical," "self-sufficient," "self-assured," and "immutable self" has been launched by the standard-bearers of postmodernism, who have claimed, for instance, that the self emerged from the "heterogeneity of language games" (Lyotard 1984, xxv, 82) and who have emphasized the importance of multiplicity, diversity, difference, and incommensurability even in connection with the self.[32] According to them, the self is "decentered" (Foucault 1988a, 1988b]); "heterogeneous" and "formless" (Stambaugh 1999); or "polymorphous" (White and Hellerich 1998). Nikolas Rose (1997, 226) argued that we "need to abandon the belief that we are 'in our very nature' discrete, bounded, self-identical creatures, inhabited and animated by an inner world whose laws and processes have begun to reveal to us. On the contrary, we are 'assembled' selves."[33]

In his book *The Multiple Self,* John Elster (1986, 1) gives a good survey of those studies that view the individual person as "a set of sub-individual, relatively autonomous 'selves,'" from the Freudian trinity of id, ego, and superego, through the concepts of "divided" or "split," "fragmented" "hierarchical," "parallel" or "successive" selves, to Foucault's or Tillich's "decentered" self. But he warns us that "barring pathological cases,[34] . . . we ought not to take the notion of 'several selves' very literally. In general, we are dealing with exactly *one* person—neither more nor less."[35] Nowadays, a number of his contemporaries would not agree: The decomposition of the SELF into selves has been a profound and sometimes shocking experience for people living in this syncretic civilization.

Some scholars maintain that the human being has ever had several selves. Others claim that the multiplication of selves has been a historical process, which has spectacularly accelerated in the past fifty years, due to the emergence of mass societies, mass media, and the civilization of consumption. Charles Taylor (1989, 502) writes, for instance, that "the individual has been taken out of a rich community life and now enters instead into a series of mobile, changing, revocable associations, often designed merely for highly specific ends. We end up relating to each other through a series of partial roles."

Television has played an important role in furthering this multiplication, or proliferation, of the human self. Its anchor people and stars, and its series and soap operas, every day offer dozens of human roles, models of behavior, selves that have a strong appeal and may prompt people to imitate them, adopt them as their own identities, own selves. Or think of clips, which appeal to our contemporary multiple selves. In each moment, there is a new stimulus, a new effect; in each moment, one has to respond to a new and unexpected visual or emotional challenge. In this experience, our self—if we have any—breaks down into a multitude of instantaneous and ephemeral selves, into a vibrating mosaic of selves, or rather protoselves, because there is no time for any of them to crystallize or mature into a real self.

The great number of horror stories on television about people changing into monsters, werewolves, or aliens calls our attention to the fact that the concept of a multiple self may refer not only to a peaceful coexistence of various selves in one person but may also indicate a hidden struggle of destructive forces within the self. Gary S. Gregg (1991, 206), argued, for instance, that psychological, cultural, and, most important, social and political forces structure the human personality, and they do so "deeply and with . . . profound and often tragic consequences." His conclusion as far as the human personality or self is concerned is rather gloomy. He claims that what we call a multiple self is not a recent, postmodern product. It is the presence of a "primitive" self that has survived over the millennia under the surface of our civilized self. It is

> a mythopoetic construction that will remain "primitive" in the space age regardless of how precise the science of behavior or how scientized society becomes. But this "primitive" self is not mere genre play, all done with mirrors. Rather it is done with instruments of power, and so the alternative representations of self that comprise it differ profoundly in their potentials for good and evil. Self-representation may be a structure of differences, but of differences that make a difference. More important than the play of symbols and masks that casts self-representation in a postmodern light is the playing out of tragedy, which reveals every self as ancient, flawed, heroic, and dangerous.[36]

And here we come back to what we discussed at the beginning of this chapter: the shocking paradox of the twentieth century simultaneously being the age of the apotheosis and that of the destruction of the human personality. We shall see that this is true also of the second part of the century, that is, of the age of consumption. Human beings may profit from the opportunities offered by, and have to struggle with the destructive forces of, the "Proletarian Renaissance."

The Second Paradox

Living in the contemporary world, one has a choice. One may enjoy the sparkling of worlds and selves, and may happily be submerged in this whirling experience. Or one may opt for constructing a rich and strong self for oneself, which will be able to positively and indomitably respond to the challenges of this storm of heterogeneous, and not at all harmless, impulses. These are two basically different human attitudes. One may need both of them. The first may help people enrich their selves by keeping them open for new emotional, intellectual, and visual adventures, and a wide gamut of roles and identities.

Beyond a certain limit, however, this experimentation may jeopardize people's autonomy, their control over their own lives, and over this other, dangerous self alluded to by Gary S. Gregg. The other, the strong-self program, has a long tradition in Western civilization. A strong and unified self may serve as an "inner compass" à la Kant or Max Weber; it may orient people in a syncretic world and help them control that other, dangerous self. But it may also confine them in their selves; it may hinder them in discovering new worlds, in experimenting with new roles and new identities.

The best solution would probably be to achieve a good balance between the two attitudes—to develop a strong self but keep it open for new, surprising experiences; or to switch to and fro between the two attitudes to optimize the outcome. The worst solution would be to have a weak self, which is lost and helpless in a chaotic world.

This latter is a bad and dangerous solution because, ironically, this modern human being, harassed by all these doubts about her or his self, has been burdened with a new and overwhelming responsibility in the twentieth and early twenty-first centuries. He or she has been forced to accept the role of being the ultimate source of meaning in a universe, which—since the "death of God," and the failure of history to redeem the world—has lost its traditional sources of purpose and meaning.

This is a radically new, and paradoxical, situation because whatever it may be, the "meaning of life" has always been something that transcended everyday human life and reality. Now, it has become immanent. Human beings have to find the meaning of their lives, and that of life in general, in themselves. This may be a difficult, if not an impossible and absurd, task. How to find something in oneself, something that transcends one's everyday existence, without reaching out to someone or something else, to God, the World of Ideas, Society, History? Charles Taylor (1989, 507) described this dilemma in the following way:

> Our normal understanding of self-realization presupposes that some things are important beyond the self, that there are some goods or purposes the furthering of which has significance for us and which hence can provide the significance a fulfilling life needs. A total and fully consistent subjectivism would tend towards emptiness: nothing would count as a fulfillment in a world in which literally nothing was important but self-fulfillment.

David Walsh (1990, 259–61) states, in the same vein, that we begin to realize, with Nietzsche and Dostoyevsky, that humans are incapable of "grounding an autonomous morality on the basis of their own assertion of will. . . . Only someone completely ignorant of our civilization's history could continue to maintain that humans create the order of their own existence."

This may be understood as a serious warning to our contemporary consumer civilization with its basic message of "self-fulfillment." But the enormous global impact of this civilization may indicate that, beyond the message of self-fulfillment, it also offers something beyond the self: the illusion of a new transcendence.

The Self and the Intensity of Life

> Live dangerously. Build your cities
> on the slopes of Vesuvius.
>
> —*Friedrich Nietzsche*

The Loss of Transcendence

It is a truism to say that human beings want to live, that they don't want to die, they cling to life, they want to have as much as possible of "sweet life," though not necessarily in the sense of la dolce vita. They want to live their lives in full. In various civilizations, and in various ages, people used various strategies to achieve this goal, to maximize their share in life: The more you observe the Law, the better and fuller your life will be (Old Testament); if you believe in Jesus Christ, you will enjoy the fullness of eternal life (New Testament); virtue and reason are the ultimate sources of a life worth living (Socrates, Kant); to work for the advancement of humankind is the only real source of the fullness of life (Hegel, Marx): These and other messages have guided hundreds of millions of people in the Western world throughout the centuries in their quest of the fullness of life. These precepts are still alive and relevant, but a fundamental change has taken place in our civilization in the past half century.[1] Let me here have a closer look at one of the main factors, or motive forces, behind this change.

It is a commonplace to state that the loss of transcendence is one of the major determinants of the existential situation of modern humankind. Since the time of Nietzsche and Weber, the thesis of the *Entzauberung* or "disenchantment" of Western civilization has been discussed and rediscussed by a great number of scholars.[2] Let me mention here only the names of Spengler, Valéry, Sorokin, Heidegger, Jaspers, Bultmann, Camus, Tillich, McIntyre, and Charles Taylor.

Peter Berger and his coauthors (Berger, Berger, and Kellner 1973, 82, 14, 12, 16) spoke in this context about the "loss of 'home,'" the breaking up of a "symbolic universe," of the "social lifeworld," of the "plausibility structure," which had surrounded people and enabled them to experience their lives as ordered and meaningful. Emmanuel Levinas (1982, 1993) wrote about the loss of "infinity." Students of postmodernism described the same process as the collapse of the great symbolic systems, "great narratives," an "overarching purpose," a "universal guidance," "universalism."[3] We are "thrown back on [our] own subjectivity as the only ultimate ethical authority," Bauman (1992, xxii) concluded.

People living in Western civilization traditionally believed in the existence of a framework—GOD, and later NATURE, REASON, HISTORY, THE FUTURE—frameworks within which human beings could find the meaning and fulfillment of their lives. With the help of these frameworks, they could "transcend"[4] the boundaries of their narrow, fragile, and transitory physical existence.[5] In the twentieth century, however, and especially in its second half, these frameworks of their lives and selves were breaking up.[6] People had to look for new ways and means to protect, develop, and actualize their selves. Consumer civilization, which was emerging in those decades, and which was partly generated by this new need, offered various new solutions and strategies.[7]

The Cult of the Moment

The collapse of the eternal framework of transcendence has increased the value of time in a dramatic way. If human life is ephemeral, then we have to find the fullness and meaning of life quickly and immediately. This speed, this urgency has become one of the dominant elements in the existential experience of people living in contemporary Western civilization. Time and space, history and society, life and the world have shrunk into one single brief moment. HIC ET NUNC could be the emblem of contemporary civilization—the emblem of a humankind without transcendence.[8]

If there is no eternity, no transcendental framework, which could protect people against mortality, there is still a way to escape. They may jump from one extreme into the other, from eternity into the moment. They may discover, or rediscover, the sacred sources of life and meaning in the mysterious depths of the moment. The idea of this existential moment as the unique source of authentic existence and meaning keeps recurring from Baudelaire, through Nietzsche, to Heidegger and others.

In his famous essay "The Painter of Modern Life," Baudelaire (1964) describes le flaneur, who strolls the streets of the modern metropolis in a meditative mood, and who is "the painter of the passing moment and of all the suggestions of eternity that it contains." He perceives, he discovers "the infinite" in the "fugitive" moment. He admires the "eternal beauty" in the "fleeting beauty" of ever-changing fashion.[9] This is not any more the ultimate harmony of classical works of art, the glorious harmony of time and timelessness, of the moment and the eternal. For Baudelaire, this is a fight and a game, a fascinating and terrifying adventure: Les flaneurs, the modern artist and modern man and woman, have to grasp the significant moment in the hectic swirl of metropolitan life, in the danse macabre of Toulouse Lautrec. And if they miss it, then they have to accept this failure with the tragic dignity and elegance of a dandy.

For Kierkegaard (1954, 1959), this significant moment is the "moment of the break-in of the wholly Other," the moment when "God bursts into life and the individual feels summoned to make the decision to risk his leap into faith."[10] For Nietzsche (1986, 7), this moment is the moment of the "breakout from the accustomed." It is the moment when the "great liberation comes . . . suddenly, like the shock of an earthquake: the youthful soul is all at once convulsed, torn loose, torn away. . . . [A] vehement, dangerous curiosity . . . flames and flickers in all its senses." In another context, he speaks of the "malady of history," that is, the inability of people to discover the eternal in the moment, and states that "the infinitely small moment is the higher reality and truth is a lightening flash out of the eternal flux."[11] "The world is complete and reaches its finality at each and every moment." "He who cannot sink down on the threshold of the moment and forget all the past . . . will never know what happiness is."[12] One has "to affirm triumphantly every moment of existence."[13] Later, Heidegger spoke of the moments of "authentic existence." In the famous Davos debate with Cassirer, he argued that "the highest form of existence of *Dasein* can be reduced to only a few rare moments in the duration of *Dasein* between life and death. . . . Man exists at the peak of his own potentialities at only a very few moments."[14]

What had been the experience of philosophers and artists in the late nineteenth and early twentieth centuries has since become the everyday experience of people living in the contemporary world. It is not a few aristocratic dandies or lonely philosophers, but hundreds of millions of people, who are looking for an ultimate source of life and meaning in the moment. And consumer civilization provides them, around the clock, with myriad intense and significant moments (or at least with the illusion that they experience these significant moments).

The world of television is, par excellence, the world of these existential moments. There is no past and no future here; there are fireworks of present moments of intensity or the semblance of intensity. In the commercials and clips, time is cut into flashing moments of intense experience; in films, frequent flashbacks and flash-forwards bring past and future together in the present.[15] People are overwhelmed by, and they have to try to shape, realize, and fulfill their selves, in this hectic fulguration of brief, evanescent moments. This is a radically new situation, a new and difficult task, which—as far as I know—has not yet received the appropriate attention of scholars.

Consumer civilization, for its part, offers people some help. It makes them feel the beauty of the moment, and the serenity of eternity, and it generates in them the illusion that these two, the moment and eternity, unite in a beautiful harmony. Let me illustrate this with a few examples taken again from the world of perfume advertisements.

Perfumes and perfume posters have the power and the magic to transform the empty and evanescent time of the real world simultaneously into magnificent eternity and meaningful and intense moments. Calvin Klein's perfume is *ETERNITY* itself, Laura Biagiotta's *ROMA* is a "breath of eternity" ("*Un soffio di eternita*"), Lancôme's *TRÉSOR* is "the perfume of precious instants,"

Dior's *DUNE* is "a moment of dream," Yves Saint Laurent's *Y* is "a fragrance for moments of intense emotion," while Chopard's *CASHMIR* promises "the magic of the moment" and Elizabeth Taylor's *WHITE DIAMONDS* an "endless brilliance." But finally Scherrer's *PERFUME* gets the gold medal by synthesizing the meaningful moment and eternity. It promises both "the passion of the moment" and the Faustian "eternal femininity" (*"La passion du moment. L'éternel féminin"*).

The Cult of Intensity

Consumer industry has developed a masterly strategy, which has become one of the main sources of its overwhelming success: It has substituted intense life experience for the meaning of life, which may get lost when the transcendental framework of people's lives collapse. It keeps offering us life experiences of the highest intensity.[16] This is a simple and extremely successful strategy; or at least people accept and are enchanted and narcotized by it. So much so that the Age of Consumption could also be called the Age of Experience. After centuries of commodity markets, financial markets, and labor markets, and decades of service markets, we now witness the emergence of an experience market.

"Experience" has recently become the watchword of the business world as well. It is certainly not a coincidence, for instance, that eBay advertised itself on the search engine Vivisimo (February 19, 2004) in the following way: "Experience on eBay. Find *experience* items at low prices. With over 5 million items for sale every day, you'll find all kinds of unique things on eBay—the World's Online Marketplace." And then it offers 158 items of direct experience like "The housebuilding experience"; "Jimi Hendrix: The total experience"; "The Alaska experience"; "The American religious experience"; "The Holy Land experience"; "The human experience"; "The synthetic experience"; "The Vietnam experience: A website that shares the emotional and spiritual experiences of the Vietnam War"; "Winston Churchill's Britain at war experience . . . recreates the LONDON BLITZ in all its fury with special effects highlighting the sites and sounds, the artifacts, and even the dust and smoke of an air raid."[17]

It is more than understandable that in a world without transcendence, people want to experience life as fully as possible. If there is no transcendence, neither "vertical" (open toward God, gods, or the World of Ideas), nor "horizontal" (open toward Nature, History, Society), if human life does not transcend its physical/biological boundaries, then there is no immortality. Then death is definitive. It is in this situation that consumer civilization comes to the aid of people. It opposes a high-voltage life experience to death and thereby soothes people's existential fears and anxieties. They are dazzled and immunized against these fears by the experience of the glowing intensity of life offered to them by their emerging new civilization.[18]

The Sources of Intensity

The media, the advertising industry, and other institutions of our contemporary civilization of consumption systematically exploit all the possible sources of intense life experience. And there is a great variety of them. Let me briefly survey a few. They are present, and bubble, everywhere in the world of the media and advertising. And people eagerly drink from them the elixir (and illusion) of life and intensity.

Physical experience. The vitality of youth, running, jumping, flying, surfing, eating, drinking, a hot or cold shower, the whirling drift of dance: They all boost our physical energies and make us feel to be very much alive.

Objects. We are attracted to objects that radiate energy and lend their energy to us, like locomotives, roaring war planes, spaceships, racing cars, guns, rockets, fire engines. We are overwhelmed by the intensity of their power. Jewels, and sacred or magic objects, like the Host or the Holy Grail, or relics and amulets, have also a deep radiation of meaning and intensity.

Predators, like jumping tigers or leopards, are symbols, and sources, of intensity. This is why they are the protagonists of so many commercials.

Visual experience. Beauty, the sight of exuberant colors, fresh fruit, sparkling of crystalline drinks, the blue Mediterranean, the brilliance of six-star hotels, the elegant gliding of luxury cars: All these radiate the experience of a life that is fuller and more intense than our everyday lives.

The forces of nature. Watching them on the screen, we experience the superhuman intensity and energy of natural catastrophes, floods, tidal waves, tornadoes, blazes, volcano eruptions. (In real life, they have the opposite effect: They make us feel weak and small.)

Speed. If in the normal flow of everyday life, we do not feel ourselves anymore, if we do not feel that we are really alive, then we may shift to top gear, accelerate our lives, speed up, and this may have a magic effect on us. It is an intense experience of (the illusion of) freedom, it is the source of euphoria of people driving fast cars may feel, it is the happy vertigo that makes people on the roller coaster shriek and laugh in ecstasy. Speeding through the world leads us through a shower of impressions, and we experience this density of impressions as a higher intensity of life. In the ecstasy of speed, we feel that we have defeated the laws of nature, we are strong, and victorious; we have overcome time and death; we are invincible and immortal: A dangerous illusion.[19]

Danger gives us a shot of adrenaline, it jump-starts our whole organism, it mobilizes all our energies: We experience our existence with a high intensity. In extreme sports, people flirt with nonbeing to intensify the feeling that they do live, they do exist. In a similar way, gamblers challenge their fate, court danger, and thereby turbo up the intensity of their life experience.

Fight. The most archaic sources of life intensity may be the fight for life, showdowns, war, murder, manhunts, flight, victory, revenge, defeat. They mobilize in us long-forgotten, but still-existing, Stone Age drives and instincts, fears and passions, which sweep away our civilized and disciplined selves with surprising ease. Consumer civilization, and the media, first of all, overwhelm us with these archaic fears and excitements. Watching television programs, thrillers, cop shows, and action movies, our metropolises are metamorphosed into dangerous jungles; we hunt together with our heroes, fly with the victims, shoot to kill the monsters, blow up houses, fortresses, the world, challenge Evil, and tear our adversaries to pieces.

Is it not strange that in the world of television, the per capita number of murdered, tortured, burnt, blown up, and drowned people is much higher than in the most murderous cities or countries of the world? And, in spite of this, we, civilized people, watch these scenes with delight. Do we love destruction, murder, torture? No, definitely not. But we love to watch the "bowdlerized," immunized, sterilized version of these horrendous events, because in this indirect, symbolic form they are powerful generators of life intensity.[20]

These techniques are not recent inventions. They have ever been used by arts and artists. Think of the fearful monsters of fairy tales. Or think of the fact that Elizabethan tragedies beat all murder statistics. Their authors wanted to shock, to move, to stagger their spectators just as the authors of our television programs do. They were not too selective in their means. They used the best, and often the cheapest, barnstorming devices. It may not have been by coincidence that one of Shakespeare's competitors called him "Shake-scene."

Passions. Revenge, atrocity, betrayal, jealousy, and envy are among the most intense emotional experiences. And so is love. It helps us experience our lives, the very essence of our selves, with exceptionally high intensity. It releases in us huge amounts of emotional energies; we feel ourselves strong, beautiful, valuable. Or, when our love fails, when we are forsaken, then we experience desperation, jealousy, and defeat on the same high level of emotional intensity.

Sex, biologically and psychologically, is one of the most intense life experiences. And beyond the physical pleasure it provides, it is the intense experience of existing, of being alive in the fullest sense of the word, that makes it almost irresistibly attractive.

Complexes and archetypes. If Freud and Jung are right, and I think they are, then complexes and archetypes are sources of exceptionally strong energies.

Crime. Is it not baffling that more than 50 percent of films shown on television turn around crime? Why are we fascinated by crime? We may be bored by the gray routine of our everyday lives. We may feel a strong urge to break out of the cage of the rigid order of the existing world. We may have an unconscious desire to plunge into the chaos of an archaic life. We may try to reduce our anxieties by flirting with, or confronting, danger. But an even stronger motive may lie in the fact that crime challenges life, threatens life with destruction, and in this critical situation, life flashes up with a high intensity. Watching these crime stories, we are swimming in a stream of intense life experience.

Destruction. Even destruction may become a source of life intensity—by contrast. The peak of intensity in almost all American action movies is a huge explosion, which seems to blow up the whole world in its black and orange flames. These scenes have a strong impact on us. We feel as if our repressed instincts exploded, as if our death instincts would blow up the world, as if an ancient chaos would triumph over our rigid civilized world. We bathe in the spectacle of these flames, we feel as if the demonic energies of these explosions were our energies.

Community. Collective and communal experience, festivals, parades, celebrations, weddings, demonstrations, riots, revolutions, carnivals: They all give us the excitement of intensity.

Religion. For thousands of years, religion was—and for many people still is— the main source of intensely experiencing their lives, their very existence. Ceremonies, the sacred, mystique experience, ecstasy, personal contact with God, the drama of sin–repentance–redemption–conversion, raptures, the adoration of saints and great teachers: They all have ever been sources of intense existential experience.[21]

Consumer civilization offers a wide range of similar experiences. The collective ecstasy of rock concerts, the adulation of stars, religious and pseudoreligious celebrations with spectacular conversions: Their main attraction is probably the fact that they are rich and easy sources of a high intensity of life.

Superhuman beings. Angels and demons, Gabriel and Satan, heroes and antiheroes, have ever been symbols and sources of fearful energies and intense life experience. Think of Milton's Satan, or Rilke's "fearful angels," about whom he writes in his *First Duino Elegy:*

> Who, if I cried, would hear me among the angelic
> Orders? And even if one of them suddenly
> Pressed me against his heart, I should fade in the strength
> of his stronger existence. For Beauty's nothing
> but beginning of Terror we're still just able to bear,
> and why we adore it so is because it serenely
> disdains to destroy us. Every angel is terrible.[22]

A sacred cause. To live and fight for a sacred cause has been the source of intense life experience for millions of people in the course of human history.

Fanaticism. The power of totalitarian ideologies and fundamentalist movements lies, to a great extent, in their ability to generate the experience of a high intensity of life in their followers. Mass rallies, a rhetoric and propaganda fanaticizing people, whipping up their passions, hatreds and nostalgias, myths of national, religious or class identity, missionary zeal, intoxication with collective power and the hope of a final victory and salvation—for many people in the twentieth century, and in other ages as well, these were among the main sources of identity and intense life experience.

Intellectual-spiritual experience. Surprise, new information, intellectual adventure, the joy of learning something new, the moments of eureka, too, are accompanied by an experience of high life intensity.

Art. In a technical language, we could say that works of art are batteries of high-intensity life experiences. They condense in themselves various life situations and experiences and, when "contacted," they re-generate these experiences, with high intensity, in their readers, listeners, or spectators.

Wealth, power, fame. The strong fascination with wealth, power, and fame may be due to the fact that the lives of the wealthy, the powerful, and the famous seem to be fuller and more intense than those of us, everyday citizens. We have the impression that more joy, adventure, pleasure, passion, and experience are condensed in their lives than in ours and that this density and wealth of experience makes their lives radiant with energy and intensity. The desire to have a fuller life, to experience life with the highest possible intensity, pushes us into the race for wealth, power, and fame. And the media help those who fail in this race identify themselves with those who have succeeded—the powerful, the rich, and the famous—and draw on the intensity of these exceptional and spectacular lives.[23]

Aristocracy, dynasty. The lives of royalty, aristocrats, famous dynasties, and the international jet set may have the same radiation of intensity, reinforced by the semisecrecy of their lives behind the walls of huge parks, penthouses, and exclusive clubs, or in the distance of private islands and luxury yachts.

Drinks and drugs. They open a dangerous and direct way to a temporary feeling of high life intensity, to intense emotions, visions, happiness, and sexual pleasure.

Contrast. Contrast is one of those formal devices that have been used by storytellers and writers of all ages and civilizations for the generation of tension, suspense, excitement—of intense life experience. Fairy tales, broadsides, tragedies, and novels have used it as much as the editors of contemporary popular magazines, television programs, and films. The contrasts of darkness and light, order and chaos, peace and war, Good and Evil, virtue and crime, the Beauty and the Beast, the strong and the weak, the young and the old, the rich and the poor, the known and the unknown, the material and the spiritual are likely to trigger in us intense emotional reactions.[24] And this is even truer in the case of the ultimate contrast, that of life and death. This is the "boundary situation" that has been at the center of philosophical thinking since Socrates. And for the human self, it may very well be the source of the highest possible life intensity: the source of a fearful and delightful existential experience, an experience that may play a major role in shaping the selves of people living in our contemporary world.

In the next chapter, I shall show the extreme importance of the intense existential experience for people's lives with the example of a trivial contemporary genre: lifestyle magazines. We shall see how these magazines do everything in their power to generate high-voltage life experience in their readers; how they mobilize powerful ancient myths and archetypes; how they dramatize ordinary people into heroes struggling with the ultimate questions of human life. We shall discover fearful existential dramas swirling under the trivial surfaces of these popular magazines. The duality of the trivial and the existential, the trivial and the tragic, keeps flashing up with high intensity, even in this "cheap," chattering genre.

The Self in Boundary Situations

In this world there is always danger
for those who are afraid of it.

—*George Bernard Shaw*

Fear and Civilization

The "boundary situation" ("*situation limite,*" "*Grenzensituation*") is one of the key concepts of Sartrian and Jaspersian existentialism.[1] It is a situation in which a human being has to make an existential choice, accepting the risks of this choice and achieving his or her freedom thereby. As if standing at the edge of a precipice, he or she has to jump in the unknown, the void; into nonbeing; into freedom. According to Sartre or Jaspers, this is the only way to achieve an authentic existence, and an authentic self.

I do not think that we have to agree with Schopenhauer (1966, vol. 2, G211), who claimed that "dying is certainly to be regarded as the real aim of life" or that the "aim of life is death." On the contrary: The aim of life is life; to stay alive; and to experience our lives with the highest possible intensity. But in the moments when our selves are threatened with annihilation, our sense of being flashes up with high intensity. The dark and frightening contrast of death enhances the value of life and intensifies in us the experience of "BEING." Death is the ultimate boundary situation, and the ultimate test of our selves. In a paper titled "Death and the Self," Jonathan Dollimore (1997, 255) argues that in a "terrible yet fascinating sense, death drives life. Which means that life at its most intense is always on the edge of its own ruin." He calls it a "paradox that disease and death are only life manifested in its most vigorous form."[2] He also quotes Thomas Mann, "who regarded Nietzsche's development as a case history of progressive syphilis, a disease which 'was to destroy his life but also to intensify it enormously.'"[3]

In an earlier book, I argued that the experience of human mortality, and the anxiety accompanying it, have played a role of primary importance in the creation and maintenance of civilizations. Let me add here the obvious fact that they play a major role in the construction of our selves as well.[4]

The ultimate source of fear and anxiety is undoubtedly the potential destruction of our lives.[5] Whenever this threat arises, existential anxiety is triggered in us. This fear of mortality and this anxiety signal the danger and mobilize our defense mechanisms. They prompt us to protect ourselves against this loss of safety, identity, self-esteem, love, freedom, and meaning—not only, and perhaps not primarily, in a defensive but also in a life-expanding and creative way. They prompt us to construct and reconstruct the protective structures, physical and symbolical, of our lives. And they prompt us to construct and continuously reconstruct our selves.

In his famous book on the history of sin and fear in Western civilization, Jean Delumeau (1990, 4, 5) stressed the role of fear in enhancing people's will to create themselves. He spoke of "creative anxiety." The "intense guilt feeling" of Western man "led him to examine his own past, to know himself better, to develop his memory, . . . and to explore his own identity." Fear has been one of the important sources of "both individualism and the sense of responsibility." Fear "has two sides. . . . It can be either salutary or destructive. As a modern philosopher wittily puts it, '*Timeo, ergo sum,*' and it is true that, when viewed in clear focus, fear is a 'call to being.' It is 'creative of being.'" It is creative of our selves.

Throughout our lives, we struggle with the dangers of this world, we try to protect ourselves against the fears and anxieties in our hearts. We develop attitudes and patterns of behavior that protect us best in a not-altogether-friendly world. We trust magic spells, superstitions, rituals. We generate symbolic systems (mythologies, religions, systems of beliefs, ideas, works of art), which surround us with a protective sphere in a cold and empty universe. And our selves, our personalities are being shaped and constructed in, and by, this process.

The fact that human beings have to protect themselves in a not-too-hospitable world, and the various human strategies of protecting themselves, have been studied in various disciplines. I briefly discussed this issue in the introduction to this book. Let me give a few further details.

According to the Nobel Prize–winning biologist S. E. Luria (1973, 150), for instance, humans have an innate immune system against fear. He concludes his book *Life: The Unfinished Experience* with the following statement:

> Humankind is justified, I believe, in suspecting that once again blind evolution has operated with subtle wisdom. While fashioning consciousness and exposing man to the ultimate terror [of inevitable death], it may by natural selection have also brought forth in the human mind some protective compensatory features. Human evolution may have imprinted into man's brain an intrinsic program that opens to him the innermost sources of optimism—art, and joy, and hope, confidence in the powers of the mind, concern for his fellow men, and pride in the pursuit of the unique human adventure.

Anxiety, and the unconscious or semiconscious psychic mechanisms with the help of which we protect ourselves against anxiety, have been at the focus of psychiatric research since the beginning. Freud, Freudians, and other experts have discovered and defined an amazingly large number of these mechanisms. They range from repression and regression to projection and introjection; identification, reaction formation, reversal, blocking and displacement; isolation, undoing, denial, depersonalization, acting out, forgetting, obsessional thinking, neurosis formation, escape into madness, paranoia, hysteria, depression, and sublimation; and even to humor and creativity, common sense and self-assuring techniques, trivialization, intoxication, and the evocation of commonly shared values.[6]

According to Ernest Becker—an eminent follower and critic of Freud, whom we have already mentioned in the introduction—much more was at stake in the ordeal of humankind than shelter and safety. In his *The Denial of Death* (1973, ix), he argues that the human being is unable to accept the fatality of death and is forced by his tragic situation and the "terror of death" to assert himself or herself, his self or her self, in a narcissistic way, as a unique—and as such, immortal—value in the universe. He "must desperately justify himself as an object of primary value in the universe; he must stand out, be a hero, make the biggest contribution to world life, show that he *counts* more than anything or anyone else."[7] He quotes William James, according to whom the world is "essentially a theater for heroism."[8] "Society itself is a codified hero system, which means that society everywhere is a living myth of the significance of human life, a defiant creation of meaning."[9] We may add that human life itself is a defiant attempt to create one's self as something that may overarch the precipice between life and death.

Peter L. Berger (1967, 1969) gives an even more dramatic account of the human condition and the human search for meaning and for an authentic self. He starts from the same proposition as Scheler and Gehlen: Human beings are "premature animals," they are being born with an inefficient instinctual structure. They suffer from "a built-in instability" and can "balance" themselves only by building up their selves and their own worlds. They attain a certain degree of maturity only in early adulthood and have to construct and reconstruct their selves throughout their lives, without ever attaining the Faustian moment of the complete fulfillment of an imagined, ideal self. In Berger's words, human society is "an enterprise of world-building."[10] And let me add: It is also a never-ending enterprise of building our selves.

In the introduction, we dealt with the "Terror Management Theory" of Tom Pyszczynski and his coauthors (Pyszczynski, Greenberg, and Solomon 1997) in some detail. They argued, and partially proved, that people try to cope with the fact, and fear, of human mortality by boosting their selves, the sense of their personal value, and their belief in a consistent and ordered, meaningful and just world, and by living up to the moral standards of their society.

We may conclude, without giving further examples, that existential fear and anxiety may have ever played a major role in shaping people's lives and selves.[11]

Death in the Consumer Civilization

Let me ask first what all this may have to do with our contemporary civilization of consumption. How can fear and existential anxiety be reconciled with what we know about consumerism? How could they have anything to do with the cheerful, lighthearted, apparently irresponsible cavalcade and hurly-burly of consumer civilization? Could it be proved that, as in the case of our traditional civilization, the forms, structures, symbolic systems, myths, and messages of consumer civilization have also been generated and are maintained by—beside other factors—people's fight with the anguish-filled experience and anxieties of their mortality?[12]

I think it could. People living in contemporary Western civilization have become especially defenseless against this experience. Their selves need the help of their civilization, of a civilization, badly. And if the traditional forms, structures, and symbols of their civilization fail to provide this protection, they may turn to a new constellation of forms, structures, and symbols, which is—in the present case—the civilization of consumption.

In the following chapters, I shall argue that the passionate and hectic cult of the human self may also have its source in people's existential anxiety, which has become deeper and stronger in a world that has lost its framework of transcendence. For lack of something else, we oppose the glorious human personality to an empty universe, and to a destiny of mortality. And I shall also try to show, and possibly prove, that even the most trivial genres of our contemporary culture have this existential deep structure and function: They help us cope with the experience of our mortality. The duality, the tension, the interaction of the trivial and the existential, the trivial and the tragic, has probably become sharper, and more intense, than it has ever been in the history of our civilization. The extent to which consumer civilization in general, and the media in particular, exploit the motif of death as a source of intense (life) experience is stupefying. One is tempted to say that the Proletarian Renaissance is a whirling carnival and a dance of death at the same time.

Believe it or not, death is one of the most frequent motifs in our contemporary popular genres. It is a recurrent and almost compulsory motif in television films and plays a major role in popular magazines as well, in spite of the fact that these magazines are thought, and expected, to present a glamorous and harmonious world modestly spiced with some well-tasting scandals and pieces of gossip.

This is true, though, only if we do not reduce the concept of life to sheer biological survival; if we take human existence in its broadest sense; if we consider human life and the human self in their wholeness and freedom, dignity and meaning. Our existence, and our selves, defined in this way, are threatened even in the trivial accidents of everyday life. If we are humiliated, or if we fail to do something, our self-esteem—that is, our existence as a human person—is impaired. If we lose our jobs, it is not only our physical existence that is threatened but also our social standing, our existence as a social being. If we lose the love of somebody whose love was essential for us, our deepest self is hurt, our existence as a feeling human being is injured. If our freedom is limited or destroyed, then our very existence as a human person is threatened, curbed, thwarted. If the purpose and meaning of our lives get blurred or are lost, the foundation of our very existence and self is shaken, and we experience the terror of chaos and absurdity. In all these situations, the foundations of our lives are shattered. We lose our feeling of safety. Our lives are impaired and threatened. We suddenly feel how fragile and perishable our lives are. We find ourselves at the edge of a precipice, the precipice of destruction and nonbeing. We are in a boundary situation, Sartre would say, where we have to make an important decision: to retreat and accept the defeat, to escape back into our everyday routines and resignation, or to have the courage to face the fact of our mortality, and have the strength to challenge a world full of suffering; and to fight for a free and authentic existence for ourselves and our fellow beings.

Let us confess that in our everyday lives we do not like these boundary situations. But, strangely enough, we tremble with delight and ecstasy if we can watch these *salti mortali* into freedom indirectly, on the screens of our TV sets, or in the pages of popular magazines.[13] We are delighted to see the tidal wave come, the volcano erupt and threaten the happy community on its slopes; we are thrilled to see the world of Evil open and crime, violence, murder, revenge overwhelm, for a moment, our world; we are fascinated by the sight of blade runners, terminators, alien monsters, demons, and Satan himself (or herself) playing havoc with our universe; we are delighted to see ambulances and police cars hysterically rushing and flashing across the cities, and we are thrilled that the clock of the terrorists' nuclear bomb is already ticking and the hero has to decide about life and death in an instant by cutting the red or the blue wire (in 99 percent of the cases, he or she cuts the right one). The ultimate pleasure is when humankind as a whole is threatened by an extreme, cataclysmic peril: This is the real boundary situation and the source of the most intense experience of being.

How to explain this overwhelming presence of destruction and death in our world so dedicated to LIFE and the joy of living? Is it a necessary psychological counterbalance? Would neo-Darwinian references to our innate aggressiveness, or Freudian references to an innate death wish in us, account for the presence of these signs of morbidity in our popular culture? Is it due to the fact that our traditional ways of coping with the fear of death have lost at least part of their relevance? Do we have an innate thirst for sensational events, and do we turn to death, especially unexpected, dramatic death, as a par excellence exciting experience? Or what? I propose a further explanation.

We are delighted to see these pictures of the destruction of the human world and the human self for two reasons. First, as we have said, in boundary situations, when we meet destruction and death—that is, virtual, immunized destruction and death—we experience life at its highest intensity. And second, these scenes give us an additional shot of energy and euphoria because they show, almost without exception, that the human being stands its ground, the hero braves the elements, and he or she ultimately defeats Evil, the monsters, death.

With its adventure series, cop shows, catastrophe films, emergency wards, and firefighter series, television permanently confronts us, shocks us, titillates us, and makes us flirt with death, with nonexistence. Seeing all these encounters with boundary situations, pace Sartre or Jaspers, we might almost speak of a "popular" or "proletarian existentialism."[14]

We enjoy these symbolic encounters, we need them, not as if we had a penchant for morbidity. We fear death, but the media reinforce us, a dozen times a day, in our belief, conviction, and illusion that though we live in an alien world, the forces of evil and destruction, danger, and death can be defeated if we have the courage and determination to prevail. Many people may die in these cataclysms. But we, the protagonists, are saved from underneath the avalanche or mudslide, from the ninety-ninth floor of the blazing tower, from the terror of an earthquake, from our aircraft that is finally landing with only one wing and the engines ablaze. We prefer to be saved in the very last moment, because to experience a genuinely existential, or even existentialist, boundary situation we have to proceed to the very edge of the precipice, of nonbeing, of the void. This is the ultimate test of strength for our selves.[15]

I am going to show with a few examples how the media use and abuse the effects inherent in these boundary situations. I shall focus on one single genre: women's magazines. To sharpen the focus even further, as a first step I have picked, in a random way, one single issue of a women's magazine and have checked how much it exploits boundary situations as sources of intense existential experience.[16] I have cross-checked; other magazines of this genre, and other issues, would provide similar results.

One would think that these magazines revolve around fashion, homes, diet, cosmetics, beauty, children, gardening, cooking, and the like. Yes, they do. But, much as it may seem incredible, death is the most, or one of the most frequent, motifs in them, if we define human life—as we did just above—in its broadest sense: in its freedom, dignity, well-being, public respect; and if we define death as the destruction of life in any of these dimensions.

The contrast of being and nonbeing, life and death, keeps flashing up in the colorful world of women's and men's magazines. It generates in the readers the experience of a high intensity of life, and the illusion that time and mortality can be defeated. This is one of the main sources of the tremendous appeal these magazines have for their readers; for people who need the experience of an intense and authentic existence, and the feeling of immortality, badly; for people who try to care for their selves in an age and civilization without the traditional forms of transcendence; for people who most of the time do not realize that while they are reading the trivial stories in their magazines, they are also battling with the ultimate concerns of the human condition.

The Beauty and the Death

One of the tricks of these popular magazines is to present life as extremely valuable in order to make the experience of its destruction more upsetting. This has ever been a staple method of the great tragic playwrights as well; they portrayed the tragic falls of great personalities, great "selves," of kings and queens, princes and princesses, and not those of everyday people. The greater and more spectacular the fall, the stronger was the impact, and the higher was the intensity of the existential experience.

This is a central and recurrent motif also in the issue of *Bunte* that we are going to analyze. Its most spectacular development is to be found in the story of a beautiful German countess, Pilar Goes.[17] The article exposes, already in the table of contents, the sharp contrast of life and death:

Pilar Goes: On the Death of a Society-Girl[18]

In the mirror of the *Bunte* article, almost all the possible values of a human life coalesce in the person of Pilar Goes: "She was so beautiful that she became world famous for it" — "She was a phenomenon in international society" — "She had a magic personality" — "She was an aristocrat, member of an ancient family" — "A star model" — "Editor of a beautiful home magazine" — "A successful business woman" — "She intensely engaged herself in Bosnia relief projects" — "She had rich lovers: the billionaire skipper Spyros Niarchos, for instance, and Karim Aga Khan" — "A brilliant woman's life in the jet set" — "Niki Lauda said: She was one of the greatest personalities."[19] All in all, she was life in its full beauty and wealth. And then, suddenly, she was diagnosed with a brain tumor and she died, in five months.

The writer of the article did a good job. As in a medieval morality play, he staged a harrowing struggle between life and death. He sharpened the contrast between them to the extreme. He opposed

YOUTH	and	DEATH
BEAUTY	and	DEATH
WEALTH	and	DEATH
POWER	and	DEATH
SUCCESS	and	DEATH
FAME	and	DEATH
STARDOM	and	DEATH
AGAPE	and	DEATH
LOVE	and	DEATH
COURAGE	and	DEATH
SPRING	and	DEATH
THE FULLNESS OF LIFE	and	DEATH

The opposition of these two columns, however, gives the wrong impression about the final impact of the article. It does not proclaim the victory of death over life, over the human being, over everything that is valuable and noble in life, but vice versa. It portrays life in its beauty, fullness, and dignity, in its glory, which suggests that life can ultimately transcend death.

To reinforce this positive impact, the author of the article describes the last, heroic days of the dying countess. These last days must have had their dignity, and nothing is reduced from the tragic greatness of the countess by the fact that the author of the article uses—to emphasize the victory of life over death—some motifs of the best traditions of sentimental literature:

> She was strong in her life and in her death. . . . She waited for her death with courage and dignity . . . Jürgen Hirzberger, . . . Pilar Goes' best friend, . . . was by her two days before her death. . . . The windows were wide open, to let the first spell of spring into the room. For two and a half hours they spoke of Life, and not of dying. "She was most beautiful. Though she had serious pains, she wanted to preserve her dignity until the last moment."
>
> Pilar Goes, 42, gathered her family around her deathbed. This is the last night. She would not survive this night, this is her doctors' diagnosis. . . . A priest administers the Last Sacrament to the faithful Catholic woman. She refuses to take heavy morphia. The good-bye has to be said with clear mind and clear heart. She wanted to die at home. . . . Shortly before her death, she was cheerful. . . . She held her parents and sisters for the last time. . . . Then it was over, exactly five months after the diagnosis. . . . A martyrdom.[20]

The open window suggests the freedom of the immortal spirit, and spring is a symbol of life, of birth, and not of death. She spoke of life, not of dying. Beauty, too, is a symbol of eternity. Death is defeated by the courage and dignity with which the dying faces it. She is raised from the ranks of ordinary mortals by being "one of the greatest personalities" in the world. Dying at home, in the circle of her family, may have protected her against the terror of an empty and dark universe. Her cheerful spirit in the last hours challenged the terror of death. Martyrdom is the final victory of the human self over death.

This multiplication of life symbols helps the magazine fulfill one of its basic functions: to help its readers experience the fullness of life and the greatness of the human person who has conquered death.

The Martyrdom of the Monster with a Golden Heart

The same contrast of life and death, the human self and destiny, is also developed into a fearful drama in another article in the same issue of *Bunte*. It is the story of the life and death of the famous German film star Horst Frank.[21] Here the method is not to enhance the value of life to the extreme in order to strike the most intense spark possible from the contrast of life and death, of the glory and the destruction of the human self. The source of an intense experience of being lies here in the fact that life and death are pressed together, into one short existential moment. And we have seen how much "the significant moment" is important for the human self in an age without transcendence.

In our everyday lives, we keep the concepts of life and death as far from each other as possible. We keep thinking of life and try to ignore death. We bring our dead out of the city, into a peaceful churchyard, which, in earlier times, was safely surrounded by stone walls.[22] The author of this article does just the contrary; she focuses on the instant in which the question of life or death has to be decided: "Is it allowed to help somebody die?" The young wife of the old and lethally sick actor has to decide whether the life-support machines should be disconnected:[23]

> The worst moment must be in which one has to utter the words: Disconnect it! This trifling interim moment. Between Life and Death. A twinkling of an eye and it has happened: crossing of a boundary. A human being dares to interfere with God's work. A taboo is broken.[24]

These lines are theatrical, but they skillfully enhance the tension. A moment — a trifling interim moment — the moment between Life and Death. And to further heighten excitement and intensity, she adds that in this moment the human being revolts against God, almost becomes a god by usurping God's privilege of deciding about life and death, and has the audacity of breaking a holy taboo. This already is a genuine *situation limite,* a boundary situation exposed in a cheap weekly magazine. Here again we are at a meeting point of the trivial and the tragic.

A series of further motifs reinforce this effect. A strong contrast flashes up already in the subtitle of the article: "A Merciful Death for the Criminal." For three decades, Horst Frank was, namely, the cruel and bloody-handed monster of German films and television series. He was Satan incarnate, and now love and mercy help him die. The archetypal motif of "the-monster-with-a-golden-heart," too, flashes up as we are told that this brutal thug was, in his real life, a sensitive man, reading and writing poetry, who did not hurt a fly.[25] The ancient motif of Fortune's Wheel emerges here as well: The celebrated star dies poor and forgotten. His fate is transformed into a romantic and existentialist metaphor: "He fell, with a divided heart, into Nothingness." I shall come back in a moment to this archetypal motif of the-fall-into-nonbeing.

The intensity of life is here further enhanced by portraying Frank as a genuine romantic and decadent hero who devoured and, at the same time, squandered life.[26] This is an especially important motif because it radiates the experience of both life and freedom. He adored life but was not enslaved by it; he dispersed it, wasted it of his own free will. He was the master of life, and not vice versa. The aristocratic and tragic, Byronian and Baudelairian, gesture of adoring and freely wasting life: Is it not surprising to encounter it here, in the world of popular magazines, in the "Proletarian Renaissance" of our contemporary consumer civilization?[27]

Women's magazines may be considered and scorned as superficial, cheap, and sloppy. But, as we see, in their best moments, they are able to convey— even if slightly mixed with, and watered down by, sentimentality—a genuine and intense human experience. And they may help people—in their own, not very authentic way—face mortality and death.

The Wheel of Fortune

The Wheel of Fortune, too, is an archetype. It expresses the experience of the fragility of human life, the transience of our existence in this world, the human drama of being born, trying to reach the peaks, and then facing, with terror or dignity, the inevitable decline into nothingness. It satisfies the human longing for justice: Behold, even the most powerful and richest in this world come to dust, like any of us. There is also a warning against pride and arrogance: One should not credit oneself with one's success. It is the Wheel of Fortune that elevates you to the heights of fame and success and lets you fall into oblivion and darkness.

At first glance, this Wheel seems to be very much out of tune with the basic message and mood of our contemporary consumer civilization. Instead of preaching the victory of the human being—his or her freedom and strength to control his or her fate, the glory of a self-actualizing human life—it suggests the fragility and mutability of the human condition. In a number of medieval illustrations, skeleton-Death, with its scythe, stands by the Wheel, while men and women are desperately trying to climb up on this side and are falling into the depths on the other side. This lurid medieval *topos* has reemerged in late-twentieth-century and early-twenty-first-century popular culture, usually combined with another archetype. This latter was called "The Fall of Princes," and it was a cherished symbol in the tormented centuries of the late Middle Ages and the early Modern Age. In the wake of Boccaccio's *De casibus illustrium virorum,* telling the story of the rise and fall of great monarchs and warlords, a series of translations, adaptations, and supplements were published. In England, for instance, Thomas Hoccleve's *The Regement of Princes* and John Lydgate's *The Fall of Princes* were the great early "best sellers," while in the sixteenth century *A Mirror for Magistrates* (1559–87) became the favorite reading of many, and an important source for Shakespeare's plays. The medieval versions had portrayed the mutability of human life and the idea of *sic transit gloria mundi,* whereas the Renaissance adaptations were much more moral lessons for the "magistrates," that is, for the rulers and high-ranking public servants of the age.

This archetype has resurfaced now and again ever since and is an important source of inspiration in contemporary popular literature as well. But the same drama of the rise and fall of the great has a new function, it conveys a new message. The aim now is not so much to suggest the frailty and vanity of human life, or to teach the "magistrates" how to behave. It is not any more a warning of *vanitatum vanitas,* and neither is it a moral lecture à la Renaissance. This ancient motif serves now the basic goal of the consumer civilization. It enhances the intensity of life to a degree at which it can already withstand the terror of death. It boosts life to heroic dimensions in order to render the fall a stunning existential experience. Just as in Greek or Shakespearean tragedies, it suggests that there is some essential dignity, meaning, and immortality in the fall of great human beings. This is why the fall of tragic heroes has an elevating and cathartic, and not a depressing, effect. The Fall-of-Princes motif, and especially its modern consumer version in our contemporary media, fully exploits this source of intense existential experience.

Heroes need not die physically. Oedipus does not die after the tragic break in his life, and neither does Electra in Sophocles' and O'Neill's plays. Nor do Gerda and Hjlamar die at the and of *The Wild Duck,* or Martha and George at the end of Albee's famous play. The fall of Horst Frank lasted several years. He died, first, a kind of public, professional, psychological death: He lost his voice, his fame, his fortune, and his role as a famous public person. And only much later did he lose his life. The destruction of the public self may be as tragic, and as "existential," as the physical death of the private self.

Popular magazines squeeze even the last drops of emotional and existential impact out of these "falls." Let us examine this with a concrete example: How a *Bunte* article presents the news that Boris Becker has concluded his tennis career.

The Fall of Princes

The title of the *Bunte* article already suggests that retiring from the glamorous world of success and fame is as if one fell from life into death:

Is There Life after Tennis?[28]

The fact that this is a boundary situation, a *situation limite,* is stressed by repeating the fact that something very important has come to a close here. "Boris Becker played here *for the last time*." "He stood there, *for the last time,* in the limelight." "This was my *last* game," Boris Becker said.[29] A few pages later, we read of Steffi Graf, a "winner in defeat," that "she played *for the last time* in Wimbledon."[30]

But this would not probably have the necessary impact. It has to be emphasized that something more important is happening here than a simple transition from one life phase to the next one. It has to be stressed that this is a fall into a precipice, from being into nonbeing. This is being done here by repeating it as a musical *Leitmotif* throughout the article, until it is deeply engraved in the readers' minds.

"And what next"? the author asks. "Will he fall in the black hole feared by everybody when giving up his profession?" We are told that Stefan Edberg had great difficulty coping with this experience. But Becker says that he "has not fallen in a black hole." His friend, Beckenbauer, confirms this, saying that "Becker has not fallen into a deep hole." This is followed by a survey of the great "falls" of recent years. Henry Maske, the famous box champion, "fell in a deep hole" after his retirement. Michael Jürgen, the former editor in chief of *Stern* magazine, says that "he fell in a black hole" when he lost his position. Henning Voscherau, on the other hand, the former mayor of Hamburg, who was not reelected in 1977, is an exception. He courageously looked into the precipice: "On the morning of the day following his defeat, at 9 o'clock sharp, he appeared in his private praxis as a public notary. "I ignored advice to go and relax somewhere in the sunshine. I did not want to exchange a black hole for a sunny hole."[31]

And, to choose a prominent example: What has happened, for instance, to Bill Clinton? For almost a decade, he was at the peak of power and fame. What kind of precipice opened under his feet when he closed the door of the White House behind him, *for the last time?* To my surprise, the popular press has not exploited the existential excitement of this spectacular boundary situation as fully as it could have done.

The Scandal

We love scandals. They are exciting, mischievous, liberating. They radiate an intense experience of life and being. They activate a whole range of motifs of a strong emotional appeal: the motifs of betrayal, vengeance, crime, lying, cheating, family tragedy, public humiliation, and so on and so forth.[32]

The strength of scandal lies in its also being a boundary situation. Scandals start as great Greek or Renaissance tragedies do. Or, vice versa, we could say that great tragedies start with scandals. It suddenly turns out that Oedipus is the most wanted murderer of the city: This is a scandal! And the scandal jolts the everyday life of the city out of its joints and pushes Oedipus to a precipice. Have you heard? It was Claudius and Gertrude who murdered the Father of Hamlet? A scandal! And Prince Hamlet, who was the symbol of Renaissance flamboyance, puts on the jet-black dress of death.[33] Desdemona has an affair with Cassio? A scandal! And Othello and Desdemona fall into nothingness.

In our everyday lives, we dread to think of the possibility that we might be involved in, and destroyed by, a scandal. But we have a more ambiguous attitude toward scandals when the victims are other people. We enjoy these scandals but, at the same time, we feel slightly uneasy and even scared. We are scared because scandals disrupt the everyday order of our world and the monsters of anarchy begin suddenly to rise. But we enjoy them as well, because it is delicious to be liberated from the routines of our everyday lives and enjoy, for a moment, the welling up of our instincts, emotions, fantasies; an experience that seems to be much more fascinating and intense then our everyday lives.[34] We enjoy this experience, though, only for a moment because if this eruption of our emotions and instincts did not end soon, if anarchy overflowed our world, we would be terrified and would desperately try to escape back into our normal lives. In a lighter and more frivolous way, we go trough the same experience under the impact of jokes. Jokes only flirt with the "alien world" of anarchy—the subconscious, the irrational, the collapse of order—but they help us back, over the bridge of laughter, into the safety of our everyday lives.[35]

Something similar happens in the wake of scandals. Hearing the news, the seams of the world burst open. The actors of public life suddenly fall out of their dignified stature and roles—they are unmasked, the carefully hidden secrets of their lives are exposed, the semblance surrounding them is lifted, the curtains of hypocrisy and lies rise. They have suddenly become fearful monsters or defenseless wrecks, ridiculous or miserable. We may laugh at them, or shudder at them. Nobody and nothing protects them any more. Predator and cannibal instincts rear in us. And we feel to be very much alive. Shame comes later, if at all.

Commercial television and the popular press blow scandals up into sensations, into exciting, moving, cataclysmic dramas.[36] They sharpen the contrast between the normal and the scandalous, between being and nonbeing to the extreme. Let us see an example again from *Bunte*.

As it is well known, about two weeks before the planned royal wedding, an English tabloid, *The Sun,* published some of those spicy photos that were taken a decade ago of Sophie Rhys-Jones, the bride of Prince Edward. *Bunte*—a bit hypocritically—joined those papers that protested against this sensationalism but used the occasion to squeeze even the last drops of sweet juice out of this scandal. It started its article[37] with a much better title than that of *The Sun:*[38]

Sophie Rhys-Jones:
Her Nude Photo Shatters the Monarchy

And then the article goes on playing on this motif. In the table of contents, we read:

Scandal about the Photo of SRJ.
Could a Nude Photo Hinder the Dream Wedding?

In the interior title, they repeat the strange metaphor:

Does a Bosom Stagger the Monarchy?[39]

This is a masterly way of blowing up a not too significant event into a sensation. Two distant concepts clash here, as two discrepant objects in a surrealist picture: a naked bosom and an empire. The collision is stunning, funny, absurd.

The intensity of the drama is heightened by the fact that this trivial incident, this passing flirtation, may scuttle the happiness of this nice girl and of her royal bridegroom, Prince Edward. In an interview with the *Daily Mail,* Sophie already admits, with resignation, that her marriage has been shipwrecked.[40] From a world of brilliant hopes, Sophie has fallen into the "black hole." Almost. Because at the very last moment, the young couple has a miraculous escape (the "it-was-a-near-miss" motif, and a "happy ending" motif). The Queen, who in such cases used to act with monarchical and puritanical rigor, unexpectedly and magnanimously pardons them (the "stern-giant-has-a-golden-heart" motif). As a last gift, the author of the article acknowledges with satisfaction that we and our world have become more and more tolerant and perfect (the "we-are-great!" motif).[41] We, readers, have also the additional satisfaction of feeling that we are great because we observe this liminal experience from a distance, as a "*communitas*" of respectful citizens, who are reinforced in their moral excellence at the sight of other people's failings.[42]

The story is further dramatized by bringing in Evil, in the person of the intriguer, a disloyal friend, who plays the same role as Ms. Tripp played in the Monica contra Bill melodrama. She is here Kara Noble, who, perhaps out of jealousy (Sophie had got a position that she also wanted), or of envy (she could not catch a royal bridegroom), or of greed (she got about £40 million for giving the pictures to *The Sun*) betrayed her friend with "premeditated cruelty," thereby committing character assassination. The reader is happy when, in the end, she or he is informed that—after all—there is justice in the world, because Kara Noble has been sacked from her lucrative job at a television station (the "Evil-will-ultimately-be-punished" motif). Catharsis.[43]

So in this case life and justice prevail. We have here a happy ending of a story that could have turned into a tragedy. Sophie found herself on the edge of the precipice, of the destruction of her hopes, her public personality, her self, her life. But she was saved in the very last moment; just like all those heroes in the emergency and catastrophe films. Life has again triumphed over death. This is, isn't it, the fundamental duty and privilege of life in the world of our contemporary consumer civilization. And this is a badly needed confirmation of our trust in life, in the human self, in a world where we have to live and where we try to experience life at its highest possible intensity.

The Myth of the Self

I don't want to make money.
I just want to be wonderful.

—*Marilyn Monroe*

The Cult of the Human Personality

Beyond intensely experiencing life, human beings also aspire to the fullness of life. This is more than understandable. Being mortal, and dreading the emptiness or the unknown that may come after they cease to be, they want to acquire, possess, and experience LIFE in its totality. One of the greatest attractions and temptations of consumer civilization lies in the very fact that it offers, twenty four hours a day, the experience, or at least the illusion, of this totality. For this purpose, it has created a special species of gods and demigods, called "celebrities," who are shaped and manipulated in a way to radiate with maximum strength the experience of fullness and immortality to us, fallible and mortal human selves. Roland Barthes' (1983, 254–55) concept of "the dream of wholeness" might be the emblem of both the Renaissance and the Proletarian Renaissance.

The rise of a certain type of human personality to this status of divine fullness goes far back in history. Pharaohs, emperors, kings, and the nobility had this radiation of a fuller and more authentic life.[1] But most of them drew their aura from a transcendental source. As a contrast, in the twentieth and early-twenty-first centuries, the everyday human individual is being prompted to find the ultimate source of this "fullness," and its radiation, in her or his own self.[2]

For people in the Western world, it was not too difficult to convince themselves that the personal existence of a human being is an absolute value and that as such it is the ultimate source of authentic life and bears its own purpose and meaning in itself.[3] It was not in the twentieth century that this formula emerged for the first time. It was already there in the work of Socrates; in the Stoa, the Renaissance, and Romanticism; in the dandyism of the nineteenth century; in the non-Christian branch of existentialism. But it became a dominant conviction, and a broad social phenomenon, only in the second half of the twentieth century.[4]

"My life is the only source of authentic life"; or, "the purpose and meaning of my life is my life": These are not very strong statements.[5] But if we say that the purpose of our lives is to realize as fully as possible the potentials of our lives and selves, then this already means something. And if we add that human life is the only possible value in a dark and empty universe, which probably is void of purpose and meaning, then to protect this life may already be accepted as a relevant goal and program.[6] And it may explain the passionate and unbridled cult of the human self in our contemporary Western civilization.[7]

Logically, the formula is still not very strong, but it seems to be working. It has, however, a great weakness. The traditional frameworks—GOD, NATURE, REASON, HISTORY, FUTURE—overarched the life and death of the individual. Human personality, conversely, does not have this transcendence. Within the short span of an individual life, how can the fullness of LIFE be reached? Is the meaning of an individual life not too fragile, questionable, finite? Does it not perish together with the individual?

Nietzsche solved the dilemma by blowing up the human being into an Übermensch. Neo-Kantians emphasized the transcendental nature of human values. Existentialists elevated human beings to the status of tragic heroes. But, and I am sorry to say, the best strategy has been found by the emerging consumer civilization. As we have just said, it consists in filling the gap left after the collapse of overarching metaphysical constructs by inflating and overinflating the human personality to mythic proportions. It did not invent, but it has transformed, the concept of "celebrity," and it has brought the methods of celebrity creation to perfection. And celebrities are, par excellence, human beings whose lives are extremely intense and full, and have (the semblance of) meaning and immortality. By identifying with them, people can experience their lives, too, as intense, meaningful, and perhaps immortal. People badly need this feeling, this experience, this illusion. They spend a substantial part of their time and energy—even without knowing that they are doing so—chasing this experience. They want to experience the fullness of life, and the full negation of nonbeing, at least by default.

Sociologists developed a different argument. They focused on the painful loss of identity, loss of roles, and loss of self and self-respect during the past century and a half of industrialization. The Industrial Revolution forced tens and hundreds of millions of farmers and craftsmen into factory halls, into the anonymous, proletarian crowd of the great cities. It uprooted people, tore them away from their traditional communities, where they had had their place, their roles, and identities, where their selves were shaped and articulated, where their lives were filled with meaning by the traditional beliefs, myths, and ceremonies of the community.[8] Industrialization deprived them of all this and ultimately robbed them of their humanity, of their human dignity, of their selves. They became nameless nonentities. Commenting on the methods of Taylorism, Stuart Ewen (1988, 80–81) described this process in the following way:

> As [Frederick] Taylor put it, "all possible brain work should be removed from the shop and centered in the planning or laying-out department."[9] Ultimately, Taylorism was a technique designed to assert absolute, managerial control over the productive sphere. . . . The key here was to undercut historic patterns of association and solidarity, to individuate the workforce. . . . Taylor's dream depended on a population that had been eviscerated of its cultural resources, community bonds, and knowledge of craft.

This depersonalization affected the eighteenth- and nineteenth-century middle classes as well, and people suffered from these changes. In Ewen's words (1988, 79):

Over the past century, an ongoing lament has been that of aloneness, iso-lation, invisibility, and insignificance; a desperate thirst for recognition, often expressed as a desire for fame. A great deal of modern literature speaks eloquently of a crisis of the spirit; a condition of anomie and di-minished meaning. Behind the democratic puffery of the modern age, the self grows dimmer. . . . The domain of freedom has been—in many ways—reduced.

To this process of depersonalization, Ewen argues, consumer civilization came as a response, offering people (the illusion of) freedom, significance, and an au-tonomous self.

This is a convincing, but only partially correct, analysis. In the eighteenth and nineteenth centuries, the loss of identity, of meaning, of one's self was not a universal and unilinear process. On the one hand, the process unfolded in different ways in the various social strata; on the other hand, destructive and constructive elements were mixing in it. In the middle classes, these centuries were much more the age of the strengthening than that of the erosion or de-struction of the human self. Yet people in the working classes underwent a deep crisis. The erosion of their identities and selves slowed down in the second half of the nineteenth century, when the rise of social democracy, with its workers' clubs, evening schools, sport clubs, newspapers, and book publishing began to reverse the trend and not only generated a new class consciousness but also strengthened people's consciousness of their rights, dignity, and individual autonomy.[10]

The two great totalitarian ideologies of the twentieth century, bolshevism and fascism, enslaved people and tried to force them into the mold of an im-personal collective being; but, at the same time, their egalitarian rhetoric rein-forced people's sense of right and ultimately thus contributed to the disinte-gration of the collective systems and the strengthening of individualism. In Eastern Europe, the emotional and moral opposition to oppression played an especially significant role in strengthening people's self-consciousness and selves. At the same time, in Western Europe, the development of the welfare state and the consolidation of democracy led to a golden age of the autonomous human personality. And, last but not least, emerging consumer civilization, with its flood of cheap mass commodities, advertising industry, popular magazines, the film industry, the radio, and finally the triumphant television, created a favorable environment for the rise of the "Proletarian Renaissance," which started to radiate new role models, identities, lifestyles, and life strategies, as well as the experience or illusion of a fuller and more authentic personal life.

"Who Are You?"

Nowadays, hundreds of lifestyle magazines and thousands of books promise to help people find their place, succeed, and be happy in this new world. They promise to teach them how to "actualize" their selves, how to "grow," how to develop their "strengths," how to overcome their anxieties, how not to deceive themselves, and so on, and so forth. And people seem to devour this self-actualization literature with the passion of addicts. If some aliens came to our planet from a faraway galaxy, they could hardly understand this craze of the natives (who call themselves *homines sapientes*) about their selves. How can they survive at all if they have so many fundamental problems with their selves, if their selves are so fragile, immature, split, fragmented, anxiety-ridden, or practically nonexistent? These benevolent and naive aliens with built-in, well-balanced, smoothly functioning digital operational systems would be seriously puzzled.

Well, the chaotic richness of problems and therapies offered by these self-construction books are indeed puzzling. Let me quote—without any comment on their content and value—several characteristic titles:

- *Who Are You? 101 Ways of Seeing Yourself* (Godwin 2000).
- *Coffee Wisdom: 7 Finely Ground Principles for Living a Full-Bodied Life* (Cheung 2003).
- *Your Road Map to Lifelong Happiness: A Guide to the Life You Want* (Keyes 1995).
- *Life's Too Short: Pull the Plug on Self-Defeating Behavior and Turn on the Power of Self-Esteem* (Twerski 1995).
- *Removing Your Mask: No More Hiding from Your Truth* (Moss 1992).
- *Struggling for Wholeness* (Anderson and Ream 1986).

- *How to Be Somebody: Open the Door to Personal Growth* (Bernhard 1975).
- *What Type Am I? Discover Who You Really Are* (Baron 1998).
- *I Want to Change, But I Don't Know How!* (Rusk 1986).
- *Overcoming Anxiety for Dummies* (Elliott and Smith 2003).
- *From Fear to Freedom: A Woman's Handbook for High Self-Esteem* (Truchses 1985).
- *Overcoming the Rating Game: Beyond Self-Love, Beyond Self-Esteem* (Hauck 1991).
- *Make It a Winning Life: Success Strategies for Love, Life, and Business* (Rinke 1992).
- *Free to Fly, Dare to Be a Success* (Rothschild and Seff 1985).
- *Executive in Passage: Career in Crisis—The Door to Uncommon Fulfillment* (Marrs 1990).
- *The Power Is Within You* (Hay and Tomchin 1991).
- *Think and Grow Rich* (Hill 1988 [1937]).
- *The Frantic Woman's Guide to Life: A Year's Worth of Hints, Tips, and Tricks* (Rulnick and Schneider 2004).
- *Becoming Real : Defeating the Stories We Tell Ourselves That Hold Us Back* (Slatz 2004).
- *The Achilles Syndrome: Turning Your Weaknesses into Strengths* (Bloomfield and Felder 1985).

Here are also some of the characteristic chapter and section titles from the Bloomfield and Felder (1985) book mentioned above:

Discovering Your Achilles Heel. You are Bigger Than Your Achilles Heel. Your Achilles Heel: An Opportunity for Growth. *I'm Always Feeling Tense and Rushed.* I Keep Finding the Wrong Person; Mending a Broken Heart. *When I Look in The Mirror, I'm Never Quite Satisfied.* Your Most Important Beauty Exercise. The Fear of Fat. "I Dread Aging." *I Can't Stand Criticism.* Overcoming the Approval Trap. Dealing with a Critical Boss. *"I'm Always Feeling Tense and Rushed."* The Fate of Ms. Late and Mr. I-Hate-to-Wait. Doing Less to Accomplish More. *I Wish I Could Be Happier.* "I Thought Loving You Would Make Me Happier." Overcoming Self-Doubt and Fear; Empowering Yourself. Where Do You Go From Here?[11]

In recent years, "self-acceptance" seems to have become even more important than "self-construction"—though, perhaps, it is only a gentle, painless, customer-friendly version of self-construction. Here are some characteristic titles:

- *Stop Being Mean to Yourself: A Story about Finding the True Meaning of Self-Love* (Beattie 1998).
- *Embracing Our Selves* (Stone and Winkelman 1985).
- *Ending the Struggle against Yourself: A Workbook for Developing Deep Confidence and Self-Acceptance* (Taubman 1994).
- *Pathological Self-Criticism: Assessment and Treatment* (Bergner 1995).
- *Soul without Shame: A Guide to Liberating Yourself from the Judge* (Brown 1999).
- *The Feeling Good Handbook* (Burn 1999).
- *Journeys to Self-Acceptance: Fat Women Speak* (Wiley 1994).
- *Body Wars: Making Peace with Women's Bodies—An Activist's Guide* (Maine 2000).
- *The Ultimate Weight Solution. The 7 Keys to Weight Loss Freedom* (McGraw 2003).

This last is a prize-winning title. There are at least four magic words in it, which appeal to the reader's basic drives and make the book irresistible. First, it promises "the solution" to people who are starved for solutions in their lives full of unsolved problems. Second, it enhances its own appeal by saying that it is offering the "ultimate" solution: Superlatives radiate intensity, and the feeling that we have reached the cosmic limits of human existence. And, in a way, they create the illusion of transcendence in a world that has lost its transcendental framework. Third, it hands over to its readers seven magic keys that can open all the secrets of the world for the reader.[12] And finally, it does not simply guarantee its readers that they will lose their weight if they follow the advice of the author; it also promises them the "freedom" of weight loss, which is something much more noble and spiritual.

Along with this self-help literature, consumer civilization has an even more powerful wonder weapon in the fight for the actualization of our selves and the fulfillment of our lives: the cult of celebrities.

Celebrities

The word "celebrity" means more than just to be famous. It derives from the Latin world *"celebrare,"* meaning to visit something or someone in the company of many other people; to celebrate a feast, a ceremony; to honor, solemnize, extol, or fete someone. Celebrities are not only famous, known by many people; they are also adored like superhuman beings, like gods. Rich mythologies are built around them by the media, mythologies that make us believe that their lives are more intense and fuller than ours, that their lives are saturated with important secrets and meaning. We can hardly resist their intense radiance. They shape our words, our attitudes, our vision of the world, our selves.[13]

There were famous people in traditional societies as well, people whom rank, power, wealth, or an extraordinary achievement surrounded with a shining aura. Think for instance of mythic heroes, prophets, god-kings, martyrs, or later of wealthy and powerful princes and counts, popes, and bishops; myths and legends, ceremonies and rituals raised them to the mysterious heights of fame. Or think of a few famous generals, admirals, adventurers, and rebels, of a Joan of Arc, Don Giovanni, Savanarola, or Till Eulenspiegel. In our contemporary mass societies, the media, television, popular magazines, advertising, and Hollywood can transform even ordinary people into stars, celebrities, gods, and goddesses. They condense into these people everything that is missing in people's lives: wealth; power and beauty; talent and high performance; pleasure and excitement; strong, fascinating selves; significant, meaningful lives; the totality of life; life triumphing over death. Or life that staggers us with the fearful tragedy of its destruction.

In this respect, the difference between traditional civilizations, on the one hand, and our contemporary civilization, on the other, is not so great as one could expect. The twentieth century did not invent advertising. Even the simplest chief of a tribe had strong public relations machinery—think of his costumes, insignia, the rituals surrounding him. Or think of kings and emperors, with their masters of ceremony, chroniclers, courtiers, symbols, and ceremonies. Or think of the self-advertising of medieval cathedrals, fairs, or monasteries on the main pilgrimage routes, the martyrologies, the *Chansons de Geste,* and the like.[14]

But as far as the range and depth of their impact, and the variety of their tools and strategies, contemporary media outstrip all these early advertising and public relations activities. They have built up the Olympic world of celebrities and broadcast to hundreds of millions of people the models, the vision, the illusion of the fulfillment of life, and the apotheosis of the human self. Walter Benjamin (1968b, 222–23) argued that photography and the modern techniques of reproduction have "desacralized" the world. According to Stuart Ewen (1988, 93), the cult of celebrity has just the opposite effect:

> The phenomenology of celebrity is nearly the opposite. If great art loses its aura in the marketplace of mass impression, the individual life of the celebrity achieves an aura through mass reproduction. In their ability to magnify, and to create near universal recognition, the mass media are able to invest the everyday lives of formerly everyday people with a magical sense of value, a secularized imprint of the *sacred*.

This is only partly true, however, because the gods of our contemporary Olympus may be important models but have no providential power: One cannot pray to them, they do not descend from heaven, and so on—though some of them have come quite close to divine status. Elvis Presley's Graceland is the destination of tens of thousands of pilgrims every year. And for many fans, celebrities' relics have the same magic power that martyrs' relics may have had for the faithful in the Middle Ages.

But the real power of stars lies in their ability to radiate the fullness of life, the glory of the human being, the meaningfulness of life:

> They have status; they are admired. They are potent. They are sexy; they live close to the edge; they step beyond the bounds; they set the bounds; they are self-directing; they are spontaneous. They are spared the limits of everyday life; they are exempt.[15]

Our contemporary consumer civilization has developed a powerful menagerie of celebrities. The creation of stars has become a profession. Media, marketing, and public relations experts first choose persons who are good material for being transformed into stars because they "have something in them"; they may be dazzlingly beautiful, may have a mysterious smile, or an enchanting voice, they may have a certain radiation or charisma, sex appeal and/or temperament. And then they create myths and concoct scandals around them, keep them in the limelight, on the screens, and in the celebrity columns of illustrated magazines. In this way, they ultimately create the semblance that these people are full of life and energy, they live an intense life, they have character, they have secrets, they are the heroes or victims of great and real human dramas, they know something. All in all, they create the illusion that these people, these stars, exist more than we ordinary people do.

And this is not the end of the process yet. Once they have been created, properly nurtured, and groomed, stars have to attract the gazes of a growing number of people. They perish if they fail to do so.

The Gaze

Social psychologists, cultural anthropologists, and even philosophers have convincingly argued—think, for instance, of the "I versus Me" theory of William James or G. H. Mead, the I and Thou concept of Martin Buber, or the argument about the "communicative action" of Jürgen Habermas—that being perceived by other people is, if not a precondition, at least an important factor in reinforcing our egos, our identities, our sense of being somebody. We live by, and in, the gazes of others. We are the sums of the gazes directed at us. The more people perceive us, the more we exist. Instead of *Cogito ergo sum,* one could say: *Percipior ergo sum.*[16]

As a matter of fact, we do not exist more if we are perceived by other people. Or do we? In a certain sense, we do. An appreciative gaze coming from a beautiful lady or an attractive gentleman, or from our boss, or the prime minister of our country, may boost our life energies. Our sense of being a person of significance may be reinforced by the gazes directed at us by the members of our community (though in a courtroom, with ourselves in the dock, these gazes may have the opposite effect; the rest of our self-assurance may be undermined by them).

In public life, being perceived by more and more people may certainly boost our sense of personality. And in our mediatized world, this is even more so. People have "ratings" in the everyday life of their community, as TV programs have in the world of the media. The more people see us, the more our public personality is inflated, the more our sense of being somebody grows stronger, the more we feel that we exist.

Think of John, who lives on a farm. He hardly goes anywhere. He is perceived by the members of his family, by some friends, by his neighbors, let's say by about hundred people altogether. This is a 0.0001 percent rating in a country of 10 million people, like Portugal or Hungary. In other words, this means that the intensity of his life is multiplied only by hundred gazes.

In the same country, the mayor of a small town may be known by 1,000 people. This is a 0.001 percent rating, and a slightly higher concentration of "gazes." If the mayor happens to be interviewed on a television program, for a certain period of time he may be recognized by, let's say, 100,000 people. This may make him feel that his life glows with a higher intensity. Let us call this the "perceptual life intensity." This is one of the attractions, and temptations, of public life. And it is one of the most cherished commodities in our consumer civilization.

The anchorwoman of a national TV network may be perceived and known by 1 million people. A famous Hollywood star may be recognized by 2 billion people. In principle, this adds a tremendous intensity to her life, if our hypothesis about the role of being "perceived" is correct. And it is due to this fact that she can shine like a "star"—or the sun. When she retires, she will be seen by fewer and fewer people and, as a consequence, her radiance will gradually fade. She will experience, in all likelihood, a gradual loss of her life intensity, and she may suffer from it.

The strength, and the ability, of gazes to reinforce our sense of existence depend on two factors. The first is the size of the relevant community within which we are perceived; and second is the importance of the people by whom we are perceived.

If the world for us consists of those hundred people who live in our village, to be known by all the members of the community may give us a feeling of importance; it may reinforce our feeling of identity. If our reference frame is the country, with 10 million inhabitants, then being perceived only by a hundred people may be frustrating and, instead of adding to the intensity of our life experience, may decrease it. In other words, this means that in recent decades, with the disappearance of local and national borders—that is, with the widening of the reference community—people need more and more "gazes" directed at them to achieve the same feeling of intensity and significance that they did before. Due to the process of "globalization," "mediatization," and "de-identification," the perceptual life intensity of everyday people and local or national celebrities has suffered painful losses. Formerly famous celebrities, with high life intensities, have shrunk to almost nonentities. They hardly exist, or do not exist at all in the global consciousness, the global media, the sphere of global celebrities. Nowadays the media, or more precisely the TV screens, are considered to be almost the unique loci of authentic human existence and self-hood. Off the screen, one hardly exists.

If the famous anchor person of, say, Lithuanian Television, who is known by everybody in her country, goes to New York, and strolls the streets, she will have lost her aura, and perhaps also her self-confidence. Her heart may sink, her self may shrink, she may realize that she is one insignificant item in an anonymous crowd, somebody of no importance, no name, no nothing. And she may have a shock of happiness when she is suddenly recognized by one of her compatriots from Vilnius; for an instant she will regain her identity, her self, the power of fame that surrounds her in her home country.

To feel one's self and life really important and intense within the global framework, one has to be perceived and known by several hundred million people. Very few people can achieve such an intense presence. In an interview given in 1999, one of the best-known Hungarian actors was asked whether he was satisfied with his life and his success. "No, absolutely not," he answered. "And why not?" came the next question. "You are a star; the whole country knows and admires you." "Well, yes. But I still am a nobody. It would be much better if I could be somebody else." Who would you like to be?" "Julia Roberts?" he answered. He smiled, but he meant it. And he was right. To be Julia Roberts means to exist, intensely, on the global level. Her existence is multiplied by billions of gazes.[17]

But not all gazes are equally important. One has to attract the attention of the right people. If you had been known and perceived by President Clinton, while he was the president, or by Julia Roberts herself, this single gaze may have been a much more powerful multiplier of your life intensity and self-intensity than the gazes of thousands of average citizens. If a Clinton or a Julia Roberts perceives you, part of his or her life intensity (due to the hundreds of millions of gazes they had attracted) may flow over to you. This is the source of their magic. They are sources of life intensity. And this high intensity of life, received from them, protects us against the malaise of being insignificant and mortal.

In traditional small communities, one was permanently under the gaze of others. And everybody had her or his traditional place, identity, and role in the community. Ewen (1988, 57–77) is right to state that identity became a crucial problem when people were thrown into the big cities of the Industrial Age and were lost in the anonymous crowds of the metropolis—crowds that now, with globalization, are becoming even more anonymous.[18]

If, in a metropolitan crowd, one wants to boost one's ego, and self-esteem, one's feeling of being important, of really existing, one has to make great efforts to attract people's attention. One can do so in various ways. A large proportion of our gestures, behavior, and personal objects serve the purpose of this strategy of attraction. We pick our pieces of clothing to make a certain impression, to attract (or to avoid, to fend off) people's gazes; we behave in certain ways, use certain gestures, and position ourselves in an environment in a way to be perceived.

We may attract people's attention by having certain physical characteristics; for instance, by being beautiful, or exceptionally tall, or a dwarf. We may attract their attention by a remarkable achievement (in sports, art, cinema, politics). We may attain the same goal by being unusually strong, powerful, or demonic like Don Giovanni; or by being rich, or unusually good and helpful. And even a juicy scandal may serve our purpose, though this may turn out to be self-destructive.

In earlier times, there were very few people who could attract the gazes of a large number of people. Beyond the boundaries of their own communities, few people could have heard of them, let alone seen them or seen their picture. Only a few kings, emperors, and warlords—a Wallerstein or a Napoleon, Byron or Victor Hugo, Queen Victoria or Bismarck, Pasteur or Lindbergh—could achieve international celebrity. The real celebrities were gods and goddesses, martyrs and saints, and the virtuous or evil heroes of folklore and the broadsides. They were media-made, just as their contemporary successors are products of the media. The techniques of transforming people into celebrities were in many ways similar, though with important differences. In earlier times, for instance, celebrity formation started, in most cases, posthumously. Nowadays, living people are selected and transformed into celebrities, that is, into virtual persons of mythic dimensions, who are likely to attract the greatest possible number of gazes. Hollywood stars and terrorists, the American president and his wife, great politicians and sopranos, Nobel Prize laureates and Olympic champions and television talk show hosts, first of all, are those who attract the greatest number of "clicks" and perceptions.

There is an interesting and important exchange, and a non-zero-sum game, going on between stars and their fans. Each fan projects emotional and spiritual energies onto the star. These individual experiences reinforce one another, until finally the star radiates with a high-voltage life intensity. And then fans may draw on this source and may (have the illusion to) experience life in its superb and almost transcendental fullness. To get in visual contact with them, or to hear their voice on a compact disc, is like touching the frock of a saint, *illo tempore*.

Let me finally add that there is a kind of irony in that we accept the fact that our existence is "real" only if we are perceived by people who exist only if they are perceived by other people (including us). We live in a "mirage," in a world of mirrors—mirrors that are facing one another. They all are empty. Emptiness mirrors emptiness, and the illusion is created, on both sides, that they mirror something. We create one another out of nothing. Nobodies create nobodies. We exist in the perception of people who do not exist.

—

In the following pages, I give a few examples of how celebrities, these mythical figures, are created by our contemporary consumer civilization. I have chosen articles from two types of magazines: from two popular weekly women's magazines, the German *Bunte* and *Gala*; and from an upscale American monthly magazine, one of the most prestigious and respected ones, *Vanity Fair*. I have analyzed hundreds of this type of article, but I shall discuss only a few of them here. My aim is only to show the techniques and tricks with which the media of our civilization of consumption create their myths and celebrities and thereby help their readers to construct their selves and achieve (the illusion of) an intense and full life.

Gods and Goddesses

There is reportage, with a great number of illustrations, on the marriage of a popular German television anchor woman from Hamburg in the 23/1999 issue of *Bunte,* which we have already analyzed.[19] Instead of a boring wedding in

Hamburg, she arranged her wedding in Las Vegas, the Gambling Paradise, but—for the sake of more excitement—with Venetian scenery. The hotel where the wedding took place is a reconstruction, on a reduced scale, of Saint Mark's Square in Venice, with the palaces and colonnades and a life-size Bridge of Sighs. As a symbol of globalization, a German girl stood in the Nevada Desert on the Bridge of Sighs. Along with wealth, luxury, and extravagance (an 8-meter-long stretch limousine, a 150-square-meter suite, a coiffure created by the hairdresser for Sharon Stone and other stars), something divine also had to flash up. Accordingly, the dinner took place on the sixty-first floor in the restaurant called Stratosphere, and from there it was only a skip and hop into a chopper where, like gods, the couple could celebrate their wedding night.[20]

Let me give also another example of this technique of divinity creation from the German magazine *Gala*.[21] The star here is Doris Schröder, the wife of the (former) German chancellor, Helmut Schröder. On the cover page, we see her as she turns her eyes toward the sky (Heaven) with a transcendental smile à la Saint Theresa on her face. And lest the celestial message get lost, we may read in big capital letters:

THAT THE WORLD GETS A BIT BETTER

In the table of contents, we see the same holy icon, with the following text:

The Angel of the Chancellor
The Heart Throbs for the Suffering Children

There are also more anthropomorphic goddesses in this popular mythology. In a *Bunte* article,[22] we meet Christina, the wife of (former) President Rau. Christina is not only an unbelievably many-sided, fantastic wife and mother, puritanical and warm hearted; she is not only the heiress of a great and wealthy German dynasty; but, on top of all that, she is an independent, autonomous, quick-witted, self-conscious, and free personality. Already the title of the article trumpets that here we have to do with a special person:

FIRST LADY—ON A ROLLING BOARD

And then we learn from the article that beyond roller skating in the streets of Bonn, she is also a deep-sea diver; excels at snowboarding, parachuting, and paragliding; cares for thirty-five domestic animals and the pets of her children (dogs, cats, rabbits, chickens, gophers); and is the first to greet women at the grocery shop. We find out also that she has inherited British culture and taste from her father—a famous German industrialist—as well as his feelings of social solidarity, thrift, and love of sports. She is a democrat. "Her children take the school bus in the morning and afternoon."

And this is not all. Mrs. Rau has got a strong, autonomous self; she is the master of her feelings and of her world. She does not let anybody interfere in her affairs. "Nobody will tell me what I should do. And she adds, in a Nietzschean tone—or quoting the God of the Old Testament: "I am who I am." Is this not the ideal that we, all of us, want to attain: the total identity with, and acceptance of, our selves? But one should not think that she is a hard, cold character. A feeling human soul dwells under the disciplined appearance. She listens to the music of Mendelssohn and loves the productions of Pina Bausch. And before I forget: She is an excellent cook as well.

And what about the temptation of power? She stands above such vanities. "Nobody will wrap me in the golden paper of power," she says. She has not yet made up her mind whether they will move into the Belvedere Palace in Berlin, the residence of the German head of state. It depends on whether they will, or will not, find a good school for the children near the palace. Modesty, too, is a divine virtue.

This deification (and its opposite, demonization) of celebrities is practically omnipresent in the popular press of our age. It is present not only in the cheap weekly fashion, lifestyle, and gossip magazines but also in the more serious monthly publications as well. To show the extent and intensity of this strategy, I now turn to *Vanity Fair,* which is a high-level monthly magazine, with a long tradition, addressed to an educated, professional, middle- and upper-middle-class readership. As we shall see, the techniques of the deification of celebrities are pushed here even farther then in the weekly magazines aimed at a broader public.

Mythology in the Superlative

To show how strong this tendency is in this magazine, I randomly selected three issues of *Vanity Fair* (January, June, September) of one year, 1999. I take all my examples from these three issues to show how strong this penchant for the mythic, the magic, the Olympic is in this famous magazine.[23]

Vanity Fair—as well as the majority of other magazines—is a breviary for people struggling with the problems of constructing their selves. The texts, the pictures, the title pages, the advertisements radiate energy, joy, success, wealth, power, and victory, and they offer a wide range of attractive roles, personalities, and life models. In their full-page photos, celebrity subjects are opulent and tempting Venuses (Charlize Theron), mysterious personalities full of energy (Baryshnikov), elegant and self-conscious (Brian Williams), serene and spiritual (Elizabeth Arden or the guitar player), manly and red-blooded (Gardner McKay), strong and concentrated (Joseph Fiennes); they have a huge ego (Will Smith), are incredibly wealthy (Bernard Arnault, Byron Nelson), are well-balanced and full of harmony (François Pinault), are world champions enthroned on their yachts or on the wings of their private jets (Jack Nicklaus, Arnold Palmer); they rise above mortality (Carolyn Bessette), they are living myths (Marlon Brando, Vivien Leigh); they are mysterious and exotic (Virginie Ledoyen); they are true friends (Kazan and Miller); they are rebels or predators (in an advertisement for Gucci); their love is gentle and beautiful (Ralph Lauren); they drink and enjoy life (the Moët Champagne family). Their fans can draw energy from them and take courage from their strength, and the fans may be prompted by these models to aim high and try to shape their own selves in their likeness.

Title pages consequently transform the stories dealt with in the magazine into great human dramas and their protagonists into mythic heroes or gods and goddesses. Let us examine several of them.

Venus. The title page of the January issue shows the famous actress, Charlize Theron, as a Venus emerging, if not from the foam of the sea, at least from the foam and waves of her white fur. She is "the White Hot Venus."[24] To call a beautiful woman Venus is not a particularly surprising and exciting turn, but the contrast of "white" and "hot," ice and fire, is an archetypal motif and may strike a chord in people's subconscious. It is a pity that the rich purple and gold of the background shifts this modern Venus in the direction of Madame Pompadour's boudoir, which belongs to another symbolic realm. The picture thus becomes a bit fuzzy, and its impact on the reader, and her self, may become contradictory and confused.

The Demon. Will Smith, clad in black, sits on a prancing black horse. This again is an archetype: It radiates demonic power, Promethean strength. Though here again, the editors made a mistake: The young man in the picture: smiles. Demons don't, and shouldn't, smile. Or at least they should have a Mephistophelean smile. If they have a nice boyish smile, they lose their demonic power and become nice young or not young men, which is the case here. Within the magazine, in the article, the young rider fits better into this demonic role. He displays an almost superhuman self-consciousness: "I absolutely believe I could be the president of the United States, I believe that if that's what I wanted to do with my life, I could win."[25]

Eurydice. On the title page of the September issue, we rise to the heights of Olympian serenity and sorrow.[26] This is a portrait of Carolyn Bessette Kennedy. She is looking upward, into the distance, into eternity, with serenity and sorrow, with resignation and hope, with clear and pensive eyes; she has a spiritual transparency, her long blond hair is blown by a gentle breeze, the stream of eternity, as someone preparing herself for a long journey, as a Eurydice, who is not with us anymore, who has passed over into the realm of timelessness. And the text, too, stresses her almost divine character:

> Bruce Weber [the photographer] immortalizes the spirit of a very private Carolyn Bessette Kennedy: "With her dazzling blond hair, . . . a face of laughter, a wealth of tenderness, . . . her brief but spirited life, . . . the looks, the charm, the style, and that wonderful voice and a sense of humor and an incredible warmth and love of conversation—she was the best company you could ever have."

The Glory and the Fall of Gods

The story of the Kennedy family was in itself a myth, or an Aeschylean tragedy. The head of the family emerging from the mythic mists of a Mafioso past. Four young Titans, who want to conquer the world. The first dies a hero's death, a fighter pilot in World War II, he falls, like Icarus, from the sky; the second and third, at the height of their careers, are cut down by deadly bullets; the fourth makes a fatal mistake, which paralyzes him for life politically; their sister dies young; their lives were gilt by the celestial smile of a Hollywood star and are overshadowed by her suicide. And finally, the young John F. Kennedy Jr., too, falls from the skies, comet-like, into the sea, taking with himself his wife, Carolyn, into their sea-grave. This is a full-blown myth as it is, but the author of the *Vanity Fair* article develops it even further. He literally lifts John F. Kennedy Jr. among the Olympian gods:

> As he grew older, authority came to him, and he wore it naturally. . . . He seemed to be surprised as a man to have become beautiful—no other word for it. He moved with Olympian grace, back rippling, stomach quilted with muscle."[27]

He must have been a divine personality, because when "he entered or left a room he did something overpowering to happen to that room and the people in it."[28] And he has his place also in the American Pantheon:

> Born a part of American history, John F. Kennedy Jr. honored a cherished myth without being consumed by it. Longtime family friend David Michaelis returns the salute a nation will never forget. . . . He had been history and he would be history.[29]

Beyond being a Greek and an American hero, he is also the hero of our age. In the article he becomes the symbol, or the emblem, of our new civilization, of a human being who does his duty toward his community. But before all, he wants to actualize himself:

> Somehow, even as John Kennedy accepted that he belonged to America, he also managed to belong to himself. . . . How hard that must have been—and how amazing the grace with which Kennedy took his place in history.
>
> But to know how to handle an intruder at your mother's deathbed, you need above all to be true to yourself. . . . Identity is the question we all have to solve, and that's why John Kennedy's triumph, his ability to be himself, despite odds no one would bet on, was a miracle to witness.[30]

"Great Expectations"—this is the title of the article—gives a painfully ironical frame to the story of this young man. Olympian beauty, strength, elegance, autonomy all together were not enough to slow down the free fall of the plane.

We are standing here, embarrassed, moved, as many centuries ago our Greek predecessors may have been watching the glory and the fall of their heroes and gods. We have experienced the destiny of a great human being, and a life that has been presented here as having had fullness and significance in spite of its shortness. And we, readers, need this experience, badly.

The "Legends" of Golf

One of the features of the July issue is a rhapsody about American golf champions. Mythic elements overflow these pages. The group of players is presented here as a pantheon of demigods; without a grain of humor or irony.

In the title of the article, they are called "The Legends of Golf." In the table of contents, they get the epithet "Green Giants: "16 of golf's current and future legends." And the inside lead continues in the same emphatic tone:

> Their names form a glorious roster of golf's American Century: passionate pioneers such as Sam Snead . . . giving way to fresh legends—Arnold Palmer, Jack Nicklaus, . . . phenomenon Tiger Woods, . . . 16 of the game's greatest champions, past and future.[31]

This is obviously not a matter-of-fact presentation of the sixteen most successful American golf players. It is, *expressis verbis,* a hagiography. The word "legend" occurs three times in these lines and will keep recurring throughout the text of the article. The protagonists are blown up to superhuman dimensions. Beyond being called "giants," "phenomena," and "greatest champions," their grandness is further emphasized by rhetorical and poetic means; by pathetic expressions or even alliterations: "glorious roaster," "American Century," "*p*assionate *p*ioneers," or "the *g*ames *g*reatest champions"). To say "past and present" would have been a pragmatic statement. "Past and future" is hyperbole; it means "eternity."

Gary Player is called THE BLACK KNIGHT, a name taken from Celtic mythology. Patty Berg is THE FIRST LADY of the world of golf, and Gene Sarazen is the PATRIARCH of the Old Testament.[32] Let alone Nancy Lopez; in her hands

> the golf club has been a magic wand, transporting young Nancy Lopez from her New Mexico home to fairy-tale places like Buckingham Palace,

where, at 19, she experienced the ultimate tea party with the Queen. Buoyed by an irrepressible game and an irresistible smile, she captured nine tournaments her first full year on tour, including an L.P.G.A.-record five in a row. . . . Her husband is former New York Mets star Ray Knight. . . . Lopez is the dominant female player of her generation.[33]

This is a world of fairy tales, magic wands, the lassie from the provinces having tea with the Queen in the Royal Palace. And this is also the world blown up by superlatives: "ultimate tea party," "irrepressible game," "irresistible smile," "she captured nine tournaments her first full year on tour," she is a "dominant player," and on top of that, even her husband is a "star."

Jack Nicklaus, too, THE GOLDEN BEAR, is elevated into the world of demigods and superlatives. We learn that "no one can claim more major titles. . . . He is also one of the game's most respected golf-course designers (170 in two dozen nations), as well as a world-class fisherman." And to emphasize his greatness, in the picture he sits on the symbol of American ultimate success, on board an oversize yacht. He smiles at us gently; his full-blooded golden retriever, too, smiles at us, mortals, with divine condescension.[34]

Bin Nelson, THE GENTLEMAN, had a "magic season." Phil Mickelson, David Duval, Justin Leonard, and Jim Furyk are called THE FOUR HORSEMEN OF THE MILLENNIUM. Arnold Palmer is simply "THE KING, who gave Americans a reason to watch and a hero to cheer."[35] And finally, Tiger Woods is the ultimate hero. He is simply (?) called: THE MAN. As if he were the embodiment, the symbol, the paragon of humankind as a whole.

Just briefly, let me return to the German weekly magazine *Bunte* and quote an article dealing with the retirement of Steffi Graf from her professional sports career.[36] The author speaks in this connection of "The Age of Heroes," and the "legend" of Steffi Graf. He calls the sportsmen and women "gods," who give meaning to our lives:

> It is not a coincidence that European sport has its origins in the sanctity of Olympic Games, and that there not only competitions were organized but animals were also sacrificed. Sport and religious faith have ever been secret sisters [?]. Even today, our sportsmen and women are not only gods, but also sacrificial animals [because advertising agencies exploit them]. . . . But this is not all and it does not explain the magic, the nos-

talgia, the dedication, the discipline, the asceticism, it does not explain the secret bond between our stars and ourselves, it does not explain the meaning they gave to our lives.[37]

Sportsmen and women as gods, sacrificial animals, who lend meaning to our lives: the mythological penchant of consumer civilization has turned here into the absurd.

Imitatio Dei

Sometimes the celebrities even deify themselves—they raise themselves to the heights of divinities. Victoria Adams, the former Spice Girl, and David Beckham, (former) star of the Manchester United soccer team, play this game. After August 1998, the world and the tabloid world have watched with excitement their "high-flying romance, . . . extravagant, exuberant, unbridled, but always elegant and stylish life," their wedding in a Scottish castle with a final check of £500,000, and the like. 'This is the biggest day of our lives—we're just going to go over the top and make it entertaining for everybody.'"[38]

They have become the symbols of the contemporary "Renaissance of the masses." They have pushed to the extreme the fundamental rule of consumer civilization: "Actualize yourself!" They are like a Renaissance duke and duchess in early-sixteenth-century Florence. They are as free, they strive for the fulfillment of their lives so happily and innocently as Greek gods did (in the mythic imagination of the Greeks). They are young, wealthy, elegant, carefree, daring; they can do whatever they want, they can satisfy all their wishes, they can live out all their whims. They enjoy and waste their wealth and lives in a divine freedom:

> Beckham and Adams continue to display a level of rampant consumerism which, in less blithe times, would have gotten them hung in effigy. [But they live in] the Eighties without bad feeling. . . . Cultural commentator Peter York is amply qualified to measure David Beckham and Victoria Adams against the laissez-unfair values of that decade. "Yes," York confirms, "Posh and Beckham are Thatcher's children. But there are no rough

edges or nastiness. They shop nicely and they look nice, and there are lots more like them—they are unstoppable people."[39]

They stepped out of the world of fairy tales. Beckham was the poor lad who went out into the world, performed unheard-of deeds, and finally gained half of a kingdom and the love of the beautiful princess. They both take themselves as seriously as if they were gods. And they are as playful as gods: They play the game with their tongues in their cheeks.

And all this is more than a show. Here we have two human beings who revolt against all the limitations of life, against the miserable poverty and shortness of life, against anxieties, inhibitions, philistine prudence and decency, social norms and constraints. A boy and a girl have decided to live as most people would like to live. They play all the possible plays, the roles of kings and queens, gods and goddesses, bohemians and dignified citizens; they do not care about anything and anybody outside themselves. But in the meantime, they lavishly scatter the diamonds of their joy and happiness around themselves. They have got the courage to aspire to the fullness of life; and thereby to challenge the power of death. Their example has certainly shaped the attitudes and selves of millions of young people around the world.

Here again, the quotidian and the mythic, the trivial and the existentially significant, meet on the pages of a weekly magazine of the Age of Consumption.

All or Nothing

While scholars speak of the demise of the autonomous human personality, of the disappearance of a genuine, essential "self," an unprecedented cult of the human personality has emerged in the Western world since the 1950s and 1960s.

But the contemporary cult of the human personality may be, itself, the sign of both strength and weakness. The scientific, technical, and economic achievements of the developed world, its unprecedented affluence, and its almost unchallenged political and military power may generate the feeling in people living in the highly developed countries that they are strong, powerful, and superb; that they are able to control the world and their own lives. If this is the case, the contemporary cult of the human personality is the self-glorification of the victors.

However, the very same people live also in a world of chaotic changes and increasing uncertainty; they are harassed by new anxieties in a globalizing and post–September 11 world; they may feel defenseless and weak in the alien world of mass societies. And if they do so, this weakness, too, may be at the source of the present passionate and hectic cult of the human personality. Their very weakness may prompt people to assert themselves, to boost their selves, to build up the myth of the strong and victorious *homo sapiens* (or *non-sapiens*). If I am nothing, I have to become everything. If I am a victim, I may be tempted to delude myself with the false belief that I am the queen or king of life. These two contradictory experiences are simultaneously present in us. We feel ourselves strong and weak at the same time. We live in the tension of these two worlds, we oscillate between pride and humiliation (not to be mistaken for humility), between the status of a superman and that of the underdog.

Strangely enough, we resemble in this respect people who lived in the age of the Renaissance. They, too, were torn and thrust between opposite poles: between joy and melancholy; the joy of life and the fear of death; between harmony and disharmony, glory and humiliation; the pomp and brilliance of Claudius' and Gertrude's court and the dark visions of Hamlet; the neoplatonic idealism of the humanists and the skepticism and daring materialism, or deism, of the "physicians";[40] the beauty of art and the terror of the plague, or that of approaching armies threatening everything with destruction.

The Self in a Reenchanted World

> There are only two ways to live your life.
> One is as though nothing is a miracle.
> The other is as though everything is a miracle.
>
> —*Albert Einstein*

Two Worlds

We live in two worlds. In the morning and early afternoon (while we are working, running after our business, organizing our lives, filling in our tax declarations, going to the bank, consulting our lawyer or physician, picking up our laundry, having our car repaired), we move around in a pragmatic world, act in a more or less rational way, behaving as modern, rational beings have learned to behave in a world organized in a more or less pragmatic and rational way.

But this is only one side of the coin. Our contemporary world also has another dimension, which is not pragmatic and rational at all. It is just the opposite: It is irrational, or nonrational, enchanted, magic—a world of symbols, myths, illusions.

Is it? After centuries of enlightenment and secularization, what may we, people of the twenty-first century, have to do with myths and symbols, with the irrational, the enchanted, the magic? We have a lot to do with them. Our selves are shaped by both these worlds. We have to survive, fare well, develop, and actualize our selves in these two worlds—in a disenchanted and a reenchanted world at the same time; both in a pragmatic and rational world, and in a mythic, magic, reenchanted world.

The Loss of Meaning

The loss of transcendence we described in chapter 11 also involved the dramatic loss of meaning. In an "enchanted" premodern world, in the world of symbols, myths, religions, it was easier to believe that both the universe and life had a purpose and meaning. The more so, because the primary function of those symbols, myths, and religions was just to enchant human beings and make them believe that both the universe and life were meaningful; that a divine intention and purposiveness was governing everything. It was easier then to believe that our personal life had a purpose, that it was meaningful and significant. With the "disenchantment" of the world, this obvious meaning disappeared from people's lives, and the quest of meaning has become one of their central preoccupations. It has become one of the main propelling forces of their lives—even if they do not wholly realize its importance—and one of the main factors shaping their selves.

Sometime in the late 1980s, Steven Weinberg, a nuclear physicist—who in a famous book (1977, 154) had described "the first three minutes" of the universe—was flying home from San Francisco to Boston.[1] Looking out the window, he was fascinated by the beauty of the landscape below, with "fluffy clouds here and there, snow turning pink as the sun sets." With a certain resignation, he mused over whether our growing knowledge about the universe will destroy forever the meaningful beauty of the world as we sometimes see it from our human perspective:

> It is very hard to realize that all this is just a tiny part of an overwhelmingly hostile universe. It is even harder to realize that this present universe has evolved from an unspeakably unfamiliar early condition, and faces a future extinction of endless cold or intolerable heat. The more the universe seems comprehensible, the more it also seems pointless.

We could add: the more it seems, and is, meaningless. The experience of this loss of meaning, the fear that the universe may have no purpose, that it may be just there, without having any "meaning," has become stronger and stronger in the age of modernization. The modern, scientific mind is unsurpassable in decomposing reality and describing the forces and laws that move it and regulate its motions. But it is rather helpless when it has to handle the whole and has to answer questions like "What is the universe?" "Why does it exist?" "Does its existence have any purpose or significance?" "Does human life, or life in general, have any meaning?" "Does our existence in the universe make any difference?" How are we to construct our selves if we do not know whether life has, or has not, a meaning?

Secularization, the gradual regression of religious beliefs, the expansion of rational and pragmatic thinking, was one of main features of the emergence of the modern world. Nietzsche spoke of the "death of God"; Max Weber described modernization as a process of "disenchantment" (*Entzauberung*). Weber discussed the economic and social importance of the spread of "goal-rationality," but he warned his readers that the eclipse of "value-rationality" and the disenchantment of the world may also have negative consequences. He argued that the "loss of meaning" (*Sinnverlust*) accompanying this process may become especially destructive. "Not summer's bloom lies ahead of us, but rather a polar night of icy darkness and hardness."[2]

In the past few decades, more and more scholars have argued that myths and magic are to be found in all civilizations and that the modernizing nineteenth and twentieth centuries were not an exception to this rule. It is a mistake to claim that in a modernized, secularized, rational world the sources of myths dry up. What happened was that traditional belief systems have been replaced by new ones, new magic, new myths. Think, for instance, of the myths of the great Romantic poets, of those of the Hegelians or Comteans; think of the socialist, nationalist, and racist myths, or of the myths of universal progress and glorious capitalism, let alone the new mythologies of contemporary consumer civilization, with its almost religious cult of stars, New Age–type penchant for mysticism, and apocalyptic visions.[3] People have to construct their selves in a world that worships rationality and, at the same time, longs for spirituality and mysticism. The systematic study of this ambivalence, of this double influence on people's selves, may become one of the most important fields of psychological and social research in the coming decades.

According to the disciples of Weber, disenchantment has never been complete. Signs and trends of a reenchantment of the world have been present since the beginnings of capitalism. Colin Campbell (1989, 153 ff.) argued, for instance, that these tendencies were already clearly distinguishable in early Calvinism, survived as latent fantasies and daydreams throughout the centuries, and prepared the ground for the "autonomous, self-illusory hedonism" of our contemporary consumer civilization.[4] Mark Schneider (1993, x), too, claimed that the magic never disappeared from Western civilization: "Enchantment . . . is part of our normal condition, and far from having fled" from our modern world, "it continues to exist."[5] And, in the wake of Baudrillard, Bauman (1993, 33) spoke already, *expressis verbis,* of "reenchantment":

> Postmodernity . . . brings "re-enchantment" of the world after the protracted and earnest, though in the end inconclusive, modern struggle to dis-enchant (or, more exactly, the resistance to dis-enchantment, hardly ever put to sleep, was all along the "postmodern thorn" in the body of modernity). The mistrust of human spontaneity, of drives, impulses, and inclinations resistant to prediction and rational justification, has been all but replaced by the mistrust of unemotional calculating reason. Dignity has been returned to emotions; legitimacy to the "inexplicable," nay *irrational.* . . . We learn again to respect ambiguity.

New Myths

The demand for nonmaterial, spiritual goods has dramatically increased in recent decades. The consumer industry producing these spiritual goods is working at full speed. It has created its Elysian Fields (the world of advertising), its New Jerusalem (America), its televised religious services, its Orphic mysteries (the New Age and occult literature),[6] its nether world (*Blade Runner*–type films), its Apocalypse (catastrophe films), and the like. And it has also its Olympus, with its gods and goddesses, heroes and heroines, called "celebrities." Thousands of books and hundreds of magazines flood us with mysticism, popular cosmology, astrology, parapsychology. Television films teem with angels, spirits, ghosts, monsters, aliens; they resurrect ancient myths or create new ones.[7] Myth generation is nowadays as intense as it may have been at the dawn of human history, in pre-Homeric Greece, or in those centuries when the great world religions emerged. With the progress of reason and rationality, the need for spirituality and mysticism has not disappeared from the human world and human hearts.

I have already analyzed some of these contemporary myths. I have discussed the mythologies surrounding cars and perfumes;[8] I have spoken of the importance of some archetypal/mythological motives in our contemporary lives ("The Wheel of Fortune," "The Fall of Princes," "The Beauty and the Beast," etc.); and I have described the "transcendental" dimensions of shopping centers.[9] And examples could be multiplied. The dominant myth of the world of advertising is the Garden of Eden myth. Its message is that this is the world of joy and freedom, happiness and harmony. Drinks sparkle as life elixirs, trees are full of dewy fruits, golden girls and boys are dancing the dance of angels, skies and seas shine with transcendental blue, souls and skirts are white as snow, children are gamboling on the deep emerald of the lawn. Here one does not have to chose between Good and Evil, here there is no suffering, Satan is not lurking behind the trees, there is no temptation or Fall, everybody and everything is good and innocent. In the Garden of Eden, the tiger and the deer loll about, together, in peace. And our selves unfold as beautiful, magic flowers.

People have ever needed myths, and they seem to need them nowadays as well. They are lost in the world and in the universe. They long for a kind of order. They grasp everything—every idea, hypothesis, creed, religion, and occult science that promises to show them the hidden order beyond the chaotic and the contingent. The saving vision may be a myth, which transforms the chaos into a simple and transparent tale, a tale about the creation and the functioning of the world or a tale that divides the chaotic grayness of the world into the sharp contrast of black and white, Evil and Good. It may be a myth about a theomachia, a fight of gods. It may be a great and holy vision of the Fall of Man, the Original Sin, which explains all the misery and suffering in this world, and stages for us the apocalyptic drama of the sacrificial death of the Son of God. It may be a vision of the world as a smoothly functioning machine, working like a universal clockwork. It may be a vision of the triumphant self-realization of the Absolute Spirit. It may be a theory about the Big Bang and the evolution of the Universe. In his famous *Psychology of World Views,* Karl Jaspers (1960) tried to understand and explain in which of these shelters various civilizations and human beings have sought refuge during the course of history. Heidegger (1962, 1990) condemned these attempts to escape from the world of uncertainty into illusory certainties.

People's inclination and wish to escape is more than understandable. Let us take as an example one of the most successful of these false illusions, astrology. It has an unbelievably strong attraction even for people who are, and praise themselves as being, utterly rational and pragmatic in their everyday lives. Astrology may catch and enthrall even them, because part of its magic lies in the fact that it projects a rational and geometric network onto the world of stars and the universe—it fascinates its addicts with real and pseudo computations about the orbits of the stars; it works with compasses and computers, schemata, and equations; and it radiates the message, soothing troubled hearts, that there is order and harmony in the universe.

And astrology does even more. It tells people that they are not lost in a chaotic and unpredictable world, and that their fates and lives are not predetermined either. They are part of the universal order, they have a certain place, a "home," in this universe, where they are free to develop their selves. And it helps them do so because it offers them a simple typology of the various possible lives, personalities, and life strategies with whose help they may gain the illusion that they can better understand and shape themselves.

Astrology offers people an easy and rosy way to (the illusion of) self-knowledge. People are delighted to recognize themselves in one or the other type or category of European or, say, Chinese astrology; they are delighted to realize that they are not random nonentities but are important creatures fitting into one of the "universal" categories. They enjoy the experience of understanding themselves, their lives, their destinies, and of even having a glance into their future. And they may even have the feeling that if the universe has this beautiful and fascinating hidden harmony and order, then human life, and their lives, may have—must have—a meaning. The faith of addicts is further boosted by the fact that each astrological type has both positive and negative features, but the balance is always tipping to the positive side. Let alone the fact that in their personal anamneses and in their weekly columns in junk or not-junk magazines, astrologers never leave their patients without a few flattering words, a glimpse of hope, thereby reducing their anxiety and boosting their selves.

Astrology is only one of the more modest magic wands of generating meaning, or the illusion of meaning, in people's minds. The consumer industry also has its heavy artillery.

The Reenchantment of the World

The real triumph of "reenchantment" of the world came with the emergence of consumer civilization in the second half of the twentieth century. Its roots reach back to the 1870s, when the first great French and American department stores were opened in Paris, Chicago, and elsewhere, though some experts consider the first World Exhibition, which took place in London in 1851, as the real starting point.[10] The department store Au Bon Marché in Paris is perhaps the best example of this early efflorescence of consumer civilization, with its brilliance, its splendid illumination, its transparent glass ceilings, its recurrent special events and happenings, concerts, carnival-like sales, and other means and tricks to enchant its customers. Rosalind H. Williams (1982) called it a "dream world." Michael B. Miller (1981, 165–87) reminds us that in the late nineteenth century, Au Bon Marché was advertised as "the World's Eighth Miracle."

Consumer civilization developed in its full wealth in the second half of the twentieth century. In recent years, a rich scholarly literature has studied it in its tiniest details.[11] A great number of authors have focused their attention on how this new civilization enchants people with its spectacular images symbols, rituals, and myths. George Ritzer, for instance, has devoted a whole book to the study of this process of reenchantment.[12] He is mainly interested in the instruments, spaces, structures, and mechanisms of mass consumption, and he focuses on the visual, spectacular side of the process of reenchantment. He gives a multitude of examples demonstrating how business flooded the spaces and centers of consumption with a dazzling world of lights and colors, images and extravagant spectacles, a whirl of symbols, visions, and myths.[13]

In Las Vegas, for instance, he writes, the Hotel Luxor rises as an Egyptian pyramid: It is "the world's largest atrium. . . . One could fit nine Boeing 747s in it." And there is "a ten-story Sphinx; taller than the original in Egypt."[14] The Hotel Excalibur is a mysterious medieval castle. "Inside the Mirage one encounters a fifty-foot aquarium (with sharks and exotic fish) behind the registration desk, a 1.5 million gallon dolphin habitat, and the 'Secret Garden'—a zoo with rare and exotic animals, including white tigers." "A volcano erupts periodically at the Mirage."[15] And there is more. In front of the Hotel Treasure Island, a "pitched sea battle, complete with the sinking of a British ship by a pirate ship, occurs several times a day."[16] And what about riding "over and through the skyscrapers that make up part of the facade of the New York, New York casino-hotel?"[17]

Restaurants, shopping centers, and airports have been "thematized" and transformed into magic worlds, fairy lands, spectacles, and theaters.[18] "If you want to imagine yourself in a tropical rainforest, Rainforest Café features 'cascading waterfalls, tropical rain showers, simulated thunder and lightning, live tropical birds, . . . animated talking trees, butterflies, and crocodiles.'"[19] Vision and reality, business and entertainment, whirl about here in a colorful cavalcade. One can amuse oneself in the shopping malls and shop in the amusement parks. Shopping centers have become Disneyesque, and Disneyland developed into a huge shopping center. Ritzer speaks of "The Las Vegasizing of America."[20]

Borderlines between reality and illusion are waning. Disney has built a traditional small town for the very rich: with a town hall, picket fences, porch swings, a wood slate water tower, a creek, wrought iron lampposts, and a home-delivery grocery store. This town does, and does not, exist. The houses, the town hall, and the streets are there, but the town does not exist and function as its nineteenth-century models did. It "is a town whose mission isn't the pursuit of commercial advantage, or religious or political freedom, or any idea more compelling than a sense of comfortable community. Its ambition is, in the end, not greater than to be like a town.[21]

The great cruise liners, too, are more than luxury ships. They are enchanted worlds. The Carnival Cruise Line's *Destiny* is a 101,000-ton ship that is 900 feet long, with a central atrium nine stories high; it has twelve passenger decks, four swimming pools, a jogging track, a 214-foot-long water slide, a 9,000-square-foot casino with more than 300 slot machines, and a 1,500-seat show lounge featuring a Las Vegas–type show with fireworks and lasers.[22]

All this dazzles and mesmerizes the passengers. They are entrapped in this magic world, and they surrender themselves to the vertigo of diversion and consumption. They lose their sense of space and time, and they lose their disciplined everyday minds and selves.

Ritzer gives an excellent description of this reenchantment of the world. His analysis has, however, two serious limitations. First, he himself limits himself to the study of the visual effects and the spectacular events of this new civilization and more or less ignores its other important aspects: the new norms and forms of behavior, for instance, the new myths and the like. This is absolutely acceptable, because one has to have a focus, and the spectacle is one of the most important elements of the process of reenchantment. It is not for nothing that our contemporary society has been called the "spectacular society" or the "society of spectacle."[23]

But Ritzer has also limited his study by consequently remaining on the phenomenological level. He brilliantly describes the process of reenchantment but does not explore the forces that are propelling this process. Or, more exactly, he discovers and studies one single motive force underlying the emergence of consumer civilization: business interest. In his interpretation, reenchantment is a business strategy, and he considers the magic, fascinating spectacles, and dazzling happenings as "selling machines." "The new means of consumption are enchanted, and they are in various ways quite spectacular, but above all they are highly effective selling machines."[24]

He devotes a few paragraphs to the discussion of the hypothesis that perhaps it is not business people who are the motive forces of this process of reenchantment but rather the consumers themselves, who want to be enchanted and thus push companies to compete with one another to provide more and more effective magic and spectacles:

Rather than having their consumption orchestrated by people like advertising executives and directors of cathedrals of consumption, it may be that it is consumers who are in control. It is the consumers who demand reenchanted cathedrals of consumption and those demands must be met if their business is to be retained. . . . In fact, it could be argued that consumers are forcing the means of consumption into a reckless and potentially destructive war to see which one can offer the most (re-)enchanted setting.[25]

But then he quickly drops the matter. Which is regrettable because, to understand the ongoing transformation of Western civilization, it is important to know more about the underlying motive forces, as studied by Baudrillard (1970, 1990, 1998), Ewen (1982, 1988), and a great number of other scholars.[26]

Let me illustrate the difference between these two approaches with an example. Speaking of the great hotels of Las Vegas, Ritzer (1999, 161) writes that "the new means of consumption manipulate the customer's sense of time in order to earn greater profits." They eliminate people's sense of time with a simple trick: "Gambling tables are open around the clock," but "clocks are forbidden in casinos."[27] And "customers who are disoriented in terms of time are likely to be disoriented in other ways, including their thinking about money."[28]

It is possible, however, that by losing their sense of time, people do not lose but gain something. They do not gain money but something that may be more important for them. They probably go to a casino because they *want to lose* their sense of time and reality. They go there because they want to step out of the depressing monotony of their everyday lives, out of a world that has lost its meaning, out of the terror of relentlessly passing time. In other words, beyond being a business trick, the timelessness of the casino may satisfy a deep human need. It may be a rare and risky way of triumphing over time. To a considerable extent, consumer civilization may owe its enormous success to the fact that—under its gay-colored, trivial surface—it offers people the illusion that time, mutability, and death can be defeated; that human life is not empty and meaningless but is full of excitement and intensity, significance and (at least the semblance of) meaning.

Throughout this book, we have discovered again and again the existential drama beneath the trivial surface of our everyday lives. We have seen how, with practically everything we do, we also protect our lives; we build, shape, and construct our selves. We, most of us, need the colorful whirl and excitement of the civilization of consumption. We need its symbols and myths, the intense experience of life radiated by it; we need the feeling that our lives have a meaning. And of course, on the other side, we also need the institutions and techniques, the efficiency and democratic order, the pragmatic ways and rational discipline of our modern, everyday world.

This situation may change. In the future, our modern, secular, and rational world may also come up with relevant answers to the ultimate questions about the human condition. And these answers will perhaps be more reliable, with fewer illusions, trickery, and delusions in them than in the spectacular "answers" of our contemporary consumer civilization. But in the meantime, we have to be forgiven for entering, again and again, the spectacular, fascinating, magical world of the civilization of consumption. We, our selves, badly need its joys, excitements, meanings, and intensities.

Proletarian Renaissance: Crisis? Transition? Revival?

What is the place and role of the "Proletarian Renaissance," or consumer civilization, in the process of the transformation of Western civilization that is taking place in these decades? Is it the symptom of a crisis? Or is it an ephemeral efflorescence of a subculture that will soon vanish without a trace? Or is it the first stage of a renewal in the history of Western civilization? It is not easy to answer these questions. However, it is important to try to answer them, because the future of the human self—the ways in which it can protect, shape, and fulfill itself—depends, to a large extent, on these answers.

If it is true that traditional Western civilization has lost, at least partly, its ability to answer the fundamental questions of human existence, then we are justified in considering the Proletarian Renaissance as an attempt to respond to this critical situation. In this case, it could be defined as a *symptom of,* and *response to, the crisis.*

It is also possible that our age is the full expansion and consummation of the individualism that has ever been present in, and has become a more and more important constituent of, Western civilization. In this case, the Proletarian Renaissance would be *an important step forward* in the evolution of this civilization. However, the situation is precarious, and troubles may lie ahead. Traditionally, individualism was only one of several important elements of Western civilization. If this single element comes to dominate all the others (and several signs seem to point in this direction), then sooner or later a functional disorder, and a critical state, may ensue, and this could seriously disturb the human personality and its attempts to actualize itself in a balanced and harmonious way.

The emergence of the Proletarian Renaissance may also be a not-peaceful evolutionary phase in the history of Western civilization. There may be a *ruth-*

less struggle going on between traditional and new cultural patterns. Disputing the thesis of Huntington (1996), one may argue that the next decades will be marked not by the clash of various great civilizations but much more by the clash of the emerging new civilization, which we have called consumer civilization, with existing traditional civilizations. Quoting Dostoyevsky, Ákos Szilágyi (2000, 91–92) argues, for instance, that the confrontation is taking place not between Europe and Russia, but between two consecutive phases of the same civilization. Thus, it is as if Europe, which has lost its way and its soul, has found itself face to face with its own earlier, religious self.[29]

The Proletarian Renaissance may also be a dangerous *cul-de-sac*. It propagates a radically individualistic lifestyle of self-fulfillment and does not develop those checks and balances and rules of conduct without which human communities cannot survive. We do not know yet, for instance, how our unrestrained consumer selves would react if the present material affluence were to be followed by a period of economic stagnation and scarcity.

There is also a fundamental *self-contradiction* in the Proletarian Renaissance, which has radically liberated instincts, desires, and aspirations. Traditionally, the concept of "civilization" or "culture" involved, *per definitionem*, an element of restraint, the taming of the natural, instinctive drives of the human being.[30] If consumer civilization proclaims the unlimited liberation of instincts and desires, *can it still be called a civilization at all?*

The exaggerated liberation of instincts has been criticized since the Age of Romanticism, and in recent decades critical voices have become louder and louder. Friedrich von Hayek (1979, 173), for instance, mentioned Freud himself as an example of how "indispensable values" may be destroyed "by scientific error." Already,

> Cartesian scientism, constructivism as developed by Auguste Comte, and logical positivism tried to prove that values are devoid of meaning. . . . But the culturally most devastating effects have come from the endeavour of psychiatrists to cure people by releasing their innate instincts. . . . I am afraid I must now concede that the logical positivism of Carnap and the legal positivism of Kelsen are far from the worst things that have come out of Vienna. Through his profound effect on education, Sigmund Freud has probably become the greatest destroyer of culture.[31]

Eugene Halton (1995) argues in the same vein, speaking of the appearance of the aggressive and hubristic ego of the modern, Faustian individual, and he emphasizes the responsibility of Simmel, Featherstone, and the postmodernist Rorty, Derrida, and Deleuze in creating the modern, irresponsible individual and celebrating the contingency of everything in human lives, including the fundamental moral values of Western civilization.[32]

There is here an interesting change of roles. Traditionally, civilization was the system that provided discipline, limits, and regulation, while everyday life was more spontaneous, free, and unrestrained. Today, the opposite seems to be true. It is our contemporary civilization that liberates our instincts and desires, and resolves our moral inhibitions, while the regulating, limiting, and restraining forces seem to be working in the routines of our everyday lives. I mean that while the Proletarian Renaissance keeps projecting its message of radical hedonism and self-fulfillment, the majority of people live a more or less "normal" and disciplined life; they do their duties, work responsibly, raise their children, respect their friends, and to a certain degree even pay attention to the affairs of their communities. This may be attributed to the survival of traditional forms, structures, and reflexes, or to the fact that people instinctively react to, and defend their selves against, the destructive forces of the radical individualism of consumer society.

The dual impact of these two factors can best be discerned in America, the home of this new, radical individualism, where, at the same time, community life has always been strong, and where more and more elements of a sense of communal responsibility are being built into the programs of personal self-fulfillment. The same process may also be observed in Western Europe, though perhaps to a slightly lesser degree. In Eastern Europe, the situation is worse. The relative lack of civic traditions, the rapid dissolution of rural communities and the rural way of life, and the destruction of social networks by the communist regimes have triggered a rampant and irresponsible individualism.[33] The situation is even more critical in the developing world, where people and societies are less able to profit from the positive message of the incoming consumer civilization and, at the same time, are almost completely defenseless against its ravaging effects. Moreover, the huge gap between reality and expectations opened by the tempting model of the Western lifestyle, as advertised and glorified in the media, has become a source of tormenting and humiliating frustration, discontent, and in some cases murderous envy and anger.

This bias and the one-sidedness are especially obvious in the world of advertising. It concentrates exclusively on the self-fulfillment of the individual and almost completely *ignores the complexities of social coexistence.* Human relationships, as portrayed in television commercials, for instance, do not go beyond happy dancing, jumping, and romping together; having fun together or exchanging tempting and flirting smiles; swallowing huge portions of spaghetti or frozen yogurt with one's family; and worshipping the latest brand of detergent together. For the time being, the world of business seems to have discovered less market value in human relationships than in individual consumption and individualistic self-fulfillment.

This is not true, however, of consumer civilization as a whole. We may like them or not, but the much-abused soap operas, for instance, deal with the *fundamental experiences of human existence:* with the situations, emotions, and dramas of love and hate, friendship and jealousy, loyalty and betrayal, birth and death, success and failure, intrigue and catharsis, revenge and forgiveness, laughing and crying together. They even present more or less valuable models of self-development, self-construction, and self-actualization. They do so not in a particularly deep way. But their enormous success proves that they provide something important for their viewers; they surround them with a virtual community, a virtual civilization of emotions and values.

The "lonely masses" seem to badly need all this. Let me give just one example. In traditional Hungary, even in my lifetime, it was almost impossible to say "I love you" to one's spouse, children, or best friends. To express one's emotions in such a direct way would have sounded almost indecent. Now, having watched for a couple of years American films and soap operas—on which people keep saying to each other "I love you, I love you"—people say more and more to their partners that they love them; and this may enrich, even if only slightly and superficially, their relationships. The same is true of the American way of cheering and expressing jubilation: People have learned in our part of the world to overcome their traditional melancholy and really rejoice when they are together and something good happens to them.[34]

It would then be a mistake to understand consumerism simply as a process of *"decivilization,"* as many do. It does fulfill civilizational functions and has generated a wealth of new forms in music, cinema, television, design, fashion, lifestyle, life strategies, behavior, "care of the self," and the like. This is so much the case that it is not completely unfounded to suggest that consumer civilization may be *an important phase in the renewal* of Western, and in the generation of a global, civilization.

Consumer civilization—and especially its radiant center, the world of advertising—is too often and too easily dismissed as a factory of cheap illusions. This criticism, too, is only partly justified. Because, in its own superficial way, consumer civilization *answers people's existential questions* that the institutions of traditional Western civilization—religion, family, school, community, publicity—are less and less able to answer. As we have seen in the preceding chapters, it projects a new vision of the world, and a new model of the human personality; it provides us with a wide range of roles, and it reduces people's anxieties; it trumpets abroad that we are free, young, beautiful, and at home in this world; and it suggests that our life has a meaning and that even the supreme Evil, mortality and death, can be defeated.

The enormous influence of consumer civilization shows that people are greatly in need of these answers, or these illusions, which does not mean that they do not also need more *authentic and reliable answers*, with less deceit and self-deception—answers that are based on facts and sound judgment and that take into account the realities of the world, the possibilities of humankind, and the real situation of the human self. But until people and societies are able to give a better response to the crisis of their traditional civilization, the symbols, goals, and aspirations of the Proletarian Renaissance are likely to play an important role in their lives.

Even if this is the case, however, the Proletarian Renaissance, as a response to the crisis of traditional Western civilization, and to the challenges of a new, globalizing world, may be only *an early phase* of a possibly emerging new civilization, a new variant of Western civilization. A real renewal, a real Renaissance or Reformation, is still to come. It might be a premature and futile effort to look for the Dantes and Petrarchs; Lope de Vegas and Shakespeares; Ficinos and Pico della Mirandolas; or Giottos, Michelangelos, and Leonardos of this new Proletarian Renaissance. Perhaps, however, we should not rule out the possibility that some of the epoch-making works of literature, art, and philosophy have already been born, works that will be elevated by history to the rank of great symbols expressing the soul and essence of our age. We do not yet know which works these will be. But think of London in, say, 1610. Who could then have known which works would be immortalized as the epitomes of their age (if a couple of hundred years of afterlife can be called "immortality")? If well-informed people in the Elizabethan Age had voted, works known today only by experts—John Lyly's *Euphues,* or the *The Faerie Queene* by Spenser, for instance—would probably have stood a better chance than Shakespeare's *Hamlet, Othello,* or *King Lear.*

I may be mixing up two things here: "high culture," that is, the culture of the humanists and the literati, on the one hand; and the "mass culture" of the age, on the other. By the latter I mean, for instance, the culture that was whirling and bubbling unrestrained, loud, morally and immorally, passionately and cynically in the theaters of outer London—the Globe, the Swan, or the Red Bull— just as the programs of our television channels do on hundreds of millions of screens. The question is, however, whether these two cultures can, and should be, separated at all.[35]

In those theaters of London, one night spectators were enthralled by the tragedies of Marlowe, Shakespeare, Ford, Webster, Beaumont, Fletcher, and others; and the next day they were entertained, in the very same theaters, by various horrendous spectacles, by "bear baiting," for instance, in which pit bulls tore to pieces bears chained to wooden poles at the center of the arena.[36] On our television screens, we have the same mixture or cacophony of art and artifice, tragedy and comedy, fun and terror, genuine value and trash.

We may not yet have the Shakespeare of cinema or television—though she may already be standing in the aisles. Imagine how Shakespeare could turn *The Taming of the Shrew* or *A Midsummer Night's Dream* into a fantastic soap opera. And what superb thrillers would come out of *Macbeth* or *Hamlet.* Or envision Shakespeare laying his hands on a movie camera!

It is therefore not impossible that, in its own way, the Proletarian Renaissance will fulfill a *positive role,* whether minor or major, in the history of Western civilization. It may deconstruct anachronistic routines and institutions and promote the development of new cultural patterns, forms, and rules of conduct; new variants of the human self; new visions of the world—a new era of our civilization.

Is the Proletarian Renaissance the symptom of a crisis? Is it a dangerous attack against the basic values of our traditional civilization? A detour or a dead alley? Or is it a new start, a new phase in the history of Western civilization? We do not yet know. The Proletarian Renaissance is so complex, and it is changing so fast, that we are not yet able to clearly describe its nature and historical significance. A period of research and debates is still ahead of us; and a difficult and fascinating period of experimenting for the human self.

Epilogue

> I shut my eyes in order to see.
>
> —*Paul Gauguin*

Care for the Self

The idea of the "care for the self"[1] has had a noble—moral and philosophical—
aura from Socrates to Foucault.[2] But caring for the self may have had also a pre-
history. In a rudimentary way, even our early ancestors must have taken care of
themselves. Vanity may not be a late civilizational development. We can hardly
imagine even Cro-Magnon women and men with a complete absence of narcissism. A kind of vanity may have, must have already been present in the competition for sexual mates and/or power in the age of hordes and early tribes.
Since the time *homo et mulier sapientes* put on the first grass skirts, caring for
one's appearance and apparel may have, must have emerged. Necklaces and
other insignia worn by our ancestors originally were magic objects, but they may
have soon served also as decoration, signs of tribal identity, objects expressing
or enhancing one's power, manliness, or feminine beauty. They were means of
an early, rudimentary process of identity formation and "self-construction."[3]

In a similar way, the fear of the unknown, natural forces, and hostile spirits
must have forced our ancestors ten or a hundred thousand years ago to think
of how they should behave to protect themselves, how to perform the rituals,

how to avoid, or get rid of, "defilement." Beyond the reconfirmation of communal values and spirit, these tribal rituals also may have had the function of shaping people's attitudes, behavior, their "selves."

Care for the self, as a concept, and as a conscious moral and philosophical exercise, emerged much later. The example that immediately comes to one's mind is the often quoted preoccupation, or even obsession, of Greek and Hellenistic thinkers with their selves, in the Socratic, Stoic, Epicurean, Cynical, Aristotelian, and other traditions.[4]

In his essay Technologies of the Self, Michel Foucault (1988b) analyzed in detail the early emergence of the concept of the care for the self:

> In 129b Alcibiades we find the first appearance of the phrase, epime-lesthai sautou.[5] In the Hellenistic and imperial periods, the Socratic notion of "taking care of oneself" became a common, universal philosophical theme. "Care of the self" was accepted by Epicure and his followers, by the Cynics, and by such Stoics as Seneca, Rufus, and Galen. The Pythagoreans gave attention to the notion of an ordered life in common.
>
> In the philosophical tradition dominated by Stoicism, askesis means not renunciation but the progressive consideration of self, or mastery over oneself, obtained not through the renunciation of reality but through the acquisition and assimilation of truth. It has as its final aim not preparation for another reality but access to the reality of this world. The Greek word for this is paraskeuazo ("to get prepared").[6]

More or less at the same time, myriad rules and norms of behavior, described and prescribed in the Old Testament (Exodus 20–23), and later in the Talmud and the Rabbinical literature, kept the faithful in a permanent process of caring for their selves. The New Testament, too, has been the vehicle for the care for one's self, or as it has been called in this context, for one's soul.[7] Even the Rules of Saint Benedict, which—seen from our secular perspective—look as if they were meant to destroy the personalities of the monks, were actually meant to help them in the care of their real, eternal selves.[8]

Care for the self has ever had its religious variants, from Saint Augustine, through Pascal, to Tillich and Buber.[9] The religious practice of the daily examen de conscience, for instance, was one of the forms of this religious care for the self.[10]

The narcissistic care of Renaissance women and men for their selves is legendary.[11] In another form, the obsession of the Puritans with their sins and the salvation of their souls was, too, an exercise in caring for their selves.[12] The principle of Cartesian cogito placed the self at the center of the world. The care for the self played a crucial role in the age of Enlightenment, too; in Locke's hypothesis of the self, as something being constructed by learning and experience; in Kant's ideas about how to achieve moral and rational perfection; in Rousseau's pedagogical ideas developed in his *Émile*; and in the Marquis de Sade's exploration of the "heart of darkness" in human beings.[13] Goethe's *Apprenticeship and Travel*, Gottfried Keller's *Green Henry*, and Jane Austen's novels were all exercises in the care, and the construction, of the self.

The idea of the care for the self was there in the melancholic narcissism and self-exploration of Pre-Romantic writers, and in the discovery of the rich fountains of inner feelings in the age of sentimentalism, Pietism, and Methodism.[14] It was there in the cult of the genius and in the splenetic self-reflection of a Byron, in the flow of emotions and the ecstasy of self-expression of the age of Romanticism. Roy Porter (1997, 5, 6–7) speaks in this connection of the journey or "odyssey of self-discovery" and remarks:

> Romanticism idealized the outsider, the Bohemian artist, the Byronic rebel, bardic visionaries—and even victims of Dr Frankenstein's monster; . . . urban man was alienated; and communing with nature was the way to get back in touch with one's self. Life must be a journey of self-discovery. That could be bitter—a Winterreise. . . .[15] In their own comparable ways, Schiller and Shelley, Coleridge and Chateaubriand, Hölderlin and Hazlitt each espoused a creed of the sacredness of the individual development. . . . Self-development was thus assuming a religious ethos, while in the philosophy of Hegel, the dialectical strivings of mind and spirit (Geist), towards autonomy or full self-awareness fused personal development with spiritual destiny: Goethe's Faust (1808) offers a dramatic parallel.

In a different way, and on a different level, the care for the self was a basic motive force in late-nineteenth-century "self-help" literature, and in the Victorian preoccupation with virtuous and civilized behavior.[16] It was there in the efforts of the Baudelairean dandy to construct himself—opposed to nature and the natural—as an artifact.[17] It became a central topic in Nietzsche's and Kierkegaard's thinking, and later, in twentieth-century philosophy and moral philosophy, from Jaspers through Tillich and Patocka to Foucault, to mention four thinkers of very different casts of mind. Caring for one's self has become a favorite subject of neo- or post-Freudian psychiatry and psychology and also of human ethology (Fromm, Erikson, Goffman), let alone the recent efforts of "positive psychology" (Diener, Seligman, Csikszentmihalyi). And then, in the second half of the twentieth century, in the emerging consumer civilization (with the slogan "Actualize yourself!"), it became the central project and all the rage for hundreds of millions of people around the world.[18]

Care for the Self: Past and Present

Comparing our present ways of caring for our selves with earlier epochs may help us better understand our own problems and opportunities. Let me use classical Greece as a point of reference. I shall focus on two concepts, "self-reflection" and "self-construction." These two concepts are different but overlap. Their weights seem to have been different in the two periods. In classical Greece, the emphasis was on self-reflection; in our contemporary civilization, self-construction is the watchword.

Self-reflection is an exercise in measuring oneself against a benchmark, a set of norms, a model, an ideal; it is a process in the course of which one reflects upon one's position, and the "human condition" in the world. Describing the classical, Greek forms of the care of the self, Nikolas Rose (1997, 242) wrote that, though in different ways,

> the practice of spiritual exercises in the service of the art of living . . . lay at the heart of the teaching of the Stoics, the Epicureans, Socratic and Platonic dialogues, in Neo-Platonism and in the Cynics. . . . One who would lead a philosophical life must practice self-examination, cultivate attention to the present moment, devote oneself to duties, cultivate indifference to indifferent things, keep certain things "before one's eyes." These spiritual exercises varied widely. They variously entailed such things as practical exercises to curb anger, gossip and curiosity and to cul-

tivate moral habits, meditation first thing in the morning and last thing at night, utilization of rhetoric and imagery to mobilize imagination, memorization of aphorisms so as to keep the fundamental dogmas at hand, the cultivation of relaxation and serenity, the practice of dialogue with others so as to be able to undertake the internal dialogue necessary to render oneself present to oneself.

As we can see, self-care was a "spiritual exercise" for the Greeks. There is less spirituality and more utilitarian consideration in our contemporary efforts of self-construction. Self-care was then a "moral exercise." Morality plays nowadays a much lesser role; self-construction is often an amoral process. We are not any more too strong at "self-examination," or at devoting ourselves to "duties." We are mesmerized by the trivialities of the age of consumption and are bad at "cultivating indifference to indifferent things." "Curbing anger, gossip and curiosity" is not part of our self-constructing exercises; living in the media age, we are overwhelmed by "gossip" and "curiosity." Yes, we "cultivate relaxation," but we forget about "serenity." We are not very strong on the "dialogue with others" and are even less so on the "dialogue with ourselves." And what about the Platonic, Socratic, Stoic, or Epicurean warnings of "know thyself," "be virtuous," "face death without fear," "cultivate harmony and resignation in your life"? Do people in the consumer age observe these principles in their daily efforts to care for their selves?[19]

Our contemporary striving for self-construction and self-actualization has a more dynamic and outward-looking character. It is a process in the course of which one builds one's body, character, and personality; develops one's "strengths" and life strategy; shapes one's behavior; develops one's views about people and the world; and strives to "actualize" oneself. The emphasis is on the active, dynamic process of "building," and not so much on "reflection." This program of dynamic self-construction was an undercurrent in most historical periods, and in most civilizations, but it was a more or less unconscious and spontaneous process. It rose to the status of a dominant program only in a few specific historical contexts—in the Age of Chivalry, for instance, or in the Renaissance, the Romantic Age, or the "dandy" subculture of the second half of the nineteenth century. And it has become the key project in our contemporary consumer civilization.

The contemporary, consumer-type preoccupation with one's self is part of a long tradition, but some major traditional elements are missing from it. It certainly is not a Socratic type of self-reflection. It has nothing to do with the moral self-examination of the Stoics or the Pythagoreans; it is not a daily checking of one's behavior in the light of basic virtues. It is certainly not the self-examination of the Jews of the Old Testament of how far they did, or did not, observe the Law. It certainly has nothing to do with the traditional Christian self-examination within the framework of monastic asceticism, and the universal sinfulness of humankind; it is not an exercise in the annihilation of one's worldly self in the hope of saving one's eternal self or soul. It does not have too much to do with the Kantian belief in the possibility of humankind's rational and moral self-improvement. It has nothing to do with the difficult exercise of introspection in Freudian analysis. It has nothing to do either with the postmodern deconstruction of the human self; it is based on a modernist, absolute, and naive belief in the glorious existence and bright opportunities of the human personality.[20] It may be an existential(ist) search for the intensity and authenticity of existence, but without the courage of the Sartrian hero at the edge of the precipice of freedom.

It has more to do, mutatis mutandis, with the Pelagian belief in the basic innocence of humankind and its opportunity and force to save itself. It is closely related to the Renaissance belief in the power of the human individual to create herself or himself. It has something in common with the narcissistic cult of the human personality of the Romantic Age, without its emphasis on the tragic fate of the genius. It has something in common also with Baudelaire's dandy, who created himself as a work of art, but without Baudelaire's inclement analysis of the human soul and his own self. It is related to the Nietzschean belief in the power of the Übermensch to conquer himself and the world, but without the tragic depths of Nietzsche's vision of the world. It is, in most of its variants, a comfortable and hedonistic program for the construction of (the illusion of) one's self.

There are scholars who claim that nowadays it is much more difficult to construct an authentic self than it was before.[21] Traditionally, people lived within a transcendental framework—in a Universe created by God, or governed by Reason, the Principle of Morality, the Laws of History—and they could find their places, their roles, their authentic selves within one of these transcendental frameworks. And then their trust and belief in these frameworks began to weaken and wither. Nietzsche declared the "death of God." The horrendous events of the twentieth century shattered people's belief in the strength of Reason and Morality, and in the triumphant progress of humankind. They have been left alone, and now they have to build up, to construct their selves in a chaotic and meaningless world, in a vacuum, in a world of uncertainty. Humankind has suffered an "existential shock," argues René J. Muller (1987, 17), a "trauma of the self facing its existence and, as an essential fact of that existence, its mortality—the certainty of its eventual annihilation in death—without delusions and false transcendences." He goes on:

> Their delusions and inauthentic transcendences no longer adequately mask their condition as existing human beings. . . . The escapes from self (inauthentic transcendences) that were successful in the past do not have the same assuasive effect as before. The Emperor is naked, i.e., we are naked. The center has not held.[22]

This shock was at the source of Kierkegaard's dread, Heidegger's anguish, and Camus's experience of the absurd. But, following Heidegger or Sartre, Bultmann or Tillich, one can add that this shock is not necessarily the sign of defeat. It may be the signal of a new beginning, of a new era when people will have the opportunity, if they have the courage, to escape from the world of false certainties and construct their genuine, authentic selves.

Other scholars contend that—in spite of temporary crises—the traditional, transcendental frameworks of our civilizations are able to renew themselves, responding to the challenges of a new age, and that there are hundreds of millions of people around the world who lead authentic lives and develop authentic personalities within these traditional frameworks.

"Highbrow" and "Lowbrow" Selves?

It may be misleading to speak in general of the contemporary way of caring for our selves. There are many different ways and styles, and even a certain social stratification of the various types of self-care may be observed. There is, for instance, a clear difference between the "highbrow" and the "lowbrow" versions of self-actualization. There are people who have the education, the incentives, the skills, and the means to embark on the adventure of a real and genuine self-construction, in which they respond to the challenges of life in an active and positive way. They explore their inner world, they reflect upon their role and place in the world, or even in the "Universe," and they may also have time and energy for self-reflection. They may emulate the great Renaissance personalities of our history.

And there are other people—and this category is not necessarily linked to a lower social status—who have less time, energy, and ability for genuine self-care. They, too, are prompted by the dominant message of our age—to "actualize themselves." But in their case, self-actualization is often a more or less passive process. They tend to be passive consumers, couch potatoes, personal music player addicts, shopping mall rats. They are more inclined to self-indulgence than to a disciplined practice of self-construction and self-realization.

If we oppose the two extreme poles, the ideal types of the highbrow and the lowbrow versions of self-actualization, then there is personality building as opposed to body building; action and creation versus passivity and consumption; self-discipline and self-limitation versus self-indulgence; an Epicurean versus a hedonistic approach to life.

Risks

Since Adorno and Horkheimer, Heidegger and Foucault, a great number of moral philosophers and theologians, sociologists, and psychologists have claimed that mass society, technical development, and consumer civilization have destroyed important political, social, moral, and cultural values; they have undermined democratic attitudes and institutions; they have led to serious social and psychological disturbances; they have distorted the human self; and they have lulled people into "oblivion," manipulating them into passive consumerism, prompting them to disperse themselves into futile activities. Baumeister (1986a, 91–92) argued, for instance, that "mass-produced goods, mass-produced and mass-mediated ideas, vicarious experience, and impersonal work leave little room" for a genuine self-actualization. He further states:

Self-actualization is one of those values that get lip service but only rare and seasonal exertion. The boxing champion's comment reflects the prevailing form of the notion of individual destiny. "I was born to be myself" implies that individuality is one's birthright, not one's achievement. This seems to be the current attitude. Individuality is not regarded as something difficult to acquire or as the final product of arduous cultivation of one's own potential. Rather, individuality is regarded as something that everyone has. If it requires anything, it requires only occasional choice and self-acceptance. . . . Two main personal goals and ideals seem to be to earn a lot of money and to become a celebrity.

It is certainly true that the project of self-actualization has its own risks. Instead of becoming the cult of the human self and personality, it may easily turn into a shortsighted, primitive, aggressive form of egoism or egotism. This is a real danger. Manuel Castells (1997, 355), for instance, warned his contemporaries that

at first sight, we are witnessing the emergence of a world exclusively made of markets, networks, individuals, and strategic organizations, apparently governed by patterns of "rational expectations" (the new, influential economic theory), except when these "rational individuals" suddenly shoot their neighbor, rape a little girl, or spread nerve-gas in the subway. No need for identities in this new world: basic instincts, power drives, self-centered strategic calculations dominate everyday life. One can see the seeds of a society whose Weltanschauung would split between the old logic of Macht and a new logic of Selbstanschauung.[23]

Castells (1997, 358) hopes that new social movements and spontaneously evolving networks will develop into real and virtual "communes of resistance," which will be able to protect the life world against various kinds of destructive forces and will develop the new cultural codes that may safeguard social values, and the human self, in the emerging Age of Information.

In the same vein, Charles Taylor (1989) convincingly argues that our efforts toward self-actualization should be tempered by moral considerations. We are not, or we should not think that we are, completely free to actualize ourselves as we please. Our community and culture have an idea of what the "good life" is, and we have to strive for our personal fulfillment within this ethico-moral framework.[24] Commenting on Taylor's ideas, Calvin O. Schrag (1997, 109, 98) wrote:

> The self in community is a self situated in this space of communicative praxis, historically embedded, existing with others, inclusive of predecessors, contemporaries, and successors. Never an island entire of itself, the self remains rooted in history but is not suffocated by the influx of historical forms and forces. The communalized self is in history but not of history. It has the resources for transcending the historically specific without arrogating to itself an unconditioned and decontextualized vision of the world.
>
> To exist ethically with others, this is the task and the norm.

Assets

These comments are relevant and worth keeping in mind. But the prevailing strong indictment of our contemporary civilization is biased and one-sided, for several reasons. First, actually, there is a continuum between the "highbrow" and "lowbrow" versions of self-actualization, with all the possible shades, mixtures, and overlapping along the line. And second—as we have seen throughout this book—even the trivial spheres of consumer civilization, which are most exposed to the impact of the media and the advertising industry, may have their own depths. In its own way, even the civilization of consumption raises and answers some of the fundamental questions of human life, and it prompts people to "construct their selves." Consumer civilization is not only an ongoing "carnival"[25] but also a pleasant, enjoyable, entertaining version of self-care and self-construction. Or it is even more: It is a desperate—though most of the time unconscious—struggle with the anxieties of a world without transcendence.

Pop music, for instance, is full of moments and elements of self-reflection. And soap operas overflow with emotions in a world that suffers from a drought of emotions. Brazilian and Mexican telenovelas are masochistic ordeals of self-reflection of people, mainly young women and men, in search of answers to the question: Why does not he or she love me? This may be not the ontologically most important question in the world, though some philosophers and theologians would claim that it is. Women's weekly magazines are full of celebrities, model personalities to whom one can measure oneself. They are full of human dramas, which for a short instant may break the ice of our everyday routines and open before our eyes the depths of our mortal condition. They give a popular version of daily caring for one's body and mind; they provide "tests" that help their readers check their abilities and draw their own psychological profiles; magazine psychologists counsel them on how to care for their selves. Horoscopes help them reflect upon the mysterious relationships between their own lives and the cosmic forces of the universe. Are all these illusions? Are they empty virtual experiences? They may be, but they fill a void left by the erosion of traditional Western civilization. If and when a more authentic and more valuable civilization emerges, consumer civilization may lose part of its appeal and its present dominant position.

Why All This Zeal?

We have followed the almost perpetual efforts of people to shape, construct, and actualize their selves throughout their lives. I have to admit that I am fascinated by the fervor, the endurance, the anguish, the inventiveness with which they find thousands of ways and means to develop their selves. But I think we have forgotten to ask one important question: Why all these efforts and exertion, why all this rage about our selves? Why are we so eager and anxious to keep constructing and "actualizing" our selves?

The most plausible answer is a truism: We want to live, we want to enjoy life, we want to have as much as possible of life; and we are convinced that the more we actualize our selves, the more valuable, powerful, smart, beautiful, and young we are, the more life we can absorb, the more we will be alive. From the opposite angle, we may state the same thing by saying—and this, too, is a blatant truism—that we cling to life because we do not want to die; we build up strong personalities and selves because we think that thus we exist more intensely and may better resist the lethal passing of time. As we have seen, one may even deify the human self to achieve a kind of virtual immortality.

It should not be forgotten, however, that human life and the self can be fulfilled, and fear and mortality can also be challenged, in ways that are ignored or neglected by the mainstream civilization of consumption. One may fulfill one's self, for instance, in an indirect way, by living according to the teaching of a great traditional religion; by curbing, punishing, and rejecting one's worldly self in exchange for an eternal life and perhaps also an eternal self. One may also identify oneself with a community, or with one's family, and hope to survive in the memory of people, in the love and the future lives of one's children and descendants. One may identify oneself with the universal and eternal harmony of the cosmos. One may be absorbed into Nature and have the feeling that one survives in the eternal return of flowers, rains, and sunshine. One may survive in a tree one has planted, or in anything one has built, constructed, or created in the world. One can accept one's mortality and try at least to help others, to reduce the misery and alleviate the suffering in the world. One can also accept one's mortality and live, in the short time span at one's disposal, with dignity, resignation, and serenity.

All these efforts turn around the human self. Directly or indirectly, the human being is motivated by the wish and hope to fulfill her or his self and protect it against the forces of mortality and death. But we should remember that other civilizations have chosen other ways. Buddhism, for instance, turned against the self and taught that the self was not the source of life and happiness but the contrary: It was the source of misery and suffering in the world; one had to get rid of it and find eternal piece in nonbeing, in nirvana.[26]

And more important, we have to think of those about whom we usually forget, those people in the poorer part of the world who have almost no chance whatever to "actualize" themselves. Think of those 800 million people around the world who do not have enough to eat. Think of the fact that about 40 (!) percent of children under age five in low-income countries are chronically undernourished and underweight for their age.[27] Think of those tens of millions of African children who are infected with malaria or HIV in infancy. Think of those tens of millions of people who spend a substantial part of their lives in countries ravaged by war. Do they have any chance to "shape," "build," and "construct" their selves? Hardly. There are people who believe that, ultimately, there is a kind of justice in the world, or at least a kind of opportunity for everybody. They may be seriously mistaken. What would have happened to Shakespeare's,

Leonardo da Vinci's, or Mozart's selves if they had grown up hungry and ill in one of the countries at the Heart of Darkness?

Questions

In the first part of this book, we observed the ways and means whereby a human person keeps constructing her or his self in her or his everyday life, and does so even without necessarily being aware of the fact that she or he is doing so. In the second part of the book, we discovered that the stakes, possibilities, and dangers of this unconscious or semiconscious process of self-construction have become even higher in our contemporary age of consumption—in an age that has lost, at least partly, its transcendental framework. We have explored the situation of the human self both in its everyday life, and in this specific age, from various angles.

After so much psychology, sociology, cultural anthropology, and whatever, let me conclude this book in a slightly more philosophical (or should I say more personal?) key. Let me ask a few shamefully unscholarly questions.

What should we do with ourselves when we have explored the world of the self from so many sides? Should we throw out the window all these ideas, theories, and problems and continue to live our lives as we have lived so far and keep diligently constructing our selves as we have done so far? Maybe. Or should we look for a framework, a religion, a philosophy, a community, within which we may find safety, some freedom and meaning, and which would probably answer the anguish-filled questions of life and death for us? Perhaps. Should we cultivate our "strengths," think "positively," thrive for success and happiness, and brush aside all kinds of "existential" nonsense? We may try. Or should we find a great issue, a great cause, for our selves and work for the betterment of the world and the alleviation of human and animal suffering in the world? This would be, beyond any doubt, a noble and meaningful activity, even if, after all, it would not tell us whether human life has, or has not, a purpose and meaning.

And further questions are lining up. We have seen that to construct our selves is not an easy task. When we are doing so, we more or less grope around in the dark. We may not be certain that the "self" exists at all, and if it does, whether we have a unified self or multiple selves. We do not know how far our selves are determined by outside factors and how far we are free to shape them. If we have a certain freedom, where should we seek and find those models, norms, and guidelines that may help us construct our selves in an optimal way? Have people ever been concerned with their selves, or is the care of the self a new, modern, contemporary phenomenon, the product of an "age of narcissism"? What are the motive forces behind or below this feverish activity of self-construction? Is our self the center of our lives? Is it a source of intensity and meaning? Or is it a dangerous trap? Why is it so important to keep constructing it day in and day out, starting with our first little tricks in the cradle and caring for our self, our appearance, our name, our memory, and our vanity even in the last days of our lives?

Do our ways of caring for our selves substantially differ from those of people who lived in earlier ages and other civilizations? And if they do, what can we learn from these differences? How do our contemporary ways of caring for our selves compare with those of a Socrates, a Saint Augustine, a Montaigne, a Byron, a Baudelaire, a Nietzsche, a Sartre, a Tillich, a Ricoeur, a Foucault? Or have we got to follow the new stars of our own age? Does contemporary consumer civilization thwart or help our efforts to achieve genuine and authentic personalities? Do we know at all how our selves are being shaped, constructed, and deconstructed in the latent sphere of our being while, on the "surface," we live our everyday lives of survival?

We have seen how, in the morning, we step out of our bathroom, out of our home, and set on our way in the world with a hangover, or with a foolish exultation, as if our lives and the world had a purpose and meaning (maybe they have); as if we were strong, autonomous, important selves and were at home in this universe (maybe we are); as if we had a mission in this world (maybe we have one). We fuss about all day, we work and talk and smile and quarrel; we solve, or fail to solve, the problems of our lives; we enjoy ourselves; and then, in the evening, we go home, we switch on the television, we go to sleep . . . and lose ourselves, our selves, again in the depths of the night.

Does all this mean that our lives are futile and trivial? Not necessarily.

My purpose in this book has been just to show that the trivialities of our everyday lives are not trivial at all. They have hidden deep structures. Beneath their practical functions, our daily activities have a level of significance as well.

We are involved, throughout our lives, in a latent existential drama. We struggle with the contingencies of the world and the uncertainties of our lives. We keep constructing and reconstructing our selves, even without knowing that we are doing so. We are running after our everyday business but, at the same time, we are also struggling, unconsciously or semiconsciously, with our anxieties about the fragility of our selves and our very existence. Beneath the trivialities of our everyday lives, and below the surface of our everyday consciousness, we keep struggling for authenticity, for the intense experience of being, for dignity, for meaning, and yes, also for (the hope of) immortality.

I do not mean that we live a double life in the sense of a French comedy or tragicomedy. Nor is the duality of our lives and selves something like the split consciousness of a Dr. Jekyll and Mr. Hyde. It may be compared much more—and I apologize for these poetic metaphors—with two melodies running parallel, and intertwining, with one another. It is the simultaneous jubilation and lamentation, laughter and sorrow of Mozart's symphonies.

It is the interplay of the joy and sadness, the playfulness and the seriousness of human life. It is the interplay of everyday life and human destiny, moment and eternity. It is the interplay of the bright colors of life and the darkness of the unknown depths of the human condition.

We have seen that this duality of our lives is even sharper and more dramatic now, in contemporary consumer civilization, which has been so aptly and appropriately described by several students as the interplay of the eternal carnival, and the dance of death, of human life. Living in this age, our selves are certainly marked by the puzzling and fascinating ambivalence of the trivial and the existential, the trivial and the tragic.

Notes

Introduction

1 As interesting examples, see Irwin (2000, 2002) and Irwin, Conard, and Skoble (2001), in which various authors explore the philosophical "depths" of everyday genres like Seinfeld's situation comedies, or *The Simpsons*. Or see the amazing book of the Reverend Chris Seay (2002), who analyzed *The Sopranos* as *The Gospel According to Tony Soprano: An Unauthorized Look into the Soul of TV's Top Mob Boss and His Family*. See also Bassham and Bronson (2003), and the volume edited by Greene and Vernezze (2004), *The Sopranos and Philosophy: I Kill Therefore I Am*, with chapters like "Bada-Being and Nothingness: Murderous Melodrama or Morality Play?" (Al Gini), and "Know Thyself, Asshole: Tony Soprano as an Aristotelian Tragic Hero" (Lippman).

2 In my *Fears and Symbols* (2001), I have dealt with the problem of "Are trivialities trivial?" in chapters 10, 11, and 12, on jokes, plays, and perfume posters.

3 See also Plessner (1965).

4 As an important and interesting early parallel see Unamuno (1921).

5 Becker (1973, 265, 269, 277, 281). I deal with these theories and hypotheses in detail in my *Fears and Symbols* (2001, 53–61).

6 I have to humbly confess that originally I wanted to speak of the dichotomy of the "trivial and the tragic." For a couple of months, I even played with the idea of giving the book the title *The Trivial and the Tragic*. This would have been a stronger and—due to the alliteration—a stylistically more elegant and emphatic statement. I liked also its slightly Nietzschean overtone. But then I discarded the idea, mainly because such a phrase, and such a title, would have been misleading. Humans' struggle for

authentic existence, meaning, and "immortality" is not so gloomy and is not necessarily tragic. It is fascinating and variegated, full of sudden turns and surprises, persistence and inventiveness, defeats and successes. And it also has its sunny sides and funny moments. Western and Eastern religions and philosophies have ever had both good and bad news for people about the human condition.

7 Readers not particularly interested in the state of the art in personal psychology may skip this and the next chapter and continue their reading with the chapter titled "The Self in Everyday Life."

8 See, e.g., Rank (1910), Mead (1935, 2001), Roheim (1943, 1950), Benedict (1946), Cassirer (1953–96), Eliade (1959, 1961, 1963, 1978–85), Dichter (1964, 1971), Bachelard (1964b, 1969), Berger and Luckmann (1966), Turner (1967), Berger (1967, 1969), Jung (1968, 1971a, 1971b), Durand (1969), Barthes (1972), Geertz (1973a), Olson (1980), Csikszentmihalyi and Rochberg-Halton (1981), Bohrer (1983), Baudrillard (1988b, 1993), Kolakowski (1989), Campbell (1993 [1972]), Samuel and Thompson (1993), Eliot (1997), and Herrick (2003). Cultural anthropology and comparative religion in general, and certain aspects of symbolic interactionism and ethnomethodology, are particularly interesting in this field.

9 Rejecting Freud's gloomy picture of the unconscious as full of dangerous and uncontrollable psychic forces, Rollo May (1969, 19) described the unconscious as a reservoir of *"those potentialities for knowing and experiencing that the individual cannot or will not actualize"* (emphasis in the original). See also Douglas, Johnson, and Altheide (1977).

10 The tradition of a more complex approach continued mainly in the field of psychiatry, in the various schools of Freudian, Neo-Freudian, and non-Freudian analysis.

11 Mischel and Morf (2003, 18). See also Cantor and Kihlstrom (1981); Devine, Hamilton, and Ostrom (1994); Wyer (1997); Adair, Bélanger, and Dion (1998); Cervone and Shoda (1999); Gollwitzer and Bargh (1996); Pléh (1999); Shohov (2002); Larsen and Buss (2002); Balota and Marsh (2003); Kellogg (2003); and Eysenck and Keane (2005).

12 See, e.g., Aronson and Pratkanis (1993); Myers (1993); Gilbert, Fiske, and Lindzey (1998); Pervin and John (1999); Hampson (2000); Forgas and Williams (2001, 2002); Cervone and Mischel (2002); Hutchison (2003); and Leary and Tangney (2003a). See also Sullivan (1953); Goffman (1974); Turner and Bruner (1986); Brehm and Kassin (1993); Hewitt (1994); Higgins and Kruglanski (1996); Hogan, Johnson, and Briggs (1997); Hall, Lindzey, and Campbell (1998); Snyder and Cantor (1998); Smith and Mackie (2000); Sedikides and Brewer (2001); Hogg and Cooper (2003); and Aronson, Wilson, and Akert (2004). For a short survey of the various fields of research, see Hoyle et al. (1999).

13 The reader will find a large selection of these books in note 21 of chapter 10.

14 See also Wyer (1997), Forgas (2000), and Birtchnell (2003).

15 In the concluding chapter of *The Social Self,* edited by Forgas and Williams (2002), Sedikides (370–71) stresses the fact that "although at several historical junctions in social and personality psychology the assertion that the self is woven into the motivational system would constitute heresy, such a statement is now considered rather trite. A sizable portion of the literature in the last 15 years has addressed the link between motivation and the self." See also Cattell and Child (1975), Deci and Ryan (1985), Sorrentino and Higgins (1986–96), Gollwitzer and Bargh (1996), Pitman (1998), Baumeister (1999), and Higgins and Kruglanski (2000). And see the extremely interesting studies of motivation in the literature discussing the advertising machinery. Among the most interesting works are two early studies by Ernest Dichter: *Handbook of Consumer Motivations. The Psychology of the World of Objects* (1964), and *Motivating Human Behavior* (1971).

16 In the words of Rollo May (1969, 30), Freud made a "radical contribution to the new image of man, namely, man as pushed by demonic, tragic, and destructive forces."

17 See, e.g., Heise (1979); Izard, Kagan, and Zajonc (1984); Sartre (1985); Frijda (1986); Ortony, Clore, and Collins (1988); Curtis (1991); Kitayama and Markus (1994); Russell et al. (1994); Damasio (1994); Goleman (1995); Tangney and Fischer (1995); Martin and Tesser (1996); Miller (1996); Hinton (1999); Baumeister (1999); Bless and Forgas (2000); Mayne and Bonano (2001); Martin and Clore (2001); Reddy (2001);Tangney (2003); Lewis and Haviland-Jones (2004); and Oatley (2004). See also the important contribution of the leading scholars of "positive psychology," Seligman (1998, 2002); Kahneman, Diener, and Schwartz (1999); Evans (2003); and Sheldon (2004).

18 Pyszczynski, Greenberg, and Solomon (1997, 2, 4, 5 and passim). See also Pyszczynski, Greenberg, and Solomon (2003). Philosophers and psychologists with a philosophical inclination have ever stressed the importance of death in shaping people's lives and selves. See, e.g., Heidegger (1962), Frankl (1963), Becker (1973), and Lifton (1979).

19 See, e.g., Mikulincer and Florian (1997, 33).

20 See Buss (1997), Baron (1997), Leary and Schreindorfer (1997), and others. In my book *Fears and Symbols* (Hankiss 2001, 32–34), I have dealt with this controversy in detail.

21 Discovering a deeper layer of motivations beneath the psychic mechanisms described by Freud, Rollo May (1969, 19) wrote for instance that "the simple mechanism of *regression* . . . is infinitely less simple than it looks; . . . it involves a complex struggle . . . of the individual's *being* against the possibility of *nonbeing.*"

22 From a fast-growing literature, see works listed in note 4 of chapter 4.

23 Let me quote here a few lines from a classical study on the experimental methodology by Aronson, Wilson, and Brewer (1998, 106): "In general, laboratory makes it easier to accomplish the random assignment of people to conditions. In addition, a laboratory setting permits the researcher to manipulate independent variables more precisely and to eliminate or minimize the intrusiveness of 'extraneous' variables. Advocates of laboratory experiments believe that the world is a complex place consisting of a great many noisy variables, a condition that impedes the chances of obtaining a pure indication of the effect of one variable upon the other. . . . Conversely, the field is generally regarded as being more 'real.' . . . Critics of the laboratory setting have suggested that it is silly to eliminate contextual variables in the interest of precision if those variables are always present in the world."

24 Mischel and Morf (2003, 29, 30) speak of a "life-long self-construction process. . . . [The self] is an interpersonal system that is constructed and re-constructed in social contexts and relationships throughout its development, maintenance, and transformation over the life course." See also works like Lipka and Brinthaupt (1992), Brinthaupt and Lipka (1994), Heckhausen and Dweck (1998), and the rich literature on "oral history."

25 I shall give a large selection of some of the most important books on the emergence of consumer and/or postmodern civilization in note 52 of chapter 9.

26 They come from various schools: Neo-Kantianism, critical theory, existentialism, neoconservatism, poststructuralism, Neo-Marxism, etc.

27 To give an idea of the enormous variety of problems, let me quote Kenneth J. Gergen (1991, 13), who gives an alarming list of concepts, attributes, and symptoms that are being used to characterize the selves in our contemporary society. Here are some of them: low self-esteem, depressed self, stressed, obsessive-compulsive, sadomasochistic, antisocial, alienated, authoritarian, repressed, burned out, paranoid, bulimic, anxious, anorexic, kleptomaniac, psychopathic deviate, voyeuristic self, etc.

28 From among the innumerable works, let me mention here only a few outstanding books: Austin (1962), Searle (1969), Foucault (1974, 1988b), Habermas (1979a, 1987), Bourdieu (1991), and Butler (1997).

29 See the works listed in note 12 above.

30 Studies in the sociology of everyday life, symbolic interaction, and ethnomethodology are especially interesting from our point of view, in spite of the fact that most of them stay on the level of the practical and the sociological. There are, though, some excellent exceptions, e.g., the works of Lefebvre (1958–81); Goffman (1959, 1966, 1970, 1972); Inkeles and Bauer (1959); Ariés (1962); Garfinkel (1967); Blumer (1969); Douglas (1973); Turner (1974); McCall and Simmons (1978); Stryker (1980); Douglas and Adler (1980); Weigert (1981); Hilbert and Collins (1992);

Heller (1984); Certau (1984); Harvey (1985); Ariés and Duby (1987–91); Certau, Giard, and Mayol (1988); Coulter (1990); Emmons (1991); Flynn (1991); Button (1991); Hewitt (1994); MacKinnon (1994); Silverstone (1994); Coulon (1995); Miller (1996); Wyer (1997); Kolakowski (1999); Gardiner (2000); Ciarrochi, Forgas, and Mayer (2001); Fivush and Haden (2003); and Newman and O'Brian (2004).

31 Out of a very rich literature see, e.g., the works of Elshtain (1981), Gilligan (1982), Tarule (1986), Nicholson (1990),Meyers (1997); Meehan and Riordan (2002), Taylor and Vintges (2004), and Heilmann and Beetham (2004); Doniger (2005).

32 In sociology and political science, there are hundreds of important works that study these various social, political, and cultural environments of the self. A growing literature on the social and cultural impact of globalization, on its ways and power of changing people's life world, is becoming particularly important for the understanding of the human self in our contemporary world.

33 See works listed in note 4 of chapter 4.

34 There are a few brilliant studies in this field. See works listed in note 2 of the epilogue.

Chapter 1. The Morning Reconstruction of the Self

1 There is a huge literature on dreaming in psychology, psychoanalysis and cultural anthropology. See, e.g., Shields (1990), Freud (1956), Roheim (1952), Eliade (1961), Jung (1974), Cohen (1979), Tedlock (1987), Foucault and Binswanger (1994), Van de Castle (1994), Domhoff (1996), Mageo (2003), and Rock (2004). See also the essay "Sleep and Self-Destruction" in Shneidman (1967).

2 See, e.g., Leary and Tangney (2003a) and the section titled "The Duality of the Self in Psychology" in the introduction to the present volume.

3 Hemingway seems to have had just the opposite experience. According to my notes [I cannot find now the exact location], he wrote somewhere that: "I love sleep. My life has the tendency to fall apart when I'm awake."

4 Quoted by Mageo (2003, 3). She speaks of "the nightly dissolution of our cultural universes" and the "dissolution of all fixed meanings."

5 *Remembrance of Things Past.* Quoted by Fraser (1978, 288).

6 A similar experience was present also in Greek and Hellenistic philosophy: "Since sleep was related to death as a kind of encounter with the gods, you had to purify yourself before going to sleep" (Foucault 1988b, 33).

7 Prayer of Father L. Lelotte in *Hitélet* (1997), a Hungarian Prayer book.

8 *Hitélet* (1997, 36–37).

9 *"Se lever"* means in French "to get up."

10 In a fascinating book, Philippe Beaussant (2000) described the intricate ceremonies accompanying the morning getting up of the Roi Soleil, i.e., Louis XIV.

11 Füst (1989).

12 See the section on "Gossip" in chapter 6.

13 See chapter 14, "The Self in a Reenchanted World."

14 See, e.g., Wetterer and Troschke (1986), Ney and Gale (1989), Bouyer and Gaffet (1997), and Eysenck (2000).

15 See, e.g., Thomas F. Cash's (1995) book *What Do You See When You Look in the Mirror? Helping Yourself to a Positive Body Image*—or Bloomfield and Felder (1985, chap. 3), "When I look in the Mirror, I'm Never Satisfied." These latter authors propose a very simple strategy against this morning shock of looking in the mirror. One has to stand nude for twenty minutes in front of a full-length mirror, observing each part of one's body, one by one, and then the body as a whole, and one has to keep saying: "I am beautiful." According to the authors, this cure may make wonders. I also remember one of the students in our university dormitory of yore who, every morning at the same time, stood in front of a mirror, took off his shirt, flexed his muscles and said: "I am strong, I am good looking, I am young"—and then, without any further ado, put on his shirt and came with us to the classes.

16 See Van Gennep (1960) and Turner (1969).

17 In Lewis Carroll's novel, the sudden and shocking changes in Alice's perception of her own body, which in one moment seems to fill the world and in the next is miniaturized, is a good example of the difficulties children may have with their body image and self-perception.

18 See, e.g., Tiemersma (1989), and his discussion of the phenomenology, hermeneutics, or ontology of the human body. From a rich literature, see Fisher (1986); Wilson (1987); Freedman (1988); Krueger (1989); Thompson (1990); Featherstone, Hepworth, and Turner (1991); Shilling (1994); Weber (2000); Falk (1994); Bermúdez, Marcel, and Eilan (1995); *Body & Society* (1995); Kaiser (1997, 97–143); Negrin (1999); Featherstone (2000); Cash and Pruzinsky (2002); and Bordo (2004). See also titles like *Body Liberation: Freeing Your Body for Greater Self-Acceptance, Health, and Sexual Satisfaction* (Coleman and Edwards 1977); *Nothing to Lose: A Guide to Sane Living in a Larger Body* (Erdman 1995); *The Body Image Workbook: An 8-Step Program for Learning to Like Your Looks* (Cash 1997); *Body Image Disturbance: Assessment and Treatment* (Thompson 1990); and *The Created Self: Reinventing Body, Persona, Spirit* (Weber 2000).

19 *GQ*, August 1998, 12.

20 In a civilization that has, at least partly, lost its belief in transcendence, people have to make the best of their immanent lives and bodies. See more about this in chapter 11.

21 Wilson (1987), Negrin (1999), Tiemersma (1989).

22 Kaiser (1997, 122–24).

23 *Webster's* (1949, 507). Under the entry "MAKE – *v.i.* – *make up.* a. To compose, . . . to constitute."

24 *Webster's* (1949, 507): "c. . . . to arrange; to adjust . . . i. . . . to compensate; to make good . . . o. To remove (a deficiency . . .)."

25 *Webster's* (1949, 507): "c. . . . to invent. . . . f . . . to assume a guise; to impersonate."

26 I have discussed another aspect of perfume advertisements in my *Fears and Symbols* (Hankiss 2001, chap. 12, 261–73).

27 "Set your spirit free" (WINGS by Giorgio), "Let it [the perfume] release the splendor in you" (VANDERBILT).

28 *"Sillage d'une femme imprévisible"* (OH LALA by Loris Azzaro).

29 *"Tendre et fougueuse amazone"* (AMAZONE by Hermes). *"Tendre et sauvage comme son parfum"* (J'AI OSÉ by Guy Laroche). On the poster, there is a young woman, with great blue eyes, with a blue-eyed panther overlooking her shoulder.

30 "Women should be bright, wild, flirty, fun, eccentric, tough, bold, and very, very dijan" (PERFUME by Dijan).

31 EAU DE GIVENCHY by Elizabeth Arden.

32 TRÉSOR by Lancôme.

33 This eau de toilette "redefines femininity and celebrates the beauty of women" (EAU DE TOILETTE by Jean Paul Gaultier).

34 ANAÏS ANAÏS, SAMSARA, SHALIMAR, YATIS, AMARIGE, or ASJA (by Fenji), "the oriental empress of sensuality," who will introduce you in this exotic world: "The Orient is fascination, mystery, magic and ancient traditions. An enchanted world, rich in colorful suggestions and intense sensations."

35 "A Woman discovers herself" (MAROUSSIA by Slava Zaitsev). "The essence of being" (VIVID by Liz Claiborne). *"L'essence d'une femme"* (INTUITION by Estée Lauder). *"Essenza di donna"* (FEMINA by Alberta Ferretti). *"Eine Frau entdeckt ihr neues Ich!"* (MAROUSSIA by Slava Zaitsev.

36 *"La sensualité à l'extrème"* (OPIUM by YSL).

37 "Life is how you change it" (Perry Ellis).

38 *"Il segreto della seduzione"* (VENEZIA by Laura Biagiotti).

39 "Living without boundary" (SAFARI by Ralph Lauren).

40 *"La passion du moment. L'éternel féminin"* (PARFUM by Jean-Louis Scherer).

41 CABOTINE by Gres.

42 "Created for the romantic woman who appreciates the natural and the authentic" (ANAïS ANAïS by Cacharel).

43 DESTINY by Marilyn Miglin.

44 [This perfume] "was created not for those who go with the trend of the moment, but for those who seek out a style of their own." HUGO by Hugo Boss).

45 *"Le parfum du succès"* (CHAMPAGNE by YSL).

46 This perfume is a "celebration of life" (SUNFLOWERS by Elizabeth Arden; it is a "celebration of laughter, love and happiness" (AMARIGE by Givenchy).

47 ". . . a fresh, soft and utterly sensual fragrance, radiant with happiness" (DOLCE VITA by Dior).

48 "Discover perfect harmony . . . an eau de toilette with fullness and clarity" (FAHRENHEIT by Dior). This is a "fragrance . . . to be worn by the easy-going and nature loving woman, at ease with life and in harmony with herself" (EAU DE GIVENCHY by Elizabeth Arden).

49 This is suggested by perfumes like INFINI and PARFUM SACRÉ by Caron, SUBLIME by Jean Patou, PERFECTION by Dijon, or PLÉNITUDE by L'Oréal.

50 EAU DE GIVENCHY by Elizabeth Arden.

51 For the psychological and social importance, cultural meaning and symbolic messages of dressing see, among others, Kroeber and Richardson (1940); Roach and Eicher (1965); Baker (1984); Simon-Miller (1985); Solomon (1985); Wilson (1987, 1990); Böhm, Lock, and Streicher (1989); Baudrillard (1990, 1993); Gaines and Herzog (1990); Featherstone, Hepworth, and Turner (1991); Finkelstein (1991); Pastoureau (1991); Shilling (1994); Benstock and Ferris (1994); Barnard (1996); Kaiser (1997); Negrin (1999); and Eicher, Evenson, and Lutz (2000).

52 For an interesting discussion of this issue see, e.g., Simon-Miller (1985).

53 Kaiser (1997, 508).

54 See also Csikszentmihalyi and Rochberg-Halton (1981, 38–45 and passim) and their interesting discussion of how the self has to balance between integrating herself/himself in the community, and at the same time to become and remain "different."

55 To show the richness of this language of fashion, let me quote a few items of his *Inventory of Genera:* "ACCESSORY—APRON Apron (blouse-, dress-). ARMHOLE—BACK—BELT Belt (corselet-), chain, tie, martingale—BLOUSE Blouse (smock-, sweater-, tunic-), blousette, brassière, caftan, canezou, caraco, casaque, chasuble,

shirt, chemise, top, jumper, sailor, polo, tunic, middy—BRACELET Bangles, bracelet, identification bracelet—CAPE Cape (pelerine-) CLIP—COAT Car coat, dustcoat, cloak, slicker, raincoat, coat (sweater-, mandarin-), overcoat, pelisse, riding coat, trenchcoat—COLLAR Collar (bertha-, cape-, hoop-, shawl, shirt-, Peter Pan-, corolla-, wing-, Byron-, scarf-, funnel-, sailor-, military-, pilgrim-, dicky-, polo-, sailor's tie-, tailored-), ruff (Pierrot-)—COLOR Simple colors (red, green, blue, etc.) to metaphorical colors (moss, lime, Pernod), and even to purely qualitative colors (gay, bright, neutral, shocking)—DETAIL—DRESS Baby-doll, smock, jumpsuit, sheath, tank, dress (blazer-, blouse-, blouson-, shirtdress, chemise, sheath, coat-, sweater-, pinafore, tunic-), overalls—EDGING Band, bias, edging, scallop, fringe, galloon, gimp, binding, hem, piping, stitching, retching, braiding, quill, ruffle—EN-SEMBLE Matching, bikini, suit, two-piece (blazer, blouson, cardigan, casaque, jumper, sailor suit), jacket-, ensemble, separates, tailored suit (blazer-, bolero-, cardigan-, kimono, safari, tunic), three-piece, twin set—FASTENERS Hooks, buckles, frogs, buttoning, buttons, studs, zippers, laces, straps, knots (hatter's-, cabbage-, butterfly-), beads— . . . etc., etc."

56 As an example, let me mention "oppositions" as important structural elements in this syntax of fashion. "With or without, natural or artificial, marked-marking or unmarked-non-marking, straight or curved, tight or loose, ascending or descending, heavy or light, supple or stiff, protruding or hollow (concave), opaque or transparent, long or short, wide or narrow, voluminous or thin, big or little, split or unsplit, fixed or movable, open or closed, turned up or turned down, horizontal or vertical, left or right, at the top or at the bottom, in front or in back, one or many, symmetrical or asymmetrical, over or under, matching or dissonant, increased by or offset by, not at all or entirely."

57 They measured historical variation of the following elements of women's evening dresses: 1. The length of the skirt. 2. The height of the waistline. 3. The depth of the neckline. 4. The width of the skirt. 5. The width of the waist. 6. The width of the neckline.

58 Quoted by Negrin (1999, 100). See also Baudrillard (1990, 1994).

59 Wilson (1987, 245), quoted by Negrin (1999, 107). See also Hollander (1993).

60 The word *"varius"* was often used as the synonym of *"virgulatus,"* *"lineatus,"* *"fasciatus,"* i.e. *"striped."*

61 Pastoureau (1991, 43).

62 Pastoureau (1991, 43–44, 10).

63 Pastoureau (1991, 17–22).

64 Pastoureau (1991, 44).

65 Pastoureau (1991, 14).

66 For the importance of objects in shaping the human self, see Csikszentmihalyi and Rochberg-Halton (1981). See also Dichter (1964, 1971) on the symbolic message of objects.

67 Wine glasses function in the same way. Their stems reach up high and lift up the wine in their bowls almost as in the ceremony of the Elevation.

68 The handbooks of social and personality psychology have chapters and a great number of references to "goals," "life goals," "personal projects," "personal strivings" (Hoyle et al. 1999, 144–46), and related topics. See, e.g., Bühler et al. (1968); Brehm and Kassin (1993); Aronson and Pratkanis (1993); Hewitt (1994); Gilbert, Fiske, and Lindzey (1998); Emmons (1999); Forgas and Williams (2001, 2002); Tesser, Stapel, and Wood (2002); Leary and Tangney (2003a); and Aronson, Wilson, and Akert (2004). See also Baumeister (1991b), Martin and Tesser (1996), Schmuck and Sheldon (2001), Waitley (2004), and the ideas of the great classics like Jung and Adler, or the members of the humanistic school of psychology—Carl Rogers, Abraham Maslow, and Rollo May (several major works of each are listed in the references and cited in the introduction). In manager training series, in popular self-help courses, and in the career planning literature, hundreds of books are used that deal with life goals. See, e.g., Dean (1991), Robbins (1992), and Ellis (1998).

69 To find one's "strengths" has become one of the main objectives of manager training. The Gallup Organization has developed a sophisticated instrument, the "Strength Finder," to help people discover their, and their employees', talents and strengths. See Clifton and Nelson (1996) and Buckingham and Clifton (2001). See also works of a more popular kind on self-actualization, like Bloomfield and Felder (1985) or Hay and Tomchin (1991).

Chapter 2. The Reconstruction of the World

1 *The Mail on Sunday,* February 27, 2000. I wrote this part of the book in 2000. Things have not changed since then. The popular or junk press (called broadsides in earlier times) is almost as eternal as Goethe's *Faust.*

2 "The Labour Party died the day Tony Blair became the leader" (p. 26). "Do yourself a big favour Tony, dump the cronies" (p. 31). "Fight this evil plot to brand us all as Nazis" (p. 57). (In this section, titles from newspapers follow the original lowercase style of these British publications.)

3 "William at 18: The making of a very modern prince" [photo with a smiling Diana].

4 "Scandal of Blue Peter charity money: £6.5 Million Raised by British children has been squandered by Bucharest charity officials" (pp. 1–2).

5 Photo of Princess Diana, who "splashes in the sea at a royal 'hideaway'" (p. 16).

6 "Turning heads on the slopes, the Onassis girl ['the richest girl in the world'] growing up fast" (p. 11). "Kents' anguish as illness hits 'golden couple'" (p. 47).

7 "The dark sex secret that tormented Dirk Bogarde . . . his ride to sexual ecstasy" (pp. 49–51). "Caught in the act" (p. 53). "How tragic Lily is set to be Britain's wealthiest woman with $1bn fortune. . . . [A] blonde with roots in the back streets of London has more money than the Queen." "Why on the eve of Leap Year Day, do many betrothed celebrity couples have no intention of ever marrying." "The heir and the ex-bra model." "A mutual love . . . of power." "Hurley and her walking handbag." (Pp. 34–35.) "Dangerous liaisons . . . Sally Farmiloe's tales of brazen trysts with Lord Archer" (p. 66). "Ken [Livingstone, the man running for mayor of London] said he needed sex morning and night" (p. 7).

8 "Racing hero John Francome betrayed me with other lovers." "Heartbroken Tracey Bailey says she dreams of beating the love-cheat racing star 'to pulp.'" (Pp. 32–33.)

9 "Veteran TV producer claims 'egomaniac' director-general forced him out" (p. 13).

10 "Revealed: the facts about how the 'indestructible' Rasputin really died" (pp. 58–59). "How Vanessa was fooled by a Communist gangster" (p. 63).

11 "'Vultures' race to take seat of MP killed in mansion blaze" (p. 5). "On the roof of the world I find the preserved hand of a woman who died in the '47 Andes plane crash" [photo of the "mummified hand" is enclosed] (p. 15). "Custody fight for baby of beheaded woman" [with photo of the "Axe of a madman: The weapon used . . . in the murder] (pp. 22–23). "Teacher's suicide after inspectors criticise school" (p. 37). "Father dies in fire trying to save girls" (p. 38).

12 "New York police who shot defenceless man 41 times are cleared of murder" (p. 44–45).

13 "Corsica's stormy start to my fine romance" (p. 90).

14 "Michelangelo created the statue of David and the Sistine Chapel . . . but a hotel as well? A miracle of the Renaissance . . . Villa San Michele, where a rich religious legacy artfully co-exists with its hedonism today" (pp. 87–88).

15 "Scandal cottage." Spring Cottage, "this charming Victorian retreat, hidden away on the Cliveden estate in Berkshire, was once a scene of wild, hedonistic orgies involving call girls, a Russian spy and some of the leading names of the English Establishment" (pp. 92–93).

16 Twelve pages of advertisements. . . .

17 "How they tore the heart and soul out of the farm I love" (pp. 64–65). "You're always on holiday in a herb garden" (p. 83).

18 "The TV Star who gave up fame and fortune to save the whale" (p. 3).

19 It occurs several dozen times in the issue of *The Mail on Sunday* we analyze here.

20 "Everyone wins a prize" with "Lucky Money Cheque" (p. 1). "£100,000 win gets Fred on the move" (p. 43). "£100,000 to be won! PLUS thousands of fabulous Bonus Prizes for everyone" (p. 81).

21 "Rusedski fails in his revenge bid" (p. 111). "Woodward hails captain fantastic" (p. 112). "I don't want to be remembered as an England player who never won anything" (p. 112). "Fiery Exiles rock Saints" (p. 114). "Hope and Gloria" (p. 115). "Swindon's agony just gets worse" (p. 122). "Duty and the Beast" (p. 123). "Rapid-fire Gunners" (p. 124). "Just a day at the office for Posh Spouse" (p. 126). "Disgrace: Fighting fans scar day to remember Sir Stan" (p. 128).

22 The world of sports is a virtual world and as such it is harmless. As opposed to the real world, nothing really hurts here. We are only spectators. But, at the same time, this virtual world creates for us a community (of fans, or simply of those who understand and discuss sports news), in which we feel at home. And, linking us up with the schedule of our favorite team, it articulates our time and gives a purpose to our lives. We always have a next match to go to, a next Cup to win, a next star to see to rise or fall. And if our team does not win this year, it may win in the next, time is reversible; there is "eternal return," there is always the prospect of a new beginning, there is no ultimate defeat, there is no death. There is the promise of resurrection every Saturday or Sunday.

23 By the way, the American Weather Channel is a fantastic tour de force: One needs genius and brilliance to be able to speak twenty-four hours a day about practically nothing.

Chapter 3. The Self in the Public Space

1 Dürrschmidt (2000, 104–12). See also Giddens (1990); Gergen (1991); Featherstone (1990); Robertson (1992); Augé (1995); Featherstone, Lash, and Robertson (1995); Beck (1997); Appadurai (2001); Urry (2003); etc.

2 I give some of his terms here in German: *"Einstellungen," "Gegenständliche Einstellung," "Selbstrekflektierte Einstellungen," "Enthusiastische Einstellung," "Weltbilder," "Das sinlich-räumliche Weltbild," "Das seelisch-kulturelle Weltbild," "Das metaphysische Weltbild," "Die Struktur des Geistestypen," "Der Halt im Begrenzten: Das*

Gehäuse," "Der Halt im Unendlichen," "Der Geist zwischen Gegensetze," "Der Geist zwischen Chaos und Form," "Der Geist zwischen Vereinzelung und Allgemeinheit: Das Individuum und das Allgemeine."

3 We have briefly discussed this change and process earlier in this book. For books in this field, see note 4 in chapter 4.

4 See, e.g., Goffman (1966, 1970), Sennett (1976), Brittan (1977), Schlenker (1985), Baumeister (1986b), Snyder (1987), Rose (1990), and Modell (1993). Here are a few titles and subtitles of this last volume: Integration of the private and public self, The influence of the private self on self-presentation, On the convergence of the public self and the self-concept, The self-concept constrains the public self, Convergence of public and private self. See also Melville and von Moos (1998), who discuss the relationship of the private and the public spheres (and selves) in the Middle Ages.

5 Among many other books, see Goffman (1959); Tedeschi (1981); Schlenker (1985); Baumeister (1986b, 1999); Snyder (1987); Giacalone and Rosenfeld (1989, 1991); Gagnier (1991); Leary (1995); Kaiser (1997, 181–209); Russell and Fernández-Dols (1997); Barker (2002). The pathological forms of "self-disclosure" are also discussed by Ames, Kasulis, and Dissanayake (1998); Coleman, Lewis, and Kowalik (2000); Weber (2000); Cholakian (2000); Mayne and Bonana (2001); Mummendey (2002); and Derlega and Berg (1987).

6 Ewen (1988) discusses the problem of "assimilation" versus "dissimilation" in the case of immigrants, who arrived in the United States in the late nineteenth and early twentieth centuries. Most of them opted for a fast assimilation in order to disappear into the American population and optimize their chances of success. Some others kept their identities and lived in their national/ethnic enclaves where they felt safe and could help one another. These two different strategies had a lasting impact on people's selves.

7 See, e.g., Taylor (1987 [1650]) and Fuller (1938 [1642]).

8 See, e.g., Overbury (1967 [1614]) and La Bruyère (1970 [1688]).

9 See more about this here below under "Etiquette" and in note 28.

10 See a few characteristic titles in chapter 13, under "Who Are You?"

11 "People attempt to create the impression that they are morally superior, virtuous, and righteous" (Brown 1998, 170).

12 "For example, in earlier times, women were expected to play helpless . . . in order to attract a male" (Brown 1998, 170).

13 "Most people confront situations in which their public identity is threatened" (Brown 1998, 175).

14 "I should probably warn you, I'm not very good at this sort of thing" (Brown 1998, 177).

15 "People may even go so far as to actively create an excuse for failure. . . . Self-hand-icapping behavior occurs when people create obstacles to their own success. Consider, for example, an athlete who fails to prepare properly for an upcoming competition. Lack of preparation makes success less likely, but it also gives the person a ready-made excuse for failure" (Brown 1998, 177). See also Hirt and McCrae (2001).

16 Leary and Kowalski (1995).

17 Sansom (1956, 230–32).

18 Due to the new means of the media, the radiation of our contemporary celebrities (and the underlying attitudinal patterns), their power of shaping people's selves, is especially great. We shall come back to them in chapter 13 on "The Myth of the Self."

19 See chapters 12 and 13.

20 This redoubling of the self is quite frequent in Greek and Elizabethan tragedies. In the final scenes, the heroes begin to speak of themselves in the third person singular. Antigone: "Luckless Antigone"; Creon: "Creon has ceased to exist"; Hamlet: "His madness is Hamlet's enemy"; and so on.

21 We shall come back to this problem in the section on "Children" in chapter 7.

22 We shall see in chapter 13 (in the section titled "Who Are You?") that "self-acceptance" is nowadays one of the key slogans—mutatis mutandis—of both psychologists and self-help gurus.

23 There are hundreds of personality tests and self-concept tests. See, e.g., Cattell (1950); Wylie (1961, 1974–79, 1989); Cloninger (1994); Baron (1998); and McCrae and Costa (2003). And see more recent works in the field of personal and developmental psychology.

24 We shall come back to this problem in chapter 14, when we discuss the role of astrology and horoscopes in forming, or deforming, people's selves.

25 Quoted by Arditi (1999, 39).

26 The methods of the study of cognitive dissonance should be further developed and applied to this field, more than they were in the 1950s and 1960s, when the theory of cognitive dissonance was at the center of scholarly interest. See, e.g., Festinger (1957), and many other important publications.

27 Arditi (1999, 44).

28 Etiquette books, and manuals of everyday morals, both traditional and contemporary, are full of good advice as to how to behave in the public space. Let me give only a few examples: Farrar (1849), Ruskin (1877), O'Reilly (1878), *Decorum* (1877), Sidgwick (1898), Conway (1904), Post (1928), Maurois (1940), Faret (1970 [1630]), Vanderbilt (1972) (929 pages!), Foster (2000), and Bridges (2003). There

are also excellent books on the history of social etiquette and etiquette books. See, e.g., Schlesinger (1947), Wildeblood and Brinson (1965), Carson (1966), Elias (1982, 1983), Aresti (1970), Bourdieu (1984), Kasson (1990), and Baudrillard (1994).

29 Arditi (1999, 34–35) describes a characteristic chapter of Post's (1928) bestseller etiquette book as follows: "A 13-page chapter on women's clothing . . . contains, for instance, 32 subtitles. . . . A few lines discoursing in 'the woman who is 'chic' are followed by a section on 'how to wear a corsage,' followed by a brief passage on 'how many jewels' a woman should wear, after which comes a diatribe against make-up called 'don't exchange a face for a mask.' This is followed by seven lines of hair-dressing, then comes a relatively long discussion on 'when one's income is limited,' then the text jumps to 'what to wear in a restaurant' and to 'clothes in the afternoon,' to return to pecuniary matters in 'don't get too much clothes.' This last is in turn followed by a very short reflection on when in doubt ('When in doubt, wear the plainer dress'), after which is discussed whether or not a woman shall wear a hat, and when should she remove her gloves, and what should she do in the countryside, . . . and so on and so forth. All this is in little more than three pages. The chapter does have coherence, but this coherence is like the one in a cookbook in which all recipes on 'salads' or 'desert' are placed together in one chapter."

30 The first edition of her book (1922) was so successful that she received about 50.000 letters from her readers.

31 According to Baumeister (1986a, 35–36) "One has a hidden, inner self, and the right to protect it against the intrusion of the outside world . . . questioning the existence of this inner self, and deconstructing the self as an autonomous entity would lead to a serious spiritual crisis." See also Derlega and Berg (1987), Christman (1989), Modell (1993).

32 "It is probably no mere historical accident that the word person, in its first meaning, is a mask. It is rather a recognition of the fact that everyone is always and everywhere, more or less consciously, playing a role. . . . It is in these roles that we know each other; it is in these roles that we know ourselves." Park (1950, 249), quoted by Goffman (1959, 17).

33 "We may practically say that he [the human being] has as many different social selves as there are distinct *groups* of persons about whose opinion he cares." Flournoy (1917) quoted by Goffman (1959, 42).

34 The study of roles has become one of the most fertile fields of research in contemporary social psychology. Theaters will never be able to compete with the wealth of roles played by people in their everyday lives.

35 There is a rich literature studying the various forms of lying, deception, and self-deception. See, e.g., Elster (1986), Lockard and Paulhus (1988), McLaughlin and

Rorty (1988), Nesse and Lloyd (1992), Barnes (1994), Zagorin (1996), Mack (1996), and Doniger (1996). In the bibliography of his book on *The Pack of Lies: Toward a Sociology of Lying,* J. A. Barnes (1994) lists more than 500 papers and books on lying, many of them on the role of lying in everyday life and with the purpose of protecting the autonomy of the human self. Sartre and Heidegger would have certainly protested against this stressing of the positive role of lying.

36 Sir Philip Sidney, *Defense of Poesie* (1835); Sir Francis Bacon, *On Truth* (1597).

37 Psychologists working for big car factories and advertising agencies keep studying the psychological effects of cars but—as far as I know—in the scholarly literature the role of cars and the automotive mythology in shaping people's selves has not yet received sufficient attention.

38 I discussed the mythology of cars in more detail in Hankiss (2001, 125–27).

39 When we do not find our cars in the street, where we left them, we lose our footing, we feel like dropping out of the world. We are lost. We feel as if we were shut out of a spaceship and were free falling in a cold and empty universe.

40 Or in their imagination, in fairy tales, traveling on Aladdin's flying carpet.

41 Though the situation had a certain indecent and almost obscene character: somebody opening her or his private world to an anonymous crowd.

42 See "Women's handbags" in chapter 1.

Chapter 4. The Limits and Freedom of Self-Construction

1 Ethnomethodologists have conducted especially interesting studies in this field. See, e.g., Garfinkel (1967), Turner (1974), Coulter (1979, 1990), Button (1991), Flynn (1991), and Coulon (1995).

2 Quoted by Gregg (1991, 184–85, 187). See also Coulter (1979) and Gergen and Davies (1985).

3 Geertz (1997, 22), quoted by Rose (1997, 225). Taylor (1989) gives a masterly survey of the history of the "self" in Western civilization.

4 Differences in the care for self in various cultures have not yet been explored thoroughly enough, though works in the field of cultural anthropology, comparative religion, cross-cultural sociology, and psychology offer an inexhaustible collection of data that can be drawn upon for further studies. See, e.g., Halbwachs (1950); Hallowell (1955); Inkeles et al. (1959); Duijker and Frijda (1960); Lipset (1960); Lipset and Lowenthal 1961); Bronfenbrenner (1970); Geertz (1973b, 1979); Inke-

les and Smith (1974); Bercovitch (1975); Spielberger and Diaz-Guerrero (1976); Bourguignon (1979); Marsella, DeVos, and Hsu (1985); Carrithers, Collins, and Lukes (1985); Abdullahi (1986); Organ (1987); Roland (1988); Hormuth (1990); Miyanaga (1991); Hamilton and Sanders (1992); Kitayama and Markus (1994); Cohen (1994); Ting-Toomey (1994); Morris (1994); Bock (1994); Pynsent (1994); Battaglia (1995); Kao and Sinha (1997); Inkeles (1997); Neisser and Jopling (1997); Allen and Malhotra (1997); Ames, Kasulis, and Dissanayake (1998); Muller (1998); Organista, Chun, and Marin (1998); Hefner (1998); Lee, Mc-Cauley, and Draguns (1999); Kim and Harrison (1999); Joseph (1999); Squire (2000); Mehrgardt and Mehrgardt (2001); Weinreich and Saunderson (2002); McCrae and Allik (2002); Berger and Huntington (2002); Steinberg (2002); and Cross and Gore (2003).

5 Of the innumerable studies on the role or absence of the self in various civilizations see the recent study by Mehrgardt and Mehrgardt (2001).

6 The quotations are mainly from chapters 4 and 7 of the *Rules*.

7 Quoted by Muller (1987, 18).

8 Hutton (1988, 126).

9 Hutton (1988, 135).

10 Lears (1992, 109). Swann (1996) uses the concept of "self-trap" in a different sense. Baker (1984) wrote a book titled *The Beauty Trap*. See also Langman (1992) and Shields (1992). For further literature, see Hankiss (2001, 127–34).

11 Levine (1992, 6).

12 Levine (1992, 8).

13 Levine (1992, 9).

14 See, e.g., Wilson (1975, 1978), Dennett (1984, 1991), and Dawkins (1976).

15 Rose here opposes traditional expressions to modern scientific terms.

16 Rose (1997, 238).

17 See, e.g., Dichter (1964, 1971), Ewen (1976, 1988), Percy and Woodside (1983), Wallen (1985 [1925]), Olson and Sentis (1986), Wernick (1991), Goldman (1992), Wagner (1995), Goldman and Papson (1996), and Peter and Olson (1996).

18 "Messenger to the King," *Collier's,* May 3, 1930, 78. Quoted by Lears (1992, 116).

19 Wallen (1985 [1925], 110–11). Quoted by Lears (1992, 115).

20 "Advertising: A Form of Organized Salesmanship," *PI 70*, March 30, 1910. Quoted by Lears (1992, 117).

21 "The Psychology of the Printed Word" (Frederick 1985 [1925], 344; quoted by Lears 1992, 118).

22 Studying the behavior of a fresh Italian immigrant in early-twentieth-century New York, Ewen and Ewen (1982, 109–251) give an excellent description of this dilemma of "to assimilate or dissimilate."

23 See, e.g., McIntosh (1994, esp. 9–18). See also works on the development of the infant mind and consciousness: Mahler, Pine, and Bergman (1975); Hetherington (1983); Damon and Hart (1988); and Damon (1998).

24 See further concepts in Howe (1992) and Sass (1992).

25 Hutton (1988, 138).

26 Martin (1988, 1).

27 "What fathoming the past teaches us is that there are options among which we are free to choose, not simply continuities to which we must adapt" Martin (1988, 1). See also Szakolczai's (1998) excellent analysis of the development of Foucault's ideas.

28 Martin (1988, 9).

29 Martin (1988, 11).

30 Martin (1988, 10).

31 Schrag (1997, 27, 18). See also Mitchell (1981), MacIntyre (1981), Jameson (1981), Ricoeur (1984–86), Sarbin (1986), Bruner (1986, 1990), Turner and Bruner (1986), Dennett (1988, 1991), Taylor (1989), Shotter and Gergen (1989), Vanhoozer (1990), Kerby (1991), Rosenwald and Ochberg (1992), Somers (1994), Benoit (1997), Delory-Momberger (2000), Cavarero (2000), Holstein and Gubrium (2000), Fivush and Haden (2003), Kundera (2003), and Pléh (2003).

32 "We have now arrived at the self's understanding of itself at the crossroads of discourse and narration as a who of discourse in the guise of a narrating self, a *homo narrans,* a storyteller who both finds herself in stories already told and strives for a self-constitution by emplotting herself in stories in the making. To be a self is to be able to render an account of oneself, to be able to tell the story of one's life" (Schrag 1997, 26.)

33 Csaba Pléh (2003) gives an excellent survey of the process in the course of which the narrative approach has gained ground in linguistics, psychology, and the cognitive sciences. He also describes how the narrative structure of the modern self disintegrated in the postmodern context. His analysis of Dennett's theory is also enlightening. See also Schank-Abelson (1977) and Kundera (2003).

34 Schrag (1997, 36).

35 Ricoeur (1992, 32).

36 Ricoeur (1992, 32).

37 Ricoeur (1992, 32–33).

38 Ricoeur (1992, 12).

39 We have already quoted the last words of Othello, Antigone, and Creon under "Models" in chapter 3.

40 In this respect, our ancestors were much wiser than we are. Think of the fact, for instance, that since the fourteenth or fifteenth century, how many "middle-class" people have kept diaries, or how Greek stoic philosophers wrote letters to their friends on an almost daily basis, in which they described and analyzed the tiniest events of their lives.

Chapter 5. The Self at Work

1 Out of an extremely rich literature on the psychological interactions at the workplace, I refer here only to a few items. See, e.g., Meyer and Scott (1983), Zucker (1988), Murnighan (1993), Hogg and Terry (2002), Handel (2003), and Thompson (2002).

2 This was discussed in note 15 of chapter 3.

3 There are a great number of studies on the role of objects in our lives, on their latent symbolic messages. I have found the *Handbook of Consumer Motivations: The Psychology of the World of Objects* by Ernest Dichter (1964) and *The Meaning of Things: Domestic Symbols and the Self* by Mihaly Csikszentmihalyi and Eugene Rochberg-Halton (1981) to be the most relevant books in this context.

Chapter 6. The Self and the Articulation of Time

1 There are a great number of books in philosophy, psychology, sociology, and anthropology on the concept and perception of time, and on the ways in which people and civilizations try to cope with it, control, and conquer it. I give here only a few titles: Eliade (1959); Heidegger (1962); Gurvitch (1964); Toulmin and Goodfield (1965); Doob (1971); Fraisse (1975); Ricoeur (1984–88); Koselleck (1985); Whitrow (1988, 2003); Wood (1988); Hawking (1988); Borst (1993); Davies (1995); Hughes and Trautmann (1995); Fraser et al. (1998); Lash, Quick, and Roberts (1998); Lippincott (1999); and Roeckelein (2003).

2 From among works analyzing the role of the urban space in shaping people's minds and selves, see, e.g., Simson (1964); Benjamin (1982); McClung (1983); Norberg-Schulz (1985); Harvey (1985); Korff (1986); Sennett (1992, 1994); Celik, Favro,

and Ingersol (1994); Tepperman (1996); Smith (1996); Källtorp et al. (1997); Huxtable (1997); Duis (1998); Dürrschmidt (2000); and Therborn (2002).

3 Zerubavel (1985, xiv, 102, and passim).

4 Peter and Olson (1996, 388).

5 E.g., Solomon, Greenberg, and Pyszczynski write essays titled "Lethal Consumption: Death Denying Materialism," and "Money: The New Ideology of Immortality" (in Kasser and Kanner 2004, 127–46, 137–38). See also Pyszczynski, Greenberg, and Solomon (2003) and the section titled "Fear and Civilization" in chapter 12.

6 See, e.g., Kowiniski (1985), Postman (1986), Ewen and Ewen (1982), Ewen (1988), Featherstone (1991), Debord (1994 [1967]), Barber (1995), Gottdiener (1997), Falk and Campbell (1989), Ritzer (1997a, 1999, 2001), and Baudrillard (1970).

7 Hankiss (2001, 127–33).

8 Langman (1992, 48).

9 Langman (1992, 40).

10 Langman (1992, 67).

11 As an interesting analysis of the role of travel in people's lives see, e.g., Ward, Bochner, and Furnham (2001).

12 See chapter 11, "The Self and the Intensity of Life."

13 The "reenchantment of the world," which is one of the major enterprises and characteristics of contemporary consumer civilization, offers people these mysteries, Gardens of Eden, and Holy Grails (see chapter 14 of this book).

14 The breakdown of social control and discipline is still much more radical in situations of war, where soldiers in occupied territories often behave like predator animals in the jungle.

15 Photography is a heavenly and devilish invention at the same time. It is the first instrument in the history of humankind that makes us feel that we, humble human beings, are able to stop time, seize and eternalize the instant, and grasp, portray, and recreate the outside world. It fills us, philistines, with the exuberance and arrogance of a great artist.

16 Hankiss (1999a, 228–32). For general studies of sports as cultural phenomena, see, e.g., Horne, Jary, and Tomlinson (1987); Tomlinson (1999, 2005); Sugden and Tomlinson (2002); and Bronson (2004).

17 This is why it is so disturbing when the referee hesitates to call a ball "in" or "out."

18 Here again I have taken over a few paragraphs, in a shortened form, from my book *Fears and Symbols* (Hankiss 2001, 229–30).

19 There is a not-too-rich, but excellent, literature on gossip, hearsay, and rumor. See, e.g., Gluckman (1963), Allport and Postman (1965 [1947]), Shibutani (1966), Ros-

now and Fine (1976), Spacks (1986), Levin and Arluke (1987), Barkow (1992), Bergmann (1993), Tebbutt (1995), Collins (1998), Kowalski (2001), Althans (2000), Camery-Hoggatt (2002), Szvetelszky (2002), and Wilkes (2002).

20 In chapter 12, I shall analyze in detail the fact that "boundary situations," in which human life is threatened with destruction, generate high-intensity life experience in us.

21 In a different context, Castells (1997, 359) also uses this metaphor. He argues that "humans are, and will be, predators."

22 In chapter 11, "The Self and the Intensity of Life," I analyze this phenomenon in detail.

23 Among "self-managing strategies," Schelling (1978) speaks of people's "striving for godlikeness and depreciation of others."

Chapter 7. The Self at Home

1 To characterize the various approaches, let me mention five excellent, but very different, books: Campbell (1968); Bachelard (1964a); Broadben, Bunt, and Jencks (1980); McClung (1983); and Norberg-Schulz (1985).

2 For several decades now, psychologists have used gardening as a therapy for their patients. I wonder how far they have studied these latent, "existential" processes underlying these therapies.

3 Quoted by Baron (1998, 181).

4 The bed trick: "You go to bed with someone you think you know, and when you wake up you discover that it was someone else."

5 See also the section titled "Models" in chapter 3.

6 In part two of this book, for the same purpose, I shall analyze popular weekly magazines. According to the experts in cultural studies, the social impact of these popular magazines compares with that of all television channels taken together.

7 Anthony Robbins, *Awake the Giant Within: How to Take Immediate Control of Your Mental, Emotional, Physical, and Financial Destiny;* Frank Bettger, *How I Raised Myself from Failure to Success in Selling.* (In this section, I quote the authors and titles of the books without giving exact bibliographical data.)

8 David Halberstam, *Powers That Be.*

9 David Dalton, *James Dean: The Mutant King.* David Dalton and Ron Cayen, *James Dean: American Icon.* Dennis Stock, *James Dean Revisited; James Dean: Max Photo Book.* Norman Mailer, *Marilyn.* Jane Ellen, *Marilyn's Men: The Private Life of Mar-*

ilyn Monroe. Michael Korda, *The Immortals* (a novel about Marilyn Monroe). Steven Bach, *Dietrich: Life and Legend*. Sophia Loren, *Living and Loving*. Sam Shaw, *Brando: In the Camera Eye*. Albert Goldman, *Elvis*. Roger Vadim, *Bardot, Deneuve, Fonda: My Life with the Three Most Beautiful Women in the World*. Lawrence Olivier, *Confessions of an Actor*. Nellie Bly, *Barbara Streisand: The Untold Story*. Shirley MacLaine, *Out on a Limb* and *My Lucky Stars: A Hollywood Memoir*. Irving Shulman, *Valentino: The True Shocking Story of America's Greatest Lover*. Rob Base and David Haslam, *The Movies of the Eighties*. Kenneth Anger, *Hollywood Babylon*. Charles Hamblett, *The Hollywood Cage*.

10 Karlheinz Jacobi, *Balconies and Terraces*. John Brookes, *The Garden Book* and *House Plants*. D. G. Hessayon, *The House Plant Expert*. Emöke Ács, *Roses*. Joseph Gerbar, *Geraniums*. Mathild Szantó, *One- and Two-Summer Flowers*. George Lazay, *Perennials*. Mária Sulyok, *Flowery Windows an Terrace*. Marjory Blamey and Philip Blamey, *Gem Guide to Fruits, Nuts and Berries and Conspicuous Seed*. Sarolta Czaka, *Evergreens and Pines*.

11 A. Z. Manfred, *Napoleon*. Julianna Zsigray, *Elizabeth, Queen of Hungary*. Thea Leitner, *The Forgotten History of the Habsburgs*. Machiavelli, *The Prince*. Isaiah Berlin, *The Hedgehog and the Fox: An Essay on Tolstoy's View on History*. Winston S. Churchill, *The Second World War, Volumes I–VI*. Antonia Fraser, *The Six Wives of Henry VIII*. Jan Smuts, *Memoirs of the Boer War*.

12 Hans-Peter Waldrich, *Secret Wisdom, Esoterics, Oriental and Western Traditions*. Carl Jung, *Memories, Dreams, Thoughts*. Catherine Aubier, *Chinese Horoscope: The Year of the Dragon*. Bruce Goldberg, *Previous Lives, Future Lives: Hypnosis, Reincarnation, Karma*. Ilma Szász, *The Shadow of the Living Light: World Religions, Esoterics, Philosophy, Psychology, and Hildegard of Bingen's Vision of the Other World*. Oswald Wirth, *Le symbolism occulte de la Franc-Maçonnerie*.

13 László Pusztay, *Love Spells, Witch-Tricks*.

14 János Szinák and István Veress, *The Dogs of the World*, 2 vols. Dominique and Serge Simon, *The World of Dogs*. Elizabeth Marshall Thomas, *The Spiritual Life of Dogs*. David Alderton, *Dogs*. Winfried Nouc, *Dog*.

15 R. T. Peterson, G. Mountfort, and P. A. D. Hollom, *A Field Guide to the Birds of Britain and Europe*. Richard Perry and Martin Woodcock, *Birds*. Egon Schmidt and Laszlo Becsy, *Thousand Nests on Thousand Boughs*.

16 The quotations are taken from the title pages of *Vanity Fair* issues.

17 Hervé Bazin, *The Power of Women*. Mary McGarry Morris, *A Dangerous Woman*. Anne Rice, *The Queen of the Damned*. Jackie Collins, *The World Is Full of Divorced Women*. Robin Norwood, *Women Who Love Too Much: A Life-Changing Book for Women*. Georgina Masson, *Courtesans of the Italian Renaissance*. Antonia Fraser,

The Six Wives of Henry VIII. Kaari Utrio, *Eve's Daughters: The History of European Women.* Tehmina Durrani, *My Master and Lord: Woman Lives.*

18 Brigitte Hamann, *Queen Elizabeth.* Emil Niederhauser, *Attempt on Queen Elizabeth's Life.*

19 Nancy Friday, *Men in Love.*

20 This book is by Octave Aubry.

21 Arthur Schnitzler, *The Return of Casanova.*

22 See also Dr. Med. Dieter Markert, *The Markert Diet: No More Yo-Yo Effect—Forever Slim with the Sensational Turbo-Program;* and Annette Wolter, *Vegetable Meals.*

23 Chris Stadtlaender, *Die geheime Schönheitsrezepte der Kaiserin und des Hofes.*

24 Freud, *Introduction to Psychoanalysis.* Frieda Fordham, *An Introduction to Jung's Psychology.* Polly Young-Eisendrath, *Jung's Self-Psychology: A Constructivist Perspective.* Peter Hildebrand, *Beyond Midlife Crisis. A Psychodynamic Approach to Aging.* Dr. Windy Dryden and Jack Gordon, *How to Cope with Difficult Parents.* M. Scott Peck, *The Road Less Traveled.*

25 I have found only a Hungarian edition. In what follows, I will try to reconstruct the English original (in some cases, certainly with humorous results).

26 This is true at least in its Hungarian version.

Chapter 8. The Self in a Changing World

1 See, e.g., Beck (1992); Adam, Beck, and Van Loon (2000); and Olson, Steiner, and Tuuli (2004).

2 Philosophers and theologians have always been concerned with the goals of human life. Psychologists and sociologists have been less interested in exploring the role goals play in shaping people's selves. This does not mean, however, that there are no interesting and important studies in this field. See, e.g., Bühler et al. (1968), Markus and Nurius (1986), Emmons (1999). Speaking about goals and life goals is much more widespread in popular self-help literature. One finds titles like *Life-Goals: Setting & Achieving Goals to Chart the Course of Your Life* (Dean 1991); *The Magic Lamp: Goal Setting for People Who Hate Setting Goals* (Ellis 1998); *Optimize Your Life with the One-Page Strategic Planner* (Dahl 2003); and the like.

3 There have been several other interpretation of this "Great Transformation." Daniel Bell (1976) described it as a transition from the Industrial to the Postindustrial Age; Inglehart (1997) spoke of a transition from modernity to postmodernity, Lyotard (1984) and Jameson (1991) described it as a transition from "capitalism" to "late

capitalism." There were experts who celebrated the final victory of liberal democracy (Fukuyama 1992) or, just on the contrary, the final decline of the capitalist ideology and world system (Wallerstein 1995). Both conservative and liberal thinkers wrote about a transition from the traditional order to a new social and moral chaos (Himmelfarb 1995; Fukuyama 1999). A substantial proportion of globalization studies also study this great transformation. The authors of the latest models of change speak of a transition from "industrial economy" to "information economy," or from "techno-economy" to "bioeconomy." See, e.g., Davis and Meyer (2000, 54–55), and a great number of other authors. A few more philosophically oriented authors outlined a process of permanent change, i.e., of permanent "liminality" (Turner 1969; Voegelin 1974; Szakolczai 2000, 215–99, and 2003).

4 For a more detailed comparison of modernism and postmodernism, see "The Modern–Postmodern Dilemma" in chapter 9.

5 Dawkins (1976). "Memes" (the concept was coined on the example of "genes" in biology) are the elementary patterns or nuclei of cultural *memory*.

6 Bertrand, Michalski, and Pench (1999).

Chapter 9. "Proletarian Renaissance"

1 The words "criterion" and "critic" derive from the same root. A good survey of the various definitions of "crisis" is found in Sills (1968–91, vol. 3, 510–14); see also Ritter and Gründer (1971–2001, vol. 4, columns 1235–45).

2 Ritter and Gründer (1971–2001, vol. 4, columns 1237–40).

3 Van Gennep (1960), Turner (1969, 1990), Girard (1977), Alexander and Seidman (1990), Shields (1990), Szakolczai (2000, 2003).

4 Béla Hamvas may have been the most significant Hungarian philosopher in the twentieth century. He is being discovered nowadays because he was forced to be silent during the forty years of communist rule. In 1936 he asked the question that would be asked later again and again: "Is there nowadays [1936] a crisis at all? Is crisis not something eternal? There is always crisis. If one takes the most ancient written texts, one already encounters the spirit and the attitude that criticizes its own age and prophecies that mankind will perish if people don't repent and reform themselves" (1983, 68–69).

5 I will return later to the question of whether or not these great crises and renewals did, or did not, break the continuity of our civilization. And I will ask if it is at all justified to speak of two or three thousand years of "Western Civilization" as a continuum and ignore, or downscale, the importance of, and the ruptures between, the

Greek and Roman, the Roman and the medieval, the medieval and the modern, the modern and the now emerging "consumer civilization."

6 Hamvas (1983, passim) gives a broad panorama of this crisis literature. Here are some characteristic titles: Walter Rathenau, *Zur Kritik der Zeit* [A Critical Appraisal of our Times], 1912; Léon Bloy, *Au seuil de l'Apocalypse* [On the threshold of Apocalypse], 1916; Richard Bie, *Diagnose unserer Zeit* [Diagnosis of Our Times], 1928; Eckaert von Sydow, *Kultur der Dekadenz* [The Culture of Decadence], 1922; and René Guénon, *La crise du monde moderne* [The crisis of the modern world], 1927. The George Circle in Germany and *La Nouvelle Revue Française* in France were also important foci of this experience of crisis in the 1920s and 1930s.

7 See also Lewis (1947); Ellul (1964); Berger, Berger, and Kellner (1973); Berman (1982); Bloom (1987); Kennedy (1987); and Walsh (1990).

8 Morin adds a whole list of these challenges and critical developments: "The accelerating expansion of the techno sciences," "the hypertrophic development of techno-bureaucracies," "the commodification and monetarization of everything," "the more and more serious problems of urbanization," "deterioration of the quality of life and environmental pollution," "the democratic regression," the process of "civilizational homogenization which destroys cultural differences," "the balkanization of ethnicities," the collapse of the great ideologies and of "the great projects," the destructive consequences of the utopia of unlimited progress and terrestrial salvation, "the loss of traditional solidarities and the atomization" of society, etc.

9 See, e.g., Tropp (1990).

10 See, e.g., Voegelin (1956), Becker (1973), Berger (1967, 1969), and Borkenau (1981).

11 Berger, Berger, and Kellner (1973); Calinescu (1977); Gumbrecht (1978); Eisenstadt (1983, 2000); Lyotard (1984); Frisby (1985); Harvey (1989); Giddens (1990, 1993); Lash (1990); Norris (1990); Jameson (1991); Bauman (1991, 1992); Featherstone (1991); Toulmin (1992); Bertens (1995); Schrag (1997); Szakolczai (2003); Arnason, Eisenstadt, and Wittrock (2004).

12 Cooke (1990). According to Edward W. Soja (1989, 185–87), the main characteristics of a postmodern economy are the following: increased flexibility, matrix structure, short-term contracts, part-time jobs, and mobile capital. "Never before has the spatiality of the capitalist city or the mosaic of uneven regional development become so kaleidoscopic, so loosened from its nineteenth-century moorings, so filled with unsettling contrariety." Quoted by Bertens (1995, 225).

13 Arac (1986).

14 Bauman (1992).

15 Frisby (1985).

16 Harvey (1989) discusses the emergence of postmodernism in great detail.

17 Discussing Troeltsch's (1911) ideas, Huizinga (1959b, 270) states that the Renaissance "illuminates only an elite, and even that elite perhaps only in a part of its complicated and contradictory essence."

18 There have been other attempts at finding good labels for consumer culture. Thomas Hine (1986), for instance, spoke of a "popoluxe" culture. See Ewen (1988, 70).

19 Huizinga (1959b, 224).

20 Huizinga (1959b, 243).

21 Huizinga (1959b, 234–44).

22 Huizinga (1959b, 245) quotes Rabelais' *Gargantua and Pantagruel,* book 1, chapter 9.

23 Huizinga (1959b, 259) quotes Burckhardt (1958). See also Burckhardt (1943).

24 Huizinga (1959b, 251) quotes Voltaire's *Age de Louis XIV.*

25 Huizinga (1959b, 253) quotes Goetz (1907, 46).

26 Huizinga (1959b, 254, 256) quotes Burckhardt (1958).

27 Huizinga (1959b, 281); speaking of the dominant Renaissance concept in the second half of the nineteenth century, he remarks (p. 264): "The concept Renaissance, identified as it is now was with individualism and a worldly spirit, had to be stretched so far that it had completely lost its elasticity. It actually meant nothing any more."

28 Huizinga (1959b, 271); see also Gurevich (1995).

29 In the course of the nineteenth century, the beginnings of the Renaissance were extended further and further back into the Middle Ages. Renaissance ideas, individualism, lifestyle, feelings, moods, and poetic forms were discovered in Abelard, Bernard of Clairvaux, Saint Francis, Joachim of Floris, Dante, Petrarch, and Giotto, and even in Gothic architecture (Huizinga, 1959b, 260–66). "Gradually everything that seemed spontaneous and singular in the later Middle Ages had been lifted out of them and given a place among the origins of the Renaissance" (p. 265). Huizinga's warnings are justified. But it cannot be denied that some of the elements of the Renaissance emerged already in the eighth and ninth centuries—in the so-called Carolingian Renaissance, in the age of chivalry, in troubadour poetry, in the twelfth-century pre-Renaissance, in the tradition of the Roman de la Rose, and in small circles of scholars enthusiastically reading, translating, and commenting on Greek classical authors. This cultural undercurrent broke gloriously to the surface in the fifteenth and sixteenth centuries. There is an ongoing controversy on the place and

function of the Renaissance in the various trends of thought of European culture. Let me mention only two major works: Kristeller (1961) and Panofsky (1962).

30 In the Renaissance, "the symbolic, sacramental way of thinking (which does not inquire first of all what is the natural causal relationship of things, but their significance in God's plan in the world) maintained itself. Two basic qualities of medieval thought, formalism and anthropomorphism, faded only very slowly. Machiavelli was just as strict a formalist as Gregory VII" (Huizinga 1959b, 282).

31 Huizinga (1959b, 283).

32 Huizinga (1959b, 283).

33 Huizinga (1959b, 283).

34 Huizinga (1959b, 282–83).

35 Huizinga (1959b, 271).

36 Huizinga (1959b, 271).

37 Huizinga (1959b, 287).

38 Huizinga (1959b, 259).

39 Huizinga (1959b, 259).

40 Huizinga (1959b, 287).

41 Huizinga (1959b, 284).

42 Huizinga (1959b, 287).

43 Huizinga (1959b, 287).

44 There is an ongoing controversy about the relationship of the Renaissance with the Reformation; about the question whether they had, at least partly, common roots; if they ran parallel with, or against, one another; whether there were common elements in their relationship with individualism, rationalism, religion, salvation, transcendence, etc. Huizinga (1959b, 273–77) gives a good account of this controversy, citing several authors. Troeltsch (1911) interpreted the Reformation as a revival, or continuation, of the spirit of the Middle Ages. Burdach (1970 [1918]), conversely, pointed out the common origins of Renaissance and Reformation and argued that they had had more in common than usually presumed; See also Huizinga (1959b, 267–87).

45 Let alone the fact that certain means and forms of the elite's lifestyle were protected by law against being used or adopted by the Tiers État.

46 New ideas, norms of conduct, and lifestyles that first appear in the upper layers of a traditional society would trickle down into the lower layers of society with several decades, or centuries, of time lag.

47 Parallels between the Renaissance and later ages have been drawn by others as well. E.g., Heller (1978, 129) writes in her book on the "Renaissance Man" that "the educational ideal of Rousseau's *Emile* is a plebeian version of Castiglione's courtier." And Ewen (1988, 76) discusses in great detail the "democratization" of the various elements of former elite civilization: "Style was in the process of being transformed from a prerogative of the few to an amusement of the millions."

48 See also Goffman (1961), Waddell (1987), Szakolczai (2000, 170–77).

49 The cultural history of the carnival and the carnivalesque has been studied by a great number of scholars. See, e.g., Caillois (1950), Bakhtin (1968), Easton et al. (1988), Shields (1990), Featherstone (1991), Buci-Glucksmann (1994), and Szakolczai (2000, 177–88).

50 See, e.g., Campbell (1989) and Illouz (1997).

51 However, this does not mean that consumer civilization is socially not structured. We shall come back to this question in the epilogue.

52 Innumerable books and papers deal with the contemporary transformation of Western Civilization, and with the emergence of the so-called consumer civilization. See, e.g., Marcuse (1955, 1964); Lukacs (1970); Ewen (1976, 1988); Baudrillard (1970, 1988a, 1988b, 1998); Lash (1979); Ewen and Ewen (1982); McKendrick, Brewer, and Plumb (1982); Lears (1983); Fox and Lears (1983); Lyotard (1984); Bellah et al. (1985); Kowinski (1985); Frisby (1985); Postman (1986); Williamson (1986); Hassan (1988); *Theory, Culture & Society* (1988); Harvey (1989); Alexander and Seidman (1990); Sanders (1990); Featherstone (1990, 1991); Inglehart (1990, 1997); Walsh (1990); Alan Tomlinson (1990); John Tomlinson (1991); Jameson (1991); Shields (1992); Bauman (1992); Friedman (1992); Lash and Friedman (1992); Gellner (1992); Gloege (1992); Kellner (1992, 1995, 2003); Kleine, Schultz-Kleine, and Kernan (1992); Brewer and Porter (1993); Smart (1993, 1999); Barber (1995); Hobsbawm (1995); Bertens (1995); Gay and Hall (1996); Lury (1996); Gottdiener (1997); Ritzer (1997a, 1997b, 1999, 2001, 2003); Best and Kellner (1997); Hefner (1998); Miles (1998); Schor (1998); Halter (2000); Corner and Pels (2003); Heilmann and Beetham (2004); and Kasser and Kanner (2004). For analyses of the interaction of postmodern and consumerist influences on contemporary selves see, among many others, the papers by Kellner (1992, 1995), and Friedman (1992); also see notes 10 and 11 in chapter 14.

53 On the democratization of dressing, see Ewen and Ewen (1982, 109–251).

54 For similar attempts at describing the contrast between the modern and the postmodern era see, e.g., Hassan (1988), Harvey (1989), and Petôfi (1997).

55 From among the many books and papers that study this historical change, see, e.g., Inkeles and Smith (1974), Lears (1983), Fox and Lears (1983), Inglehart (1997), and Szakolczai (2003).

56 For an analysis of the role of guilt in Western civilization, see Hankiss 2001, chap. 7 ("The World of Guilt"), 157–80.

57 Quoted by Wechsler (1990, 13).

58 This was the name given to natural scientists experimenting with the human body, the physical laws of nature, and the heretical ideas of an Averroes and a reinterpreted Aristotle.

59 One might object that a similar contradiction also underlay medieval Christian thought, because the human being, whom God created in His own image, had a distinguished place even if not he or she, but God, was at the center of the universe; the great drama of the Fall and Redemption turned around him or her. But after the Fall, Adam and Eve were expelled from the Garden of Eden to the periphery, into the wilderness, where they became the most miserable creatures in the world. This contradiction has been an important factor throughout the history of Western Civilization. But today a growing number of people feel a strong affinity with the melancholy-tragic-absurd-stoic experience of Renaissance poetry and tragedy.

60 Agnes Heller (1978, 101–45) refers to these principles of Stoicism and Epicureanism in her book on the "Renaissance man."

61 Huizinga (1959b, 270) accepted, with a certain reserve, Troeltsch's (1911) idea that "the Renaissance did not by any means determine the culture of the sixteenth century as a whole, but only one important aspect of it. Merely to mention such names as Savonarola, Luther, Thomas Münzer, Calvin, and Loyola is enough to deny that Renaissance is synonymous with sixteenth-century culture. All these forceful personalities are very sixteenth-century and very un-Renaissance."

62 Hankiss (2001, chap. 12).

63 However, the influence is reciprocal: People's selves, too, shape the way in which they see the world.

64 Patocka (1989). It is worth remembering that "to live within the truth" became one of the central ideas of the Czech dissidents. See Vaclav Havel's "The Power of the Powerless" (1985a). Their "silent revolution" was, in its essence, the program of an existential transformation of the self.

65 See note 5 in chapter 8.

66 See also chapter 1 above, and Hankiss (2001, 261–76).

67 See chapters 12 and 13.

68 See titles like *Seinfeld and Philosophy: A Book about Everything and Nothing* (Irwin 2000); *The Simpsons and Philosophy: The D'oh! of Homer* (Irwin, Conard, and Skoble 2001); and *The Matrix and Philosophy: Welcome to the Desert of the Real* (Irwin 2002). See also *The Gospel According to Tony Soprano* (Seay 2002); *The Gospel Reloaded: Exploring Spirituality and Faith in the Matrix* (Seay and Garrett 2003);

Bond and Beyond: The Political Career of a Popular Hero (Bennet and Woollacott 1987); and *Cover Stories: Narrative and Ideology in the British Spy Thriller* (Denning 1987).

69 I have referred to some of these works already in the introduction of this book.

70 Cultural anthropologists have done much more in this field.

Chapter 10. The Self in a Syncretic Age

1 Deriving from the Greek verb *synkrétizein* (to combine), syncretism is an effort to reconcile conflicting and heterogeneous beliefs, faiths, tenets, and rites.

2 For an introduction to the early emergence of the individual, and on the history of individualism see Huizinga (1959b), MacIntyre (1981), Elias (1982, 1983, 1991), Taylor (1989), and others. See also Heller, Sosna, and Wellbery (1986); Baumeister (1986a); Foucault (1988b); Solomon (1988); Birnbaum and Leca (1990); Le Goff (1993); Porter (1997); Klemm and Zöller (1997); Nehamas (1998); Bürger (1998); Carr (1999); Melville and Schürer (2002); Strozier (2002); and several other important works.

3 Baumeister (1986a, 40).

4 Baumeister (1986a, 35–36). Baumeister mentions among the new developments also "the incipient cultivation of privacy," which symbolized the separation of social life and personal life; the fact that "attitudes to death underwent a basic change, suggesting a growing concern over individual life"; the fact that "people began to have an increasing role in the selection of their own spouses"; and finally the fact that "there emerged a heightened awareness of individual development and potentiality, symbolized by new attitudes toward children" (pp. 36–46).

5 Hume questioned the existence of a consistent self that would have continuity over time.

6 Csaba Pléh (1999) gives an excellent survey of these early attempts at questioning the existence of the self. Among others, he quotes Mach (1897, 21; 1910, 234–35), according to whom the self is only a "hypothetical entity." "We feel that the real pearls of life lie in the ever changing contents of consciousness, and that the person is merely an indifferent symbolic thread on which they are strung."

7 See Rorty's (1989, 27–29) analysis of Nietzsche's ideas about self-creation.

8 Rorty (1989, 30).

9 Rorty (1989, 33).

10 Rorty (1989, 41).

11 Rorty (1989, 32).

12 Rorty (1989, 28).

13 "Man, in a word, has no nature; what he has is . . . history" Ortega (1936). See also the section titled "Crises" in chapter 9.

14 See also Jaspers (1978). From among the numerous Jaspers interpretations, see, e.g., Olson (1979).

15 See also Adorno et al. (1969 [1950]); Husserl (1970); Camus (1971 [1951]); Fromm (1969); Habermas (1979b, 1979c, 1987a, 1987b); Berman (1982); Hamvas (1983); Ricoeur (1986); Michalski (1986); Tillich (1988); Beelman (1990); Kolakowski (1991); Cadava, Connor, and Nancy (1991); Maffesoli (1996); Voegelin (2000); and see books and essays by the great midwar generation of Paul Valéry, Ortega y Gasset, Unamuno, and others.

16 The authors in Shneidman's volume (1967) deal mainly with suicide, but some of the papers also discuss nonphysical ways of self-destruction. A few titles: "Death as a Motive of Philosophical Thought," "Buddha and Self-Destruction," "Sleep and Self-Destruction."

17 About the destruction, or nonexistence, of the self see, e.g., Collins (1982); Kolm (1986); Elster (1986); Barrett (1987); Baumeister (1991a); Cadava, Connor, and Nancy (1991); Schrag (1997); Anderson (1997); Muller (1998); and White and Hellerich (1998). The death wish studied by Freud and the human penchant for suicide, however, are other categories, because they suppose the existence of a self that can be annihilated.

18 Castells (1997, 355) speaks also of the "dissolution of shared identities, which is tantamount to the dissolution of society as a meaningful social system."

19 Baumeister (1986a, 87).

20 Quoted by Baumeister (1986a, 67). The loss of self has also its seriously pathological forms, which have little to do with these philosophical, sociological, and psychological concepts and arguments. There are extreme situations in which people may effectively lose their "selves." In an accident, for instance, they may lose their memory, their ability to coordinate their behavior, to act as a conscious human being. Various nervous diseases and brain injuries may have the same effect. Oliver Sacks's (1987) *The Man Who Mistook His Wife for a Hat and Other Clinical Tales* is a curious link between the two domains, i.e., between the pathological and the nonpathological forms of the "loss of self." See also Schreiber (1973); Curtis (1989); and Higgins, Snyder, and Berglas (1990).

21 There is a wide variety of approaches to the concept of "self," ranging across studies in psychiatry; clinical, personal, developmental, and social psychology; sociology; cultural anthropology; ethnomethodology; communication studies; history; lit-

erature and the arts; etc. Out of the rich literature, let me mention first a few classical titles: James (1890), Lewin (1935), Allport (1937, 1961), Stagner (1937), Freud (1937), Adler (1941, 1967, 1979), Cattell (1950), Erikson 1959, 1968), Mead (1962 [1934]), Jung (1968, 1971a, 1971b), Skinner (1971), Berne (1972), Scheler (1973), Bronfenbrenner (1979), and Freud (1989).

Since the late 1970s, the number of important books on the self has increased so fast that I can give only a short, and contingent, selection of them (I shall refer to most of these studies later in this book): Marcuse (1955); Sennett (1976, 1992, 1994); Rosenberg (1979); Ickes and Knowles (1982); Kegan (1982); Lynch, Norem-Hebeisen, and Gergen (1981); Ricoeur (1984–86, 1992); White and Kirkpatrick (1985); Baumeister (1986a, 1986b, 1998, 1999); Elster (1986); Snyder (1987); Muller (1987, 1998); Foucault (1988a, 1988b, 2001); Hampson (1988); Taylor (1989); Danziger (1990); Prost and Vincent (1991); White (1991); Gergen (1991); Young-Eisendrath (1991); Gregg (1991); Featherstone, Hepworth, and Turner (1991); Elias (1991); Kolak and Raymond (1991); Levin (1992); Levine (1992); Hattie (1992); Lash and Friedman (1992); Csikszentmihalyi (1993); Giddens (1993); Morris (1994); Wiley (1994); Cohen (1994); Berofsky (1995); Kellner (1995); Hacking (1995); Grodin and Lindlof (1996); Rose (1990, 1996, 1997); Porter (1997); Schrag (1997); Castells (1997); Kaiser (1997); Pyszczynski, Greenberg, and Solomon (1997); White and Hellerich (1998); Bermúdez (1998); Seligman (1998); Smelser (1998); Carr (1999); Innes (1999); Gallagher and Shear (1999); Weber (2000); Featherstone (2000); Dürrschmidt (2000); Cavarero (2000); Seligman (2000); Strozier (2002); Goldberg (2002); Sedikides and Brewer (2001); Weinreich and Saunderson (2002); Burr (2002); Mageo (2002); Tesser, Stapel, and Wood (2002); Tesser, Wood, and Stapel (2005); Pervin (2003); Sheldon (2004); and Petersen and Seligman (2004); Morf and Ayduk (2005).

Some of the recent handbooks and collections of essays may also be important guides for those who want to get an overview of the field. See, e.g., Aronson and Pratkanis (1993); Myers (1993); Gilbert, Fiske, and Lindzey (1998); Pervin and John (1999); Hampson (2000); Cervone and Mischel (2002); Forgas and Williams (2001, 2002); Hutchison (2003); Leary and Tangney (2003); and Carver and Scheier (2004). For a short survey of the various fields of research, see Hoyle et al. (1999),

22 Leary and Tangney (2003b, 7, 6).

23 Leary and Tangney (2003b, 11). In the same year, and the same connection, Mischel and Morf (2003, 33) spoke about a "rapidly spreading prefix disease."

24 Jung, (1971b, 142) proposed a simple way out of this labyrinth. He suggested simply calling "the total personality which, though present, cannot be fully known, the *self*." But the discussion on how these various concepts (person, psyche, self, subject, ego, "I," "soul," "individual") relate to one another is still going on. Scholars have

made great efforts to find, or introduce, some order into this almost chaotic richness and complexity. E.g., Baumeister (1998, 683–700, 700–12, 712–27) discussed the various concepts according to the functions the self may play in people's lives (*reflexive functions, interpersonal functions,* and *executive functions*). Others classify the concepts of self in different ways. Sedikides and Brewer (2001) work with the main categories of the *individual self,* the *relational self,* and the *collective self.* Leary and Tangney's (2003b) main categories are the *individual and intrapsychic;* the *interpersonal and relational;* and the *intergroup, cultural, and collective* aspects of the self. In a similar way, Forgas and Williams (2002) speak of the *cognitive, interpersonal,* and *intergroup* perspectives. Mischel and Morf (2003, 33) propose a slightly different classification, when they argue that the self is "an agentic doing system, an organized cognitive-affective (knowing-thinking-feeling) system, and it is an interpersonal system."

25 The word "transcendent" is not used here in its religious sense. In Csikszentmihalyi's terminology (1993, 212–13), "transcendenters" are persons who "have been able to fulfill the potential complexity of their lives," who "learned to transform entropy into memes that create order in the consciousness of those who attend to them" and because of whom "the world is a little more harmonious than it would have been otherwise," because their lives increase harmony in the world and diminishes chaos.

26 See also Nietzsche (1983, 1989, 1995).

27 The "I" is the self as we internally experience it, and the "me" is the self as we think other people see us. Donald McIntosh (1994, 18) describes the "me" as follows: "The 'me' is formed of physical traits (e.g., 'little'), category membership (e.g., gender, family), characteristic modes of actions (e.g., playing with dolls), and the child's name, which is taken to be an essential aspect of the self."

28 James (1981, 282). Quoted by Gregg (1991, 182).

29 Mead (1962, 142). Quoted by Gregg (1991, 184).

30 See, e.g., Baumeister (1986a), Muller (1987), and White (1991).

31 The question of what does hold the self together over time and change has ever puzzled philosophers and later psychologists and psychoanalysts. There are many possible answers: my body, my genes, my skin, my name, my routines, my idiosyncrasies, my illusions about myself, my family, my home, my profession, my job, my position in society, my life goals, my roles, a "narrative," my memory. Let me quote a strong, though not expert, statement: "You have to begin to lose your memory, if only in bits and pieces, to realize that memory is what makes our lives. Life without memory is no life at all. . . . Our memory is our coherence, our reason, our feeling, even our action. Without it, we are nothing." Luis Bunuel, quoted by Sacks (1987, 23).

32 Schrag (1997, 26–27, 32–33).

33 From among the hundreds of works dealing with the possible multiplicity of the self, see Cervona and Shoda (1999), Hoyle et al. (1999), and Mischel and Morf (2003).

34 As, e.g., the case of the Dr. Jekyll / Mr. Hyde–type split personalities.

35 Elster (1986, 30). In his *Rewriting the Soul: Multiple Personality and the Science of Memory,* Ian Hacking (1995) also stresses that in psychiatric practice the "multiple self" is a serious disease and has nothing, or very little, to do with the "multiple self" used more or less in a metaphoric or sometimes almost in a poetic way by philosophers and personality theorists. See also Laing (1965).

36 Gregg (1991, 208).

Chapter 11. The Self and the Intensity of Life

1 See chapter 8.

2 See chapter 14, "The Self in a Reenchanted World."

3 Lyotard (1984, passim), Lash (1990, 79–81), Bertens (1995, 185–96), Bauman (1992, 193).

4 I use the term "to transcend" here in its original meaning, i.e., to indicate something that transcends its own boundaries.

5 For a detailed analysis, see Brown (1959), Berger (1967), Becker (1973), Lifton (1979), and Hankiss (2001).

6 See also Olson and Rouner (1981). However, we should not overemphasize the "loss of transcendence," because the existence of a divine transcendence is still a major fact, hope, and consolation for hundreds of millions of people living in the Western world.

7 One of the blatant examples of people's need, and almost desperate search for, a lost transcendence is the success of "transcendental" TV series, which in these days are overflowing the TV channels in America (and more and more also in Europe). The cover story of the January 24–30, 2004, issue of the American *TV Guide* has the following title: "God and TV: Joan of Arcadia Talks to the Almighty and Her Ratings Soar" (Nollinger 2004, 41–45). And within the issue, we learn that an amazing number of transcendental series are running on the various channels. "On Fox's *Tru* [sic] *Calling* talking corpses seek help from a morgue attendant." "On ABC's *The Practice,* Sharon Stone appeared in a recurring role as a lawyer who claimed to be in contact with the Big Judge in the Sky." In *Still Life,* a murdered cop "observes his loved ones beyond the grave." The hero of *Dead Like Me* has to search for the meaning of

his life after he has died. In *Wonderfalls,* unspecified transcendental powers instruct the heroine through talking toys how she has to help other people; etc.

8 Koselleck (2004), Laïdi (1994, 2000), Virilio (1994), Lash, Quick, and Roberts (1998).

9 Baudelaire (1964, 4, 9, 13, 11, 32). Quoted by Frisby (1985, 16–18).

10 Quoted by Safranski (1998).

11 Nietzsche (1983, nos. 80, 92). See also Nietzsche (1980, vol. 7, 817) and Frisby (1985, 32, 35).

12 Nietzsche (1983, nos. 79, 78).

13 Nietzsche (1983, no. 91). Quoted by Stambaugh (1972, 25). Frisby (1985, 6) has shown that, according to Georg Simmel, too, "the key to the contemporary analysis of modernity . . . (lies) . . . in diverse 'momentary images' or 'snapshots' (*Moment-bilder*) of modern social life that are to be viewed *sub specie aeternitatis.*" "Simmel states quite explicitly that 'the unity of these investigations lies . . . in the possibility . . . of finding in each of life's details the totality of its meaning.'" See Simmel (1998).

14 Heidegger (1990, 290). See also Safranski's (1998, 183–88) description of the Davos debate.

15 The existential moment, and the timeless present, also play an important role in the subculture of the New Age. Think, for instance, of the hyperintensive moments of spiritual enlightenment, or of the timeless present of meditation and mystique experience.

16 Let me mention here that the intensity of life may be both joyful (success, love, joy, youth, religious experience, speed, etc.) and painful (physical suffering, passion, death, despair, fright).

17 See also the fast-growing literature on the importance of life experience versus possessing material goods. See titles like *To Have or to Be?* (Fromm 1976); *Luxury Fever: Why Money Fails to Satisfy in an Era of Excess* (Frank 1999); *Well-Being: The Foundations of Hedonistic Psychology* (Kahneman, Diener, and Schwartz 1999); *Authentic Happiness: Using the New Positive Psychology to Realize Your Potential for Lasting Fulfillment* (Seligman 2002); and *To Do or to Have? That Is the Question* (Boven and Gilovitch 2003).

18 Baudrillard (1988a, 48) speaks in this connection of the "maximization of existence by . . . the intensive use of signs and objects, and by the systematic exploitation of all the possibilities of pleasure."

19 We might listen to Mahatma Gandhi's remark: "There is more to life than increasing its speed." See also Zaki Laïdi's (1994) excellent book on "urgency" as a dominant feature of our contemporary world.

20 George Bernard Shaw said once somewhere: "Cruelty would be delicious if one could only find some sort of cruelty that didn't really hurt." We have found the solution: We have invented the virtual world of Television.

21 The importance of intense life experience has been discovered also by modern theology. See, e.g., Tillich (1952, 1965).

22 Rilke (1975). The German original: Wer, wenn ich schriee, hörte mich denn aus der Engel / Ordnungen? und gesetzt selbst, es nähme /einer mich plötzlich ans Herz: ich verginge von seinem / stärkeren Dasein. Denn das Schöne ist nichts / als des Schrecklichen Anfang, den wir noch gerade ertragen, / und wir bewundern es so, weil es gelassen verschmäht, / uns zu zerstören. Ein jeder Engel ist schrecklich.

23 See chapter 13 below.

24 In the next chapter, we shall study an issue of the well-know German women's weekly, *Bunte*. There we shall see how systematically the editors of this magazine work with contrasts. Here are a few examples: World-famous star singer ↔ and she is lonely and unhappy. The macho kick-box champion ↔ who is a henpecked husband. The bosom of a young lady ↔ which shattered the British monarchy in its foundations. The German First Lady ↔ who roller-skates in the streets of Berlin. A chain of sex shops ↔ on the stock exchange. Robust football players ↔ cry. A beautiful young woman ↔ has to die.

Chapter 12. The Self in Boundary Situations

1 The French and German terms of *"situation limite"* and *"Grenzensituation"* are translated into English both as "boundary situation" and "limit situation."

2 Dollimore (1997, 257).

3 Dollimore (1997, 257); see also Mann (1959, 146).

4 This role may be positive as well as negative. Here we shall mainly discuss its positive impact on the development of our selves but should not forget that fear may also distort not only human personalities but also whole communities, societies, and polities.

5 In a shortened form, I shall use here a few paragraphs of one of my earlier books (Hankiss 2001, 32–34, 55–61). There is a large body of literature on the role of fear in human life. See, e.g., May (1950), Haefner (1971), Rachman (1978), Tuan (1979), Scruton (1986), Marks (1987), and Delumeau (1990).

6 Among others, see Freud (1959a), Freud (1937), Horney (1937), Miller and Swanson (1960). For an excellent survey of Freudian and non-Freudian research in this

field, see Smelser (1987). Anxiety and panic are also important variables in Smelser's *Theory of Collective Behavior* (1962). See also Hankiss (2001, 55–57).

7 Becker (1973, 7, 2, 4).

8 Becker (1973, 1).

9 Becker (1973, 4–5, 7).

10 Berger (1967, 3, 6, 19, 27).

11 There are, of course, other factors as well. In our lives, and in the process of self-construction, we are pulled and pushed by various forces. Depending on their academic backgrounds, experts speak of God's creative will and our duties in this world—or of the Schopenhauerian or Nietzscheian will; the Bergsonian élan vital; Adler's "striving for superiority," "self-enhancement," and "self-perfection"; the more prosaic genetic factors; instincts; the Freudian libido; the Faustian aspiration to the fulfillment of our lives; socially programmed motivations; and so on and so forth.

12 I think that the same could be said and proved about all the civilizations that have ever existed. This is, however, only a hypothesis to be tested.

13 Boundary situations played an important role in the traditional European novel and drama as well. As far as Greek, Elizabethan, or modern tragedies are concerned, their very essence was to expose a boundary situation and to display how the heroes try to cope with this predicament. See, e.g., Hankiss (2001, 209–16) on the tragic catharsis or the section of chapter 11 titled "The World of Jokes." See also the section in Hankiss (1977, 31–57) titled "Boundary Situations in Animated Cartoons."

14 The use of the philosophical concept of "boundary situation" is not wholly justified here, because, e.g., for Sartre a boundary situation is a par excellence situation of decision, the danger, and the freedom of an authentic choice, while in the world of television, boundary situations are just catastrophes, sudden turns in a human life, a treason, a shocking discovery, the fall of a human being out of her or his everyday life.

15 Intellectuals, who usually disparage such television programs as shallow and junk, could help people a lot by analyzing these programs and disclosing the hidden human situations and existential dramas underlying their trivial surface.

16 It is a popular German women's magazine, *Bunte,* and its 1999 no. 23 issue. I could as well use other issues of *Bunte,* and other popular magazines like *People, Paris Match,* and *Gala.* I have cross-checked my results by analyzing thirty issues of each of these magazines. There are a few extremely interesting books on the history, and present role, of women's magazines. See, e.g., Winship (1987), Beetham (1996), Zuckerman (1998).

17 Kindel (1999, 46–49): "*Sie lebte und starb—so stark.*"

18 "*Pilar Goess: Tod eines Society-Girls—Die reichen Freunde zeigen Herz.*" Later a nice metaphor enhances the impact: "Many of her famous friends surrounded her with the protective wall of love."

19 Kindel (1999, passim).

20 Kindel (1999, 48–49).

21 Kohlrusch (1999, 38–41): "*Darf man beim Sterben helfen?*"

22 In a great number of traditional civilizations, the living feared that the dead might come back and haunt them, threaten them, and destroy them. Tombstones did not only mark graves; they also kept the dead from getting out of their graves too easily (at least before the Last Judgment).

23 Kohlrusch (1999, 38).

24 Kohlrusch (1999, 38).

25 Kohlrusch (1999, 41).

26 Kohlrusch (1999, 41).

27 The various popular magazines have, of course, their own version of this "popular existentialism." *GQ*, for instance, radiates a tragic dandyism, with its young men and women staring, with a stoic dignity and gloom, into a dark and bleak and empty universe. *Bunte* is more sentimental and romantic.

28 "*Gibt es ein Leben nach dem Tennis?*" *Bunte* 27 (1999). Let me admit that I cheat here a bit because I promised to study articles in just one single issue of *Bunte* and this article is from another issue.

29 *Bunte* 27 (1999): 20.

30 *Bunte* 27 (1999): 94.

31 *Bunte* 27 (1999): 22–23.

32 See, e.g., Ebbinghausen and Neckel (1989), Cohen (1996), Holler (1999), Kohn (2001), and Vargo (2003).

33 See, e.g., Wilson Knight's (2001) studies of the symbolic messages of Shakespeare's plays. In his essay on *Hamlet,* he argues that Claudius, Gertrude, and their joyful royal court are the symbols of life and Hamlet, morbid and clad in black, is the Ambassador of Death.

34 This is the fascination of situations of "liminality" and of the eruption of the "carnivalesque" latent in our civilization. See Van Gennep (1960), Turner (1969), Bakhtin (1968), Easton et al. (1988), Shields (1990), and Featherstone (1991).

35 I discussed the "mechanism of jokes" in my book on *Fears and Symbols* (Hankiss 2001, 245–57).

36 The Latin word *sensatio* originally meant sensation, perception, emotional experience. Later, in French, English, and other modern languages, it already indicated
the event as well, which triggered off the strong emotional impact, i.e., which was
sensational.

37 Englert (1999, 24–27).

38 The title in *The Sun* (May 26, 1999) was "Sophie Topless: Star Tarrant's Sexy Fun
with Edward's Bride."

39 Englert (1999, 24–27).

40 Englert (1999, 27).

41 Englert (1999, 27).

42 Victor Turner (1990) points out that in liminal situations, people experience a strong
feeling of "communitas." Let me add, in brackets, that in these moments of happy
self-apotheosis we should not forget, however, that in spite of our elevated spirits,
we are champing this juicy scandal as our scavenger ancestors did champ the mar-
row from the broken bones of their prey. And we should not forget either that, yield-
ing to a proletarian envy deeply hidden under the surface of our middle-class aloof-
ness, we do not mind too much that even royal families have their problems—let
alone the fact that surreptitiously we even enjoy, a tiny bit, the view of that blouse
flapping up for a second. However, *Bunte* reproduces only an almost virginally decent version of this scene.

43 A close parallel with traditional folktales enhances the impact of this story. The
prince falls in love with the beautiful orphan girl. He wants to marry her. But the
wicked witch pours poison in the idyllic story. She slanders her in the court. The
happiness of the couple is ruined. But the queen has a golden heart; she forgives
the youthful mistake of the orphan girl and gives her blessing to the marriage. The
wicked witch gains her deserved punishment. And the prince and the princess live
happily ever after.

Chapter 13. The Myth of the Self

1 "Notabilities" have been more recent predecessors of our contemporary "celebrities."
They were important and well-known public persons, politicians, rich businessmen,
dignitaries of the state and the church. In the nineteenth century, and in the first part
of the twentieth, they practically ruled the public space and it was only in the second
half of this century that they had to share this space with the stars and celebrities of
the consumer age. The change has been rapid and almost shocking. To give only one
example: From 1927 to the early 1980s, the title pages of the *Time* magazine showed

almost exclusively the portraits of notabilities. The influx of star and celebrity images (and various topical images of the consumer age) took place in the 1980s.

2 There were a great number of reasons why people might want to exalt the human personality. In his famous book *The Treason of the Intellectuals,* the French philosopher Julien Benda (1969, 64) opposed the free, autonomous individual to the rising tide of totalitarian ideologies and movements. "Man belongs neither to his language, nor to his race; he belongs only to himself, for he is free, that is, a moral being." Other thinkers—e.g., Berdyaev, Heidegger, and Tillich—saw a sign of crisis in this shrinking of the world into the human individual.

3 Charles Taylor (1989) analyzed this process in detail. The European Renaissance was not the only age in which radical individualism and the fulfillment of the human self was a conscious and central project. Various historical and social contexts—classical Athens, the life of the elites in imperial Rome, China, or Persia, the age of chivalry, etc.—offer embarrassing and only partly explored parallels. The program of the fulfillment of human life has also had its religious versions. The claim that the Renaissance is unique in this respect is obviously questionable. But it may be nevertheless true that the program of self-fulfillment was stronger and more systematic in the age of the Renaissance, and in the circles of Renaissance lifestyle, than in most of the other ages and other social environments. With an obvious and remarkable exception: the consumer civilization at the turn of the twentieth and twenty-first centuries.

Actualize yourself! Realize your potentials! Construct your life like a work of art! This was one of the fundamental rules of Renaissance life, and it is one of the fundamental messages of the Proletarian Renaissance as well. Ever since the 1950s new and new waves of revivals have swept through Western civilization. The hippies, Flower Power, the Beatles, Punk, the New Age, aerobics, parapsychological sit-ins, transcendental meditation: each of them was a micro-Renaissance in the sign of self-actualization and the search for harmony and meaning.

4 Zygmunt Bauman (1992, xxii) speaks in this connection of a dual process. On the one hand, we witness the disintegration and "deconstruction" of the human personality, and, on the other, the reemergence of "the fullness of moral choice and responsibility." There have been also outstanding thinkers who saw in this inflation of the human personality or self a sign of crisis. Heidegger argued that the self, entangled in the trivialities of everyday life, makes it extremely difficult for the human being to submerge in the real and genuine depths of Being.

5 The problem whether human life may have its own purpose and meaning in itself has been discussed by a great number of authors. See again Taylor (1989).

6 The existentialists' concept of Being has a certain transcendental character. By experiencing "authentic existence," one steps over into the sphere of, if not immor-

tality, at least timelessness. This Being, or "authentic existence," is the framework within which human life finds its purpose and meaning.

7 In other civilizations, the role of self may be different, though the irradiation of almost all contemporary civilizations by Western consumer civilization has been very strong.

8 There were, of course, huge differences between the sense of self and identity of the rich farmer and the poor cottar but even the beggar or the clown of the village had a name, a function, a kind of identity.

9 Ewen quotes here Braverman (1974, 113).

10 Ewen (1988, 78–106 and passim) gives and excellent description of this rise, this resurrection, of the ways in which working-class people worked more and more consistently on the construction of their selves.

11 In the audiovisual version of the book, there are some further chapters that may strongly appeal to people: Maximum Power and Inner Joy; Expressing Love, Trust and Intimacy; Overcoming Emotional Hurt; Making Peace with Your Parents; From Resentment to Forgiveness; Expressing Anger and Love with Your Family; Martyrs, Dictators, and Other Difficult Parents.

12 In the same November 2003 flyer of the Borders bookshop, there is another self-help book working with this magic number: Cheung's (2003) *Coffee Wisdom: 7 Finely Ground Principles for Living a Full-Bodied Life.*

13 Out of the hundreds of books on the making, role, and social impact of celebrities, I cite here only a few recent ones: Marshall (1997), Hills (2002), Barbas (2002), Corner and Pels (2003), Orth (2004), Turner (2004), and Schroeder (2004).

14 According to a strongly supported hypothesis, the famous French *Chansons de Geste* served (also) to advertise the monasteries along the roads that had been taken by the Christian armies in their crusades against the Arabs in Spain; the monasteries were interested in hosting as many pilgrims as possible.

15 Ewen (1988, 107).

16 Bishop Berkeley stated already in the mid–eighteenth century that "to be is to be perceived." Quoted by Ewen (1988, 76). When social psychologists study the self as "Me," i.e., as perceived by other people, or as the individual believes that he or she is perceived by other people, then they deal, in a certain respect, with this "gazing" problem. Thomas Gilovich (2002) speaks in this connection of a "spotlight effect." An interesting attempt at dealing with the problem is to be found in Bourdieu (1998, "3ᵉ partie: La genèse sociale de l'oeil," 510–22). See also Denzin's (1995) *The Cinematic Society: The Voyeur's Gaze.*

17 Zétényi (1999).

18 Elias (1991, 164) remarked that "the problem of the relation of the individual and society poses itself in some respects differently now than it did fifty years ago. There were less than half as many people in the world: more exactly, about 40 per cent of the present world population. The number of people now alive is not without significance for the theoretical, and practical discussion of the actual relation of individual, and society." To construct oneself in a community of, say, 500 inhabitants may be very different from constructing oneself in a global community of six or seven billion people.

19 See chapter 12 on "The Self in Boundary Situations."

20 Siewert and Sahner (1999): *"Exklusiv die Fotos der intimen Feier im amerikanischen Spielerparadies . . . mit einer Flitternacht im Hubschrauber."*

21 Junkersdorf (1998, 12–15).

22 Boenisch (1999, 30–32).

23 To sharpen the focus further, I will analyze only the title pages, the titles, the leads, the pictures, and the captions—i.e., those elements that were set off by the editors. They are likely to carry the main message of this publication and to play a major role in shaping their readers' selves.

24 Sessums (1999, title page).

25 Zeman (1999, title page, 78, 82).

26 Peretz and Webber (1999, title page, 7, 115, 121).

27 Michaelis (1999, 36). In the illustration, these muscles can be clearly seen.

28 Michaelis (1999, 37).

29 Michaelis (1999, 7, 38).

30 Michaelis (1999, 36, 40).

31 O'Neill and Gummer (1999, title page, 5–7, 111).

32 O'Neill and Gummer (1999, 112, 116).

33 O'Neill and Gummer (1999, 120).

34 O'Neill and Gummer (1999, 110–11).

35 O'Neill and Gummer (1999, 118–19, 122–23).

36 Schuller (1999).

37 Schuller (1999, 94).

38 Daily (1999, 136, 138).

39 Daily (1999, 143). Daily cites also Will Self's remarks.

40 See note 58 in chapter 9. This was the name given to natural scientists experimenting with the human body, the physical laws of nature, and the heretical ideas of Averroes and a reinterpreted Aristotle.

Chapter 14. The Self in a Reenchanted World

1 I quote here a few paragraphs from chapter 8 of my book *Fears and Symbols* (2001).

2 Quoted by Gerth and Mill (1958, 128) and Ritzer (1999, 63).

3 Let me give a few titles for all tastes, all fears, all seasons now (November 2003) on the shelves of bookstores: *Advanced Candle Magic; Talking to Heaven; The Hidden Truth of Your Name; Numerology; Tarot Basics; To Stir a Magic Cauldron; Green Witchcraft; The 21 Lessons of Merlin; Celtic Wisdom; Everyday Karma; The New Revelations; Visits from the Afterlife: The Truth about Hauntings, Spirits, and Reunions with Lost Loved Ones; The Art of Shen Ku; The New Chinese Astrology; Astrology for the Soul; Technology of Gods; Atlantis;* and *The Secret Doctrine.* The popularity of films about catastrophes, space wars, and time travel also testifies to this penchant for the irrational and the unpredictable.

4 Quoted by Ritzer (1999, 68–69).

5 Quoted by Ritzer 1999, 69).

6 See, e.g., Campbell and Holt-Underwood (1994), Singer (1995), Faver (1996), Lane (1996), Saliba (1996), Parrish-Harra (2002), and York (2004). See also note 12 in chapter 7.

7 Amazon.com lists the following subjects, and hundreds if not thousands of books under the headings of Aliens, Astral Projection, Auras and Colors, Controversial Knowledge, Crop Circles, Cults and Demonism, ESP, Kabbalah, Magic, Metaphysical phenomena, Occultism, Parapsychology, Rosicrucianism, Satanism, Shamanism, Spiritualism, Supernatural, UFOs, Unexplained Mysteries, Wicca, and Witchcraft.

8 Hankiss (2001, chaps. 5, 12).

9 See the corresponding section of chapter 12 entitled "The Self in Boundary Situations," and chapter 6 entitled "The Self and the Articulation of Time." See also Hankiss (2001, 127–33).

10 There are excellent works studying the origins and early decades of the civilization of consumption. See, e.g., Williams (1958); Bailey (1978, 1986); Miller (1981); Benjamin (1982); McKendrick, Brewer, and Plumb (1982); Williams (1982); Bennett et al. (1983); Chaney (1983); Seigel (1986); Easton et al. (1988); Urry (1988); Strasser (1989); Gardner and Sheppard (1989); and Leach (1993).

11 I mention here only a few of the most important books: Berger (1967, 1969), Horton (1984), Kowinski (1985), Strasser (1989), Mullen and Johnson (1990), Adams (1991), Zukin (1991), Featherstone (1991), Sorkin (1992), Tobin (1992), Beck (1992), Baudrillard (1993, 1998), Debord (1994 [1967]), Barber (1995), Bryman (1995), Denzin (1995), Fellman (1995), Lury (1996), Gottdiener (1997), Zepp

(1997), Corrigan (1997), Illouz (1997), Clammer (1997), Ritzer (1997a, 1999, 2001, 2003), Miles (1998), Goldman and Papson (1998), Smart (1999), Lee (2000), Brooks (2000), and Couldry (2003). See also note 52 in chapter 9.

12 The term "reenchantment" was used earlier by other authors; see, e.g., Berman (1981).

13 Ritzer (1999, chaps. 3, 5, 7, pp. 68–76, 104–69). See also Ritzer (1997a, 2001, 2003).

14 Ritzer (1999, 169).

15 Ritzer (1999, 169–210).

16 Ritzer (1999, 108).

17 Ritzer (1999, 169).

18 Gottdiener (1997).

19 Ritzer (1999, p. 110). The quotation is from the "Rainforest Café" Web site.

20 Ritzer (1999, 169).

21 Rhymer (1996, 75), quoted by Ritzer (1999, 130).

22 Ritzer (1999, 167–68).

23 Chaney (1983), Debord (1994 [1967], Ritzer (1999, 105–8).

24 Ritzer (1999, 214).

25 Ritzer (1999, 75–76).

26 Gottdiener (1997, 6) studies both factors: "I am especially interested in the inter-mixing of creation and use; that is, how milieus designed for profit interact with the dreams, fantasies, and forms of popular entertainment for people in our society."

27 Ritzer (1999, 160, 159).

28 Ritzer (1999, 161).

29 See also Groys (1993).

30 The concept of "agriculture" referred to an activity, or process, in the course of which the human being subdued, tamed, shaped, improved, polished, trimmed, and "civilized" the raw forces of nature. But the notion of culture appeared in an extended sense already in the works of Cicero, who wrote about the "*cultura deorum*," or "*cultura animi*" ("culture of the gods," "culture of the soul"). In the age of the Renaissance and the Enlightenment, the concept of culture was largely used to mean the polishing of human nature. The notion of "civilization," conversely, referred to the polished and cultivated behavior of the "*cives*," i.e., the city dwellers. Two hundred years later, Norbert Elias (1982, 1983) studied in great detail a certain segment of this civilizing process in Europe.

31 Hayek (1979, 173–74).

32 See also Featherstone, Lash, and Robertson (1995, 1–24).

33 In a national survey conducted in 1980, we found that in this "negative" way, Hungarian people were more individualistic than people in the United States (we used the famous Rokeach survey in our survey). See Hankiss et al. 1982).

34 The American epidemics of OK-ing in every possible and impossible situation is also there, but we are still far from the American hero who answers the question "Are you OK?" dutifully with a "Yes, I am OK."—even if he has been shot, has lost one of his legs, and the blazing tower is falling on his head.

35 The opposition of "high" and "low" culture is questionable, both in the Renaissance and in the Proletarian Renaissance. Shakespeare, as a playwright, was part of the "popular culture" (though theater companies were sponsored by the queen, the king, and their courtiers, and the very same companies performed also at the court), but as a poet writing sonnets he belonged to the highbrow culture of the Renaissance court. The greatest masterpieces of the age, written for these popular stages, became later part of the "high" culture of humankind. In our own age, cinema, television, design, and advertising are the "popular" genres, but they may have already produced some masterpieces (we, their contemporaries, may not know which they are) that will later be included in the canon of the highest art and the common heritage of humankind.

And there are cultural domains where the separation of high and popular art is not feasible at all. Architecture is the most democratic art, because most of its main creations—temples, churches, aqueducts, amphitheaters, thermal baths, triumphal arches, town halls, bridges—were built for communities. In the same way, in our own day, it is impossible, and it would be absurd to exclude people from the magnificent atriums of the shopping malls; from the ground floor of the steel and glass towers of banks; from airports, museums, sports domes, etc. As far as their style is concerned, they may be the monuments of a late modernism, or those of a highbrow postmodernism, but they provide an excellent framework also for the human selves wandering around in the world of the Proletarian Renaissance.

36 One night, spectators were frustrated because a lion, imported for that purpose from Nubia, and a bear from the English forests were, in spite of all prompting, unwilling to tear each other to pieces.

Epilogue

1 In French: "*souci de soi*"; Montaigne speaks of "*le soing que nous avons de nous*" and "*le soing pour soy-mesmes.*" Foucault speaks of the "technologies of the self" and the "hermeneutics of the subject." In German, the term "*Selbstsorge*" is used.

2 Taylor's (1989) and Baumeister's (1986a) books are among the best histories of the concept, and care, of the self. But there are many important studies focusing on specific problems and periods of this history. See, e.g., Geertz (1973b, 1979); Spacks (1976); Lyons (1978); Greenblatt (1980); Cox (1980); MacIntyre (1981); Elias (1982, 1983, 1991); Marsella, DeVos, and Hsu (1985); Carrithers, Collins, and Lukes (1985); Heller, Sosna, and Wellbery (1986); Foucault (1988b, 2001); Solomon (1988); Roland (1988); Birnbaum and Leca (1990); Danziger (1990); Le Goff (1993); Cohen (1994); Battaglia (1995); Porter (1997); Klemm and Zöller (1997); Nehamas (1998); Bürger (1998); Carr (1999); Cassirer (2000); Coleman, Lewis, and Kowalik (2000); Melville and Schürer (2002); Strozier (2002); and several other studies in the history of individualism.

3 Cultural anthropologists have described thousands of interesting cases of these early and timid attempts at self-construction, which were strictly controlled by the traditions and belief systems of the various communities. The importance of the destruction and the regeneration of the self is obvious, e.g., in the "rites of passage" and initiation ceremonies, described, among many other anthropologists, by Van Gennep (1960) and Turner (1969).

4 Among others, see Nehamas (1998) and Foucault (1988b).

5 Foucault (1988b, 19) translates and/or interprets this Greek expression as "to take care of yourself," "the concern with self," "to be concerned, to take care of yourself."

6 Foucault (1988b, 24, 26, 35). See also Hutton (1988).

7 The *Legenda Aurea* and other martyrologies were lessons of how a true Christian had to care for her or his real self, her or his immortal soul.

8 Saint John of the Cross also spoke of the "annihilation of the self," Porter (1997, 2). See also Foucault (1988b, 35, 44–45).

9 For some excellent recent studies, see Innes (1999), Mehrgardt and Mehrgardt (2001), Stein (2001), and Melville and Schürer (2002).

10 Jan Patocka's (1989) concept of the "care of the soul" also has religious overtones.

11 Self-discovery and self-fulfillment became key concepts, and the appearance of a whole range of new genres indicate the growing importance of the care for the self (Porter 1997, 3). See, e.g., Castiglione (1950 [1528]), Kai Ka'us (1951 [1082–83]), Erasmus (1982 [1520]), Elyot (1970 [1531]), Dorset (1960 [1563]), Montaigne (1958 [1595]), Bacon (1985 [1597]), and Faret (1970 [1630]).

A beautiful example of the idea of self-construction in the Renaissance is to be found in Pico della Mirandola's *Oration on the Dignity of Man*. God says: "We have made thee neither of heaven nor of earth, Neither mortal nor immortal, So that with freedom of choice and with honor, As though the maker and molder of thyself, Thou mayest fashion thyself in whatever shape thou shalt prefer. Thou shalt have the power out of thy soul's judgment, To be reborn into the higher forms, which are divine." Characteristically, these lines are quoted by Anthony Robbins (1992, 361–62), one of the great gurus of contemporary manager and personality training.

12 See the fascinating drama of soul searching in their spiritual diaries in Porter (1997, 3).

13 Porter (1997, 5).

14 Taylor (1989, 301).

15 This is an allusion to Schubert's famous cycle of songs, *Winterreise.*

16 Smiles (1958 [1858]). See also Ransom (1886) and Craik (1972 [1831]).

17 Taylor (1989, 300–2).

18 Hundreds, if not thousands, of books on self-actualization have been published in the last half a century. Let me refer here to a few of recent titles (of various levels and quality): Cawelti (1965), Bloomfield and Felder (1985), Rusk (1986), Marrs (1990), Hauck (1991. 1998), Robbins (1992), Moss (1992), Wiley (1994), Bergner (1995), Twerski (1995), Baron (1998), Godwin (2000), and Maine (2000). See also further titles in chapter 13, "The Myth of the Self."

19 We have seen earlier in this book (chapters 13 and 14) that—in strangely distorted forms—some of these principles play an important role in our lives, and that, for instance, one of the main sources of the hectic happyism of consumer civilization is the fear of death.

20 As we have seen in the section on "The emergence and disappearance of the self," according to deconstructionists in chapter 10, efforts of "self-reconstruction" are futile because there is no such thing as an essential human self that could be "reconstructed."

21 See, e.g., Stein, Vidich, and Manning (1960); Lash (1984); and Gergen (1991).

22 Muller (1987, 19, 16). The last sentence is an allusion to a line in the famous poem of W. B. Yeats, "The Second Coming": "Things fall apart; the center cannot hold."

23 "*Macht* = strong power; *Weltanschauung* = culture-centered view of the world: *Selbstanschauung* (proposed neologism) = self-centered view of the world" (Castells 1997, 355).

24 See also Kiros (1998).

25 See note 49 in chapter 9.

26 For a concise but excellent comparison of the Western and the Buddhist conceptions of the self, see Kolm (1986).

27 World Bank (2000, table 2.17).

References

Abdullahi, Ramatu. 1986. *Self-Concept and Cultural Change among the Hausa.* Ibadan: Ibadan University Press.

Aboulafia, Mitchell. 1986. *The Mediating Self: Mead, Sartre, and Self-Determination.* New Haven, Conn.: Yale University Press.

Adair, John G., David Bélanger, and Kenneth Dion, eds. 1998. *Advances in Psychological Science, I: Social, Personal and Cultural Aspects.* Philadelphia: Psychology Press.

Adam, Barbara, Ulrich Beck, and Joost Van Loon, eds. 2000. *The Risk Society and Beyond.* London: Sage.

Adams, Judith A. 1991. *The American Amusement Park Industry: A History of Technology and Thrills.* Boston: Twayne.

Adler, Alfred. 1941. *Understanding Human Nature.* New York: World Publishing Co. (German original, 1927.)

——. 1967. *The Individual Psychology of Alfred Adler,* ed. Heinz L. Ansbacher and Rowena Ansbacher. New York: Harper & Row.

——. 1979 (1964). *Superiority and Social Interest. A Collection of Later Writings,* 3rd rev. edition, ed. Heinz L. Ansbacher and Rowena Ansbacher. New York: W. W. Norton.

Adorno, Theodor W. 1991. *The Culture Industry.* London: Routledge.

—— W., et al. 1969 (1950). *The Authoritarian Personality.* New York: W. W. Norton.

Alexander, Jeffrey C., Bernhard Giesen, Richard Münch, and Neil J. Smelser, eds. 1987. *The Micro–Macro Link.* Berkeley: University of California Press.

Alexander, Jeffrey C., and Steven Seidman, eds. 1990. *Culture and Society: Contemporary Debates.* Cambridge: Cambridge University Press.

Allen, Douglas, and Ashok Malhotra, eds. 1997. *Culture and Self: Philosophical and Religious Perspectives, East and West.* Boulder, Colo.: Westview Press.

Allport, Gordon W. 1937. *Personality: A Psychological Interpretation.* New York: Holt.

———. 1961. *Pattern and Growth in Personality.* New York: Holt, Rinehart and Winston.

Allport, Gordon W., and Leo Postman. 1965 (1947). *The Psychology of Rumor.* New York: Russell & Russell.

Althans, Brigit. 2000. *Der Klatsch, die Frauen und das Sprechen bei der Arbeit.* Frankfurt: Campus.

Ames, Roger T., and Thomas P. Kasulis, and Wimal Dissanayake, eds. 1998. *Self-Image in Asian Theory and Practice.* Albany: State University of New York Press.

Amy Vanderbilt's Etiquette. 1972 (1952). New York: Doubleday, Anchor Books.

Anderson, Ann Kiemel, and Jean Kiemel Ream. 1986. *Struggling for Wholeness.* Nashville: Oliver-Nelson Books.

Anderson, Walt. 1997. *The Future of the Self: Inventing the Postmodern Person.* New York: J. P. Tarcher.

Appadurai, Arjun, ed. 2001. *Globalization:* Durham, N.C.: Duke University Press.

Arac, Jonathan, ed. 1986. *Postmodernism and Politics.* Minneapolis: University of Minnesota Press.

Arato, Andrew, and Eike Gebhardt, eds. 1978. *The Essential Frankfurt School Reader.* New York: Urizen Books.

Arditi, Jorge. 1999. Etiquette Books, Discourse and the Deployment of an Order of Things. *Theory, Culture and Society* 16, no. 4: 25–48.

Aresti, Esther. 1970. *The Best Behavior: The Course of Good Manners. From Antiquity to the Present—As Seen through Courtesy and Etiquette Books.* New York: Simon & Schuster.

Ariés, Philippe. 1962. *Centuries of Childhood: A Social History of Family Life,* trans. Robert Baldick. New York: Vintage.

Ariés, Philippe, and Georges Duby, eds. 1987–91. *A History of Private Life,* 5 vols. Cambridge, Mass.: Belknap Press.

Arnason, Johann P., S. N. Eisenstadt, and Björn Wittrock, eds. 2004. *Axial Civilization and World History:* Leiden: Brill.

Aronson, Elliot, and Anthony R. Pratkanis, eds. 1993. *Social Psychology,* 3 vols. New York: New York University Press.

Aronson, Elliot, Timothy D. Wilson, and Robin M. Akert. 2004. *Social Psychology,* 5th ed. Upper Saddle River, N.J.: Prentice-Hall.

Aronson, Elliot, Timothy D. Wilson, and Marylinn B. Brewer. 1998. Experimentation in Social Psychology. In *The Handbook of Social Psychology,* vol. 1, ed. Daniel T. Gilbert, Susan T. Fiske, and Gardner Lindzey. New York: McGraw-Hill.

Augé, Marc. 1995. *Non-Places: Introduction to the Anthropology of Supermodernity.* Cambridge: Polity.

Austin. J. L. 1962. *How to Do Things With Words.* Oxford: Basil Blackwell.

Bachelard, Gaston. 1964a. *The Poetics of Space,* trans. Maria Jolas. Foreword by Étienne Gilson. New York: Orion Press.

———. 1964b. *The Psychoanalysis of Fire,* trans. Alan C. M. Ross. Boston: Beacon Press.

———. 1969. *The Poetics of Reverie,* trans. Daniel Russell. New York: Orion Press.

Bacon, Francis, Sir. 1985 (1597). *Essays,* ed. Michael Kiernan. Cambridge, Mass.: Harvard University Press.

Bailey, Peter. 1978. *Leisure and Class in Victorian England: Rational Recreation and the Contest for Control, 1830–1885* London: Routledge & Kegan Paul.

———. 1986. *Music Hall: The Business of Pleasure.* Milton Keynes, U.K.: Open University Press.

Baker, Nancy C. 1984. *The Beauty Trap.* New York: Franklin Watts.

Bakhtin, Mikhail Mikhailovich. 1968. *Rabelais and His World.* Cambridge, Mass: MIT Press.

Balota, David A., and Elizabeth J. Marsh, eds. 2003. *Cognitive Psychology: Key Readings.* New York: Psychology Press.

Barbas, Samantha. 2002. *Movie Crazy: Fans, Stars, and the Cult of Celebrity.* New York: Palgrave Macmillan.

Barber, Benjamin R. 1995. *Jihad vs. McWorld.* New York: Times Books.

Bargh, John A. 1986–96. Auto-Motives: Preconscious Determinants of Social Interaction. In *Handbook of Motivation and Cognition,* vol. 2, ed. Richard M. Sorrentino and Raymond L. Higgins. New York: Guilford Press.

Barker, Rodney S. 2001. *Legitimating Identities: The Self-Presentation of Rulers and Subjects.* New York: Cambridge University Press.

Barkow, Jerome H. 1992. Beneath New Culture Is Old Psychology: Gossip and Social Stratification. In *The Adapted Mind. Evolutionary Psychology and the Generation of Culture,* ed. Jerome H. Barkow, Leda Cosmides, and John Tooby. New York: Oxford University Press.

Barkow, Jerome H., Leda Cosmides, and John Tooby, eds. 1992. *The Adapted Mind. Evolutionary Psychology and the Generation of Culture.* New York: Oxford University Press.

Barnard, Malcolm. 1996. *Fashion as Communication*. London: Routledge.

Barnes, John. A. 1994. *A Pack of Lies. Toward a Sociology of Lying*. Cambridge: Cambridge University Press.

Baron, Renee. 1998. *What Type Am I? Discover Who You Really Are,* illustrated by Miriam Fabbri. New York: Penguin Books.

Baron, Reuben M. 1997. On Making Terror Management Theory Less Motivational and More Social. *Psychological Inquiry* 8, no. 1: 21–22.

Barrett, William. 1987. *Death of the Soul. Philosophical Thought from Descartes to the Computer*. Oxford: Oxford University Press.

Barth, Karl. 1953 (1919). *Der Römerbrief*. Zürich: EVZ Verlag.

Barthes, Roland. 1972. *Mythologies*. New York: Hill and Wang.

———. 1983. *The Fashion System,* trans. Matthew Ward and Richard Howard. Berkeley: University of California Press. (French original, 1967.)

Bassham, Gregory, and Eric Bronson, eds. 2003. *The Lord of the Rings and Philosophy: One Book to Rule Them All*. Chicago: Open Court.

Battaglia, Debbora, ed. 1995. *Rhetorics of Self-Making*. Berkeley: University of California Press.

Baudelaire, Charles. 1964. *The Painter of Modern Life and Other Essays,* trans. J. Mayne. London: Phaidon.

Baudrillard, Jean. 1970. *La société de consommation*. Paris: Gallimard.

———. 1988a. Consumer Society. In *Selected Writings,* by Jean Baudrillard, ed. Mark Poster. Oxford: Polity Press.

———. 1988b. *Selected Writings,* ed. Mark Poster. Oxford: Polity Press.

———. 1990. *Seduction*. London: Macmillan.

———. 1993. *Symbolic Exchange and Death*. London: Sage.

———. 1994. *Simulacra and Simulations*. Ann Arbor: University of Michigan Press.

———. 1998. *The Consumer Society. Myths and Structures*. London: Sage. (French original, 1970.)

Bauman, Zygmunt. 1991. *Modernity and Ambivalence*. Oxford: Polity Press.

———. 1992. *Intimations of Postmodernity*. London: Routledge.

———. 1993. *Postmodern Ethics*. Oxford: Blackwell.

Baumeister, Roy F. 1986a. *Identity: Cultural Change and the Struggle for Self*. New York: Oxford University Press.

———, ed. 1986b. *Public and Private Self*. New York: Springer.

———. 1991a. *Escaping the Self: Alcoholism, Spirituality, Masochism, and Other Flights from the Burden of Selfhood*. New York: Basic Books.

———. 1991b. *Meanings of Life*. New York: Guilford Press.

———, ed. 1993. *Self-Esteem: The Puzzle of Low Self-Regard*. New York: Plenum Press.

———. 1998. The Self. In *The Handbook of Social Psychology*, vol. 1, ed. Daniel T. Gilbert, Susan T. Fiske, and Gardner Lindzey. New York: McGraw-Hill.

———, ed. 1999. *The Self in Social Psychology. Key Readings*. Philadelphia: Psychology Press.

Beattie, Melody. 1998. *Stop Being Mean to Yourself: A Story about Finding the True Meaning of Self-Love*. Center City, Minn.: Hazelden.

Beaussant, Philippe. 2000. *Le Roi-Soleil se lève aussi*. Paris: Gallimard.

Beck, Ulrich. 1992. *Risk Society: Towards a New Modernity*. London: Sage.

———. 1997. *The Reinvention of Politics: Rethinking Modernity in the Global Social Order*. Cambridge: Polity.

Becker, Ernest. 1973. *The Denial of Death*. New York: Free Press.

Beelman, Axel. 1990. *Die Krisis des Subjekts: Cartesianismus, Phänomenologie und Existenzanalytik unter anthropologischen Aspekten*. Bonn: Bouvier.

Beetham, Elizabeth. 1996. *A Magazine of Her Own? Domesticity and Desire in the Women's Magazine, 1800–1914*. New York: Routledge.

Belk, Russell W. 1989. Extended Self and Extending Paradigmatic Perspective: Comment. *Journal of Consumer Research. An Interdisciplinary Quarterly* 16, no. 1: 129–32.

Bell, Daniel. 1976. *Coming of Post-Industrial Society: A Venture in Social Forecasting*. New York: Basic Books.

Bellah, Robert, et al. 1985. *Habits of the Heart*. Berkeley: University of California Press.

Benchetritt, Paul. 1952. A History of Hamlet in France. Diss., University of Birmingham, Birmingham.

Benda, Julien. 1969. *The Treason of the Intellectuals*, trans. R. Aldington. New York: W. W. Norton. (French original: *La trahison des clercs*, 1927.)

Benedict, Ruth. 1946. *The Chrysanthemum and the Sword*. Boston: Houghton Miffin.

Benedict, Saint, Abbot of Montecassino. 2001. *Saint Benedict's Rule for Monasteries*, trans. L. J. Doyle. Collegeville, Minn.: St. John's Abbey Press.

Benjamin, Walter. 1982. *Das Passagen-Werk*, 2 vols., ed. R. Tiedemann. Frankfurt: Suhrkamp.

———. 1986a (1968). *Illuminations*, ed. Hannah Arendt and trans. Harry Zohn. New York: Schocken Books.

———. 1986b. The Work of Art in the Age of Mechanical Reproduction. In *Illuminations* by Walter Benjamin, ed. Hannah Arendt and trans. Harry Zohn. New York: Schocken Books.

Bennett, Tony, and Janet Woollacott. 1987. *Bond and Beyond: The Political Carrier of a Popular Hero.* New York: Methuen.

Bennett, Tony, et al., eds. 1983. *Formations of Pleasure.* London: Routledge & Kegan Paul.

Benoit, Pamela J. 1997. *Telling the Success Story: Acclaiming and Disclaiming Discourse.* Albany: State University of New York Press.

Benstock, Shari, and Suzanne Ferris, eds. 1994. *On Fashion.* New Brunswick, N.J.: Rutgers University Press.

Bercovitch, Sacvan. 1975. *The Puritan Origins of the American Self.* New Haven, Conn.: Yale University Press.

Berdyaev, Nicolas. 1927. *Das neue Mittelalter.* Darmstadt: O. Reichl. (Russian original: Berlin, 1924.)

Berger, Peter L. 1967. *The Sacred Canopy: Elements of a Sociological Theory of Religion.* New York: Doubleday. (Reprinted in 1990 as an Anchor Book.)

———. 1969. *A Rumor of Angels: Modern Society and the Rediscovery of the Supernatural.* New York: Doubleday. (Reprinted in 1990 as an Anchor Book.)

Berger, Peter L., Brigitte Berger, and Hansfried Kellner. 1973. *The Homeless Mind: Modernization and Consciousness.* New York: Random House.

Berger, Peter L., and Samuel P. Huntington, eds. 2002. *Many Globalizations: Cultural Diversity in the Contemporary World.* Oxford: Oxford University Press.

Berger, Peter L., and Thomas Luckmann. 1966. *The Social Construction of Reality: A Treatise in the Sociology of Knowledge.* Garden City, N.Y.: Doubleday.

Bergmann, Jorg R. 1993. *Discreet Indiscretions: The Social Organization of Gossip.* New York: Aldine de Gruyter.

Bergner, Raymond M. 1995. *Pathological Self-Criticism: Assessment and Treatment.* New York: Plenum Press.

Berman, Marshall. 1982. *All That Is Solid Melts into Air.* New York: Simon & Schuster.

Berman, Morris. 1981. *The Reenchantment of the World.* Ithaca, N.Y.: Cornell University Press.

Bermúdez, Jose Luis. 1998. *Paradox of Self-Consciousness.* Cambridge, Mass.: MIT Press.

Bermúdez, Jose Luis, Anthony Marcel, and Naomi Eilan, eds. 1995. *The Body and the Self.* Cambridge, Mass.: MIT Press.

Berne, Eric. 1972. *What Do You Say After You Say Hello? The Psychology of Human Destiny.* New York: Grove Press.

Bernhard, Yetta. 1975. *How to Be Somebody: Open the Door to Personal Growth.* Millbrae, Calif.: Celestial Arts.

Berofsky, Bernard. 1995. *Liberation from Self: A Theory of Personal Autonomy.* New York: Cambridge University Press.

Bertens, Hans. 1995. *The Idea of the Postmodern: A History.* New York: Routledge.

Bertrand, Gilles, Anna Michalski, and Lucio R. Pench. 1999. *Scenarios Europe 2010: Five Possible Futures for Europe.* Working Paper, Forward Study Unit. Brussels: European Commission.

Best, Steven, and Douglas Kellner. 1997. *The Postmodern Turn.* New York: Guilford Press.

Birnbaum, Pierre, and Jeane Leca, eds. 1990. *Individualism: Theories and Methods,* trans. John Gaffne. New York: Oxford University Press.

Birtchnell, John. 2003. *The Two of Me: The Rational Outer Me and the Emotional Inner Me.* London: Routledge.

Bless, Herbert, and Joseph P. Forgas, eds. 2000. *The Message Within: The Role of Subjective Experience in Social Cognition and Behavior.* Philadelphia: Psychology Press.

Bloom, Allan. 1987. *The Closing of the American Mind.* New York: Simon & Schuster.

Bloomfield, Harold H., and Leonard Felder. 1985. *The Achilles Syndrome: Transforming Your Weaknesses into Strengths.* New York: Random House.

Blumer, Herbert. 1969. *Symbolic Interactionism.* Englewood Cliffs, N.J.: Prentice-Hall.

Bock, Philip K., ed. 1994. *Handbook of Psychological Anthropology.* Westport, Conn.: Greenwood Press.

Body & Society. 1995. Vol. 1, no. 1 (March). Thousand Oaks, Calif.: Sage Publications.

Boenisch, Julia. 1999. First Lady auf Rollerblades: "Christina Rau, die Gattin des neuen Bundespräsidenten." *Bunte* 3: 30–32.

Böhm, Thomas, Birte Lock, and Thomas Streicher, eds. 1989. *Die Zweite Haut: Über Moden.* Hamburg: Rohwolt.

Bohrer, Karl Heinz, ed. 1983. *Mythos und Moderne.* Frankfurt: Suhrkamp.

Bordo, Suzan. 2004. *Unbearable Weight: Feminism, Western Culture, and the Body.* Berkeley: University of California Press.

Borkenau, Franz. 1981. *End and Beginning: On the Generation of Cultures and the Origins of the West,* ed. Richard Lowenthal. New York: Columbia University Press.

Borst, Arno. 1993. *The Ordering of Time: From the Ancient Computus to the Modern Computer,* trans. Andrew Winnard. Cambridge: Polity Press.

Bourdieu, Pierre. 1984. *Distinction: A Social Critique of the Judgment of Taste.* Cambridge, Mass.: Harvard University Press.

———. 1991. *Language and Symbolic Power.* Cambridge: Polity Press.

———. 1998. *Les règles de l'art: Genèse et structure du champs littéraire.* Paris: Seuil.

Bourguignon, Erika. 1979. *Psychological Anthropology.* New York: Holt, Rinehart and Winston.

Bouyer, Sylvain, and Alain Gaffet, eds. 1997. *Anthropologie du tabac.* Paris: L'Harmattan.

Boven, Leaf Van, and Thomas Gilovitch. 2003. To Do or to Have? That Is the Question. *Journal of Personality and Social Psychology* 85, no. 6: 1193–1202.

Branam, George C. 1956. *Eighteenth-Century Adaptations of Shakespearean Tragedy.* Berkeley: University of California Press.

Braudel, Ferdinand. 1972–73. *The Mediterranean and the Mediterranean World in the Age of Philip II,* 2 vols., trans. Siân Reynolds. London: Collins.

———. 1992. *Civilization and Capitalism, 15th–18th Century,* 3 vols., trans. Siân Reynolds. Berkeley: University of California Press.

Braverman, Harry. 1974. *Labor and Monopoly Capital: The Degradation of Work in the Twentieth Century.* New York, Monthly Review Press.

Brehm, Sharon S., and Saul M. Kassin. 1993. *Social Psychology,* 2nd ed. Boston: Houghton Mifflin.

Brewer, John, and Roy Porter, eds. 1993. *Consumption and the World of Goods.* London: Routledge.

Bridges, John. 2003. *A Gentleman Gets Dressed Up: What to Wear, When to Wear It, How to Wear It.* Nashville: Rutledge Hill Press.

Brinthaupt, Thomas M., and Richard P. Lipka, eds. 1994. *Changing the Self: Philosophies, Techniques, and Experiences.* Albany: State University of New York Press.

Brittan, Arthur. 1977. *The Privatised World.* London: Routledge & Kegan Paul.

Broadben, Geoffrey, Richard Bunt, and Charles Jencks, eds. 1980. *Signs, Symbols, and Architecture.* New York: John Wiley and Sons.

Bronfenbrenner, Urie. 1970. *Two Worlds of Childhood: U.S. and U.S.S.R.* New York: Russell Sage Foundation.

———. 1979. *The Ecology of Human Development: Experiments by Nature and Design.* Cambridge, Mass.: Harvard University Press.

Bronson, Eric, ed. 2004. *Baseball and Philosophy: Thinking Outside the Batter's Box.* Chicago: Open Court.

Brooks, David. 2000. *Bobos in Paradise: The New Upper Class and How They Got There.* New York: Simon & Schuster.

Brown, Byron 1999. *Soul without Shame: A Guide to Liberating Yourself from the Judge.* Boston: Shambhala.

Brown, Jonathan D. 1998 (1975). *The Self.* New York: McGraw-Hill.

Brown, Norman O. 1959. *Life Against Death: The Psychoanalytical Meaning of History.* New York: Viking Books.

Bruner, Jerome S. 1986. *Actual Minds, Possible Worlds.* Cambridge, Mass.: Harvard University Press.

———. 1990. *Acts of Meaning.* Cambridge, Mass.: Harvard University Press.

Brunner, Otto, Werner Conze, and Reinhart Koselleck, eds. 1978. *Geschichtliche Grundbegriffe: Historisches Lexikon zur politisch-sozialen Sprache in Deutschland.* Stuttgart: Klett-Cotta.

Bryman, Alan. 1995. *Disney and His Worlds.* London: Routledge.

Brzezinski, Zbigniew. 1990. Post-Victory Blues. Lecture, Academy of World Inquiry, School of Foreign Service, Georgetown University, Washington, October 25.

Buber, Martin. 1970. *I and Thou.* New York: Charles Scribner.

Buci-Glucksmann, Christine. 1994. *Baroque Reason: The Aesthetics of Modernity,* trans. Patrick Camiller. London: Sage.

Buckingham, Marcus, and Donald O. Clifton. 2001. *Now, Discover Your Strengths.* New York: Free Press.

Bühler, Charlotte Malachowski, James F. T. Bugentak, and Fred Massarik. 1968. *The Course of Human Life: A Study of Goals in Humanistic Perspective.* New York: Springer.

Burckhardt, Jacob. 1943. *Force and Freedom: Reflections on History,* trans. James H. Nichols. New York: Pantheon Books. (German original: *Weltgeschichtliche Betrachtungen,* 1905.)

———. 1958. *The Civilization of the Renaissance in Italy,* 2 vols., trans. S. G. C. Middlemore. New York: Harper Brothers. (German original, 1860.)

Burdach, Konrad. 1970 (1918). *Reformation, Renaissance, Humanismus: Zwei Abhandlungen über die Grundlage moderner Bildung und Sprachkunst.* Darmstadt: Wissenschaftliche Buchgesellschaft.

Bürger, Peter. 1998. *Die Verschwinden des Subjekts: Eine Geschichte der Subjektivität von Montaigne bis Barthes.* Frankfurt: Suhrkamp.

Burn, David D. 1999. *The Feeling Good Handbook,* rev. ed. New York: Penguin.

Burr, Vivien. 2002. *The Person in Social Psychology* . Philadelphia: Psychology Press.

Buss, David M. 1997. Human Social Motivation in Evolutionary Perspective: Grounding Terror Management Theory. *Psychological Inquiry* 8, no. 1: 22–26.

Butler, J. 1997. *Excitable Speech: A Politics of the Performative*. New York: Routledge.

Button, Graham, ed. 1991. *Ethnomethodology and the Human Sciences*. Cambridge: Cambridge University Press.

Cadava, Eduardo, Peter Connor, and Jean-Luc Nancy, eds. 1991. *Who Comes after the Subject*. New York: Routledge.

Caillois, Roger. 1950. *L'homme et le sacré,* ed. augmentée. Paris: Gallimard.

Calinescu, Matei. 1977. *Five Faces of Modernity: Modernism—Avant Garde—Decadence —Kitsch—Postmodernism*. Bloomington: Indiana University Press.

Camery-Hoggatt, Jerry A. 2002. *Grapevine: The Spirituality of Gossip*. Scottdale, Pa.: Herald Press.

Campbell, Colin. 1989. *The Romantic Ethic and the Spirit of Modern Consumerism*. Oxford: Blackwell.

Campbell, Eileen, and Fran Holt-Underwood. 1994. *Body, Mind and Spirit: A Dictionary of New Age Ideas, People, Places, and Terms,* new ed. Boston: C. E. Tuttle.

Campbell, Joseph. 1968. *The Hero with a Thousand Faces*. Princeton, N.J.: Princeton University Press.

———. 1993 (1972). *Myths to Live By: How We Re-create Ancient Legends in Our Daily Lives to Release Human Potential*. New York: Penguin.

Camus, Albert. 1971. *The Rebel*. New York: Alfred A. Knopf. (French original, 1951.)

Canfield, John V. 1990. *The Looking-Glass Self: An Examination of Self-Awareness*. New York: Praeger.

Cantor, Nancy, and John F. Kihlstrom, eds. 1981. *Personality, Cognition, and Social Interaction*. Hillsdale, N.J.: Lawrence Erlbaum Associates.

Carr, David. 1999. *The Paradox of Subjectivity: The Self in the Transcendental Tradition*. New York: Oxford University Press.

Carrithers, Michael, Steven Collins, and Steven Lukes, eds. 1985. *The Category of the Person: Anthropology, Philosophy, History*. New York: Cambridge University Press.

Carson, Gerald. 1966. *The Polite Americans: A Wide-Angle View of Our More or Less Good Manners over 300 Years*. New York: Morrow.

Carver, Charles S., and Michael F. Scheier. 2004. *Perspectives on Personality,* 5th ed. Boston: Pearson.

Cash, Thomas F. 1995. *What Do You See When You Look in the Mirror? Helping Yourself to a Positive Body Image*. New York: Bantam Books.

———. 1997. *The Body Image Workbook: An 8-Step Program for Learning to Like Your Looks*. Oakland: New Harbinger.

Cash, Thomas F., and Thomas Pruzinsky, eds. 2002. *Body Image: A Handbook of Theory, Research, and Clinical Practice*. New York: Guilford Press.

Cassirer, Ernst. 1944. *An Essay on Man: An Introduction to the Philosophy of Human Culture*. New Haven, Conn.: Yale University Press.

———. 1953–96. *The Philosophy of Symbolic Forms*, 4 vols., trans. Ralph Manheim and John Michael Krois. New Haven, Conn.: Yale University Press.

———. 2000. *The Individual and the Cosmos in Renaissance Philosophy*, trans. Mario Dormandi. Mineola, N.Y.: Dover Publications.

Castells, Manuel. 1997. *The Power of Identity* (vol. 2 of *The Information Age: Economy, Society, and Culture*). London: Blackwell.

Castiglione, Baldesar. 1959. *The Book of the Courtier*, trans. Friench Simpson. New York: F. Ungar. (Italian original, 1528; first English translation, 1561.)

Cattell, Raymond B. 1950. *Personality: A Systematic Theoretical and Factual Study*. New York: McGraw-Hill.

Cattell, Raymond B., and Dennis Child. 1975. *Motivation and Dynamic Structure*. New York: John Wiley and Sons.

Cavarero, Adriana. 2000. *Relating Narratives: Storytelling and Selfhood*, trans. Paul Kottman. London: Routledge.

Cawelti, John G. 1965. *Apostles of the Self-Made Man*. Chicago: Chicago University Press.

Celik, Zeynep, Diane Favro, and Richard Ingersol, eds. 1994. *Streets: Critical Perspectives on Public Space*. Berkeley: University of California Press.

Certau, Michel de. 1984. *The Practice of Everyday Life*, trans. Steven Rendall. Berkeley: University of California Press.

Certau, Michel de, Luce Giard, and Pierre Mayol. 1988. *The Practice of Everyday Life, Volume 2: Living and Cooking*, trans. Timothy J. Tomasik. Minneapolis: University of Minnesota Press.

Cervone, Daniel, and Walter Mischel, eds. 2002. *Advances in Personality Science*. New York: Guilford Press.

Cervone, Daniel, and Y. Shoda, eds. 1999. *The Coherence of Personality: Social-Cognitive Bases of Consistency, Variability, and Organization*. New York: Guilford Press.

Chaney, David. 1983. The Department Store as a Cultural Form. *Theory, Culture and Society* 1, no. 3.

Ciarrochi, Joseph P., John Forgas, and D. Mayer, eds. 2001. *Emotional Intelligence in Everyday Life: A Scientific Inquiry*. Philadelphia: Psychology Press.

Cheung, Theresa. 2003. *Coffee Wisdom: 7 Finely Ground Principles for Living a Full-Bodied Life*. Boston: Conari Press.

Cholakian, Patricia Francis. 2000. *Women and the Politics of Self-Representation in Seventeenth-Century France.* Newark: University of Delaware Press.

Christman, John Philip, ed. 1989. *The Inner Citadel: Essays on Individual Autonomy.* New York: Oxford University Press.

Clammer, John. 1997. *Contemporary Urban Japan: A Sociology of Consumption.* Oxford: Blackwell.

Clifton, Donald O., and Paula Nelson. 1996. *Soar with Your Strengths.* New York: Dell.

Cloninger, C. Robert. 1994. *The Temperament and Character Inventory (TCI): A Guide to Its Development and Use.* Saint Louis: Center for Psychobiology of Personality, Washington University.

Cohen, Anthony P. 1994. *Self-Consciousness: An Alternative Anthropology of Identity.* New York: Routledge.

Cohen, David B. 1979. *Sleep and Dreaming.* Oxford: Pergamon Press.

Cohen, Richard. 1993. Waiting for New Meaning in a Post–Cold War World. *International Herald Tribune,* October 27.

Cohen, William A. 1996. *Sex Scandal: The Private Parts of Victorian Fiction.* Durham, N.C.: Duke University Press.

Cole, J. Preston. 1971. *The Problematic Self in Kirkegaard and Freud.* New Haven, Conn.: Yale University Press.

Coleman, Emily, and Betty Edwards. 1977. *Body Liberation: Freeing Your Body for Greater Self-Acceptance, Health, and Sexual Satisfaction.* Los Angeles: J. P. Tarcher.

Coleman, Patrick, Jayne Lewis, and Jill Kowalik, eds. 2000. *Representations of the Self from the Renaissance to Romanticism.* New York: Cambridge University Press.

Collins, Gail. 1998. *Scorpion Tongues: Gossip, Celebrity, and American Politics.* New York: William Morrow.

Collins, Steven. 1982. *Selfless Persons. Imagery and Thought in Theravada Buddhism.* New York: Cambridge University Press.

Conklin, P. S. 1947. *A History of "Hamlet" Criticism, 1601–1821.* New York, King's Crown Press.

Conway, Katherine E. 1904. *The Christian Gentlewoman and Its Social Apostolate.* Boston: Thomas J. Flynn.

Cooke, Philip. 1990. *Back to the Future: Modernity, Postmodernity and Locality.* London: Unwin Hyman.

Corner, John, and Dick Pels, eds. 2003. *Media and the Restyling of Politics: Consumerism, Celebrity and Cynicism.* Thousand Oaks, Calif.: Sage.

Corrigan, Peter. 1997. *The Sociology of Consumption: An Introduction.* London: Sage.

Couldry, Nick. 2003. *Media Rituals: A Critical Approach*. New York: Routledge.

Coulon, Alain. 1995. *Ethnomethodology*, trans. Jacqueline Coulon and Jack Katz. Thousand Oaks, Calif.: Sage.

Coulter, Jeff. 1979. *The Social Construction of the Mind: Studies in Ethnomethodology and Linguistic Philosophy*. London: Macmillan.

———, ed. 1990. *Ethnomethodological Sociology*. Brookfield, Vt.: Edward Elgar.

Cox, Stephen D. 1980. *"The Stranger Within Thee": The Concept of the Self in Late Eighteenth Century Literature*. Pittsburgh: Pittsburgh University Press.

Craik, George L. 1972 (1831). *Pursuit of Knowledge under Difficulties*, rev. ed. London: Bell and Daldy.

Cross, Susan E., and Jonathan S. Gore. 2003. Cultural Models of the Self. In *Handbook of Self and Identity*, ed. Mark L. Leary and June Price Tangney. New York: Guilford Press.

Csikszentmihalyi, Mihaly. 1975. *Beyond Boredom and Anxiety*. San Francisco: Jossey-Bass.

———. 1990. *Flow: The Psychology of Optimal Experience*. New York: Harper & Row.

———. 1993. *The Evolving Self: A Psychology for the Third Millennium*. New York: HarperCollins.

———. 1997. *Finding Flow. The Philosophy of Engagement with Everyday Life*. New York: Basic Books.

———. 2003. *Good Business: Leadership, Flow, and the Making of Meaning*. New York: Viking.

Csikszentmihalyi, Mihaly, and Eugene Rochberg-Halton. 1981. *The Meaning of Things: Domestic Symbols and the Self*. Cambridge: Cambridge University Press.

Curtis, Rebecca C., ed. 1989. *Self-Defeating Behaviors: Experimental Research, Clinical Impressions, and Practical Implications*. New York: Plenum.

———. 1991. *The Relational Self: Theoretical Convergences in Psychoanalysis and Social Psychology*. New York: Guilford Press.

Dahl, Bernhoff A. 2003. *Optimize Your Life with the One-Page Strategic Planner*. Bangor, Me.: Wind-Breaker Press.

Dahrendorf, Ralf. 1997. *After 1989: Morals, Revolution, and Civil Society*. New York: St. Martin's Press.

Daily, Steven. 1999. Posh and Becks. *Vanity Fair*, September, 136–43.

Damasio, Antonio R. 1994. *Descartes' Error: Emotion, Reason, and the Human Brain*. New York: Putnam.

Damon, William, ed. 1998. *Handbook of Child Psychology*, 5th ed., 4 vols. New York: John Wiley and Sons.

Damon, William, and Daniel Hart. 1988. *Self-Understanding in Childhood and Adolescence*. Cambridge: Cambridge University Press.

Danziger, Kurt. 1990. *Constructing the Subject: Historical Origins of Psychological Research*. Cambridge: Cambridge University Press.

Davies, Paul. 1995. *About Time*. London: Penguin.

Davis, Stan, and Christopher Meyer. 2000. What Will Replace the Techno-Economy. *Time,* May 29.

Dawkins, Richard. 1976. *The Selfish Gene*. Oxford: Oxford University Press.

Dean, Amy. 1991. *LifeGoals: Setting and Achieving Goals to Chart the Course of Your Life*. Santa Monica, Calif.: Hay House.

Debord, Guy. 1994 (1967). *The Society of the Spectacle*. New York: Zone Books.

Deci, Edward L., and Richard M. Ryan. 1985. *Intrinsic Motivation and Self-Determination in Human Behavior*. New York: Plenum Press.

Decorum: A Practical Treatise on Etiquette and Dress of the Best American Society. 1877. Chicago: J. A. Ruth.

Delory-Momberger, Christine. 2000. *Les histoires de vie: De l'invention de soi au projet formation*. Paris: Anthropos.

Delumeau, Jean. 1990. *Sin and Fear: The Emergence of a Western Guilt Culture, 13th–18th Centuries*. New York: St. Martin's Press.

Dennett, Daniel C. 1984. *Elbow Room: The Varieties of Free Will Worth Wanting*. Cambridge. Mass.: MIT Press.

———. 1988. Why Everyone Is a Novelist. *Times Literary Supplement* 49, no. 4: 1016, 1028–29.

———. 1991. *Consciousness Explained*. Boston: Little, Brown.

Denning, Michael. 1987. *Cover Stories: Narrative and Ideology in the British Spy Thriller*. London: Routledge.

Denzin, Norman K. 1995. *The Cinematic Society: The Voyeur's Gaze*. London: Sage.

Derlega, Valerian J., and John H. Berg, eds. 1987. *Self-Disclosure. Theory, Research, and Therapy*. New York: Plenum Press.

Derrida, Jacques. 1973. *Speech and Phenomena,* trans. David B. Allison and Newton Garver. Evanston, Ill.: Northwestern University Press.

———. 1976. *Of Grammatology,* trans. G. Ch. Spivak. Baltimore: Johns Hopkins University Press.

———. 1978. *Writing and Difference,* trans. Alan Bass. Chicago: Chicago University Press.

Devine, P. G., D. C. Hamilton, and T. M. Ostrom, eds. 1994. *Social Cognition: Impact on Social Psychology.* New York: Academic Press.

Devos, Thierry, and Mahzarin R. Banaji. 2003. Implicit Self and Identity. In *Handbook of Self and Identity,* ed. Mark L. Leary and June Price Tangney. New York: Guilford Press.

Dichter, Ernest. 1964. *Handbook of Consumer Motivations: The Psychology of the World of Objects.* New York: McGraw-Hill.

———. 1971. *Motivating Human Behavior.* New York: McGraw-Hill.

Dillon, Robin S., ed. 1995. *Dignity, Character, and Self-Respect.* New York: Routledge.

Dollimore, Jonathan. 1997. Death and the Self. In *Rewriting the Self: Histories from the Renaissance to the Present,* ed. Roy Porter. London: Routledge.

Domhoff, G. Williams. 1996. *The Meaning of Dreams.* New York: Plenum Press.

Doniger, Wendy. 1996. Sex, Lies, and Tall Tales. In *Truth-Telling, Lying and Self-Deception,* ed. Arien Mack. *Social Research* 63, no. 3.

———. 2000. *The Bedtrick: Tales of Sex and Masquerade.* Chicago: Chicago University Press.

———. 2005. *The Woman Who Pretended to Be Who She Was: Myths of Self-Imitation.* New York: Oxford University Press.

Doob, Leonard W. 1971. *Patterning of Time.* New Haven, Conn.: Yale University Press.

Dorset, Thomas Sackville, Earl of. 1960 (1563). *The Mirror for Magistrates,* ed. Lily B. Campbell. New York: Barnes & Noble.

Douglas, Jack D., and Patricia A. Adler. 1980. *Introduction to the Sociology of Everyday Life.* Boston: Allyn and Bacon.

Douglas, Jack D., John M. Johnson, and David L. Altheide, eds. 1977. *Existential Sociology.* New York: Cambridge University Press.

Douglas, Mary, ed. 1973. *Rules and Meanings: The Anthropology of Everyday Knowledge.* Harmondsworth, U.K.: Penguin.

Duijker, H. C. J., and Nico H. Frijda. 1960. *National Character and National Stereotypes: A Trend Report Prepared for the International Union of Scientific Psychology.* Amsterdam: North-Holland.

Duis, Perry. 1998. *Challenging Chicago: Coping with Everyday Life, 1987–1920.* Urbana: University of Illinois Press.

Durand, Gilbert. 1969. *Les structures anthropologiques de l'imaginaire.* Grenoble: Dunod.

Dürrschmidt, Jorg. 2000. *Everyday Lives in the Global City: The Delinking of Locale and Milieu.* New York: Routledge.

Dweck, Carol S. 1999. *Self-Theories: Their Role in Motivation, Personality, and Development*. Philadelphia: Psychology Press.

Easton, Susan, A. Hawkins, S. Laing, and H. Walker. 1988. *Disorder and Discipline. Popular Culture from 1955 to the Present*. London: Temple Smith.

Ebbighausen, Rolf, and Sighard Neckel, eds. 1989. *Anatomie des politischen Skandals*. Frankfurt: Suhrkamp.

Eicher, Joanne B., Sandra Lee Evenson, and Hazel A. Lutz, eds. 2000. *The Visible Self: Global Perspectives on Dress, Culture, and Society*, 2nd ed. New York: Fairchild.

Eisenstadt, Shmuel N. 1983. *Tradition, Change and Modernity*. New York: John Wiley and Sons.

———. 2000. Multiple Modernities. *Daedalus* 129: 1–29.

Eliade, Mircea. 1959. *The Sacred and the Profane. The Nature of Religion*, trans. W. R. Trask. New York: Harcourt Brace.

———. 1961. *Myths, Dreams, and Mysteries: The Encounter between Contemporary Faiths and Archaic Realities*, trans. Philip Mairet. New York: Harper & Row.

———. 1963. *Myth and Reality*, trans. Willard R. Trask. New York: Harper & Row.

———. 1978–85. *A History of Religious Ideas*, 3 vols. Chicago: Chicago University Press.

Elias, Norbert. 1982. *The Civilizing Process: State Formation and Civilization*, trans. Edmund Jephcott. Oxford: Blackwell. (Original edition, 1939.)

———. 1983. *The Court Society*, trans. Edmund Jephcott. New York: Pantheon.

———. 1991. *The Society of Individuals*, ed. Michael Schröter and trans. Edmund Jephcott. Oxford: Blackwell.

Eliot, Alexander. 1997. *The Timeless Myths: How Ancient Legends Influence the Modern World*. New York: Meridian.

Eliot. T. S. 1934. *After Strange Gods: A Primer of Modern Heresy*. London: Faber and Faber.

Elliott, Charles H., and Laura L. Smith. 2003. *Overcoming Anxiety for Dummies*. New York: John Wiley and Sons.

Ellis, Keith. 1998. *The Magic Lamp: Goal Setting for People Who Hate Setting Goals*, rev. ed. New York: Three Rivers Press.

Ellul, Jacques. 1964. *The Technological Society*. New York: Vintage.

Elshtain, Jean. 1981. *Public Man, Private Woman: Women in Social and Political Thought*. Princeton, N.J.: Princeton University Press.

Elster, John, ed. 1986. *The Multiple Self*. Cambridge: Cambridge University Press.

Elyot, Thomas, Sir. 1970 (1531). *The Book Named the Governor*, ed. John M. Major. New York: Teachers College Press.

Emmons, Robert A. 1991. Personal Strivings, Daily Life Events, and Psychological and Physical Well-Being. *Journal of Personality* 59: 453–72.

———. 1999. *The Psychology of Ultimate Concerns: Motivation and Spirituality in Personality.* New York: Guilford Press.

Englert, Andreas C. 1999. Sophie Rhys-Jones: Ihr Nacktfoto erschüttert die Monarchie. *Bunte* 23: 24–27.

Erasmus. 1982 (1520). *Adagia,* trans. Margaret Mann Philips. Toronto: University of Toronto Press.

Erdman, Cheri K. 1995. *Nothing to Lose: A Guide to Sane Living in a Larger Body.* San Francisco: Harper San Francisco.

Erikson, Erik H. 1959. *Identity and the Life Cycle.* New York: International Universities Press.

———. 1968. *Identity, Youth, and Crisis.* New York: W. W. Norton.

Estés, Clarissa Pinkola. 1995. *Women Who Run with the Wolves: Myths and Stories of the Wild Woman Archetype.* New York: Ballantine Books.

Evans, Dylan. 2003. *Emotion: A Very Short Introduction.* Oxford: Oxford University Press.

Ewen, Stuart. 1976. *Captains of Consciousness: Advertising and the Social Roots of the Consumer Culture.* New York: McGraw-Hill.

———. 1988. *All-Consuming Images: The Politics of Style in Contemporary Culture.* New York: Basic Books.

Ewen, Stuart, and Elizabeth Ewen. 1982. *Channels of Desire: Mass Images and the Shaping of American Consciousness.* New York: McGraw-Hill.

Eysenck, Hans Jürgen. 2000. *Smoking, Health and Personality.* With a new foreword by Stuart Brady. New Brunswick, N.J.: Transaction Publishers.

Eysenck, Michael W., and Mark T. Keane. 2005. *Cognitive Psychology: A Student's Handbook,* 5th ed. New York: Psychology Press.

Falk, Pasi. 1994. *The Consuming Body.* London: Sage.

Falk, Pasi, and Colin Campbell, eds. 1997. *The Shopping Experience.* London: Sage.

Faret, Nicolas. 1970 (1630). *L'honneste-homme, ou l'art de plaire à la court.* Paris: Toussaincts Du Bray. Slatkine Reprints.

Farrar, Eliza. (Farrar, Mrs. John) 1849. *The Young Lady's Friend.* New York: Samuel S. and William Wood.

Faver, Mel D. 1996. *New Age Thinking: A Psychoanalytic Critique.* Ottawa: University of Ottawa Press.

Featherstone, Mike, ed. 1990. *Global Culture, Nationalism, Globalization and Modernity.* London: Sage.

————. 1991. *Consumer Culture and Postmodernism*. London: Sage.

————. 1995. *Undoing Culture: Globalization, Postmodernism and Identity.* London: Sage.

————, ed. 2000. *Body Modification*. London: Sage.

Featherstone, Mike, Mike Hepworth, and Bryan S. Turner, eds. 1991. *The Body: Social Process and Cultural Theory.* London: Sage.

Featherstone, Mike, and Scott Lash. 1995. Globalization, Modernity and the Spatialization of Social Theory: An Introduction. In *Global Modernities,* ed. Mike Featherstone, Scott Lash, and Roland Robertson. Thousand Oaks, Calif.: Sage Publications.

Featherstone, Mike, Scott Lash, and Roland Robertson, eds. 1995. *Global Modernities.* Thousand Oaks, Calif.: Sage Publications.

Fellman, Stephen M. 1995. *Vinyl Leaves: Walt Disney World and America*. Boulder, Colo.: Westview Press.

Festinger, Leon. 1957. *A Theory of Cognitive Dissonance*. Evanston, Ill.: Row, Peterson.

Fingarette, Herbert. 1969. *Self-Deception*. London: Routledge & Kegan Paul.

Finkelstein, Joanne. 1991. *The Fashioned Self*. Oxford: Polity Press.

Fisher, Seymour. 1986. *Development and Structure of the Body Image,* 2 vols. Hillsdale, N.J.: Lawrence Erlbaum Associates.

Fivush, Robyn, and Catherine A. Haden, eds. 2003. *Autobiographical Memory and the Construction of the Narrative Self: Developmental and Cultural Perspectives.* Mahwah, N.J.: Lawrence Erlbaum Associates.

Fleissner, P., and J. K. Nyiri. 1999. *Philosophy of Culture and Electronic Networking,* vol. 1. Innsbruck: Studien-Verlag–Áron Kiadó.

Flournoy, Théodore. 1917. *The Philosophy of William James*. London: Constable.

Flynn, Pierce Julius. 1991. *The Ethnomethodological Movement: Sociosemiotic Interpretations.* New York: Mouton de Gruyter.

Ford, Stephen. 1672. *The Evil Tongue Tryed and Found Guilty, or, The Hainousness and Exceeding Sinfulness of Defaming and Back-Biting Opened and Declared: Wherein Is Shewed That a Defaming and Back-Biting Tongue Is a Most Pernicious and Grievous Plague to Man-Kind / Published for the Common Good . . . by Stephen Ford.* London: Printed for Nath. Crouch.

Forgas, Joseph P., ed. 2000. *Feeling and Thinking: The Role of Affect in Social Cognition.* New York: Cambridge University Press.

Forgas, Joseph P., and Kipling D. Williams, eds. 2001. *Social Influence: Direct and Indirect Processes.* Philadelphia: Psychology Press.

————. 2002. *The Social Self: Cognitive, Interpersonal, and Intergroup Perspectives.* New York: Psychology Press.

Foster, Dean. 2000. *The Global Etiquette Guide to Europe: Everything You Need to Know for Business and Travel Success.* New York: John Wiley and Sons.

Foucault, Michel. 1974. *The Order of Things: An Archeology of the Human Science.* London: Tavistock. (French original, 1966.)

———. 1982. *Michel Foucault: Beyond Structuralism and Hermeneutics,* ed. Hubert L. Dreyfus and Paul Rabinow. Chicago: Chicago University Press.

———. 1988a. *The Final Foucault,* ed. James Bernauer and David Rasmussen. Cambridge, Mass.: MIT Press.

———. 1988b. *Technologies of the Self: A Seminar with Michel Foucault,* ed. Luther H. Martin, Huck Gutman, and Patrick H. Hutton. Amherst: University of Massachusetts Press.

———. 2001. *L'herméneutique du sujet: Cours au Collège de France, 1981–1982,* ed. François Ewald, Alessandro Fontana, and Frédéric Gros. Paris: Gallimard.

Foucault, Michel, and Ludwig Binswanger. 1994. *Dream and Experience.* Atlantic Highlands, N.J.: Humanities Press.

Fox, Richard W., and T. Jackson Lears, eds. 1983. *The Culture of Consumption: Critical Essays in American History, 1889–1980.* New York: Pantheon.

Fraisse, Paul. 1975. *The Psychology of Time,* trans. Jennifer Leith. Westport, Conn.: Greenwood Press.

Frank, Robert H. 1999. *Luxury Fever: Why Money Fails to Satisfy in an Era of Excess.* New York: Free Press.

Frankl, Victor E. 1963. *Man's Search for Meaning.* Boston: Beacon Press.

Fraser, Julius Thomas. 1978. *Time as Conflict: A Scientific and Humanistic Story.* Basel: Birkhäuser.

Fraser, J. T., Marlene P. Soulsby, and Alexander J. Argyros. 1998. *Time, Order, Chaos.* Madison, Conn. : International Universities Press.

Frederick, J. George. 1985 (1925). *Masters of Advertising Copy.* New York: Garland.

Freedman, Rita. 1988. *Beauty Bound: Why Women Strive for Physical Perfection.* London: Columbus Books.

Freud, Anna. 1937. *The Ego and the Mechanisms of Defense.* London: Hogarth Press.

Freud, Sigmund. 1956 (1900). *The Interpretation of Dreams.* New York: Basic Books.

———. 1959a. Inhibitions, Symptoms and Anxiety. In *The Standard Edition of the Complete Psychological Works of Sigmund Freud,* vol. 20, ed. James Strachey. London: Hogarth Press.

———. 1959b. *The Standard Edition of the Complete Psychological Works of Sigmund Freud,* vol. 20, ed. James Strachey. London: Hogarth Press.

————. 1989. *The Ego and the Id,* trans. Joan Riviere. New York: W. W. Norton.

Friedman, Jonathan. 1992. Narcissism, Roots and Postmodernity: The Constitution of Selfhood in the Global Crisis. In *Modernity and Identity,* ed. Scott Lash and Jonathan Friedman. Oxford: Blackwell.

Frijda, Nico H. 1986. *The Emotions.* Cambridge: Cambridge University Press.

Frisby, David. 1985. *Fragments of Modernity: Theories of Modernity in the Work of Simmel, Kracauer and Benjamin.* Oxford: Polity Press.

Fromm, Erich. 1969 (1941). *Escape from Freedom.* New York: Holt.

————. 1976. *To Have or to Be?* New York: Harper & Row.

Fukuyama, Francis. 1992. *The End of History and the Last Man.* New York: Free Press.

————. 1999. *The Great Disruption: Human Nature and the Reconstruction of Social Order.* New York: Free Press.

Fuller, Thomas. 1938 (1642). *The Holy State,* trans. Maximilian Graf Walten. New York: Columbia University Press.

Füst, Milan. 1989. *The Story of My Wife: The Reminiscences of Captain Störr: A Novel,* trans. Ivan Sanders. New York: Vintage Books.

Gagnier, Regenia. 1991. *Subjectivities: A History of Self-Representation in Britain, 1832–1920.* New York: Oxford University Press.

Gaines, Jane, and Charlotte Herzog, eds. 1990. *Fabrications: Costume and the Female Body.* New York: Sage.

Gallagher, Shaun, and Jonathan Shear, eds. 1999. *Models of the Self.* Thorverton, U.K.: Academic.

Gardiner, Michael. 2000. *Critiques of Everyday Life.* New York: Routledge.

Gardner, C., and J. Sheppard. 1989. *Consuming Passion: The Rise of Retail Culture.* London: Unwin Hyman.

Garfinkel, Harold. 1967. *Studies in Ethnomethodology.* Englewood Cliffs, N.J.: Prentice-Hall.

Garton-Ash, Timothy 2004. *Free World : America, Europe, and the Surprising Future of the West.* New York: Random House.

Gay, Paul du, and Stuart Hall. 1996. *Doing Cultural Studies: The Story of the Sony Walkman.* London: Sage.

Geertz, Clifford. 1973a. The Impact of the Concept of Culture on the Concept of Man. In *The Interpretation of Cultures: Selected Essays.* New York: Basic Books.

————. 1973b. *The Interpretation of Cultures: Selected Essays.* New York: Basic Books.

————. 1979. From the Native's Point of View: On the Nature of Anthropological Understanding. In *Interpretive Social Science: A Reader,* ed. Paul Rabinow and William M. Sullivan. Berkeley: University of California Press.

Gehlen, Arnold. 1988. *Man: His Nature and Place in the Universe.* New York: Columbia University Press. (German original, 1940.)

Gellner, Ernest. 1992. *Postmodernism, Reason and Religion.* London: Routledge.

Gergen, Kenneth J. 1991. *The Saturated Self: Dilemmas of Identity in Contemporary Life.* New York: Basic Books.

Gergen, Kenneth J., and K. E. Davies, eds. 1985. *The Social Construction of the Person.* New York: Springer.

Gerth, Hansm, and Charles Wright Mill, eds. 1958. *From Max Weber.* New York: Oxford University Press.

Giacalone, Robert A., and Paul Rosenfeld, eds. 1989. *Impression Management in the Organization.* Hillsdale, N.J.: Lawrence Erlbaum Associates.

———. 1991. *Applied Impression Management: How Image-Making Affects Managerial Decisions.* Newbury Park. Calif.: Sage.

Giddens, Anthony. 1990. *The Consequences of Modernity.* Oxford: Polity Press.

———. 1993. *Modernity and Self-Identity: Self and Society in the Late Modern Age.* Cambridge: Polity Press.

Gilbert, Daniel T., Susan T. Fiske, and Gardner Lindzey, eds. 1998. *The Handbook of Social Psychology,* 4th ed., 2 vols. New York: McGraw-Hill.

Gilligan, Carol. 1982. *In a Different Voice: Psychological Theory and Women's Development.* Cambridge, Mass.: Harvard University Press.

Gilovich, Thomas. 2002. Egocentrism and the Social Self. Anchoring (and Adjustment) in Self and Social Judgments. In *The Social Self: Cognitive, Interpersonal, and Intergroup Perspectives,* ed. Joseph P. Forgas and Kipling D. Williams. New York: Psychology Press.

Girard, René. 1977 (1972). *Violence and the Sacred,* trans. Patrick Gregory. Baltimore: Johns Hopkins University Press.

Gloege, Martin E. 1992. The American Origins of the Postmodern Self. In *Constructions of the Self,* ed. George Levine. New Brunswick, N.J.: Rutgers University Press.

Gluckman, Max. 1963. Gossip and Scandal. *Current Anthropology* 4: 307–16.

Godwin, Malcolm. 2000. *Who Are You? 101 Ways of Seeing Yourself.* New York: Penguin Books.

Goetz, Walter. 1907. Mittelalter und Renaissance. *Historische Zeitschrift* 97: 30–54.

Goffman, Erving. 1959. *The Presentation of Self in Everyday Life.* Garden City, N.Y.: Doubleday.

———. 1961. *Asylums.* Garden City, N.Y.: Doubleday.

———. 1966. *Behavior in Public Spaces: Notes on the Social Organization of Gatherings.* New York: Free Press.

———. 1970. *Strategic Interaction.* Oxford: Blackwell.

———. 1972. *Relations in Public: Microstudies of the Public Order.* Harmondsworth, U.K.: Penguin.

———. 1974. *Frame Analysis: An Essay on the Organization of Experience.* New York: Harper & Row.

Goldberg, Arnold, ed. 2002. *Postmodern Self Psychology.* Hillsdale, NJ: Analytic Press.

Goldman, Robert. 1992. *Reading Ads Socially.* London: Routledge.

Goldman, Robert, and Stephen Papson, eds. 1996. S*ign Wars: The Cluttered Landscape of Advertising.* New York: Guilford Press.

———. 1998. *Nike Culture: The Sign of the Swoosh.* London: Sage.

Goleman, Daniel. 1995. *Emotional Intelligence.* New York: Bantam Books.

Gollwitzer, Peter M. 1986. Striving for Specific Identities: The Social Reality of Self-Symbolizing. In *Public and Private Self,* ed. Roy F. Baumeister. New York: Springer.

Gollwitzer, Peter M., and John A. Bargh, eds. 1996. *The Psychology of Action: Linking Cognition and Motivation to Behavior.* New York: Guilford Press.

Gombár, Csaba, and Hédi Volosin, eds. 2000. *A kérdéses civilizáció* [The questionable civilization]. Budapest: Helikon.

Gottdiener, Mark. 1997. *The Theming of America: Dreams, Visions, and Commercial Spaces.* Boulder, Colo.: Westview Press.

Greenblatt, Stephen. 1980. *Renaissance Self-Fashioning: From More to Shakespeare.* Chicago: University of Chicago Press.

Greene, Richard, and Peter Vernezze, eds. 2004. *The Sopranos and Philosophy: I Kill Therefore I Am.* Chicago: Open Court.

Gregg, Gary S. 1991. *Self-Representation: Life Narrative Studies in Identity and Ideology.* New York: Greenwood Press.

Grodin, Debra, and Thomas R. Lindlof (ed.). 1996. *Constructing the Self in a Mediated World.* Thousand Oaks, CA: Sage.

Groys, Boris. 1993. Rosszija kak podszoznanyije Zapada [Russia, the Subconscious of the West]. In *Utopija I obmne* (Moscow).

Gumbrecht, Hans Ulrich. 1978. Modern, Modernität, Moderne. In *Geschichtliche Grundbegriffe: Historisches Lexikon zur politisch-sozialen Sprache in Deutschland,* vol. 4, ed. Otto Brunner, Werner Conze, and Reinhart Koselleck. Stuttgart: Klett-Cotta.

Gurevich, Aron Yakovlevich. (1995). *The Origins of European Individualism,* trans. Katherine Judelson. Cambridge, Mass.: Blackwell.

Gurvitch, Georges. 1964. *The Spectrum of Social Time,* ed. and trans. Myrtle Korenbaum. Dordrecht: D. Reidel.

Habermas, Jürgen. 1979a. *Communication and the Evolution of Society.* Boston: Beacon Press.

———. 1979b. Einleitung. In *Stichworte zur "Geistigen Situation der Zeit."* Frankfurt: Suhrkamp.

———. 1979c. *Stichworte zur "Geistigen Situation der Zeit."* Frankfurt: Suhrkamp.

———. 1987a. *The Philosophical Discourse of Modernity: Twelve Lectures,* trans. Frederick Lawrence. Cambridge, Mass.: MIT Press.

———. 1987b. *The Theory of Communicative Action, Volume Two: Lifeworld and System; A Critique of Functionalist Reason,* trans. Thomas McCarthy. Boston: Beacon Press.

Hacking, Ian. 1995. *Rewriting the Soul: Multiple Personality and the Science of Memory.* Princeton, N.J.: Princeton University Press.

Haefner, H. 1971. Angst, Furcht. In *Historisches Wörterbuch der Philosophie,* vol. 1, ed. Joachim Ritter and Karlfried Gründer. Basel: Schwabe.

Halbwachs, Maurice. 1950. *La mémoire collective.* Paris: Presses Universitaires de France.

Hall, Calvin S., Gardner Lindzey, and John B. Campbell. 1998. *Theories of Personality.* New York: Wiley.

Hallowell, A. I. 1955. *Culture and Experience.* Philadelphia: University of Pennsylvania Press.

Halter, Marilyn. 2000. *Shopping for Identity: The Marketing of Ethnicity,* New York: Shocken.

Halton, Eugene. 1995. The Modern Error: Or, the Unbearable Enlightenment of Being. In *Global Modernities,* ed. Mike Featherstone, Scott Lash, and Roland Robertson. Thousand Oaks, Calif.: Sage Publications.

Hamilton, V. Lee, and Joseph Sanders. 1992. *Everyday Justice: Responsibility and the Individual in Japan and the United States.* New Haven, Conn.: Yale University Press.

Hampson, Sarah E. 1988. *The Construction of Personality: An Introduction,* 2nd ed. London: Routledge.

———, ed. 2000. *Advances in Personality Psychology,* vol. 1. Philadelphia: Psychology Press.

Hamvas, Béla. 1983. *Világválság* [World Crisis]. Budapest: Magvető.

Handel, Michael J., ed. 2003. *The Sociology of Organizations: Classic, Contemporary, and Critical Readings.* Thousand Oaks, Calif: Sage.

Hankiss, Elemér. 1977. *Érték és társadalom* [Values and society]. Budapest: Magvető.

———. 1999a. Proletár Reneszánsz [Proletarian Ranaissance]. In *Proletár Reneszánsz:*

Tanulmányok az európai civilizációról és a magyar társadalomról [Proletarian Renaissance: Essays in European Civilization]. Budapest: Helikon.

———. 1999b. *Proletár Reneszánsz: Tanulmányok az európai civilizációról és a magyar társadalomról* [Proletarian Renaissance: Essays in European Civilization]. Budapest: Helikon.

———. 2001. *Fears and Symbols: An Introduction to the Study of Western Civilization.* Budapest: Central European University Press.

Hankiss, Elemér, Róbert Manchin, László Füstös, and Árpád Szakolczai. 1982. *Kényszerpályán? A magyar társadalom értékrendszerének alakulása 1930 és 1980 között* [On a Forced Path? The Transformation of Value Beliefs in Hungary between 1930 and 1980]. Budapest: Institute of Sociology, Hungarian Academy of Sciences.

Hanson, Karen. 1986. *The Self Imagined: Philosophical Reflections on the Social Character of Psyche.* New York: Routledge & Kegan Paul.

Harvey, David R. 1985. *Consciousness and the Urban Experience: Studies in the History and Theory of Capitalist Urbanization.* Baltimore: Johns Hopkins University Press.

———. 1989. *The Condition of Postmodernity: An Enquiry into the Origins of Cultural Change.* Oxford: Blackwell.

Hassan, Ihab. 1988. *The Postmodern Turn: Essays in Postmodern Theory and Culture.* Columbus: Ohio State University Press.

Hattie, John. 1992. *Self-Concept.* Hillsdale, N.J.: L. Earlbaum Associates.

Hauck, Paul A. 1991. *Overcoming the Rating Game: Beyond Self-Love, Beyond Self-Esteem.* Louisville: Westminster / John Knox Press.

———. 1998. *How to Cope with People Who Drive You Crazy.* London: Sheldon Press.

Havel, Václav. 1985a. The Power of the Powerless. In *The Power of the Powerless: Citizens against the State in Central Eastern Europe,* ed. John Keane. Armonk, N.Y.: M. E. Sharpe.

Havel, Václav, et al. 1985b. *The Power of the Powerless: Citizens against the State in Central Eastern Europe,* ed. John Keane. Armonk, N.Y.: M. E. Sharpe.

Hawking, Stephen W. 1988. *A Brief History of Time.* London: Bantam.

Hay, Louise L., and Linda Carwin Tomchin. 1991. *The Power Is Within You.* Carson, Calif.: Hay House.

Hayek, Friedrich von. 1979. *Law, Legislation and History, Volume 3: The Political Order of a Free People.* London: Routlege & Kegan Paul.

Heckhausen, Jutta, and Carol S. Dweck, eds. 1998. *Motivation and Self-Regulation across the Life Span.* New York: Cambridge University Press.

Hefner, Robert, ed. 1998. *Market Cultures: Society and Moralities in the New Asian Capitalisms.* Boulder, Colo: Westview Press.

Heidegger, Martin. 1962. *Being and Time,* trans. John Macquarrie and Edward Robinson. New York: Harper & Row. (German original, 1927.)

———. 1990. *Kant and the Problem of Metaphysics,* trans. Richard Taft. Bloomington: Indiana University Press.

Heilmann, Ann, and Margaret Beetham. 2004. *New Woman Hybridities: Femininity, Feminism ad International Consumer Culture, 1880–1930.* New York: Routledge.

Heise, David R. 1979. *Understanding Events: Affect and the Constitution of Social Action.* Cambridge: Cambridge University Press.

Heller, Agnes. 1978. *Renaissance Man,* trans. Richard E. Allen. London: Routledge & Kegan Paul. (Hungarian original, 1967.)

———. 1984. *Everyday Life,* trans. G. L. Campbell. London: Routledge & Kegan Paul.

———. 1992. The Death of the Subject. In *Constructions of the Self,* ed. George Levine. New Brunswick, N.J.: Rutgers University Press.

Heller, Thomas. C., Morton Sosna, and David E. Wellbery, eds. 1986. *Reconstructing Individualism: Autonomy, Individuality and the Self in Western Thought.* Stanford, Calif.: Stanford University Press.

Herrick, James A. 2003. *The Making of the New Spirituality: The Eclipse of the Western Religious Tradition.* Downers Grove, Ill.: InterVarsity Press.

Hetherington, E. Mavis. 1983. *Handbook of Child Psychology: Socialization, Personality, and Social Development.* New York: John Wiley and Sons.

Hewitt, John P. 1994. *Self and Society: A Symbolic Interactionist Social Psychology,* 6th ed. Boston: Allyn and Bacon.

Higgins, Raymond L., C. R. Snyder, and Steven Berglas. 1990. *Self-Handicapping. The Paradox that Isn't.* New York: Plenum.

Higgins, E. Tory, and Arie W. Kruglanski, eds. 1996. *Social Psychology: Handbook of Basic Principles.* New York: Guilford Press.

———. 2000. *Motivational Science: Social and Personality Perspectives.* Philadelphia: Psychology Press.

Hilbert, R. A., and R. Collins. 1992. *The Classical Roots of Ethnomethodology: Durkheim, Weber and Garfinkel.* Chapel Hill, N.C.: University of North Carolina Press.

Hill, Napoleon, 1988 (1937). *Think and Grow Rich.* New York: Fawcett.

Hill, Thomas E. 1991. *Autonomy and Self-Respect.* Cambridge: Cambridge University Press.

Hills, Matt. 2002. *Fan Cultures.* New York: Routledge.

Himmelfarb, Gertrude. 1995 (1994). *The De-Modernization of Society. From Victorian Virtues to Modern Values.* New York: Alfred A. Knopf.

Hine, Thomas. 1986. *Populuxe*. New York: Alfred A. Knopf.

Hinton, A. L., ed. 1999. *Biocultural Approaches to the Emotions*. New York: Cambridge University Press.

Hirt, Edward R., and McCrae, Sean. 2001. Positioning Self-Handicapping within the Self-Zoo: Just What Kind of Animal Are We Dealing With Here? Draft of paper to be presented at the Fourth Sydney Symposium on Social Psychology, The Social Self: Cognitive, Interpersonal, and Intergroup Perspectives, Sydney, March 20–22 (http://www.sydneysymposium.unsw.edu.au/2001/downloads/sydney.paper.txt).

Hitélet. 1997. *Hitélet: Imakönyv népénekeskönyv melléklettel* [Life of the Faithful: Prayer and song book], 4th ed. Szeged: Agapé.

Hobsbawm, Eric. 1995 (1994). *Age of Extremes: The Short Twentieth Century, 1914–1991*. London: Michael Joseph.

Hogan, Robert, John A. Johnson, and Stephen R. Briggs, eds. 1997. *Social Psychology: Handbook of Basic Principles*. San Diego: Academic Press.

Hogg, Michael A., and Joel Cooper, eds. 2003. *The Sage Handbook of Social Psychology*. 2 vols. Thousand Oaks, Calif: Sage.

Hogg, Michael A., and Deborah J. Terry, eds. 2002. *Social Identity Processes in Organizational Contexts*. Philadelphia: Psychology Press.

Hollander, Anne. 1993. *Seeing through Clothes*. Berkeley: University of California Press.

Holler, Manfred J., ed. 1999. *Scandal and Its Theory*. Munich: Accedo-Verlag-Gesellschaft.

Horkheimer, Max. 1947. *Eclipse of Reason*. New York: Oxford University Press.

———. 1972. *Critical Theory: Selected Essays*. New York: Herder and Herder.

———. 1978. The End of Reason. In *The Essential Frankfurt School Reader,* ed. Andrew Arato and Eike Gebhardt. New York: Urizen Books.

Hormuth, Stefan E. 1990. *The Ecology of the Self: Relocation and Self-Concept Change*. New York: Cambridge University Press.

Horne, John, David Jary, and Alan Tomlinson, eds. 1987. *Sport, Leisure, and Social Relations*. New York: Routledge & Kegan Paul.

Horney, Karen. 1937. *The Neurotic Personality of Our Time*. New York: W. W. Norton.

———. 1950. *Neurosis and Human Growth: The Struggle Toward Self-Realization*. New York: W. W. Norton.

Horton, Raymond L. 1984. *Buyer Behavior: A Decision Making Approach*. Columbus: Charles E. Merrill.

Howe, Irving. 1992. The Self in Literature. In *Constructions of the Self,* ed. George Levine. New Brunswick, N.J.: Rutgers University Press.

Hoyle, Rick H., M. H. Kernis, M. R. Leary, and M. W. Baldwin. 1999. *Selfhood: Identity, Esteem, Regulation.* Boulder, Colo.: Westview Press.

Hughes, Diane Owen, and Thomas R. Trautmann, eds. 1995. *Time: Histories and Ethnologies.* Ann Arbor: University of Michigan Press.

Huizinga, Johan. 1959a. *Men and Ideas: History, the Middle Ages, the Renaissance—Essays.* New York: Meridian Books. (Dutch original, 1920.)

————. 1959b. The Problem of the Renaissance. In *Men and Ideas: History, the Middle Ages, the Renaissance—Essays.* New York: Meridian Books. (Dutch original, 1920.)

Huntington, Samuel. 1996. *The Clash of Civilizations and the Remaking of World Order.* New York: W. W. Norton.

Husserl, Edmund. 1970. *The Crisis of European Sciences and Transcendental Phenomenology.* Evanston, Ill.: Northwestern University Press.

Hutchison, Elizabeth D., ed. 2003. *Dimensions of Human Behavior: Volume 1, Person and Environment;* and *Volume 2, The Changing Life Course,* 2nd ed. Thousand Oaks, Calif.: Sage.

Hutton, Patrick H. 1988. Foucault, Freud, and the Technologies of the Self. In *The Final Foucault,* ed. James Bernauer and David Rasmussen. Cambridge, Mass.: MIT Press.

Huxtable, Ada Louise. 1997. *The Unreal America: Architecture and Illusion.* New York: New Press–W. W. Norton.

Ickes, William, and Eric S. Knowles, eds. 1982. *Personality, Roles, and Social Behavior.* New York: Springer.

Illouz, Eva. 1997. *Consuming the Romantic Utopia.* Berkeley: University of California Press.

Inglehart, Ronald. 1990. *Culture Shift in Advanced Industrial Society.* Princeton, N.J.: Princeton University Press.

————. 1997. *Modernization and Postmodernization: Cultural, Economic and Political Change in 43 Societies.* Princeton, N.J.: Princeton University Press.

Inkeles, Alex, ed. 1997. *National Character: A Psycho-Social Perspective.* With contributions by D. J. Levinson et al. New Brunswick, N.J.: Transaction Publishers.

Inkeles, Alex, and Raymond Bauer (with David Gleicher and Irving Rosow). 1959. *The Soviet Citizen: Daily Life in a Totalitarian Society.* Cambridge, Mass.: Harvard University Press.

Inkeles, Alex, and David Smith. 1974. *Becoming Modern: Individual Change in Six Developing Countries.* Cambridge, Mass.: Harvard University Press.

Innes, Robert. 1999. *Discourses of the Self: Seeking Wholeness in Theology and Psychology.* New York: P. Lang.

Irwin, William, ed. 2000. *Seinfeld and Philosophy: A Book about Everything and Nothing*. Chicago: Open Court.

———. 2002. *The Matrix and Philosophy: Welcome to the Desert of the Real*. Chicago: Open Court.

Irwin, William, Mark T. Conard, and Aeon J. Skoble, eds. 2001. *The Simpsons and Philosophy: The D'oh! of Homer*. Chicago: Open Court.

Izard, Carroll E., Jerome Kagan, and Robert B. Zajonc, eds. 1984. *Emotions, Cognition, and Behavior*. Cambridge: Cambridge University Press.

James, William. 1890. *The Principles of Psychology,* 2 vols. New York: H. Holt.

———. 1981. *The Principles of Psychology*. Cambridge, Mass.: Harvard University Press.

Jameson, Frederic. 1981. *The Political Unconscious. Narrative as a Socially Symbolic Act*. Ithaca, N.Y.: Cornell University Press.

———. 1991. *Postmodernism, or, the Cultural Logic of Late Capitalism*. Durham, N.C.: Duke University Press.

Jaspers, Karl. 1960 (1919). *Die Psychologie der Weltanschaungen,* 5th ed. Berlin: Springer.

———. 1965. *Die geistige Situation der Zeit* [The Spiritual Situation of the World] (5th ed.). Berlin: Walter de Gruyter. (Written in 1930, revised in 1932.)

———. 1978. *Man in the Modern Age*. New York: AMS Press.

Jones, Edward E., and Harold B. Gerard. 1967. *Foundations of Social Psychology*. New York: John Wiley and Sons.

Joseph, Suad (ed.). 1999. *Intimate Selving in Arab Families: Gender, Self, and Identity*. Syracuse, NY: Syracuse University Press.

Jung, Carl G. 1968. *The Archetypes and the Collective Unconscious,* vol. 9.1 in *The Collected Works of Carl G. Jung*. Princeton, N.J.: Princeton University Press.

———. 1971a. Aion: Phenomenology of the Self. In *The Portable Jung,* ed. Joseph Campbell. New York: Viking.

———. 1971b. *The Portable Jung,* ed. Joseph Campbell. New York: Viking.

———. 1971c. The Spiritual Problem of Modern Man. In *The Portable Jung,* ed. Joseph Campbell. New York: Viking. (German original, 1928.)

———. 1974. *Dreams,* trans. R. F. C. Hull. Princeton, N.J.: Princeton University Press.

Junkersdorf, Tom. 1998. Damit die Welt ein wenig besser wird. *Gala* 22: 12–15.

Kahneman, Daniel, Ed Diener, and Norbert Schwartz, eds. 1999. *Well-Being: The Foundations of Hedonic Psychology*. New York: Russell Sage Foundation.

Kai Ka'us ibn-Iskandr (Prince of Gurgan). 1951 (1082–83). *A Mirror for Princes: The Qabus Nama*. New York: Dutton.

Kaiser, Susan B. 1997. *The Social Psychology of Clothing. Symbolic Appearances in Context,* 2nd rev. ed. New York: Fairchild.

Kålltorp, Ove, et al., eds. 1997. *Cities in Transformation—Transformation in Cities: Social and Symbolic Change of Urban Space.* Brookfield, Vt.: Avebury.

Kao, H. S. R., and D. Sinha, eds. 1997. *Asian Perspectives on Psychology.* New Delhi: Sage.

Kasser, Tim, and Allen D. Kanner, eds. 2004. *Psychology and Consumer Culture: The Struggle for a Good Life in a Materialistic World.* Washington, D.C.: American Psychological Association.

Kasson, John, F. 1990. *Rudeness and Civility: Manners in Nineteenth-Century America.* New York: Hill and Wang.

Kegan, Robert. 1982. *The Evolving Self: Problem and Process in Human Development.* Cambridge, Mass.: Harvard University Press.

Kellaway, Lucy. 2002. How to Talk Yourself Up. *Financial Times,* July 3.

Kellner, Douglas. 1992. Popular Culture and the Construction of Postmodern Identities. In *Modernity and Identity,* ed. Scott Lash and Jonathan Friedman. Oxford: Blackwell.

———. 1995. *Media Culture: Cultural Studies, Identity, and Politics between the Modern and the Postmodern.* New York: Routledge.

———. 2003. *Media Spectacle.* New York: Routledge.

Kellogg, Ronald T. 2003. *Cognitive Psychology,* 2nd ed. London: Sage.

Kennedy, Paul. 1987. *The Rise and Fall of the Great Powers: Economic Change and Military Conflict from 1500 to 2000.* New York: Random House.

Kerby, Anthony Paul. 1991. *Narrative and the Self.* Bloomington: Indiana University Press.

Kernis, M. H., ed. 1995. *Efficacy, Agency, and Self-Esteem.* New York: Plenum.

Keshen, Richard. 1996. *Reasonable Self-Esteem.* Montreal: McGill–Queen's University Press.

Keyes, Ken. 1995. *Your Road Map to Lifelong Happiness: A Guide to the Life You Want.* Coos Bay, Ore.: Love Line Books.

Kierkegaard, Søren. 1954. *The Sickness Unto Death,* trans. W. Lowry. New York: Anchor Books.

———. 1959. *Either/Or,* 2 vols., trans. W. Lowry. New York: Anchor Books.

Kihlstrom, John F., Jennifer S. Beer, and Stanley B. Klein. 2003. Self and Identity as Memory. In *Handbook of Self and Identity,* ed. Mark L. Leary and June Price Tangney. New York: Guilford Press.

Kim, Tae-Chang, and Harrison, Ross eds. 1999. *Self and Future Generations: An Intercultural Conversation.* Cambridge: White Horse Press.

Kindel, Georg. 1999. Sie lebte und starb—so stark [She lived and died so strong]. *Bunte* 23: 46–49.

Kiros, Teodros. 1998. *Self-Construction and the Formation of Human Values: Truth, Language, and Desire.* Westport, Conn.: Greenwood Press.

Kitayama, Shinobo, and Hazel R. Markus, eds. 1994. *Emotion and Culture: Empirical Studies of Mutual Influence.* Washington, D.C.: American Psychological Association.

Klages, Ludwig. 1929–32. *Der Geist als Widersacher der Seele,* 3 vols. Leipzig: J. A. Barth.

Kleine, Robert E., Susan Schultz-Kleine, and Gerome B. Kernan. 1992. Mundane Everyday Consumption and the Self: A Conceptual Orientation and Prospects for Consumer Research. *Advances in Consumer Research* 19: 411–15.

Klemm, David E., and Günter Zöller, eds. 1997. *Figuring the Self: Subject, Absolute, and Others in Classical German Philosophy.* Albany: State University of New York Press.

Klibansky, Raymond, and H. J. Paton, eds. 1936. *Philosophy and History: Essays Presented to Ernst Cassirer.* Oxford: Clarendon Press.

Knight, G. Wilson. 2001 (1949). *The Wheel of Fire: Interpretations of Shakespearian Tragedy* (with an introduction by T. S. Eliot). New York: Routledge.

Kohlrusch, Eva. 1999. Darf man beim Sterben helfen? *Bunte* 23: 38–41.

Kohn, George Childs, ed. 2001. *The New Encyclopedia of American Scandal.* New York: Checkmark Books.

Kolak, Daniel and Raymond Martin. 1991. *Self and Identity: Contemporary Philosophical Issues.* New York: Macmillan.

Kolakowski, Leszek. 1989. *The Presence of Myth.* Chicago: Chicago University Press.

———. 1991. *Die Moderne auf der Anklagebank.* Zürich: Menessa Verlag.

———. 1999. *Freedom, Fame, Lying and Betrayal: Essays on Everyday Life.* Boulder, Colo.: Westview Press.

Kolm, Serge-Christophe. 1986. The Buddhist Theory of "No-self." In *The Multiple Self,* ed. John Elster. Cambridge: Cambridge University Press.

Korff, Rudiger. 1986. *Bangkok: Urban System and Everyday Life.* Fort Lauderdale: Breitenbach.

———. 2004. *Futures Past: On the Semantics of Historical Time,* trans. Keith Tribe. New York: Columbia University Press.

Kowalski, Robin M., ed. 2001. *Behaving Badly: Aversive Behaviors in Interpersonal Relationships.* Washington, D.C.: American Psychological Association.

Kowinski, William S. 1985. *The Malling of America. An Inside Look at the Great Consumer Paradise.* New York: William Morrow.

Kristeller, Paul Oskar. 1961. *Renaissance Thought, I.: The Classic, Scholastic, and Humanistic Strains.* New York: Harper & Row.

Kristeva, Julia. 1991. *Strangers to Ourselves.* New York: Columbia University Press.

Kroeber, A. L., and J. Richardson. 1940. *Three Centuries of Women's Dress Fashions.* Berkeley: University of California Press.

Krueger, David W. 1989. *Body Self and Psychological Self: A Developmental and Clinical Integration of Disorders of the Self.* New York: Brunner/Mazel.

Kundera, Milan. 2003. *The Art of the Novel,* trans. Linda Asher. New York: Perennial Classics.

La Bruyère, Jean de. 1970 (1688). *Characters,* trans. Jean Stewart. Baltimore: Penguin Books.

Laïdi, Zaki. 1994. *Un monde privé de sens.* Paris: Fayard.

———. 2000. *Le sacré du présent.* Paris: Flammarion.

Laing, Ronald. 1965. *The Divided Self: An Existential Study of Sanity and Madness.* Baltimore: Penguin.

Lane, David. J. 1996. *The Phenomenon of Teilhard: Prophet for a New Age.* Macon, Ga.: Mercer University Press.

Langman, Lauren. 1992. Neon Cages. Shopping for Subjectivity. In *Lifestyle Shopping: The Subject of Consumption,* ed. Rob Shields. London: Routledge.

Larsen, Randy J., and David Buss. 2002. *Personality Psychology: Domains of Knowledge About Human Nature.* New York: McGraw-Hill.

Lash, Christopher. 1979. *The Culture of Narcissism.* New York: W. W. Norton.

———. 1984. *The Minimal Self.* New York: W. W. Norton.

Lash, Scott. 1990. *Sociology of Postmodernism.* London: Routledge.

Lash, Scott, and Jonathan Friedman, eds. 1992. *Modernity and Identity.* Oxford: Blackwell.

Lash, Scott, Andrew Quick, and Richard Roberts, eds. 1998. *Time and Value.* London: Blackwell.

Leach, William. 1993. *Land of Desire: Merchants, Power, and the Rise of a New American Culture.* New York: Pantheon Books.

Lears, T. J. Jackson. 1983. From Salvation to Self-Realization. In *The Culture of Con-*

sumption: Critical Essays in American History,1889–1980, ed. Richard W. Fox and T. Jackson Lears. New York: Pantheon.

———. 1992. The Ad-Man and the Grand Inquisitor: Intimacy, Publicity, and the Managed Self in America, 1880–1940. In *Constructions of the Self,* ed. George Levine. New Brunswick, N.J.: Rutgers University Press.

Leary, Mark R. 1995. *Self-Presentation: Impression Management and Interpersonal Behavior.* Boulder, Colo.: Westview Press.

Leary, Mark R., and Robin M. Kowalski. 1995. *Social Anxiety.* New York: Guilford Press.

Leary, Mark R., and Lisa S. Schreindorfer. 1997. Unresolved Issues with Terror Management Theory. *Psychological Inquiry* 8, no. 1: 26–29.

Leary, Mark L., and June Price Tangney, eds. 2003a. *Handbook of Self and Identity.* New York: Guilford Press.

Leary, Mark L., and June Price Tangney. 2003b. The Self as an Organizing Construct in the Behavioral and Social Sciences. In *Handbook of Self and Identity,* ed. Mark L. Leary and June Price Tangney. New York: Guilford Press.

Lee, Martyn J., ed. 2000. *The Consumer Society Reader.* London: Blackwell.

Lee, Yueh-Ting, Clark R. McCauley, and Juris G. Draguns. 1999. *Personality and Person Perception across Cultures.* Mahwah, N.J.: Lawrence Erlbaum Associates.

Lefebvre, Henri. 1958–81. *Critique de la vie quotidienne,* 3 vols. Paris: L'Arche.

Le Goff, Jacques. 1993. *Intellectuals in the Middle Ages,* trans. Teresa Lavender Fagan. Cambridge, Mass.: Blackwell.

Leicester, Henry Marshall. 1990. *The Disenchanted Self: Representing the Subject in the Canterbury Tales.* Berkeley: University of California Press.

Levesque, C., and L. G. Pelletier. 2000. On the Investigation of Conscious and Nonconscious Regulatory Processes Underlying Intrinsic and Extrinsic Motivation. Manuscript submitted for publication.

Levin, Jack, and Arnold Arluke. 1987. *Gossip: The Inside Scoop.* New York: Plenum Press.

Levin, Jerome D. 1992. *Theories of the Self.* Washington, D.C.: Hemisphere.

Lévinas, Emmanuel. 1982. *Éthique et infini.* Paris: Fayard.

———. 1993. *Dieu, la mort et le temps.* Paris: Bernard Grasset.

Levine, George, ed. 1992. *Constructions of the Self.* New Brunswick, N.J.: Rutgers University Press.

Lewin, Kurt. 1935. *A Dynamic Theory of Personality.* New York: McGraw-Hill.

———. 1951. *Field Theory and Social Science,* ed. Dorwin Cartwright. New York: Harper and Brothers.

Lewis, C. S. 1947. *The Abolition of Man*. New York: Macmillan.

Lewis, Michael, and Jeanette M. Haviland-Jones, eds. 2004. *Handbook of Emotions*, 2nd ed. New York: Guilford Press.

Lifton, Robert Jay. 1979. *The Broken Connection: On Death and the Continuity of Life*. New York: Simon & Schuster.

———. 1993. *The Protean Self: Human Resilience in an Age of Fragmentation*. New York: Basic Books.

Lipka, Richard P., and T. M. Brinthaupt, eds. 1992. *Self-Perspectives Across the Life Span*. Albany: State University of New York Press.

Lippincott, Kristen, ed. 1999. *The Story of Time*. London: Merrell Holberton.

Lipset, S. Martin. 1960. *Political Man: The Social Bases of Politics*. Garden City, N.Y.: Doubleday.

Lipset, S. Martin, and Leo Lowenthal. 1961. *Culture and Social Character: The Work of David Riesman Reviewed*. New York: Free Press.

Lirondelle, André. 1912. *Shakespeare en Russie, 1748–1840*. Étude de littérature comparée. Paris: Hachette.

Lockard, Joan S., and Delroy L. Paulhus, eds. 1988. *Self-Deception: An Adaptive Mechanism?* Englewood Cliffs, N.J.: Prentice Hall.

Lukacs, John. 1970. *The Passing of the Modern Age*. New York: Harper & Row.

Luria, Salvador E. 1973. *Life: The Unfinished Experiment*. New York: Scribner.

Lury, Celia. 1996. *Consumer Culture*. London: Polity Press.

Lynch, Mervin D., Ardyth A. Norem-Hebeisen, and Kenneth J. Gergen, eds. 1981. *Self-Concept, Advances in Theory and Research*. Cambridge, Mass.: Ballinger.

Lyons, John O. 1978. *The Invention of the Self: The Hinge of Consciousness in the Eighteenth Century*. Carbondale: Southern Illinois University Press.

Lyotard, Jean-François. 1984. *The Postmodern Condition: A Report on Knowledge*, trans. Geoff Bennington and Brian Massumi and foreword by Fredric Jameson. Minneapolis: University of Minnesota Press. (French original, 1979.)

Mach, Ernst. 1897. *Contributions to the Analysis of Sensations*, trans. C. M. Williams. Chicago: Chicago Open Court.

MacIntyre, Alasdair. 1981. *After Virtue. A Study in Moral Theory*. Notre Dame, Ind.: University of Notre Dame Press.

Mack, Arien, ed. 1996. Truth-Telling, Lying and Self-Deception. *Social Research* 63, no. 3.

MacKinnon, Neil J. 1994. *Symbolic Interaction as Affect Control*. Albany: State University of New York Press.

Maffesoli, Michel. 1996. *The Time of the Tribes: The Decline of Individualism in Mass Society*, trans. Don Smith. London: Sage.

Mageo, Jeannette Marie, ed. 2002. *Power and the Self*. New York: Cambridge University Press.

―――. 2003. *Dreaming and the Self: New Perspectives on Subjectivity, Identity, and Emotion*. Albany: State University of New York Press.

Mahler, Margareth S., Fred Pine, and Anni Bergman. 1975. *The Psychological Birth of the Human Infant*. New York: Basic Books.

Maine, Margo. 2000. *Body Wars: Making Peace With Women's Bodies—An Activist's Guide*. Carlsbad, Calif.: Gürze Books.

Mander, Raymond, and Joe Mitchenson. 1952. *Hamlet through the Ages. A Pictorial Record from 1709*. London: Rockliff.

Mann, Thomas. 1959. *Last Essays*, trans. Richard Winston, Clara Winston, Tania Stern, and James Stern. London: Secker and Warburg.

Marcuse, Herbert. 1955. *Eros and Civilization: A Philosophical Inquiry into Freud*. Boston: Beacon Press.

―――. 1964. *One-Dimensional Man: Studies in the Ideology of Advanced Industrial Society*. Boston: Beacon Press.

Marks, Isaac M. 1987. *Fears, Phobias, and Rituals*. New York: Oxford University Press.

Markus, H., and P. Nurius. 1986. Possible Selves. *American Psychologist* 41: 954–69.

Marrs, Donald. 1990. *Executive in Passage: Career in Crisis—The Door to Uncommon Fulfilment*. Los Angeles: Barrington Sky.

Marsella, Anthony J., George DeVos, and Francis Hsu, eds. 1985. *Culture and Self: Asian and Western Perspectives*. New York: Tavistock.

Marshall, P. David. 1997. *Celebrity and Power: Fame in Contemporary Culture*. Minneapolis: University of Minnesota Press.

Martin, Leonard L., and Gerald L. Clore, eds. 2001. *Theories of Mood and Cognition: A Users Handbook*. Mahwah, N.J.: Lawrence Erlbaum Associates.

Martin, Leonard L., and Abraham Tesser, eds. 1996. *Striving and Feeling: Interactions among Goals, Affect, and Self-Regulation*. Hillsdale, N.J.: Lawrence Erlbaum Associates.

Martin, Rux. 1988. Truth, Power, Self: An Interview with Michel Foucault, October 25. In *The Final Foucault*, ed. James Bernauer and David Rasmussen. Cambridge, Mass.: MIT Press.

Maslow, Abraham H. 1954. *Motivation and Personality*. New York: Harper & Row.

―――. 1999 (1968). *Toward a Psychology of Being*, 3rd ed. New York: John Wiley and Sons.

Maurois, André. 1940. *The Art of Living*. New York: Harper and Brothers.

May, Rollo. 1950. *The Meaning of Anxiety*. New York: Ronald Press.

———. 1953. *Man's Search for Himself*. New York: W. W. Norton.

———, ed. 1969 (1960). *Existential Psychology*, 2nd ed. New York: Random House.

———. 1983. *The Discovery of Being: Writings in Existential Psychology*. New York: W. W. Norton.

May, Rollo, Ernest Angel, and Henry Ellenberger, eds. 1958. *Existence: A New Dimension in Psychiatry and Psychology*. New York: Basic Books.

Mayne, Tracy J., and George A. Bonano. 2001. *Emotions: Current Issues and Future Directions*. New York: Guilford Press.

McCall, G. J., and J. L. Simmons. 1978. *Identities and Interactions*. New York: Free Press.

McClung, William A. 1983. *The Architecture of Paradise. Survivals of Eden and Jerusalem*. Berkeley: California University Press.

McCrae, Robert R., and Jüri Allik. 2002. *The Five-Factor Model of Personality Across Cultures*. New York: Kluwer Academic / Plenum Publishers.

McCrae, Robert R., and Paul T. Costa Jr. 2003. *Personality in Adulthood: A Five-Factor Theory Perspective*, 2nd ed. New York: Guilford Press.

McGraw, Phil. 2003. *The Ultimate Weight Solution: The 7 Keys to Weight Loss Freedom*. New York: Free Press.

McIntosh, Donald. 1994. Language, Self, and Lifeworld in Habermas's "Theory of Communicative Action." *Theory and Society* 23: 1–33.

McKendrick, Neil, J. Brewer, and J. H. Plumb. 1982. *The Birth of a Consumer Society: The Commercialization of Eighteenth-Century England*. London: Europa.

McLaughlin, Brian P., and Amélie Rorty, eds. 1988. *Perspectives on Self-Deception*. Berkeley: University of California Press.

Mead, George Herbert. 1962 (1934). *Mind, Self, and Society from the Standpoint of a Social Behaviorist*. Chicago: University of Chicago Press.

Mead, Margaret. 1935. *Sex and Temperament in Three Primitive Societies*. New York: William Morrow.

———. 2001 (1928). *Coming of Age in Samoa: A Psychological Study of Primitive Youth for Western Civilisation*. New York: Perennial Classics.

Mecca, Andrew M., Neil J. Smelser, and John Vasconcellos, eds. 1989. *The Social Importance of Self-Esteem*. Berkeley: University of California Press.

Meehan, Eileen R., and Ellen Riordan, eds. 2002. *Sex and Money: Feminism and Political Economy in The Media*. Minneapolis: University of Minnesota Press.

Mehrgardt, Michael, and Eva-Maria Mehrgardt. 2001. *Selbst und Selbstlosigkeit: Ost und West im Spiegel ihrer Selbsttheorien.* Cologne: Edition Humanistische Psychologie.

Melville, Gert, and Peter von Moos, eds. 1998. *Das Öffentliche und Private in der Vormoderne.* Cologne: Böhlau.

Melville, Gert, and Markus Schürer, eds. 2002. *Das Eigene und das Ganze: Zum Individuellen im mittelalterlichen Religiosentum.* Münster: Lit.

Meyer, John W., and W. Richard Scott. 1983. *Organizational Environments: Ritual and Rationality.* Beverly Hills, Calf.: Sage.

Meyers, Diana Tietjens (ed.). 1997. *Feminists Rethink the Self.* Boulder, Colo.: Westview Press.

Michaelis, David. 1999. Great Expectations. *Vanity Fair,* September, 36–40.

Michalski, Krzysztof, ed. 1986. *Über die Krise: Castelgandolfo-Gespräche, 1985.* Stuttgart: Klett-Cotta.

Mikulincer, Mario, and Victor Florian. 1997. Do We Really Know What We Need? A Commentary on Pyszczynski, Greenberg, and Solomon. *Psychological Inquiry* 8, no. 1: 33–36.

Miles, Steve. 1998. *Consumerism as a Way of Life.* London: Sage.

Miller, Daniel R., and Guy E. Swanson. 1960. *Inner Conflict and Defense.* New York: Holt.

Miller, Michael B. 1981. *The Bon Marché. Bourgeois Culture and the Department Store.* Princeton, N.J.: Princeton University Press.

Miller, Rowland S. 1996. *Embarrassment: Poise and Peril in Everyday Life.* New York: Guilford Press.

Mischel, Walter, and Carolyn C. Morf. 2003. The Self as a Psycho-Social Dynamic Processing System: A Meta-Perspective on a Century of the Self in Psychology. In *Handbook of Self and Identity,* ed. Mark L. Leary and June Price Tangney. New York: Guilford Press.

Mitchell, W. J. Thomas, ed. 1981. *On Narrative.* Chicago: Chicago University Press.

Mitroff, Ian I., and Warren Bennis. 1989. *The Unreality Industry: The Deliberate Manufacturing of Falsehood and What It Is Doing to Our Lives.* New York: Carol Publishing.

Miyanaga, Kuniko. 1991. *The Creative Edge: Emerging Individualism in Japan.* New Brunswick, N.J.: Transaction Books.

Modell, Arnold H. 1993. *The Private Self.* Cambridge, Mass.: Harvard University Press.

Montaigne, Michel de. 1958 (1595). *Essays,* trans. J. M. Cohen. London: Penguin Books.

Morf, Carolyn C. and Ozlem Ayduk, eds. 2005. *Current Directions in Personality Psychology.* Upper Saddle River, N.J.: Pearson/Prentice Hall.

Morin, Edgar. 1993. La pensée socialiste en ruine. *Le Monde,* April 21.

Morris, Brian. 1994. *Anthropology of the Self: The Individual in Cultural Perspective.* Boulder, Colo.: Pluto Press.

Moss, Marion. 1992. *Removing Your Mask: No More Hiding from Your Truth.* Seattle: Orion.

Mullen, Brian, and Johnson, Craig. 1990. *The Psychology of Consumer Behavior.* Hillsdale, N.J.: Lawrence Erlbaum Associates.

Muller, René J. 1987. *The Marginal Self: An Existential Inquiry into Narcissism.* Atlantic Highlands, N.J.: Humanities Press International.

———. 1998. *Beyond Marginality: Constructing the Self in the Twilight of Eastern Culture.* Westport, Conn.: Praeger.

Mumford, Lewis. 1963. *Technics and Civilization.* New York: Harcourt, Brace & World.

Mummendey, Hans Dieter. 2002. *Psychologie der Selbstdarstellung.* Göttingen: Hofgrefe-Verlag für Psychologie.

Murnighan, J. Keith, ed. 1993. *Social Psychology in Organizations: Advances in Theory and Research.* Englewood Cliffs, N.J.: Prentice-Hall.

Musil, Robert. 1979. *The Man Without Qualities,* trans. Eithne Wilkins and Ernst Kaiser. London: Secker & Warburg.

Myers, David G. 1993. *Social Psychology,* 4th ed. New York: McGraw-Hill.

Negrin, Llewellyn. 1999. The Self as Image: A Critical Appraisal of Postmodern Theories of Fashion. *Theory, Culture, and Society* 16, no. 3: 99–118.

Nehamas, Alexander. 1998. *The Art of Living: Socratic Reflections from Plato to Foucault.* Berkeley: University of California Press.

Neisser, Ulric, and D. A. Jopling, eds. 1997. *The Conceptual Self in Context: Culture, Experience, Self-Understanding.* Cambridge: Cambridge University Press.

Nesse, Randolph M., and Alan T. Lloyd. 1992. Evolution of Psychodynamic Mechanisms. In *The Adapted Mind: Evolutionary Psychology and the Generation of Culture,* ed. Jerome H. Barkow, Leda Cosmides, and John Tooby. New York: Oxford University Press.

Newman, David M., and Jodi O'Brian, eds. 2004. *Sociology: Exploring the Architecture of Everyday Life,* 5th ed. Thousand Oaks, Calif: Pine Forge Press.

Ney, Tara, and Anthony Gale, eds. 1989. *Smoking and Human Behavior.* New York: John Wiley and Sons.

Nicholson, Linda, ed. 1990. *Feminism/Postmodernism.* New York: Routledge.

Niebuhr, Reinhold. 1941. *The Nature and Destiny of Man.* New York: Scribner.

Nietzsche, Friedrich. 1968. *The Will to Power,* trans. Walter Kaufmann. New York: Vintage.

———. 1980. *Sämtliche Werke: Kritische Studienausgabe in 15 Bänden,* ed. Giorgio Colli and Mazzino Montinari. New York: De Gruyter.

———. 1983. *Untimely Meditations,* trans. R. J. Hollingdale and ed. Daniel Breazeale. New York: Cambridge University Press.

———. 1986. *Human, All Too Human: A Book for Free Spirits,* trans. R. J. Hollingdale. Cambridge: Cambridge University Press.

———. 1989. *Beyond Good and Evil,* trans. Walter Kaufmann. New York: Vintage.

———. 1995. *Thus Spoke Zarathustra: A Book for All and None,* trans. Walter Kaufmann. New York: Modern Library.

Nollinger, Mark. 2004. On Shows Like *Joan of Arcadia,* Spiritual Matters Suddenly Matter. *TV Guide,* January 24, 41–45.

Norberg-Schulz, Christian. 1985. *The Concept of Dwelling: On the Way to Figurative Architecture.* New York: Rizzoli.

Norris, Christopher. 1990. *What's Wrong with Postmodernism: Critical Theory and the Ends of Philosophy.* Baltimore: Johns Hopkins University Press.

Oatley, Keith. 2004. *Emotions: A Brief History.* Malden, Mass.: Blackwell.

Olson, Alan M. 1979. *Transcendence and Hermeneutics: An Interpretation of the Philosophy of Karl Jaspers.* The Hague: M. Nijhoff.

———, ed. 1980. *Myth, Symbol, and Reality.* Notre Dame, Ind.: University of Notre Dame Press.

Olson, Alan M., and Leroy Rouner. 1981. *Transcendence and the Sacred.* Notre Dame, Ind.: University of Notre Dame Press.

Olson, Alan M., David M. Steiner, and Irina S. Tuuli, eds. 2004. *Educating for Democracy: Paideia in an Age of Uncertainty.* Lanham, Md.: Rowman & Littlefield.

Olson, Jerry, and Keith Sentis, eds. 1986. *Advertising and Consumer Psychology,* vol. 3. New York: Praeger.

O'Neill, Michael, and Scott Gummer. 1999. The Legends of Golf: Green Giants. *Vanity Fair,* July, 5–7, 110–23.

O'Reilly, Bernard. 1877. *The Mirror of True Womanhood: A Book of Instruction for Women in the World.* New York: P. F. Collier.

Organ, Troy Wilson. 1987. *Philosophy and the Self: East and West.* Cranbury, N.J.: Associated University Presses.

Organista, Pamela Balls, Kevin M. Chun, and Gerardo Marin, eds. 1998. *Readings in Ethnic Psychology*. New York: Routledge.

Ortega y Gasset, José. 1936. History as a System. In *Philosophy and History: Essays Presented to Ernst Cassirer*, ed. Raymond Klibansky and H. J. Paton. Oxford: Clarendon Press.

————. 1957. *The Revolt of the Masses*, trans. J. R. Carey. New York: W. W. Norton. (Spanish original: *La Rebelion de las masas*, 1930.)

Orth, Maureen. 2004. *The Importance of Being Famous: Behind the Scenes of the Celebrity-Industrial Complex*. New York: Henry Holt.

Ortony, Andrew, Gerald L. Clore, and Allan Collins. 1988. *The Cognitive Structure of Emotions*. New York: Cambridge University Press.

Overbury, Sir Thomas. 1967 (1614). *Characters or Witty Descriptions of the Properties of Sundry Persons,* illustrated by Eric Artlander. Chicago: Frumious Press.

Panofsky, Erwin. 1962. *Studies in Iconology, Humanistic Themes in the Art of the Renaissance*. New York: Harper & Row.

Park, Robert Ezra. 1950. *Race and Culture*. Glencoe, Ill.: Free Press.

Parrish-Harra, Carol E. 2002. *The New Dictionary of Spiritual Thought,* 2nd ed. Tahlequah, Okla.: Sparrow Hawk Press.

Pastoureau, Michel. 1991. *L'étoffe du Diable: Une histoire des rayures et des tissus rayés*. Paris: Éditions du Seuil.

Patocka, Jan. 1985a. La conception de la crise spirituelle de l'humanité européenne chez Masaryk et chez Husserl. In *La crise du sens*. Brussels: Ousia.

————. 1985b. *La crise du sens*. Brussels: Ousia.

————. 1989. *Ketzerische Essais über die Geschichte der Philosophie*. Stuttgart: Klett-Cotta.

Percy, Larry, and Arch G. Woodside, eds. 1983. *Advertising and Consumer Psychology,* vol. 1. Lexington, Mass.: Lexington Books.

Peretz, Evgenia, and Bruce Webber. 1999. The Private Princess. *Vanity Fair,* September, 7, 114–23.

Pervin, Lawrence A. 2003. *The Science of Personality,* 2nd ed. New York: Oxford University Press.

Pervin, Lawrence A., and Oliver P. John, eds. 1999. *Handbook of Personality: Theory and Research,* 2nd ed. New York: Guilford Press.

Peter, J. Paul, and Jerry C. Olson. 1996. *Consumer Behavior and Marketing Strategy*. Chicago: Irwin.

Peterson, Christopher, and Martin E. P. Seligman. 2004. *Character Strength and Virtues: A Handbook of Classification.* New York: Oxford University Press.

Petôfi, Sándor János. 1997. Non scholae sed vitae . . . [in Hungarian]. *Vigilia* 6: 409–17.

Pitman, Thane S. 1998. Motivation. In *The Handbook of Social Psychology,* vol. 1, ed. Daniel T. Gilbert, Susan T. Fiske, and Gardner Lindzey. New York: McGraw-Hill.

Pléh, Csaba. 1999. Ernst Mach and Daniel Dennett: Two Evolutionary Models of Cognition. In *Philosophy of Culture and Electronic Networking,* vol. 1, ed. P. Fleissner and J. K. Nyiri. Innsbruck: Studien-Verlag–Áron Kiadó.

Pléh, Csaba. 2003. Narrativity in Text Construction and Self Construction. *Neohelicon* 30, no. 1: 187–205.

Plessner, Helmuth. 1965. *Die Stufen des Organischen und der Mensch: Einleitung in die philosophische Anthropologie.* Berlin: De Gruyter.

Porter, Roy, ed. 1997. *Rewriting the Self: Histories from the Renaissance to the Present.* London: Routledge.

Post, Emily. 1928 (1922). *Etiquette: The Blue Book of Social Usage.* New York: Funk & Wagnalls.

Postman, Neil. 1986. *Amusing Ourselves to Death: Public Discourse in the Age of Show Business.* New York: Penguin.

Prost, Antoine, and Gérard Vincent, eds. 1991. *Riddles of Identity in Modern Times.* Cambridge, Mass.: Harvard University Press.

Pynsent, Robert B. 1994. *Questions of Identity: Czech and Slovak Ideas of Nationality and Personality.* Budapest-London: CEU Press.

Pyszczynski, Tom, Jeff Greenberg, and Sheldon Solomon. 1997. Why Do We Need What We Need? A Terror Management Perspective on the Roots of Human Motivation. *Psychological Inquiry* 8, no. 1: 1–20.

———. 2003. *In the Wake of 9/11: The Psychology of Terror.* Washington, D.C.: American Psychological Association.

Rabinow, Paul, and William M. Sullivan, eds. 1979. *Interpretive Social Science: A Reader.* Berkeley: University of California Press.

Rachman, Stanley J. 1978. *Fear and Courage.* San Francisco: Freeman.

Rank, Otto. 1910. *The Myth of the Birth of the Hero: A Psychological Interpretation of Myth,* trans. Gregory C. Richter and E. James Lieberman. Baltimore: Johns Hopkins University Press.

Ransom, J. Clinton. 1886. *The Successful Man in His Manifold Relations with Life.* Baltimore: Hill and Harvey.

Reddy, William M. 2001. *The Navigation of Feeling: A Framework for the History of Emotions.* New York: Cambridge University Press.

Rhymer, Russ. 1996. Back to the Future: Disney Reinvents the Company Town of Celebration, Florida. *Harper's Magazine,* October, 75.

Ricoeur, Paul. 1984–86. *Time and Narrative,* 2 vols., trans. Kathleen McLaughlin and David Pellauer. Chicago: Chicago University Press.

———. 1986. Ist "die Krise" ein spezifisch modernes Phänomen? In *Über die Krise: Castelgandolfo-Gespräche,1985,* ed. Krzysztof Michalski. Stuttgart: Klett-Cotta.

Ricoeur, Paul. 1992. *Oneself as Another* Chicago: Chicago University Press.

Rilke, Rainer-Maria. 1975. *Duino Elegies (Duineser Elegien),* trans. J. B. Leishman and Stephen Spender. London: Chatto & Windus.

———. 1982. *Poems, 1912–1926,* trans. Michael Hamburger. Redding Ridge, Conn.: Black Swan Books.

Rinke, Wolf J. 1992. *Make It a Winning Life: Success Strategies for Love, Life, and Business.* Rockville, Md.: Achievement Publishers.

Ritter, Joachim, and Karlfried Gründer, eds. 1971–2001–. *Historisches Wörterbuch der Philosophie,* 11 vols. Basel: Schwabe.

Ritzer, George. 1997a. *The McDonaldization Thesis: Explorations and Extensions.* London: Sage.

———. 1997b. *Postmodern Social Theory.* New York: McGraw-Hill.

———. 1999. *Enchanting a Disenchanted World: Revolutionizing the Means of Communication.* London: Sage.

———. 2001. *Explorations in the Sociology of Consumption: Fast Food, Credit Cards and Casinos.* London: Sage.

———. 2003. *The Globalization of Nothing.* Thousand Oaks, Calif.: Pine Forge Press.

Roach, Mary E., and Joanna B. Eicher. 1965. *Dress, Adornment, and the Social Order.* New York: John Wiley and Sons.

Robertson, Roland. 1992. *Globalization: Social Theory and Global Culture.* London, Sage.

Robbins, Anthony. 1992. *Awaken the Giant Within: How to Take Immediate Control of Your Mental, Emotional, Physical, and Financial Destiny.* New York: Simon & Schuster.

Rock, Andrea. 2004. *The Mind at Night: The New Science of How and Why We Dream.* New York: Basic Books.

Roeckelein, Jon E. 2000. *The Concept of Time in Psychology: A Resource Book and Annotated Bibliography.* Westport, Conn.: Greenwood Press.

Rogers, Carl R. 1951. *Client-Centered Therapy: Its Current Practice, Implications and Theory.* Boston: Houghton Mifflin.

———. 1961. *On Becoming a Person.* Boston: Houghton Mifflin.

———. 1980. *A Way of Being.* Boston: Houghton Mifflin.

Roheim, Geza. 1943. *The Origin and Function of Culture.* New York: Nervous and Mental Disease Monographs.

———. 1950. *Psychoanalysis and Anthropology: Culture, Personality and the Unconscious.* New York: International Universities Press.

———. 1952. *The Gates of the Dream.* New York: International Universities Press.

Roland, Alan. 1988. *In Search of Self in India and Japan.* Princeton, N.J.: Princeton University Press.

Rorty, Amélie Oksenberg. 1988. The Deceptive Self: Liars, Layers, and Lairs. In *Perspectives on Self-Deception,* ed. Brian P. McLaughlin and Amélie Rorty. Berkeley: University of California Press.

Rorty, Richard. 1989. *Contingency, Irony, and Solidarity.* Cambridge: Cambridge University Press.

Rose, Margaret A. 1991. *The Post-Modern and the Post-Industrial: A Critical Analysis.* Cambridge: Cambridge University Press.

Rose, Nikolas. 1990. *Governing the Soul: The Shaping of the Private Self.* London: Routledge.

———. 1996. *Inventing Our Selves: Psychology, Power and Personhood.* New York: Cambridge University Press.

———. 1997. Assembling the Modern Self. In *Rewriting the Self: Histories from the Renaissance to the Present,* ed. Roy Porter. London: Routledge.

Rosenberg, Morris. 1979. *Conceiving the Self.* New York: Basic Books.

Rosenwald, George C., and Richard L. Ochberg, eds. 1992. *Storied Lives: The Cultural Politics of Self-Understanding.* New Haven, Conn.: Yale University Press.

Rosnow, Ralph L., and Gary Alan Fine. 1976. *Rumor and Gossip: The Social Psychology of Hearsay.* New York: Elsevier Scientific Publishing.

Rothschild, Helene, and Marsha Kay Self. 1985. *Free to Fly, Dare to Be a Success.* Saratoga, Calif.: R & E Publishers.

Rudy, John G. 1996. *Wordsworth and the Zen Mind: The Poetry of Self-Emptying.* Albany: State University of New York Press.

Rulnick, Mary Jo, and Judith Burnett Schneider. 2004. *The Frantic Woman's Guide to Life: A Year's Worth of Hints, Tips, and Tricks.* New York: Warner Books.

Rusk, Tom. 1986. *I Want To Change, But I Don't Know How!* Los Angeles: Price/Stern/Sloan.

Ruskin, John. 1877. *The Ethics of the Dust: Ten Lectures to Little Housewives on the Elements of Crystallisation.* New York: Thomas Y. Crowell.

Russell, James A., and José Miguel Fernández-Dols, eds. 1997. *The Psychology of Facial Expression*. New York: Cambridge University Press.

Russell, James A., J. M. Fernández-Dols, A. S. R. Manstead, and J. C. Wellenkamp, eds. 1994. *Everyday Conceptions of Emotion: An Introduction to the Psychology, Anthropology and Linguistics of Emotion*. Dordrecht, the Netherlands: Kluwer.

Ryan, Alan. 1996. Professional Liars. In *Truth-Telling, Lying and Self-Deception*, ed. Arien Mack. *Social Research* 63, no. 3.

Sacks, Oliver. 1987. *The Man Who Mistook His Wife for a Hat and Other Clinical Tales*. New York: Harper & Row.

Safranski, Rüdiger. 1998. *Martin Heidegger: Between Good and Evil*, trans. Ewald Osers. Cambridge, Mass.: Harvard University Press.

Saliba, John A. 1996. *Understanding New Religious Movements*. Grand Rapids: Eerdmans.

Saltz, Gail. 2004. *Becoming Real: Defeating the Stories We Tell Ourselves That Hold Us Back*. New York: Riverhead Books.

Sampson, E. 1989. The Deconstruction of the Self. In *Texts of Identity*, ed. John Shotter and Kenneth J. Gergen. London: Sage.

Samuel, Raphael, and Paul Thompson, eds. 1993. *The Myths We Live By*. London: Routledge.

Sanders, Clinton R., ed. 1990. *Marginal Conventions: Popular Culture, Mass Media and Social Deviance*. Bowling Green, Ohio: Bowling Green State University Popular Press.

Sandra, Jane. 2000. *Kantian Moral Theory and the Destruction of the Self*. Boulder, Colo.: Westview Press.

Sansom, William. 1956. *A Contest of Ladies*. London: Hogarth.

Sarbin, Theodore R., ed. 1986. *Narrative Psychology: The Storied Nature of Human Conduct*. New York: Praeger.

Sartre, Jean Paul. 1953. *Existential Psychoanalysis,* trans. Hazel E. Barnes. Chicago: Regnery.

Sartre, Jean Paul. 1985. *Sketch for a Theory of the Emotions*. London: Methuen & Co.

———. 1956. *Being and Nothingness. An Essay on Phenomenological Ontology,* ed. and trans. Hazel E. Barnes. New York: Philosophical Library. (French original, 1943.)

Sass, Louis A. 1992. The Self and Its Vicissitudes in the Psychoanalytic Avant-Garde. In *Constructions of the Self,* ed. George Levine. New Brunswick, N.J.: Rutgers University Press.

Schank, Roger C., and Robert P. Abelson. 1977. *Scripts, Plans, Goals, and Understand-*

ing: *An Inquiry into Human Knowledge Structures.* Hillsdale, N.J.: Lawrence Erlbaum Associates.

Scheler, Max. 1961. *Man's Place in Nature.* Boston: Beacon Press. (German original, 1928.)

———. 1973. *Formalism in Ethics and Non-Formal Values: A New Attempt Toward the Foundation of an Ethical Personalism.* Evanston, Ill.: Northwestern University Press.

Schelling, Thomas. C. 1978. Egonomics, or the Art of Self-management. *American Economic Review, Papers and Proceedings* 68: 290–94.

Schlenker, Barry R., ed. 1985. *Impression Management: The Self-Concept, Social Identity, and Interpersonal Relationship.* New York: McGraw-Hill.

Schlesinger, Arthur M. 1947. *Learning How to Behave: A Historical Study of American Etiquette Books.* New York: Macmillan.

Schmuck, Peter, and Kennon M. Sheldon, eds. 2001. *Life Goals and Well-Being: Towards a Positive Psychology of Human Striving* . Seattle: Hogrefe & Huber.

Schneider, Mark A. 1993. *Culture and Enchantment.* Chicago: University of Chicago Press.

Schopenhauer, Arthur. 1966 (1819–44). *The World as Will and Idea,* 2 vols., trans. E. F. J. Payne. New York: Dover.

Schor, Juliet B. 1998. *The Overspent America: Upscaling, Downshifting, and the New Consumer.* New York: Basic Books.

Schrag, Calvin O. 1997. *The Self after Postmodernity.* New Haven, Conn.: Yale University Press.

Schreiber, Flora. 1973. *Sybil.* New York: Warner Books.

Schroeder, Alan. 2004. *Celebrity-in-Chief: How Show Business Took Over the White House.* Boulder, Colo.: Westview Press.

Schuller, Alexander. 1999. Das Ende der Helden-Ära: "Steffi, eine Legende tritt von der Bühne ab." *Bunte* 36: 93–94.

Schutz, Alfred, and Thomas Luckmann. 1989. *The Structures of the Life-World,* 2 vols., trans. M. Richard Zauer and David J. Parent. Evanston, Ill.: Northwestern University Press.

Scruton, David L., ed. 1986. *Sociophobics: The Anthropology of Fear.* Boulder, Colo.: Westview Press.

Searle, John R. 1969. *Speech Acts: An Essay in the Philosophy of Mind.* Cambridge: Cambridge University Press.

Seay, Chris. 2002. *The Gospel According to Tony Soprano: An Unauthorized Look into the Soul of TV's Top Mob Boss and His Family.* New York: Jeremy P. Tarcher / Putnam.

Seay, Chris, and Greg Garrett. 2003. *The Gospel Reloaded: Exploring Spirituality and Faith in "The Matrix."* Colorado Springs: Pion Press.

Sedikides, Constantine. 2002. Putting Our Selves Together: Integrative Themes and Lingering Questions. In *The Social Self: Cognitive, Interpersonal, and Intergroup Perspectives*, ed. Joseph P. Forgas and Kipling D. Williams. New York: Psychology Press.

Sedikides, Constantine, and Marilyn B. Brewer, eds. 2001. *Individual Self, Relational Self, Collective Self.* Philadelphia: Psychology Press.

Sedikides, Constantine, and John J. Skowronski. 2003. Evolution of the Symbolic Self: Issues and Prospects. In *Handbook of Self and Identity*, ed. Mark L. Leary and June Price Tangney. New York: Guilford Press.

Seigel, Jerrold E. 1986. *Bohemian Paris: Culture, Politics, and the Boundaries of Bourgeois Life, 1830–1930.* New York: Viking.

Seligman, Adam. 2000. *Modernity's Wager: Authority, the Self and Transcendence.* Princeton, N.J.: Princeton University Press.

Seligman, Martin E. P. 1998. *Learned Optimism: How to Change You and Your Life.* New York: Pocket Books.

———. 2002. *Authentic Happiness: Using the New Positive Psychology to Realize Your Potential for Lasting Fulfillment.* New York: Free Press.

Sennett, Richard. 1976. *The Fall of Public Man.* New York: W. W. Norton.

———. 1992. *The Uses of Disorder: Personal Identity and City Life.* New York: W. W. Norton.

———. 1994. *Flesh and Stone: The Body and the City in Western Civilization.* New York: W. W. Norton.

Sessums, Kevin. 1999. White Hot Venus: The Lean, Sexy Glamour of Charlize Theron. *Vanity Fair,* January, 54–61.

Sheldon, Kennon M. 2004. *Optimal Human Being : An Integrated Multi-Level Perspective.* Mahwah, N.J.: Lawrence Erlbaum Associates.

Shibutani, Tamotsu. 1966. *Improvised News: A Sociological Study of Rumor.* Indianapolis: Bobbs-Merrill.

Shields, Rob. 1990. "The System of Pleasure": Liminality and the Carnivalesque in Brighton. *Theory, Culture and Society* 7, no. 1.

———, ed. 1992. *Lifestyle Shopping: The Subject of Consumption.* London: Routledge.

Shilling, Chris. 1994. *The Body and Social Theory.* London: Sage.

Shneidman, Edwin S. 1967. *Essays in Self-Destruction.* New York: Science House.

Shohov, Serge P., ed. 2002. *Trends in Cognitive Psychology.* New York: Nova Science Publishers.

Shotter, John, and Kenneth J. Gergen, eds. 1989. *Texts of Identity.* London: Sage.

Sidgwick, Henry. 1898. *Practical Ethics.* London: Swan Sonnenschein.

Siewert, Beate, und Sahner, Paul. 1999. Die Las-Vegas-Hochzeit der Susan Stahnke: "Exklusiv die Fotos der intimen Feier im amerikanischen Spielerparadies . . . mit einer Flitternacht im Hubschrauber." *Bunte* 33: 1, 3, 18–21.

Sills, David L., ed. 1968–91. *International Encyclopedia of the Social Sciences.* New York: Macmillan.

Silverstone, Roger. 1994. *Television and Everyday Life.* London: Routledge.

Simmel, Georg. 1998. *Momentbilder sub specie aeternitatis: Philosophische Miniaturen,* ed. Christian Wehlte. Heidelberg: Manutius.

Simon-Miller, F. 1985. Commentary: Signs and Symbols in the Fashion System. In *The Psychology of Fashion,* ed. Michael R. Solomon. Lexington, Mass.: Lexington Books.

Simson, Otto von. 1964. *The Gothic Cathedral: Origins of Gothic Architecture and the Medieval Concept of Order,* 2nd ed. New York: Harper & Row.

Singer, Margaret T. 1995. *Cults in Our Midst.* San Francisco: Jossey-Bass.

Skinner, B. F. 1971. *Beyond Freedom and Dignity.* New York: Alfred A. Knopf.

Smart, Barry. 1993. *Postmodernity.* New York: Routledge.

———, ed. 1999. *Resisting McDonaldization.* London: Sage.

Smelser, Neil J. 1962. *Theory of Collective Behavior.* London: Routledge & Kegan Paul.

———. 1987. Depth Psychology and the Social Order. In *The Micro–Macro Link,* ed. Jeffrey C. Alexander, Bernhard Giesen, Richard Münch, and Neil J. Smelser. Berkeley: University of California Press.

———. 1998. *The Social Edges of Psychoanalysis.* Berkeley: University of California Press.

Smiles, Samuel. 1958 (1859). *Self-Help: With Illustrations of Conduct and Perseverance.* London: John Murray.

Smith, Anthony. 1996. *Software for the Self: Culture and Technology.* London: Faber.

Smith, Eliot R., and Diane M. Mackie. 2000. *Social Psychology,* 2nd ed. Philadelphia: Psychology Press.

Smith, Joseph H., Harold A. Durfee, Gloria Parloff, and Katherine S. Henry. 1981. *Kierkegaard's Truth: The Disclosure of the Self.* New Haven, Conn.: Yale University Press.

Snyder, Mark. 1987. *Public Appearances, Private Realities: The Psychology of Self-Monitoring.* New York: Freeman.

Snyder, Mark, and Nancy Cantor. 1998. Understanding Personality and Social Behavior: A Functionalist Strategy. In *The Handbook of Social Psychology,* vol. 1, ed. Daniel T. Gilbert, Susan T. Fiske, and Gardner Lindzey. New York: McGraw-Hill.

Snyder, Stephen. 1994. *The Transparent I: Self/Subject in European Cinema.* New York: P. Lang.

Soja, Edward W. 1989. *Postmodern Geographies: The Reassertion of Space in Critical Social Theory.* London: Verso.

Solomon, Michael R., ed. 1985. *The Psychology of Fashion.* Lexington, Mass.: Lexington Books.

Solomon, Robert C. 1988. *Continental Philosophy: The Rise and Fall of the Self.* New York: Oxford University Press.

Somers, Margaret R. 1994. The Narrative Constitution of Identity. *Theory and Society* 23: 605–45.

Sorkin, Michael, ed. 1992.*Variations on a Theme-Park.* New York: Hill and Wang.

Sorokin, Pitrim A. 1962 (1937–41). *Social and Cultural Dynamics,* 4 vols. New York: Bedminster Press.

Sorrentino, Richard M., and Raymond L. Higgins, eds. 1986–96. *Handbook of Motivation and Cognition,* 3 vols. New York: Guilford Press.

Spacks, Patricia Ann Meyer. 1976. *Imagining a Self: Autobiography and Novel in Eighteenth Century England.* Cambridge, Mass.: Harvard University Press.

———. 1986. *Gossip.* Chicago: University of Chicago Press.

Spengler, Oswald. 1926. *The Decline of the West: Perspectives of World History,* 2 vols., trans. C. F. Atkinson. New York: Alfred A. Knopf. (German original, 1918–23.)

Spielberger, Charles D., and Robelio Diaz-Guerrero, eds. 1976. *Cross-Cultural Anxiety.* Washington, D.C.: Hemisphere.

Squire, Corinne, ed. 2000. *Culture in Psychology.* New York: Routledge.

Stagner, Ross. 1937. *Psychology of Personality.* New York: McGraw-Hill.

Stambaugh, Joan. 1972. *Nietzsche's Thought of Eternal Return.* Baltimore: Johns Hopkins University Press.

———. 1999. *The Formless Self.* Albany: State University of New York Press.

Stein, Craig C. 2001. *Schleiermacher's Construction of the Subject in the Introduction to the Christian Faith: In Light of M. Foucault's Critique of Modern Knowledge.* Lewiston: Edwin Mellon Press.

Stein, Maurice R., Arthur J. Vidich, and David Manning, eds. 1960. *Identity and Anxiety: Survival of the Person in Mass Society.* Glencoe, Ill.: Free Press.

Steinberg, Mark D. 2002. *Proletarian Imagination: Self, Modernity, and the Sacred in Russia, 1910–1925.* Ithaca. Cornell University Press.

Stone, Hal, and Sidra Winkelman. 1985. *Embracing Our Selves.* Marina del Rey, Calif.: Devorss.

Strasser, Susan. 1989. *Satisfaction Guaranteed: The Making of the American Mass Market.* New York: Pantheon Books.

Stryker, Sheldon. 1980. *Symbolic Interactionism: A Social Structural Version.* Menlo Park, Calif.: Benjamin/Cummings.

Strozier, Robert M. 2002. *Foucault, Subjectivity, and Identity: Historical Constructions of Subject and Self.* Detroit: Wayne State University Press.

Sugden, John, and Alan Tomlinson, eds. 2002. *Power Games: A Critical Sociology of Sport.* New York: Routledge.

Sullivan, H. S. 1953. *The Interpersonal Theory of Psychiatry.* New York: W. W. Norton.

Swann, William B. 1996. *Self-Traps: The Elusive Quest for Higher Self-Esteem.* New York: Freeman.

Sypher, Wylie. 1962. *Loss of Self in Modern Literature and Art.* New York: Random House.

Szakolczai, Árpád. 1998. *Max Weber and Michel Foucault: Parallel Life-Works.* New York: Routledge.

———. 2000. *Reflexive Historical Sociology.* London: Routledge.

———. 2003. *The Genesis of Modernity.* New York: Routledge.

Szilágyi, Ákos. 2000. Civilizációk civilizálódása [Civilizations civilized]. In *A kérdéses civilizáció* [The questionable civilization], ed. Csaba Gombár and Hédi Volosin. Budapest: Helikon.

Szvetelszky, Zsuzsanna. 2002. *A pletyka* [The gossip]. Budapest: Gondolat K. Kör.

Tangney, June Price. 2003. Self-Relevant Emotions. In *Handbook of Self and Identity,* ed. Mark L. Leary and June Price Tangney. New York: Guilford Press.

Tangney, June Price, and K. W. Fischer, eds. 1995. *Self-Conscious Emotions: The Psychology of Shame, Guilt, Embarrassment, and Pride.* New York: Guilford Press.

Tarule, Jill M. 1986. *Women's Ways of Knowing: The Development of Self, Voice, and Mind.* New York: Basic Books.

Taubman, Stan. 1994. *Ending the Struggle Against Yourself: A Workbook for Developing Deep Confidence and Self-Acceptance.* New York: Putnam.

Taylor, Charles. 1989. *Sources of the Self: The Making of the Modern Identity.* Cambridge: Cambridge University Press.

Taylor, Diana, and Karen Vintges, eds. 2004. *Feminism and the Final Foucault*. Urbana: University of Illinois Press.

Taylor, Jeremy. 1987 (1650). *Holy Living and Dying: With Prayers; Containing the Whole Duty of a Christian, and the Parts of Devotion Fitted to All Occasions and Furnished for All Necessities*. London: G. Bell and Sons.

Taylor, Mikko. 2003. *Self-Seduction: Your Ultimate Path to Inner and Outer Beauty*, with photographs by Paul Lange. New York: One World.

Tebbutt, Melanie. 1995. *Women's Talk? A Social History of "Gossip" in Working-Class Neighbourhoods, 1880–1960*. Brookfield, Vt.: Ashgate.

Tedeschi, James T., ed. 1981. *Impression Management: Theory and Social Psychological Research*. New York: Academic Press.

Tedlock, Barbara, ed. 1987. *Dreaming*. Cambridge: Cambridge University Press.

Tepperman, Lorne. 1996. *Choices and Chances: Sociology for Everyday Life*. Boulder, Colo.: Westview Press.

Tesser, A., L. L. Martin, and D. P. Cornell. 1996. On the Substitutability of Self-Protective Mechanisms. In *The Psychology of Action: Linking Cognition and Motivation to Behavior*, ed. Peter M. Gollwitzer and John A. Bargh. New York: Guilford Press.

Tesser, Abraham, Diederik A. Stapel, and Joanne V. Wood, eds. 2002. *Self and Motivation: Emerging Psychological Perspectives*. Washington, D.C.: American Psychological Association.

Tesser, Abraham, Joanne V. Wood, and Diederik A. Stapel. 2005. *On Building, Defending, and Regulating the Self: A Psychological Perspective*. New York: Psychology Press.

Theory, Culture & Society. 1988. *Special Issue on Postmodernism*. Vol. 5, nos. 2–3.

Therborn, Göran. 2002. Monumental Europe: The National Years—On the Iconography of European Capital Cities. *Theory and Society* 19: 26–47.

Thompson, J. Kevin. 1990. *Body Image Disturbance: Assessment and Treatment*. Elmsford, N.Y.: Pergamon Press.

Thompson, Leigh L. 2002. *The Social Psychology of Organizational Behavior*. New York: Routledge.

Tice, Diane M., and Harry M. Wallace. 2003. The Reflected Self: Creating Yourself as (You Think) Others See You. In *Handbook of Self and Identity*, ed. Mark L. Leary and June Price Tangney. New York: Guilford Press.

Tiemersma, Douwe. 1989. *Body Schema and Body Image. An Interdisciplinary and Philosophical Study*. Amsterdam: Swets and Zeitlinger.

Tillich, Paul. 1936. *The Interpretation of History*. New York: Scribner.

———. 1951–63. *Systematic Theology,* 3 vols. Chicago: University of Chicago Press.

———. 1952. *The Courage to Be.* New Haven, Conn.: Yale University Press.

———. 1965. *Ultimate Concern: Tillich in Dialogue,* ed. T. M. Brown. New York: Harper & Row.

———. 1988 (1957–65). *The Spiritual Situation in our Technical Society.* Macon, Ga.: Mercer University Press.

Ting-Toomey, Stella, ed. 1994. *The Challenge of Facework: Cross-Cultural and Interpersonal Issues.* Albany: State University of New York Press.

Tobin, Joseph, ed. 1992. *Remade in Japan: Everyday Life and Consumer Taste in a Changing Society.* New Haven, Conn.: Yale University Press.

Tomlinson, Alan, ed. 1990. *Consumption, Identity and Style: Marketing, Meanings and the Packaging of Pleasure.* London: Comedia.

———. 1999. *The Game's Up: Essays in the Cultural Analysis of Sport, Leisure, and Popular Culture.* Brookfield, Vt.: Ashgate/Arena.

———. 2005. *Sport and Leisure Cultures.* Minneapolis : University of Minnesota Press.

Tomlinson, John. 1991. *Cultural Imperialism.* London: Pinter.

Toulmin, Stephen. 1992. *Cosmopolis: The Hidden Agenda of Modernity.* Chicago: University of Chicago Press.

Toulmin, Stephen, and June Goodfield. 1965. *The Discovery of Time.* London: Hutchinson.

Toynbee, Arnold. 1934–61. *A Study of History,* 12 vols. New York: Oxford University Press.

Troeltsch, Ernst. 1911. *Die Bedeutung des Protestantismus für die Entstehung der moderner Welt.* München: R. Oldenbourg.

Tropp, Martin. 1990. *Images of Fear: How Horror Stories Helped Shape Modern Culture (1818–1918).* Jeffers, N.C.: McFarlan.

Truchses, Darlene Deer. 1985. *From Fear to Freedom: A Woman's Handbook for High Self-Esteem.* Denver: New Option.

Tuan, Yi-fu. 1979. *Landscapes of Fear.* New York: Pantheon Books.

Turner, Graeme. 2004. *Understanding Celebrity.* London: Sage.

Turner, John C., and Michael A. Hogg. 1987. *Rediscovering the Social Group: A Self-Categorization Theory.* Oxford: Blackwell.

Turner, Roy, ed. 1974. *Ethnomethodology: Selected Readings.* Baltimore: Penguin.

Turner, Victor W. 1967. *The Forest of Symbols.* Ithaca, N.Y.: Cornell University Press.

———. 1969. *The Ritual Process: Structure and Antistructure.* New York: Aldine de Gruyter.

————. 1990. Liminality and Community. In *Culture and Society: Contemporary Debates,* ed. Jeffrey C. Alexander and Steven Seidman. Cambridge: Cambridge University Press.

Turner, Victor W., and Edward M. Bruner, eds. 1986. *The Anthropology of Experience.* Urbana: University of Illinois Press.

Twerski, Abraham J. 1995. *Life's Too Short: Pull the Plug on Self-Defeating Behavior and Turn on the Power of Self-Esteem.* New York: St. Martin's Press.

Uleman, James S., and John A. Bargh, eds. 1989. *Unintended Thought.* New York: Guilford Press.

Unamuno y Jugo, Miguel de. 1921. *The Tragic Sense of Life in Men and in Peoples,* trans. J. E. Crawford Flitch. New York: Dover Publications. (Spanish original: *Del sentimiento tragico de la vida,* 1912.)

————. 1928. *The Agony of Christianity,* trans. Pierre Loving. New York: Payson & Clark. (Spanish original: *La agonia del Cristianismo,* 1924.)

Urry, John. 1988. Cultural Change and Contemporary Holiday-Making. *Theory, Culture and Society* 5, no. 1.

Urry, John. 2003. *Global Complexity.* Malden, Mass.: Polity Press.

Valéry, Paul. 1924. La crise de l'esprit. In *Oeuvres 1–2* (1957–60). Édition établie et annotée par Jean Hytier. Paris: Gallimard.

————. 1951. *Reflections on the World Today,* trans. F. Scarfe. London: n.p. (French original: *Regards sur le monde actuel;* Paris: Stock–Delamain et Boutelleau, 1931.)

Van de Castle, Robert L. 1994. *Our Dreaming Mind.* New York: Ballantine Books.

Van Gennep, Arnold. 1960. *The Rites of Passage.* Chicago: University of Chicago Press.

Vanderbilt, Amy. 1972–52. *Amy Vanderbilt's Etiquette.* Garden City, N.Y.: Doubleday.

Vanhoozer, Kevin J. 1990. *Biblical Narrative in the Philosophy of Paul Ricoeur: A Study in Hermeneutics and Theology.* New York: Cambridge University Press.

Vargo, Marc. 2003. *Scandal: Infamous Gay Controversies of the Twentieth Century.* New York: Harrington Park Press.

Virilio, Paul. 1994. *The Vision Machine.* Bloomington: Indiana University Press.

Voegelin, Eric. 1956. *Order and History, Volume 1: Israel and Revelation.* Baton Rouge: Louisiana State University Press.

————. 1974. *Order and History, Volume 4: The Ecumenic Age.* Baton Rouge: Louisiana State University Press.

————. 2000. *Order and History,* 5 vols. Columbia: University of Missouri Press.

Waddell, H. 1987. 1934. *The Desert Fathers.* London: Constable.

Wagner, Roy. 1995. If You Have the Advertisement You Don't Need the Product. In *Rhetorics of Self-Making,* ed. Debbora Battaglia. Berkeley: University of California Press.

Waitley, Denis. 2004. *Psychology of Success: Finding Meaning in Work and Life,* 4th ed. Boston: McGraw-Hill Higher Education.

Wallen, James. 1985. Emotion and Style in Copy. In *Masters of Advertising Copy,* ed., J. George Frederick. New York: Garland.

Wallerstein, Immanuel. 1995. The End of What Modernity? Guest Commentary. *Theory and Society* 24: 471–88.

Walsh, David. 1990. *After Ideology: Recovering the Spiritual Foundations of Freedom.* San Francisco: Harper San Francisco.

Ward, Colleen, Stephen Bochner, and Adrian Furnham. 2001. *The Psychology of Culture Shock.* London: Routledge.

Weber, Robert J. 2000. *The Created Self: Reinventing Body, Persona, Spirit.* New York: W. W. Norton.

Webster's New Collegiate Dictionary. 1949. Springfield, Mass.: Merriam-Webster.

Wechsler, Harlan J. 1990. *What's So Bad about Guilt?* New York: Simon & Schuster.

Weigert, Andrew. J. 1981. *Sociology of Everyday Life.* New York: Longman.

Weinberg, Steven. 1977. *The First Three Minutes: A Modern View of the Origin of the Universe.* New York: Basic Books.

Weinreich, Peter, and Wendy Saunderson, eds. 2002. *Analysing Identity: Cross-Cultural, Societal and Clinical Contexts.* London: Routledge.

Wernick, Andrew. 1991. *Promotional Culture: Advertising, Ideology, and Symbolic Expression.* London: Sage.

Wetterer, Angelika, and Jürgen von Troschke. 1986. *Smoker Motivation: A Review of Contemporary Literature.* New York: Springer Verlag.

White, Daniel R., and Gert Hellerich. 1998. *Labyrinths of the Mind: The Self in the Postmodern Age.* Albany: State University of New York Press.

White, Geoffrey M., and John Kirkpatrick, eds. 1985. *Person, Self, and Experience.* Berkeley: University of California Press.

White, Stephen L. 1991. *The Unity of the Self.* Cambridge, Mass.: MIT Press.

Whitehead, George I., and Stephanie H. Smith. 1986. Competence and Excuse-Making as Self-Presentational Strategies. In *Public and Private Self,* ed. Roy F. Baumeister. New York: Springer.

Whitrow, G. J. 1988. *Time in History: The Evolution of Our General Awareness of Time and Temporal Perspective.* New York: Oxford University Press.

—————. 2003. *What Is Time?* With a new bibliographic essay by J. T. Fraser and Marlene P. Soulsby. New York : Oxford University Press.

Wicklund, Robert A., and Martina Eckert. 1992. *The Self-Knower: A Hero under Control.* New York: Plenum Press.

Wicklund, Robert A., and Peter M. Gollwitzer. 1982. *Symbolic Self-Completion.* Hillsdale, N.J.: Lawrence Erlbaum Associates.

Widmann, Wilhelm. 1931. *Hamlets Bühnenlaufbahn, 1601–1877,* ed. Joseph Schick and Werner Deetjen. Leipzig: B. Tauchnitz.

Wilde, Oscar. 1988 (1890). *The Picture of Dorian Gray.* New York: W. W. Norton.

Wildeblood, Joan, and Peter Brinson. 1965. *The Polite World: A Guide to Manners and Deportment from the Thirteenth to the Nineteenth Centuries.* London: Oxford University Press.

Wiley, Carol, A., ed. 1994. *Journeys to Self-Acceptance: Fat Women Speak.* Freedom, Calif.: Crossing Press.

Wiley, Norbert. 1994. *The Semiotic Self.* Chicago: University of Chicago Press.

Wilkes, Roger. 2002. *Scandal: A Scurrilous History of Gossip, 1700–2000.* London: Atlantic.

Williams, Raymond. 1958. *Culture and Society 1780–1950.* Harmondsworth, U.K.: Penguin.

Williams, Rosalind H. 1982. *Dream Worlds: Mass Consumption in Late Nineteenth Century France.* Berkeley: California University Press.

Williamson, Judith. 1986. *Consuming Passions: The Dynamics of Popular Culture.* London: Marion Boyars.

Wilson, Elisabeth. 1987. *Adorned in Dreams: Fashion and Modernity.* London: Virago.

—————. 1990. These New Components of the Spectacle: Fashion and Postmodernism. In *Fabrications: Costume and the Female Body,* ed. Jane Gaines and Charlotte Herzog. New York: Sage.

Wilson, Edward O. 1975. *Sociobiology: The New Synthesis.* Cambridge: Mass.: Harvard University Press.

—————. 1978. *On Human Nature.* Cambridge: Mass.: Harvard University Press.

Winship, Janice. 1987. *Inside Women's Magazines.* London: Pandora.

Wood, David. 1988. *The Destruction of Time.* Atlantic Highlands, N.J.: Humanities Press.

World Bank. 2000. *World Development Indicators.* Washington, D.C.: World Bank.

Wyer, Robert S., Jr., ed. 1997. *The Automaticity of Everyday Life: Advances in Social Cognition.* Mahwah, N.J.: Lawrence Erlbaum Associates.

Wylie, Ruth C. 1961. *The Self-Concept: A Critical Survey of Pertinent Research Literature.* Lincoln: University of Nebraska Press.

———. 1974–79. *The Self-Concept: A Review of Methodological Considerations and Measuring Instruments,* 2 vols. Lincoln: University of Nebraska Press.

———. 1989. *Measures of Self-Concept.* Lincoln: University of Nebraska Press.

York, Michael. 2004. *Historical Dictionary of New Age Movements.* Lanham, Md: Scarecrow Press.

Young-Eisendrath, Polly. 1991. *Jungs's Self-Psychology: A Constructivist Perspective.* New York: Guilford Press.

Zagorin, Perez. 1996. The Historical Significance of Lying and Dissimulation. In *Truth-Telling, Lying and Self-Deception,* ed. Arien Mack. *Social Research* 63, no. 3.

Zajonc, Robert B. 1998. Emotions. In *The Handbook of Social Psychology,* vol. 1, ed. Daniel T. Gilbert, Susan T. Fiske, and Gardner Lindzey. New York: McGraw-Hill.

Zeman, Ned. 1999. Will Smith Rides High. *Vanity Fair,* July, 78, 82.

Zepp, Ira G., Jr. 1997. *The New Religious Image of Urban America: The Shopping Mall as Ceremonial Center,* 2nd ed. Niwot: University Press of Colorado.

Zerubavel, Eviatar. 1985 (1981). *Hidden Rhythms: Schedules and Calendars in Social Life.* Chicago: University of Chicago Press.

Zétényi, Lili. 1999. Mi van velünk (Interjú Kern Andrással) [What about Us? An Interview with András Kern]. *Nők Lapja* 50, no. 49: 22–24.

Zimmerman, Michael E. 1981. *Eclipse of the Self: The Development of Heidegger's Concept of Authenticity.* Athens: Ohio University Press.

Zucker, Lynn G., ed. 1988. *Institutional Patterns and Organization: Culture and Environment.* Cambridge, Mass.: Ballinger.

Zuckerman, Mary Ellen. 1998. *A History of Popular Women's Magazines in the United States, 1792–1995.* Westport, Conn.: Greenwood Press.

Zukin, Sharon. 1991. *Landscapes of Power: From Detroit to Disney World.* Berkeley: University of California Press.

Zurcher, Louis A. 1977. *The Mutable Self: A Self-Concept for Social Change.* Beverly Hills, Calif.: Sage.

Index

archetypes (*continued*)
194, 218, 221; Wheel of Fortune as, 234–35
Arditi, Jorge, 73, 76
Aristotle, 189, 327, 340
art and artworks, 2–3, 134, 220
articulation of time, 5, 107–22; gossip and, 119–22; pub and, 115–16; shopping center and, 108–13; sports and, 116–19; street and, 107–8; travel and, 113–14
astrology, 270–71
Augustine (Saint), 132, 194, 284, 296
authentic: choice, 335; civilization, 113, 293; existence, 2–6, 36, 68, 98, 100, 109–11, 135–36, 194, 213–14, 223, 228–30, 234, 242, 245, 252, 282, 288, 297, 300, 338–39; happiness, 333, 335; self, 2, 6, 11, 67–69, 76, 111, 114, 125–30, 139, 169, 188, 198–201, 206, 223–28, 252, 288–89, 296, 306. *See also* boundary situations; Jaspers, Karl; Sartre, Jean-Paul
autonomous: choice, 5; hedonism, 268; morality, 210; self, 41–42, 44, 67–68, 74, 77–78, 81, 91–98, 128, 159, 171, 179, 187, 191, 194, 204–9, 244, 255–56, 259, 263, 285, 296, 313–14, 338
autonomy: fight for, 40; loss of, 91–92, 263; sunglasses and, 81, 89
avarice, 73, 74
Awake the Giant Within (Robbins), 138–39

Bachelard, Gaston, 123
background of knowledge, 57. *See also* framework
Bacon, Francis, 79
baldness, 34–35
Balzac, Honoré de, 67

Barkow, James H., 57
Baroque Age, 181–82
Barth, Karl, 164
Barthes, Roland, 40, 81, 241
Baudelaire, Charles, 50, 172, 213, 285, 288. *See also* dandyism
Baudrillard, Jean, 13, 40, 90, 170–73, 268, 274, 333
Bauman, Zygmunt, 171, 173, 212, 268, 338
Baumeister, Roy F., 198–206, 290, 301, 311, 313, 328, 331, 344
The Beauty and the Beast, 220, 269
Becker, Boris, 236–37
Becker, Ernest, 5, 225–26
Beckett, Samuel, 122
Beckham, David, 262–63
"bed trick," 127
The Bedtrick: Tales of Sex and Masquerade (Doniger), 205
behavioral sciences, achievements and limitations of, 6–10
Being: authentic sense of, 136; contrast of Nonbeing, 230, 238; depths of, 338; essence of, 36, 305; existentialist concept of, 125, 338; experience of, 2, 229, 233–34, 237, 297; fear as creative of, 224; as framework of meaning, 339; Heidegger on, 6; timeless, 137; toward-death, 99; void of, 122
Bellah, Robert, 66
Bellum Americanum, 147–48
Benedict (Saint), 88–89, 188, 284
Benjamin, Walter, 10
Bennis, Warren, 92, 111
Berdyaev, Nicolas, 200
Berg, Patty, 260
Berger, Peter L.: "enterprise of world-building," 5, 226; homeless self, 199, 212; meaning, 47, 57, 212, 226;

cell phones, 84–85
center of life and five worlds scenarios, 157
"center of narrative gravity," self as, 98
change over time, 16–17. *See also* trends
changing world, 145–59; "The Great Transformation," 185–88; possible and impossible futures, 145–51; self in various worlds, 151–59, 185–88
"Characters," seventeenth century, 61
Chateaubriand, François-René de, 285
Chekhov, Anton, 69, 79
children, 128–29
chivalry, age of, 287
cigarettes, 26–27
city environment and articulation of time, 107–8
clash of civilizations, 149
Clinton, Bill, 237, 252
clothing, 37–43, 183–84
coffee, morning cup of, 27–28
cognitive psychology, 7–8
Cohen, Richard, 166
coiffure, 33–35
Coleridge, Samuel Taylor, 285
community, 55–56, 60, 62, 219
conscious and unconscious realms of self, 7
construction of the self. *See* self-construction; self, shaping of
consumer civilization: advertising in, 278; America and, 277; assessment of, 13, 283–97; authentic self, search for, 69; boundary situations in, 223–40; care of self in, 286–89; celebrities and, 241–43, 248–64, 268; changing world and, 145–59; crisis of Western civilization and, 172–73, 179, 275–81; death in, 226–30; defining, 172; development of full wealth of, 271; emergence of, 1, 74, 199, 245;

entertainment and, 184–85; Europe and, 277; existential depths in, 2, 6, 9–12, 78–86, 100, 119, 140, 167, 212–27, 236, 274, 297, 319, 335; experience in, 219; generally, 12–14; impact in Eastern Europe, 277; influence of, 279; loss of self in, 69; "manufacturing people," 92; meaning through consumption in, 108; myth of the self and, 241–64; as new civilization, 275–81; parallels with Renaissance, 182–95; physical transformation of human body and, 30–33; postmodernity and, 172–73; questions of life and death, 162, 169, 279; as reenchanted world, 6, 26, 265–82; as renewal of Western civilization, 275–81; role playing in, 78; search for intensity and, 288; self-construction in, 12–14, 211–21; shock, 289; situation, 212; social interaction and, 15; sphere of life, 2, 125, 227; as syncretic age, 197–210; transcendent and, 338; transformation of self, 327; as transition, 275–81; travel in, 113; trend toward, 150–51; trivialities and, 287; values of, 67. *See also* carnival; "Proletarian Renaissance"
contemporary and traditional values compared, 173–75, 186–88
contingency: books on, 330; of everything, 277; of home, 123; in postmodernity, 171, 277; search for order beneath contingencies, 296; self as web of contingencies (Freud), 199; of word, 297
contrast, 220–21. *See also* boundary situations
Cosmides, Leda, 57
creative energies, flow of, 47
creative societies scenario, 152–58

entertainment in "Proletarian Renaissance," 184–85

envy, 74

Epicureanism: care of self, 284, 286–87; codes of behavior, 191–92; in consumer civilization, 191–93; versus hedonism, 191, 290; mentality, 155; in Renaissance, 191–93, 327; self, 186

Erikson, Erik, 286

eschatological prophecies about future of Western civilization, 165

Estés, Clarissa Pinkola, 137–38

eternal return (Nietzsche), 109, 117, 310

eternity: beauty as symbol of, 232; etiquette, 75–78; human condition and, 57; illusion of, 109; jewels and, 42; moment and, 109, 213–15, 297, 333; objects and, 43, 106; perfumes and, 37, 214–15; stream of, 258; world of, 108

Etiquette: The Blue Book of Social Usage (Post), 76

Eulenspiegel, Tyl, 80

Europe: consumer civilization and, 277; Russia, confrontation with, 276

everyday life, self-construction in, 11–12, 21–141

evil: challenging, 217; good and, 168–69, 220, 269; heroes of folklore, 253; punished, 240; in self, 208; in shopping mall, 110–13; spirits, 23, 25; victory over, 133, 229, 279; in world, 26, 164, 228

Ewen, Stuart, 95, 201, 243–44, 249, 253, 274, 311, 316, 326, 339

examination of conscience, 284

exercise, 30–33, 83

existentialism, 99, 223, 302; attitude, 66; boundary situation and, 229, 237; choice, 223; Christian, 242, 302; dance of death and, 12; destruction, 236; dilemma, 4, 9; drama underlying everyday life, 2, 6, 11–12, 78–86, 100, 119, 140, 221, 274, 297, 319, 335; experience, 212, 219, 221, 230, 236; fear and anxiety, 9, 82, 167, 216, 224, 226–27; moment, 213–14, 233, 333; needs, 4; proletarian, 14, 182, 229, 336; questions of life and death, 162, 169, 279; search for intensity, 288; self, 14, 207; shock, 289; situation, 212; sphere of life, 2, 125, 227; transcendent and, 338; transformation of self, 327; world, 139

existentialists, 5, 17, 164, 200, 242

experience: advertisement and, 215–16; age of, 215–16; of anxiety, 90; of apotheosis of self, 111; of Being, 6, 9; of carnival and dance of death, 141; celebrities and, 131; children and, 128; as commodity, 215; consumer civilization and, 151, 215; of crisis, 162, 165, 167; of duality of life, 189–90; existential, 212, 219, 221, 230, 236; of fear and hope, 190; of freedom, 72, 120; home and, 123; intellectual, 220; of intensity, 120, 215–18; of life, 120, 212, 215–16; of loss of self, 69, 72, 202, 207–8; love and, 126; market of, 215; metaphysical, 83; of the moment, 211, 214; physical, 216; of power, 102; roles and, 129; of self, 95, 97, 198, 201, 209, 218; of self-reflection, 108; shopping center and, 108–9, 111; of significance, 101, 107; spiritual, 6, 77, 220; stream of, 108; of strolling in street, 107; television and, 129; of time, 116; tragic, 163; travel and, 113–16; visual, 216

Freud, Sigmund: on complexes and archetypes, 218; destruction of values by, 276; on happiness, 194; motivation research and, 8; on trivial phenomena of everyday life, effect of, 7; view of self, 97, 199

Fromm, Erich: care of self, 137, 286; escape from freedom, 201; *To Have or to Be,* 333

fulfillment of life and self: advertising and, 278; books on, 245–46; celebrities and, 247–48; children and, 128–29; communal responsibility and, 277; consumption and, 182, 278; within ethico-moral framework, 292; existential drama and, 140; experimenting with selves and, 71; Faustian, 226, 335; fundamentalist movements and, 170; hedonism and, 277; lack of framework and, 212; loss of transcendence and, 210; perfumes and, 36–37; positive psychology and, 333; precondition of, 159; "Proletarian Renaissance" and, 141, 180, 186–88, 210; Protestantism and, 180; radical individualism and, 276; religious version of, 338; Renaissance and, 180, 338, 344; Saint Benedict's Rule and, 89; shopping center and, 110; totalitarian ideologies and, 169; unsuccessful, 11–112; Victorian morals and, 199. *See also* self-actualization

fundamentalist movements, 169

Furyk, Jim, 261

future: five worlds prediction for, 151–59; possible and impossible, 145–51

Gadamer, Hans-Georg, 98

Gala magazine, 255

gardening: defeating world of chaos in, 124; interaction of the trivial and the existential in, 124–25

Garden of Eden, 5, 56, 114, 132, 269, 327

Garton Ash, Timothy, 168

gaze, 250–54

Geertz, Clifford, 5, 10, 88

Gehlen, Arnold: on humans as handicapped beings, 5; on humans as premature animals, 32, 226

gender: amulets and, 42–43; body image and, 32–33; change in myth and story, 205; clothes and, 38–39, 40; coiffure and, 34; makeup and, 35–36; perfumes and, 36; self-construction and, 15; shoes and, 44; sunglasses and, 81–82

genetics and human behavior, 92

Gergen, Kenneth J., 98, 200–201

Giddens, Anthony, 172

globalization, 55, 56, 150–53

gloves, 45

gluttony, 74

goals and life goals, 46–47, 57, 83, 146, 154, 279, 291, 321, 331

Goes, Pilar, 231–32

Goethe, Johann Wolfgang von, 70, 71, 285

Goffman, Erving, 10, 55, 59, 64, 286

Golding, William, 70

golf legends, 260–62

gossip, 51, 102–3, 119–22, 227, 256, 286–87, 318–19

Graff, Steffi, 261–62

great transformation of Western civilization, 185–88

Greece, classical: care of self in, 286–87; spiritual crisis in, 164

Greek myths, 205

Greenberg, Jeff, 9, 226, 301, 318

Iago, 72, 79
Ibsen, Henrik, 69, 79, 236
The Iceman Cometh (O'Neill), 79, 122
ID cards, 46, 86
ideal world, construction of, 5
identity, 26, 46; achieved, 99; books and,
    136; bounded, 201; construction of,
    39, 99, 283; crisis of, 167; as crucial
    problem, 253, 259; destruction of, 38;
    dream of, 201; erosion of, 243–45;
    explored, 224; invention of, 90; job
    and, 102; lack of, 80–81, 199, 201;
    local, 38–39, 56, 84, 201, 224,
    243–44; loss of, 38–39; myth of, 219;
    narrative self-, 95, 98–99; patriotic,
    51; permanence of, 207;
    predicaments, 62; public, 311;
    rebellious, 67; reconfirmed, 84;
    reconstruction of, 24–25; regained,
    252; repair tactics, 62; sense of, 252,
    339; social, 102, 112, 159; source of,
    67; sunglasses and, 80–81; tribal, 283;
    unacceptable, 70
ideologies, age of, 147–48
illness and distorting of self, 32
immortality: celebrities and, 241–43;
    consumer civilization and, 316;
    creation and, 158; hope of, 2; illusion
    of, 2, 169; jewels and, 42; magazines
    and, 230; narration and, 99; shopping
    and, 108; struggle for, 297, 300;
    toothpaste of, 29–30; transcendence
    and, 216; virtual, 293; Wheel of
    Fortune and, 236
"implicit" processes in psychological
    theory, 8
impression management, art of, 59. *See
    also* self-presentation
inauthenticity, 6
Indian myths about multiplication of
    self, 205

individualism: amorality and, 177;
    bourgeois, 199; emergence of, 176;
    fear and, 224; history of, 328, 338;
    "Proletarian Renaissance" and, 198,
    275; radical, 90, 125, 151, 165, 177,
    197–98, 277; Reformation and, 325;
    Renaissance and, 176, 182, 324, 325;
    self-actualization and, 176; totalitarian
    ideologies and, 244; victory of, 90, 275
individuality: as birthright, 291; desire
    for, 201; loss of, 201; as major value,
    198; semblance of, 201; sham, 201
indolence, 74
Industrial Revolution, 164, 243
inmates, 38, 42
innocence, contemporary myth of, 188
innocent lamb role, 104
intensity: archetypes and, 218; artistic
    experience and, 220; books and, 247;
    boundary situation and, 230–40, 319;
    catastrophes and, 217; celebrities and,
    133–35, 181, 220, 248–50, 252,
    254–64; community and, 219;
    contrast and, 220; crime and, 218;
    cult of, 173, 215–16; danger and, 217;
    death and, 223, 227–30; destruction
    and, 218; drugs and, 220; explosions,
    218–19; fame and, 220; fanaticism,
    219; fight and, 217; freedom and, 210;
    gaze and, 250–56; of life, 42, 113,
    116, 133–35, 181, 211–21, 230–40,
    333; loss of transcendence, 211–12,
    216, 266, 288–89; meaning and, 274;
    moment and, 212–15; of Nietzsche's
    life, 71; passions and, 218; perceptual,
    251; personality and, 241–49; power
    and, 220; religion and, 219; sacred
    cause and, 219; scandal and, 237–39;
    search for, 288; self and, 241–49, 296,
    311, 318–19; sex and, 218; sources of,
    216–22; speed and, 217; spiritual

literature: beat, 201; "Fall of Princes" motif in, 235–37; highbrow and lowbrow, 279–80; *"jeux de l'amour"* in, 127–28; loss of self in, 201–2; lying and, 79–80; narrative and, 98–99; New Age, 268–69; of prayer, 23; rabbinical, 284; self-help, 61, 245–47, 285, 321; sentimental, 202; source of life strategies, 66–73; spiritual crisis in, 233–34; Wheel of Fortune motif in, 234–36; as "world builder," 133

Locke, John, 285

Lopez, Nancy, 260–61

The Lord of the Flies (Golding), 70

loss of meaning, 266–68. *See also* meaning

loss of transcendence. *See* transcendence, books and

love and shaping of self, 126–27

Love thyself! principle, 188

Löwith, Karl, on permanent crisis, 163

Luria, Salvador E., 225

lying, 78–80

Lyotard, Jean-François, 9, 98, 170, 173, 207, 321

Madame Bovary, 70

magazines (lifestyle and women's), 31, 39, 69, 72, 75, 91, 131, 135–36, 167, 195, 220–21, 227–50, 254–58, 261, 263, 268, 270, 293, 319, 334–37

The Magic Flute (Mozart), 11, 28–29

The Magic Mountain (Mann), 71

magic power and small objects, 42–43

Mahin, John Lee, 93

makeover programs, 30, 32

makeup, 35–36

Mann, Thomas: on intensity of Nietzsche's life, 224; on self-education, 71

manufacturing people, modern society as, 92

The Man Without Qualities (Musil), 50, 71

Marcuse, Herbert, 124

marketing. *See* advertising

Márquez, Gabriel García, 202

Martha and George *(Who's Afraid of Virginia Woolf?)*, 2, 68, 236

Marx, Karl, 199, 211

Maslow, Abraham, 4, 7, 8–9, 95, 204, 308

masquerades, 80–81

May, Rollo, 7, 9, 300, 301, 308

Mead, George Herbert, 87, 206, 250

Mead, Margaret, 10

meaning: astrology and, 271; "background radiation" of, 124; Being as framework of, 339; books and, 130, 133; celebrities and, 243, 248; city environment and, 108; concepts of, 154, 204; consumer civilization and, 108, 110, 275; creation of, 97, 226; crisis and, 169; deeper layers of, 7, 29, 139, 297; heroes and, 236; hidden, 7; illusion of, 271, 274; importance of, 306; life and, 7, 28, 45, 47, 57, 86, 100, 103, 108, 110, 115, 124, 128, 134, 139, 150, 162, 166, 181, 193, 210–15, 228, 242–43, 248–49, 261, 266–67, 270, 274, 279, 295–96, 332–33, 338–39; loss of, 167, 190, 209, 224, 244, 266–68, 274, 289, 303, 329; magic world of, 115; narrative and, 100; objects and, 317; overarching framework and, 57, 210; plausibility structures and, 212; progress and, 295; quest for, 97, 100, 129, 141, 166, 195, 226, 266–300, 338; self and, 204–5, 228, 236, 242–44, 261–62; shopping center and,

meaning (*continued*)
110; shortage of, 110, 169; sources of,
213–14, 296; suffering and, 295;
symbols and, 124; time and, 107,
214–15; values and, 276; world and,
101, 110, 113, 130, 209, 226, 266,
289. *See also* significance
media, 216, 238. *See also* magazines;
papers; television
medieval "carnivalesque," 181
medieval monasticism and modernity, 181
membership in social groups versus
autonomy, 60
memes, 151, 195, 322, 331
mentality and *habitus* in five worlds
scenarios, 155
Mephistopheles, 70, 79
The Metamorphosis (Kafka), 70–71
Methodism, 285
method of study, 10–11
Mickelson, Phil, 261
Middle Ages and concept of self, 198
milieu (Scheler), 55
mind in five worlds scenarios, 156
The Mirror of True Womanhood
(O'Reilly), 75–76
mirrors, 28, 54
Mischel, Walter, 8
Mitroff, Ian I., 92, 111
models for self-construction: in
literature, 6–73; in magazines,
245–50, 254–64
modern inquisitors (Foucault), 91
modernity: Baudelaire on, 213; belief in
self in, 288; Benjamin, Walter, on,
249; body image in, 30–31; boundary
situations in, 335; care of self in, 296;
characteristics of, 146, 173–74;
civilization of, 74; crisis of, 164–68,
323; crisis of self in, 165; crisis of
Western civilization, 165, 244;

democratic puffery in, 244; as
desacralized world, 249;
disenchantment in, 268; enchantment
in, 268; end of, 167, 210; existential
situation in, 210; Fall of Princes in,
236–37; Faustian individual in, 277;
frame of mind of, 91; "Great Project"
of, 168; human beings in, 209–19;
ideology of, 168; individuation in, 200;
intense life experience in, 334;
irresponsible individual in, 277;
medieval monasticism and, 181; moral
greed in, 91; mutation of, 174; myths
in, 267; narrative structure of self in,
316; political liberation in, 91; politics
in, 165; rational behavior in, 265, 267,
274; self-apotheosis in, 90–91; self in,
198; self-reflection in, 133; Simmel,
Georg, on, 333; skepticism in, 177;
spiritual problems of human beings in,
200; stoicism in, 192; superstitions in,
26; tragedies in, 2, 235; women in, 81;
world of, 85, 193
modern-postmodern dilemma, 91,
146–47, 170–73, 326
moment: beauty of, 214; cult of, 212–15;
eternity and, 213–15, 297, 333;
existential, 213–15, 233, 333;
Faustian, 226; Heidegger and, 214;
infinite and, 213; of intensity, 214–15,
333; Kierkegaard and the significant,
213; of liberation, 213; magic of, 215;
meaning and, 214–15; of meditation,
27, 108, 292; mysterious depths of,
213; Nietzsche and, 213; significant,
2, 213–14, 233; of silence, 27; of
spiritual enlightenment, 237; of
ultimate questions, 193
monasticism and modernity, 181
moral considerations and self-
actualization, 291–92

Nonbeing (*continued*)
228–29; struggle against, 301; world
of, 22–23
nonconscious "automaticies," 8
"nonterritorial" virtual lifeworld, 55–56
Nora (*Doll's House*), 69
norms of conduct, 73–75, 185–88; of
Saint Benedict, 88–89, 188, 284
"no-self" theories, 200; age of, 197
nothingness, 17, 122, 234–35, 238

objects: as amulets, 43; eternity and, 43;
home and, 123; magic power of, 25,
42–43, 45, 283; maximization of
existence and, 333; meaning and, 45,
105, 124; self-enhancement and, 283;
self-presentation and, 253; shaping of
self, 308; sources of intensity, 216;
symbolic message of, 317; world of, 92
oblivion, human penchant for, 6, 67,
130, 164, 290
"odyssey of the self" (Schrag), 96
Oedipus, 2, 69, 70, 122, 236, 238
Old Testament, 211, 284, 288
Onegin, 70
One Hundred Years of Solitude
(Márquez), 202
O'Neill, Eugene, 79, 122
Ophelia, 69, 202
O'Reilly, Bernard, 75–76
Original Sin, 4, 164, 194, 200, 269
Orlando (Woolf), 71, 206
Ortega y Gasset, José, 165, 319
Othello, 68, 238

"The Painter of Modern Life"
(Baudelaire), 213
panem et circenes (bread and circuses), 2
papers, 50–53. *See also* media
paradox, 33, 39, 78, 197–202, 209–10,
224

passions, 218
Pastoureau, Michel, 41
pathologies of self, 14
Patocka, Jan, 194–95, 200, 286
patterns of human attitudes, 65–66
Pax Americana, 147, 148
Pelagianism, 288
perfumes, 36–37, 305–6; eternity and,
214–15, 299; Neoplatonism and,
192–93; self-construction and, 36–37,
139, 188; triviality and, 299
persona, 58
personality. *See* self
philosophical anthropology, 5
physical experience as source of
intensity, 216
The Picture of Dorian Gray (Wilde), 127,
206
Pietism, 285
Plato, 79, 118, 189, 191–92, 286–87
Player, Gary, 260
playing with selves, 72
poor, the, and their chances of self-
actualization, 277–78, 294–95
pop music, 292
"popoluxe" culture, 324
Popper, Karl, 132–33, 168
Porter, Roy, 22, 92, 199, 285
positive psychology, 286, 301
Post, Emily, 76
postmodernity: age of, 13, 76;
ambiguities in, 13; characteristics of,
146–47, 173, 323; clash of
civilizations in, 149; collapse of "great
narratives," 212; consumer civilization
and, 172–73, 326; contingency in, 41,
277; creative societies and, 155; cult
of artificial in, 41; deconstruction of
self in, 200–201; disenchantment and,
266, 268; disintegration of self in, 316;
eclecticism in, 78; emergence of, 302,

A *Streetcar Named Desire* (Williams), 71
stripes, message of, 41–42
structuralists, 92, 200
structuring time. *See* articulation of time
The Stuff of the Devil (Pastoureau), 41
suffering and the self, 294
sunglasses, 46, 81–82
superhuman beings as sources of
intensity, 219
superstitions, 26
symbolic animals, human beings as, 5
"symbolic revolution," 25–26, 177, 224
symbolic space, 25–26, 55, 57
symbols, shaping people's lives, 7
syncretic age, 197–210; concepts and
strategies of, 202–5; emergence and
disappearance of self in, 198–202;
first paradox, 197–98; multiple self
in, 205–9, 296; second paradox,
209–10
Sypher, Wylie, 201
Szilágyi, Ákos, 276

Talmud, 284
Tangney, June Price, 202–3
Tartuffe, 72, 79
Taylor, Charles: on care of self, 344; on
disenchantment, 212; on ethico-moral
framework, 292; on history of self,
314; on loss of meaning, 212; on
meaning, 210, 338; on models of
behavior, 66; on multiple selves, 207;
on myths of self, 205; on self-
fulfillment, 210, 291–92; on self-
interpreting animal, 205; on self-
narration, 99; on self-seduction, 95
"Technologies of the Self" (Foucault),
205, 284
Teilhard de Chardin, Pierre, 194
television: attraction of, 202; boundary
situations on, 228–29, 335; care of

self and, 136; celebrities and, 248;
crime and, 218; crisis of Western
civilization and, 167; death on,
227–30; demonic characters on, 70;
destruction and, 217–18; destruction
of self and, 112, 130, 201; duality and,
190; existential drama and, 335;
existential moments and, 214; gaze
and, 251–54; high and low culture
and, 343; home viewing, 129–30;
human body and, 30; human relations
and, 278; loss of meaning of life and,
167; modernists and, 91;
multiplication of self and, 207–8;
myths and, 269; "Proletarian
Renaissance" and, 184, 185, 245;
ratings, 250–52; scandals and, 69,
238; self-construction and, 129–30;
Shakespeare and, 280; stoicism and,
192; study of programs on, 195; as
typology, 72; virtual world of, 334
tennis, 116–19
terror management theory, 9, 226
theater, workplace as, 103
Theron, Charlize, 257
Tillich, Paul: ambiguities of human life,
5, 194; ambiguity of sacrifice, 129;
care of self, 284, 286, 289; "courage to
be," 194; decentered self of, 207;
disenchantment, 212; evil in world,
164; existential shock, 289; experience
of intensity, 334; method, 10; modern
self-apotheosis, 90; permanent crisis,
163–64; radical individualism's
dangers, 90, 338; self-sacrifice, 129
time: acceleration of, 62; to articulate,
51, 107–22, 310, 341; to control, 43,
119, 317; to defeat, 4, 35, 122, 133,
217, 230, 274; eternity and, 57, 214;
to experience, 116; to fight, 98, 122;
flow of, 110, 113, 115, 122; to kill,

115, 122; loss of, 113, 129, 274; mortality and, 34, 42, 82; neurosis of, 115; passing of, 27, 115–17, 122, 217, 230, 274; profane and sacred, 108; to reverse, 3–4, 114, 118, 133, 310; self-construction and, 82; to slow down, 107; spirit of (*Zeitgeist*), 174; to stop, 30, 35, 109, 122, 318. *See also* articulation of time

Timeo ergo sum, 224

Tooby, John, 57

toothpaste of immortality, 29–30

totalitarian ideologies, 166, 168–69, 244

Toynbee, Arnold, 165

tragedy: absurdity and ambiguity of human life, 190; catharsis, 335; comic and, 190; confrontation with death, 66; depths of human condition, 67, 225, 288; destiny, 198; destruction of life, 236; dignity of dandy, 213, 336; duality of self, 70–71; experience in Renaissance, 327; fall of genius, 288; fall of heroes, 69, 230, 236; heroes, 242, 299; life experience, 163; search for self, 65; trivial and, 13, 122, 221, 227, 234, 297, 299; uncertainties of life, 53; wasting of life, 234; world, 5

transactionalist approach to life, 65–66

transcendence: books and, 132–33; false, 289; loss of, 166, 173, 200, 210–12, 216, 227, 230, 233, 247, 266, 288–89, 292, 305, 332; search for, 332; self and, 210, 242; travel and, 114

transformation: of human body, 30–33; shopping center and, 110; travel and, 114; of Western civilization, 121, 185–88

travel, 113–14, 318

trends: age of ideologies to age of pragmatism, 147–48; free world to "fortress West," 149; global democracy to decline of democracy, 149–50; history to end of history, 148; information age to age of misinformation, 150; modernity to postmodernity, 170–73; multicultural world to clash of civilizations, 149; nation states to globalization, 150; new world order to new world disorder, 148; open society and minds to closed society and minds, 149; traditional civilization to consumer civilization, 150–51; world of peace to world of uncertainty, 148–49

tribal societies, 67

triumphant markets scenario, 152–58

the trivial and the existential, 1–10, 12–14, 29–30, 37, 77–78, 110, 115–19, 122–26, 138–41, 221, 227–30, 234, 239, 263, 274, 292, 296–99, 335, 338

trivialities: duality of self in philosophy, 5–6; duality of self in psychology, 6–10; focus of book and, 14–17; method of study, 10–11; self in consumer civilization and, 12–14; self in everyday life and, 11–12; shopping center and, 111

turbulent neighborhoods scenario, 152–58

Twain, Mark, 126

typologies of selves, 72–73

tyranny of things, 124

Übermensch, 242, 288

ultimate concerns. *See* questions

Umwelt (Goffman), 55

Unamuno y Jugo, Miguel de, 165

UN and UNESCO optimism, 166

unconscious and conscious realms of self, 7

unreality industry, 111–12

Also by Elemér Hankiss

Values and Societies: Essays in the Sociology of Values
Social Traps
Diagnoses: Essays in Social Pathology
Hongrie: Diagnostiques—Essai en pathologie sociale
East European Alternatives
Abenteuer Menschheit: Skizze einer Zivilisationstheorie
Europe After 1989: A Culture in Crisis?
Essays in Contemporary Civilization
Fears and Symbols: An Introduction to the Study of Western Civilization